Artificial Consciousness

A Journey Beyond AI

Artificial Consciousness
A Journey Beyond AI

Researched and Written By

James V Luisi

Author of

Sensitive by Nature: Understanding Intelligence and the Mind (2002)

Pragmatic Enterprise Architecture: Strategies to Transform Information Systems in the Era of Big Data (2014)

ABSTRACT

Understanding consciousness requires a synthesis of ideas from many disciplines, including the obvious ones like psychology, biology, evolution, neurology, and neuroscience, as well as less obvious ones like protozoology – the study of protozoans; botany – the study of plant life; entomology – the study of insects; carcinology - a branch of zoology that studies crustaceans and anthropods; herpetology – the study of reptiles and amphibians; mammalogy – the study of mammals; and the computer sciences.

As a helpful backdrop, we can better understand this subject matter by seeing how philosophy and science collaborated in the earliest studies into consciousness, eventually only to lose that bond. However, we realize the value of re-establishing that lost bond hundreds of years later.

Although this is not a philosophy book, we must acknowledge that organized thinking about consciousness first emerged in ancient philosophy. As it turns out, the ancients had called it correctly on many consciousness-related topics, which we will help illustrate at the appropriate times along this scientific journey.

The earliest documented forms of philosophy are Eastern philosophy. These are the first teachings of Buddhism for their relevance regarding early thought about the nature of consciousness, which is quite different from what modern Buddhism is today.

As consciousness is a complex topic, the ideas expressed in the book are presented in a multi-level framework to illustrate consciousness within a tapestry of building blocks that explain how humans evolved to understand reality.

The purpose of any organism for understanding reality is to survive. In the case of *Homo sapiens*, it happens to have moved well beyond meeting the basic needs of daily and even multi-generational survival. Our understanding of reality is so extensive that it borders on the possibility of surviving beyond our planet's life.

As we shall see, the main ingredient for any organism to understand reality rests entirely upon consciousness. Hence, we cannot overstate the importance of consciousness.

However, understanding consciousness is not a small task. You cannot glean it from a dictionary or encyclopedia with an easy-to-understand synopsis. Instead, it requires the reader to embark on a scientific journey that exposes us to a thought-provoking sequence of experiences.

That said, the journey starts early in our history when science and philosophy collaborate. The fact that these two disciplines began in collaboration helps reveal the natural symbiotic relationship they each have as systems of thought and reasoning.

As we shall see, this journey will traverse through a framework of consciousness, gathering some of the key elements regarding the evolution of consciousness along with the emergence of *free will* and its other related freedoms.

Readers are encouraged to think for themselves about the issues we will explore and to question every facet presented, as even with this material, much further exploration is needed.

The subject of consciousness will continue to evolve into the distant future, and it is arguably in the interests of all intelligent beings to consider attaining the ability and willingness to participate in the conversation to extend their journey beyond the pages of this book.

DEDICATION

Any book of this size and magnitude can never be perfect. Much like a painting, one of the most challenging aspects of writing a book is deciding when it attains the point on its path of improvement that the author is willing to consider as close to perfection as it will ever be.

The same thing can be said when I was a young man searching for a life partner who searched for that perfect partner.

However, unlike the process of laboring over any painting or book, I hit the jackpot on a warm summer day in Staten Island, New York. That was the day I found someone who embodied the definition of perfection.

Since this is my third book, which I believe is the best I may ever produce, I dedicate it to my perfect wife, Onita. Onita has given me an interesting forty years and counting, a perfect daughter, Olivia, and an unrelenting stare I get whenever I tell one of my many jokes.

Thank you, Onita. The only consolation I can offer is that I have heard that the first forty years are the toughest.

TABLE OF CONTENTS

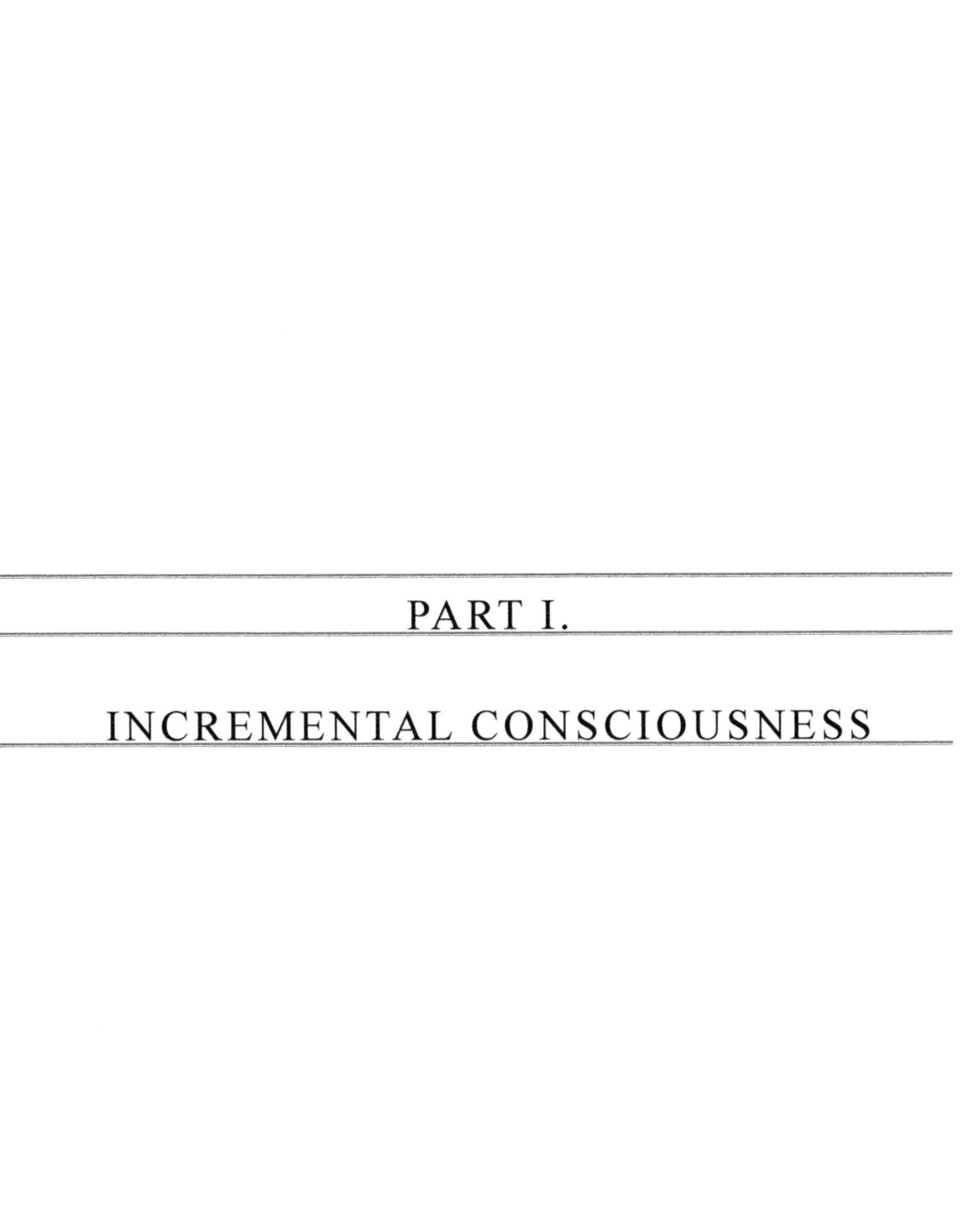

PART I.

INCREMENTAL CONSCIOUSNESS

INTRODUCTION

There are several ways of looking at consciousness, and many of those can go deep into various realms of neuroscience, computer science, and philosophy, to name a few. For our journey, we will need to cover a spectrum of disciplines that are necessarily interconnected, as the most constructive way to view consciousness is step by step as a tapestry of these disciplines.

Stated another way, this is a journey that begins with unicellular life that travels to human experience and beyond.

The intended audience includes the general reader and expert, particularly information technology professionals and thought leaders.

The reader will not need expertise except for a high school education and life experience. For those academically inclined, the sources of material are placed in the text immediately following either an exact quote or a paraphrasing of the original material to make it easier to read.

We will explicitly call out areas where informational gaps in the scientific record prevent conclusions from being drawn. When doing so, we will identify the type of additional research that we would encourage to close those gaps.

We will begin our journey by introducing consciousness as ancient scholars understood it 2,500 years ago. Given the level of scientific knowledge present at that time, it is remarkable how much we can learn from that early period that continues to offer pertinent intellectual value to this day.

Once we accomplish this, we will contrast the ancient perspective with our more modern views, giving us a glimpse into the challenges of expounding upon and explaining consciousness.

Upon aligning the ancient and contemporary perspectives with one another, we begin again at the beginning of life, where consciousness first emerged and then evolved.

As we journey through the evolution of consciousness, we embark on a path that takes us through twenty-four levels of consciousness. This journey is brief, though of sufficient duration, to allow the reader to see how consciousness continually evolves and then continues to influence the evolution of organisms into the future.

Once equipped with the twenty-four levels of consciousness, we explore one of consciousness's most hotly debated topics, namely that of *qualia,* and the five types of *qualia* illustrated in the framework.

We then arrive at one of the most contentious topics regarding consciousness, which is the subject of *free will*, where we provide valuable perspectives on *freedom of attention, freedom of will, freedom of action, freedom of emotion, freedom of thought*, and *freedom of paradigm*.

So as not to leave significant gaps in our coverage of consciousness, we explore awareness, intelligence, sentience, and sapience through the framework's lens before exploring some of the ethical issues that naturally arise when contemplating artificial consciousness.

To wrap up our journey, we provide a glimpse into how computer science can approach our levels of consciousness; we journey into the conceptual design of computer components that can support artificial consciousness.

ONE ANCIENT PERSPECTIVE

A well-developed form of philosophical thought had already emerged in the East a hundred years before the emergence of Socrates, Plato, and Aristotle.

Buddhism was founded in the sixth century BCE by the Buddha (i.e., Siddhartha Gautama, born 563 BCE) as a minor tradition near the foothills of the Himalayas in an area that is present-day Nepal. This area was a Silicon Valley of religions where many beliefs and philosophical practices emerged in opposition to the then-dominant Vedic religion.

Initially, Buddhism remained a minor tradition with the scarcity of written documents until 268-232 BCE when Ashoka the Great (304-232 BCE), a Mauryan Indian Emperor, saw the value of philosophy and the ideas of Buddhism.

Upon realizing this, Ashoka the Great declared Buddhism the state religion of India, establishing an extensive written record of Buddhist monks from various sects of Buddhist schools that ranged in degrees between secular and religious.

In short, having a philosophy can lead to guiding principles with measurable outcomes. Philosophy can help individuals or large organizations set a more consistent direction. In contrast, the absence of an overarching philosophy can lead to inconsistent decisions that conflict with one another in various ways.

As a guide, the ancient Buddhist writings about consciousness address the subject of 'consciousness' as one of "The Five Aggregates" (i.e., The Five Skandhas) that explain personal experience and cognition from a secular Buddhist perspective.

These Five Aggregates consist of form, sensation, perception, mental formation, and consciousness. According to the Buddhist Universal Truth of No-Self, these aggregates work together to form physical and mental personal experiences, such as our emotions, ideas, opinions, and attitudes, that render individuals an impression of self.

The first aggregate 'form' (i.e., *'rupa'* in Sanskrit) is associated with experiencing the physical world, including our body and its components that sense the physical world with sight, sound, scent, taste, and touch.

The second aggregate, 'sensation' (i.e., *'vedana'* in Sanskrit), is associated with the experience of feeling, such as a feeling that is pleasant, unpleasant, or indifferent.

The third aggregate' perception' (i.e., *'samjna'* in Sanskrit) is associated with conceptualizing a particular experience into an idea distinct from others, such as identifying different tones of pleasant sounds.

The fourth aggregate, 'mental formation' (i.e., *'caitasika'* in Sanskrit), is associated with choosing an action or inaction, where these volitions have moral consequences when intentions and choices are involved.

The fifth aggregate, 'consciousness' (i.e., *'chetna'* in Sanskrit), pertains to awareness. It is when we combine the fifth aggregate with perception and mental formation that allows psychological experience (a.k.a. *qualia*) to manifest itself within 'mind' as thoughts, ideas, and sensations (e.g., the scent, taste, texture, temperature, and weight of vanilla ice cream when its surface sparkles as sunlight reflects off its fine ice crystals) to create a pleasant feeling.

In ancient Buddhism, there are a total of six senses that comprise the fifth aggregate of consciousness, with the sixth being the sense of mind. These senses follow the sequence of 'eye consciousness' (i.e., *'cakṣurvijñāna'* in Sanskrit), 'ear consciousness' (i.e., *'śrotravijñāna'* in Sanskrit), 'nose consciousness' (i.e., *'ghrāṇavijñāna'* in Sanskrit), 'tongue consciousness' (i.e., *'jihvāvijñāna'* in Sanskrit), 'body consciousness' (i.e., *'kāyavijñāna'* in Sanskrit), and finally 'mind consciousness' (i.e., *'manovijñāna'* in Sanskrit).

The mind sense (i.e., the sixth sense) renders thoughts about the other bodily senses, involving thoughts within one's mind, creating thoughts about thoughts, which are called meta-thoughts.

During the ensuing two and a half thousand years since Buddhism, scientific methods have revealed a wealth of new information in the fields of biology, neurology, brain chemistry, physics, quantum mechanics, psychology, and so much more, yet the Buddhist framework is nearly as sensible today as it was before the advent of science.

THE ADVENT OF SCIENCE

The scientific method is an empirical approach to knowledge acquisition formalized as recently as the 17th century. However, this approach wholly depends on the fact that the terms employed must be sufficiently defined to make any exchange of ideas clear and meaningful.

Likewise, just as different sects of Buddhism established many different secular and nonsecular conceptions of the Buddha and his teachings over time, scientists and academia have established significantly disparate conceptions of consciousness, rendering it challenging to agree upon a set of terms with clear and meaningful definitions.

To paraphrase Professor Susan Greenfield, Oxford University, in her Closer to Truth.com interview:

> *As an alternative to agreeing upon clear and meaningful definitions, some scientists and philosophers have retreated to focus on identifying the various capabilities of consciousness. At the same time, others have more strategically attempted to determine what consciousness is and is not, while others still focus on identifying the different types of consciousness and the associated capabilities.*
>
> *[Susan Greenfield, Professor of Pharmacology, Oxford University, https://www.closertotruth.com/series/what-consciousness-part-2]*

Our approach is to identify the different types of consciousness and define each in clear and meaningful ways. The significance of this approach is three-fold.

From the perspective of manageability, identifying the types of consciousness may make it easier to facilitate a working model that defines each level of consciousness, including how they cooperate or build upon one another. This approach avoids the daunting task of agreeing on one unified definition for a concept of consciousness.

As we shall see, this approach also dovetails into being integrated with the evolutionary path that formed each level of consciousness.

To illustrate this, let's assume that we have two types of consciousness, reptilian and mammalian, as differences at each stage of evolution that can be more readily identified and explored.

An example of this can be expressed succinctly in the psychophysiological research of Stephen Porges into polyvagal theory.

The tenth cranial nerve (a.k.a. vagus nerve) has two neural fibers that connect numerous primary organs to the brain.

One neural strand, large and coarse, originates in primitive lizard anatomy and is part of a defensive mechanism that helps the organism to be dormant and blend into the environment; the other strand, fine and smooth, only emerges in mammalian anatomy and operates the fight and flight response as well as the majority of facial muscles.

The point is that evolution demonstrates that it builds new add-ons on top of old components, sometimes modifying or strengthening old ones.

This approach also speaks to the Buddhist notion of *dependent origination,* which is a core concept in the teachings of the Buddha that overlaps with the idea of building blocks.

To quote the 2018 book by Chokyi Nyima Rinpoche, Sadness, *Love Openness: The Buddhist Path of Joy:* Quote.

"Dependent origination means that everything comes into being dependent on something else. In other words, all existence is conditioned and contingent ... dependent origination lies at the very heart of the teachings of the Buddha." End Quote.

[Sadness, Love Openness: The Buddhist Path of Joy, pg. 10, 2018, Chokyi Nyima Rinpoche, Shambhala Publications]

Similarly, some types of consciousness will be relatively primitive, best studied from within the primitive organisms they first emerge. This approach also causes us to realize that many specialized disciplines within science are necessary to cover the range of organisms involved and the importance of collaboration between and across these disciplines if we hope to understand consciousness.

Then, as Jim Collins advises in his books and seminars, it is crucial to get the right people on the bus and equally essential to get the wrong people off the bus, keeping only the individuals interested in going on the journey with their fellow passengers. Failing this, we will be no closer to having a working definition of consciousness in another two and a half thousand years.

Quote. "If we get the right people on the bus, the right people in the right seats, and the wrong people off the bus, then we'll figure out how to take it someplace great." End Quote. Jim Collins

ANCIENT AND MODERN PERSPECTIVES

At a fundamental level, ancient and modern perspectives on consciousness automatically align in various ways. One is that our senses are distinct from the emotional responses associated with them.

Another is that our senses and emotional responses are distinct from conceptualizing ideas about these sensations and emotions. Yet another is that these are distinct from our choice of action or inaction.

These distinctions depict the layers of capabilities supporting our lizard brain as different sensory systems are laid upon and integrated, just as additional mammalian components build upon those of our most recent common ancestor with reptilians.

How organisms perceive their environment is through psychological experiences known as *qualia*. The psychological effects of *qualia* pertain to an eye for sight, an ear for sound, a nose for scent, a tongue for taste, and a body for tactile sensations. These are part of the ancient Buddhist world's fifth Buddhist aggregate of consciousness.

The fifth aggregate of consciousness also supports *manovijñāna* (i.e., the sixth sense *mind* within the fifth aggregate *consciousness*), rendering thoughts about the other senses, including meta-thoughts and meta-meta-thoughts.

These Buddhist aggregates ultimately lead to the subject of *free will*, though depending upon the Buddhist sect, views on *free will* do differ significantly. However, as different sects of Buddhism have other ideas of *free will*, so do areas of specialization in science across various scientific disciplines.

The choice we face as participants in this journey is whether we find a way to identify and build upon areas where we agree or dwell upon the subjects we do not.

To return momentarily to Tony, this doesn't mean that we let everyone onto the bus, nor does it mean that there should be only one bus. There could easily be different buses that take somewhat different paths. The goal is to learn as much as possible by building upon our experiences and conversations, even if these conversations are with the various voices within ourselves.

Just as there are disparate frameworks of thought we know as philosophies, some relatively compatible and some not, there is always an opportunity to have another bus other than what we are currently on.

My experiences may have formed fundamentally different philosophies than many other researchers, while some researchers will realize we share a common philosophy. Which one it is, the journey itself will decide.

A USEFUL PERSPECTIVE
(LIFE BEFORE CELL FORMATION)

The ancient world did not offer the Buddha the advantages of today's science and technology. However, many of the conclusions would be the same if it had.

At this point, it is safe to conclude that, thus far, the foundation for all consciousness is life. A stone has no life, though under the stone, on top of a stone, in the crevices of the stone, and sometimes deep within the stone, evidence of life may be present.

The best that modern science can tell us at this time is that the following scientific discoveries represent the earliest signs of life on Earth.

Scientists have found biogenic molecules in Western Greenland dating back 3.7 billion years ago; fossilized cyanobacteria found in Precambrian stromatolites in the Siyeh formation, Glacier National Park, US, and Canada dating 3.5 billion years ago; and microbial mat fossils (bacteria) found in Western Australia dating 3.48 billion years ago.

Since then, 99% of all species that ever lived are extinct, with roughly 12 million species estimated to live today. Our singular subspecies, *Homo sapiens*, is the most advanced of the 1.2 billion species ever to emerge. *Homo sapiens* have significantly surpassed our closest extinct *Homo* relatives.

> *The genus' Homo,' in the family Hominidae, includes many species now extinct, and we are the only surviving subspecies of Homo sapiens as Homo sapiens neanderthalensis are extinct. All races of humans are in (genus species subspecies) Homo sapiens sapiens.*

> *Our closest surviving relatives, overlapping in 98.8% of our DNA structure, are the species' common chimpanzee' and 'bonobo,' in the genus' Pan' (a.k.a. 'chimpanzee' as a genus should not be confused with the species' common chimpanzee'), in the family Hominidae. The few surviving species of Hominidae (the great apes) include [Genus-species]: Homo sapiens, Pan common chimpanzee, Pan bonobo, Gorilla eastern gorilla, Gorilla western gorilla, and Pongo orangutan.*

Unicellular forms of life and pre-cellular organisms are at opposite ends of the evolutionary spectrum. These organisms do not get placed into species. Although most scientists do not consider pre-cellular or non-cellular life (e.g., viruses) to be forms of life necessarily, these collections of molecules were precursors to cellular life forms with cell membranes. Chemical systems formed symbiotic relationships within a free-floating chemical soup, facilitating their continued survival and evolution until and after cell membranes formed.

The first of five things living cells have in common is a cell membrane. Cell membranes protect and organize cells and regulate what and how much a given substance can enter and leave. Additionally, internal membranes encase the organelles of cell components, which are packages within cells with membranes that keep their parts bundled together.

> *The five components all cells share include a <u>cell membrane</u>; <u>cytoplasm</u> within the cell, within which the other components float; <u>DNA</u>, which defines the genetic code; <u>ribosomes</u>, which synthesize proteins; and <u>organelles</u> with their membranes.*

Before the formation of cell membranes, parts that would eventually become organelles would already have to collaborate with the elements that would ultimately become other organelles in their environmental soup.

Unfortunately, we know little about organelle parts' formation, collaboration, and eventual packaging.

The opposing view would seem to stipulate that these parts formed randomly, and a collection of specialized functions came together haphazardly. Some would then believe a cell membrane randomly formed around these collaborative parts. However, as we shall see much later, self-organizing systems are far more likely the force behind much of our evolution to this point and into the future.

FIRST LEVEL OF CONSCIOUSNESS (UNICELLULAR)

Our journey into consciousness starts here, at which consciousness first emerges and builds upon this fundamental level.

Scientists classify the first unicellular organisms as prokaryotic. These prokaryotic cells lack membrane-bound organelles, such as a nucleus or mitochondria, compared to the more advanced eukaryotic cells possessing them. Whether organelles formed membranes before or after having been collected within the confines of the larger cell membrane is unclear.

PARAMECIUM

Eukaryotes are at the other end of the evolutionary continuum of unicellular organisms, such as the genus *Paramecium* of the family *Parameciidae*, the phylum *Ciliophora*, and the kingdom *Protista*.

To paraphrase Christine Wilcox in *Researchers Rethink the Ancestry of Complex Cells:*

However, Paramecium did not evolve from other eukaryotes, as all single-cell eukaryotes evolved from a collection of various primitive prokaryotes as far back as two billion years ago.

> *[Researchers Rethink the Ancestry of Complex Cells, April 9, 2019, Christie Wilcox Ph.D. in Cell and Molecular Biology from the University of Hawaii, Quantum Magazine,* https://www.quantamagazine.org/rethinking-the-ancestry-of-the-eukaryotes-20190409/*]*

Eukaryotes such as *Paramecium* feed on microorganisms, such as algae, bacteria, euglena, water fleas, amoebas, yeasts, and decaying matter by using cilia to sweep them into an oral groove, leading to the mouth of the cell, and then nutrients of these materials are extracted chemically in the cell gullet.

Even as an individual cell, *Paramecium* is highly advanced among unicellular organisms, sensing various materials in its environment using chemical sensors along with other sensors that detect light and energy, allowing it to identify concentrations of food, a nearby predator, temperature differentials, brightness levels of light, and levels of electrical current.

When relying upon signals from chemical sensors, *Paramecia* exhibit non-random motion propelled by an array of cilia in response to changes in its surrounding environment, either by moving toward favorable or away from unfavorable factors. Another use of cilia is for the cell to control the motion of fluids surrounding it to either ingest or repel material in its immediate surroundings.

To paraphrase Howard Armus, Amber Mongomery, Jenny Jellison in *"Discrimination Learning in Paramecia (P. caudatum)"* and Simona Ginsburg, Eva Jablonka in *"Epigenetic learning in non-neural organisms."*

> *Under normal conditions, a Paramecium undergoes asexual reproduction two to three times a day, except when its surrounding environment becomes unfavorable. At this point, they switch modes and engage in sexual reproduction.*

> *Within the single cell of Paramecium, there may also be the capacity for learning and memory. A 2006 study demonstrates that Paramecium caudatum exhibits cell memory or epigenetic learning in an organism without neuronal structures.*

> *["Discrimination Learning in Paramecia (P. caudatum)", Armus, Harvard L.; Montgomery, Amber R.; Jellison, Jenny L. (Fall 2006). The Psychological Record. **56** (4): 489–498., University of Toledo]*

> *["Epigenetic learning in non-neural organisms." Ginsburg, Simona; Jablonka, Eva (2009). Journal of Biosciences. **34** (4): 633–646. doi:10.1007/s12038-009-0081-8]*

Paramecium also demonstrates symbiotic relationships with green algae, which float freely inside the protection of the *Paramecium's* cell membrane mixed in with the cytoplasm, providing nutrition to the *Paramecium* from photosynthesis.

While no one is claiming that a one-celled eukaryote can experience *qualia*, such as the blend of flavors from its various sources of food, the most primitive form of consciousness in our framework starts here in the individual eukaryote cell, *'Unicellular Consciousness.'*

The cytoskeleton is among the sub-cellular structures of the *Paramecium* that may be responsible for supporting communication and control functions. The cytoskeleton, with many active microfilaments, microtubules, and intermediate fibers, causes chemicals within the cytoplasm to flow to specific destinations in different parts of the cell.

As we shall discuss, it is the cytoskeleton of the *Paramecium* and the cytoskeleton within all eukaryotic cell types, including that of neurons, that is potentially the starting point for the phenomenon of awareness.

As Professor Stuart Hameroff, MD, professionally an anesthesiologist and professor at the University of Arizona, asserts when it pertains to consciousness studies, the cytoskeleton requires deep scientific study as the operations of microtubules within the cytoskeleton of eukaryotic cells are remarkably complex and their role pervasive in cellular processes.

The average human brain possesses about a hundred billion individual neurons surrounded by about an equal number of glial cells. However, some brain regions have four times as many glial cells as others.

But what do glial cells do?

Glial cells attenuate physical and chemical effects on neurons, and they help determine what connections a neuron should establish. Though it varies greatly, the typical central nervous system (CNS) neuron has roughly 10,000 connections to other neurons.

If *Unicellular Consciousness* participates at the most fundamental level of consciousness, then it may be a critical building block upon which all other types of consciousness depend. When we discuss the brain, we will take the opportunity to touch upon the many types and configurations of neurons, whether they participate in the CNS, including whether they transport signals toward or away from the CNS.

There is an often-expressed notion within the field of artificial intelligence (AI) that claims each neuron in the brain is analogous to an individual bit of information in a computer. However, this is woefully inaccurate and misleading. Within one eukaryotic cell, such as a neuron, a *Paramecium* processes many signals from many sensory nodes, considering many things vying for its attention and making many decisions.

As a result, to claim any eukaryotic cell is equivalent to one bit of information (i.e., '0' or '1') is entirely nonsensical.

Suppose the microtubules of the cytoskeleton within an individual cell are as active as they would appear. In that case, a one-celled *Paramecium* is an entire system of capabilities like a complex' *control system,*' we are dealing with more than a million bits of information.

But what exactly is a *control system* in the field of computer sciences?

> *A 'control system' is a software system that automates the operation of physical machinery guided by streams of signal data emanating from sensors instead of information systems that automate information processing.*
>
> *For example, a PC is operated by an information system, whereas a control system operates a robotic Roomba floor vacuum.*

We could go on about our first level of consciousness for some time, but we have a long and exciting journey ahead. But before we do, there is one more important topic to discuss in *Unicellular Consciousness.*

The topic is whether *Paramecium* can learn. For example, can it learn to anticipate the difference in electrical current from different light levels?

To quote the 2021 NIH article by Gershman, Balbi, Gallistel, and Gunawardena, *Reconsidering the evidence for learning in single cells*: Quote.

> *"Pavlovian conditioning is particularly interesting for our purposes because of the prevailing theory that it is mediated by synaptic plasticity. This theory has been criticized on several grounds: that synaptic plasticity cannot account for the behavioral features of Pavlovian conditioning (Gallistel and Matzel, 2013); that it is too unstable to implement long-term memory storage due to molecular turnover (Crick, 1984; Mongillo et al., 2017); that it can be experimentally dissociated from behavioral measures of memory (Chen et al., 2014; Ryan et al., 2015); and that behaviorally relevant information is not stored in a readable format (Gallistel, 2017). Furthermore, a synaptic memory substrate requires that computations operate via the propagation of spiking activity, incurring an energetic cost roughly 13 orders of magnitude greater than the cost incurred if the computations are implemented using intracellular molecules (Gallistel, 2017)."*

> *"As an alternative (or complement), it has been proposed that memory may be stored using a cell-intrinsic substrate, such as polynucleotide sequences (e.g. RNA), post-translational histone modifications, or DNA methylation patterns (Landauer, 1964; Crick, 1984; Day and Sweatt, 2010; Abraham et al., 2019; Gräff and Tsai, 2013; Gallistel, 2017). These theories posit a mapping from experienced quantities, like the duration of the interval between the onset of the conditioned stimulus and the onset of the unconditioned stimulus, to the hypothesized changes in molecular level structures that encode them. The biochemical processes that produce these changes in response to relevant synaptic input and that later convert the encoded information to appropriately timed output signals remain unknown, although recent work revealing a CamKII-dependent tunable event timer provides a possible biochemical mechanism for interval timing (Thornquist et al., 2020)."*

> *"The possibility of a cellular-level mechanism for storing acquired information with delayed behavioral consequences is exciting from an evolutionary perspective because it suggests that the mechanisms for memory storage in complex multicellular organisms may have been inherited from much simpler organisms, possibly even protozoa, that share the same intracellular molecular repertoire." End Quote.*

> *[Reconsidering the evidence for learning in single cells, Samuel J Gershman, Petra EM Balbi, C Randy Gallistel, Jeremy Gunawardena,*

Jan 4, 2021, eLife, NIH, National Library of Medicine, PMID 33395388, https://www.ncbi.nlm.nih.gov/pmc/articles/PMC7781593/]

Note: I recommend that students and researchers become familiar with the abovementioned article for its ability to put the scientific record of Beatrice Gelber, NIH Postdoctoral Fellow in the Department of Psychology, into perspective.

To further quote the 2021 NIH article, *Reconsidering the evidence for learning in single cells*:

Quote.

"Fast forward to the 21st century, and it is now banal for cell biologists to think of the cell as a miniature computer, capable of sophisticated information processing (Bray, 2009). Among their many capabilities, it is now appreciated that cells have memory, possibly in the form of a 'histone code' (Jenuwein and Allis, 2001; Turner, 2002), though a precise computational understanding of this code has remained elusive. Whatever the memory code may be, its implications for neuroscience are far-reaching: we may finally be poised to link cellular memory codes with cognitive information processing. In this context, the studies by Gelber and others of learning in Paramecia become freighted with significance. They suggest that single cells have the ability to carry out a form of information processing that neuroscientists have traditionally attributed to networks of cells. We still do not understand how Paramecia accomplish this feat. If the hypothesis is correct, then single cells hold more surprises in store for us." End Quote.

[Reconsidering the evidence for learning in single cells, Samuel J Gershman, Petra EM Balbi, C Randy Gallistel, Jeremy Gunawardena, Jan 4, 2021, eLife, NIH, National Library of Medicine, PMID 33395388, https://www.ncbi.nlm.nih.gov/pmc/articles/PMC7781593/]

To summarize *Unicellular Consciousness*, all eukaryotic cells, including the cells of all plants and animals, contain cytoskeletal structures that may contribute to myriad operations, potentially including memory and learning.

Research into cytoskeletal structures is in its infancy among the various types of cytoskeletons across the many known species of cells. We can barely glimpse the computing power of what may be possible within single-cell eukaryotes, such as *Paramecia*.

As for a Buddhist view of *Unicellular Consciousness*, the chemical sensors of the *Paramecium* are primitive forms of taste receptors consistent with the first aggregate of form (i.e., 'rupa') for experiencing the physical world, followed by the second aggregate of sensation (i.e., 'vedana') to categorize the form as pleasant, unpleasant, or indifferent, thereby leading the *Paramecium* to move away from hostile or toward favorable conditions.

Regarding learning, even though the Buddha would not have known about the potential for recording learned information with macromolecules or histones of single-cell organisms that get passed onto their offspring, the Buddha would have pointed to the third aggregate of perception (i.e., '*samjna*') associating a particular experience and conceptualizing it into an idea that is distinct from other ideas and experiences.

Then, and surprising to many for a species of protozoan, the Buddha would likely have pointed to the fourth aggregate of mental formation (i.e., 'caitasika') when choosing an action or inaction when it comes to learning, as science has shown the behavior of even the single cell *Paramecium* learns from prior experience.

SECOND LEVEL OF CONSCIOUSNESS (MULTICELLULAR CONSCIOUSNESS)

Our next level of consciousness, also pre-neuronal, is *Multicellular Consciousness,* which establishes some degree of consciousness of the surrounding environment supported by a collection of cells that operate in collaboration, requiring a method of communication with adjoining cells.

While this might be easier to demonstrate within the animal kingdom, to prove the point clearly, we will select two species of plants, the first of which is *Dionea muscipula,* within the genus *Dionea.*

Dionea muscipula is a plant in a tiny subtropical wetland region along a 700-mile stretch of coast where North and South Carolina meet (a.k.a. The Venus flytrap). It is one of a handful of plants that exhibit easily observable behavior involving rapid movement, as seen with the naked eye.

The second species we will select is the *Mimosa pudica* (a.k.a. sensitive plant), native to South and Central America as a problematic weed. However, over time, it has become pantropical, which means it is in both hemispheres' tropical regions.

DIONEA MUSCIPULA (VENUS FLYTRAP)

As for our first plant species, many of us are familiar with the Venus flytrap, which is among a handful of carnivorous plants that consume insects. However, the largest species of *Dionea muscipula* consumes small amphibians and rodents, using leaves that have evolved a unique clamping ability.

To avoid false triggering, two events involving the same individual hair-like structure, termed mechanosensor by Alexander Volkov – plant physiologist, Oakwood University, Alabama, must come in physical contact with a solid or liquid within a 30-second window to cause the plant to clamp the modified leaves closed with a hinged midrib.

These mechanosensors send a tiny electrical charge toward the midrib of the leaf, causing specialized pores within the outermost layer of cells of the leaf to open, allowing water to rush out from inner to outer cells, creating a rapid change of turgor or internal cell pressure, flipping the lobes of the leaf to snap shut as quickly as within one twenty-fifth of a second (i.e., 0.04 seconds). This flipping of the lobes surrounds its prey with no avenue for escape before it could have sufficient time to react.

If the prey is of insignificant size, thereby of insignificant nutritional value to the plant, it should be able to escape the cage bars. However, when the prey is sufficiently sized and struggles to push free, the mechanosensors cause the plant to clamp down on its captive with increasing pressure.

Once the prey is trapped, the leaf releases an array of acidic digestive enzymes that dissolve the tissues of its meal, excluding insect exoskeleton or skeleton of small amphibians and rodents, to absorb nutrients, such as nitrogen, not available in the nutrient-poor soil that it inhabits in the coastal marshland.

MIMOSA PUDICA (SENSITIVE PLANT)

The second species of plant chosen to help us illustrate *Multicellular Consciousness*, also a pre-neuronal multicellular organism, is *Mimosa pudica* (a.k.a. the sensitive plant).

Mimosa pudica is well known for its rapid movement of leaves successively closing when stimulated tactilely by touching, jarring, shaking, sudden blowing, or the rapid warming of even a single leaflet.

Like *Dionea muscipula*, the tactile receptors of the leaf release electrically charged ions that travel through to the base, causing cell membranes to alter their permeability, thus shifting turgor with the transit of water through cell membranes. These differences in turgidity cause the leaflets to fold to the leaf's stem, where they are more protected, resting against the stronger stems of the plant.

The reason for choosing the species *Mimosa pudica* (a.k.a. the sensitive plant) is its capability to demonstrate habitual learning in carefully controlled experiments when plants are dropped from a height of 15 centimeters.

After a few successive iterations, the plant no longer closes its leaves because it learns when the stimuli do not threaten its leaves.

Scientists shook the plants to test if the leaves were suppressing their leaf folding reflex from habitual learning and not energy exhaustion, after which the leaves closed. They concluded that it was not due to energy exhaustion.

Moreover, upon retesting the same plant hours, days, weeks, and months after, the plants remembered what they had learned and did not close their leaves when dropped from a height of 15 centimeters.

Mimosa pudica (a.k.a. the sensitive plant) expends significant energy closing and opening leaflets. However, it demonstrates that it can recall and compare new stimuli to the memory of non-threatening stimuli versus the memory of other threatening stimuli to differentiate among them.

Since there is a 40% reduction in photosynthesis when *Mimosa pudica* folds its leaves closed, plants conditioned to lower light levels need to conserve more energy than plants conditioned to higher light levels.

Scientists correctly predicted, therefore, that plants conditioned to low light levels might exhibit a faster learning mechanism, such as learning with even fewer iterations.

When comparing these two plant species, the tactile sensors of *Dionea muscipula* (a.k.a. Venus flytrap) consistently detect the presence of food on the inner fold of its leaves using a more primitive mechanism before communicating with adjacent cells using the release of ions to close the leaf, trapping, digesting, and releasing the remains of its prey.

On the other hand, the tactile sensors of Mimosa pudica demonstrate an ability to distinguish between the various types of tactile stimuli, including those that present no harm to the plant, with the ability to learn and recall the experience when appropriate.

In summarizing *Multicellular Consciousness*, all eukaryotic cells, including all plants and animals, contain cytoskeletal structures that may contribute to myriad operations, including memory and learning. The primary difference involving *Multicellular Consciousness* of these two plant species is that *Mimosa pudica* has the physical ability to demonstrate a learned response. In contrast, *Dionea muscipula* physically lacks the same capacity.

As for the Buddhist view of *Multicellular Consciousness*, if the Buddha knew what science has learned about *Dionea muscipula* and *Mimosa pudica*, the Buddha's ideas would remain unchanged.

The hair-like sensors of *Dionea muscipula* act as primitive types of touch receptors consistent with the first aggregate of form (i.e., '*rupa*') for experiencing the physical world, followed by the second aggregate of sensation (i.e., '*vedana*') to categorize the form as pleasant, unpleasant, or indifferent, thereby leading *Dionea muscipula* to close its trap and begin the digestive cycle.

The ability of tactile sensors of *Mimosa pudica* to detect being dropped would also be consistent with the first aggregate of form (i.e., '*rupa*') for experiencing the physical world, followed by the second aggregate of sensation (i.e., '*vedana*') to categorize the form as pleasant, unpleasant, or indifferent, thereby leading *Mimosa pudica* to close its leaves when unpleasant.

Given the scientific evidence of *Mimosa pudica* being able to detect the difference between being dropped as compared to other stimuli that its tactile senses could detect, the Buddha may have pointed to the third aggregate of perception (i.e., '*samjna*') associating a particular experience and conceptualizing it into an idea that is distinct from other ideas and their experiences.

Then, and surprising to many for a species of plant, the Buddha may have pointed to the fourth aggregate of mental formation (i.e., '*caitasika*') with choosing an action or inaction when it comes to learning influenced by prior experience.

THIRD LEVEL OF CONSCIOUSNESS (NERVE NET)

Continuing along the path of evolution, the next level of consciousness is *Nerve Net Consciousness.* Before the emergence of nerve nets, a diffuse net-like nervous system, cells of multicellular organisms could only communicate with physically adjacent cells via spreading a wave of electrically charged ions.

However, this level of consciousness marks the emergence of a new type of cell, the neuron. Neuron cells are unique, with dendrites having finger-like extensions, a cell body called a soma, and an axon with an axon terminal.

There are hundreds of types of neurons specialized in a variety of ways. Structurally, they can be unipolar, bipolar, multipolar, or pseudo-unipolar. Functionally, they can be sensory neurons, motor neurons, or interneurons that sit between other neurons in a reflex arc. They can also vary genetically in size and shape and how they form connections with other cells. However, the neurons that support *Nerve Net Consciousness* are limited to the unipolar and multipolar neuron types.

The emergence of neuronal cells marked the first time rapid transmission of electrical signals to various locations within an organism could occur. The first cells classified as neurons were simple nerve nets in the phylum cnidarian marine animals, comprising over 10,000 marine species, including jellyfish, gorgonian, coral, and sea anemones.

Jellyfish belong to the invertebrate animal group called gelatinous zooplankton because of their delicate physical form, which is easily damaged or destroyed, though not all gelatinous zooplankton are jellyfish.

Jellyfish have sensory neurons that detect the presence of chemicals, tactile interactions, and visual signals, with corresponding motor neurons that activate body contractions and intermediate neurons that transport stimuli from sensory neurons.

TRIPEDALIA CYSTOPHORA (BOX JELLYFISH)

The most advanced of nerve net organisms originated in the Middle Cambrian period, the box jellyfish, of which there are 51 species organized across two orders (e.g., *Carybdeida* and *Chirodropida*) with eight families therein (i.e., five and three families respectively).

For our purposes, we chose *Tripedalia cystophora*, a species of box jellyfish, to illustrate *Nerve Net Consciousness* because it predates the development of neural bundles and brains. Yet, with scant neuronal structures, the box jellyfish is equipped with no fewer than twenty-four eyes of four different types, grouped in clusters of six on the four sides of their bell, with each set including a pair of eyes already equipped with a sophisticated lens, retina, iris, and cornea.

Four of the twenty-four eyes of this species are exclusively to peer above the water's surface. Unlike most jellyfish that can only flow with the current, box jellyfish use their remaining eyes to navigate shallow waters around the various obstacles they encounter, using the location of the tree canopy above as a point of reference. When obscuring the canopy from view, the organisms cannot navigate, leading scientists to suspect that each set of eyes supports a small number of specific behaviors.

Each eye group directly supports a small set of behaviors. Thus, the organism circumvents the need for a neural bundle to process sensory signals. All that exists is a simple network of neurons communicating signals from the eyes to specific physical locations within the organism's body.

Box jellyfish are more advanced than other jellyfish species as they demonstrate the ability to hunt and capture prey with directional control of their mobility to rates of travel as high as two meters per second (i.e., 4.5 mph) while also coordinating venomous tentacles that extend up to ten feet in length.

The visual array of box jellyfish as a sensory system is consistent with the first aggregate of form (i.e., '*rupa*') for experiencing the physical world, followed by the second aggregate of sensation (i.e., '*vedana*') to categorize the form as pleasant, unpleasant, or indifferent. These features allow box jellyfish to make choices of where to move independently of the flow of the current physically.

Given that the organism can perceive prey, obstacles, and tree canopies within its local environment, the Buddha would have pointed to the third aggregate of perception (i.e., '*samjna*'), associating a particular experience and conceptualizing it into an idea that is distinct from other ideas and their experiences.

Being equipped with an array of eyes renders an extensive visual awareness of the environment, and its network of neurons creates the ability to rapidly communicate this awareness to the pertinent motor neurons within the organism.

The next question is whether the box jellyfish can learn, and the answer is yes, as one would expect from a predator.

To quote Doctor Sofie Dam Nielsen in her 2018 article, *Learning in the Box Jellyfish Tripedalia cystophora*: Quote.

> *"In the present study, we wanted to test the hypothesis that T. cystophora can learn and remember changes in the relationship between contrast and distance. Through a series of behavioral experiments where*

contrast and distance can be controlled separately, we are able to show that they do change their behavior over time. Further, they can only learn a given 'contrast: distance' relationship when they are allowed the combined information from visual and mechanical stimuli. Our results also show that even one of the most advanced features of nervous systems, the ability to learn and remember, is a fundamental property of nervous systems present already in cnidarians, the earliest branch in the animal kingdom." End Quote.

[Learning in the Box Jellyfish Tripedalia cystophora, Feb 8, 2018, Sofie Dam Nielsen Ph.D. Marine Biology Section, Biology Department, Copenhagen University, Univisen - Kobenhavns Universitet]

As a result, the Buddha would have pointed to the fourth aggregate of mental formation (i.e., '*caitasika*') for the ability to choose an action or inaction when it comes to learning, influenced by prior experience.

To paraphrase Katsuki and Greenspan in their Current Biology article *Jellyfish nervous systems*:

Though this represents the emergence of neural structures, we are at the point where evolution has developed the full battery of molecular machinery for neurotransmission and neuromodulation (e.g., ion channels, traditional neurotransmitters, peptides, amino acids, small molecules, and their receptors). Specialized pacemaker neurons are even present to provide a rhythmic pulse to signal motor neurons to contract sheaths of muscle tissue in time to effect efficient motion.

[Jellyfish nervous systems, Takeo Katsuki and Ralph J. Greenspan, Kavli Institute for Brain and Mind, UCSD, La Jolla, California, USA, Current Biology Vol 23 No 14 R592]

FOURTH LEVEL OF CONSCIOUSNESS (NERVE CORD)

The next evolutionary step is *Nerve Cord Consciousness,* which began with the emergence of bilaterians, where a long line of organisms developed a left and right side that mirror one another, descending from a common marine wormlike ancestor some 600 million years ago. Nearly all animals belong to this group, sharing a design pattern where a neuronal nerve cord traverses from the organism's front to back, with a hollow gut cavity running in the same direction from mouth to anus.

PHYLUM NEMATODA

Phylum Nematoda is a suitable candidate to help illustrate *Nerve Cord Consciousness* as it contains a transparent group of nematodes (i.e., roundworm) about 1 mm in length belonging to the species *Caenorhabditis elegans* (a.k.a. C. elegans) within the genus *Caenorhabditis* and phylum *Nematoda*.

C. elegans is among the most studied organisms, second only to the volume of studies performed on *Drosophila melanogaster*, the common fruit fly, for its complex behaviors supported by 302 neurons having roughly 7,000 synapses.

To paraphrase J. Hodgkin in the 2001 article *Caenorhabditis elegans* in the Encyclopedia of Genetics:

> *This nematode possesses sensory capabilities at the nose supporting light detection, tactile, thermal, osmotic pressure, tiny electrical current, and chemical detecting excitatory neurotransmitters, social behaviors, mating, sleep, motor, drug-dependence behaviors, learning, and memory.*

> *By 1998, sequencing of the 97 million DNA base pairs of the C. elegans genome was complete.*

> *Scientific estimates of the number of species of nematodes go into the millions, as four out of every five animals on our planet are a nematode. Nematology is a recognized discipline within zoology encompassing plant and animal parasitic nematodes, entomopathogenic nematodes that kill insects, and many individual marine and land nematodes.*

> *[Caenorhabditis elegans, 2001, J. Hodgkin, Encyclopedia of Genetics]*

We observe most behaviors in response to stimuli of *C. elegans* in terms of locomotion.

For example, the worm usually initiates backward movement to alter direction, called a reversal. A small group of command interneurons is responsible for reversals, as laser ablation of interneurons renders *C. elegans* incapable of reversals.

The design of the *C. elegans* nervous system has sensory neurons sending signals to the first two layers of interneurons for decision-making. Command interneurons then receive signals from both interneuron layers and directly from sensory neurons to transmit signals down the ventral cord (i.e., the remaining length of the neural cord) to drive locomotion.

To paraphrase Piggott, Liu, Feng, Wescott, and Xu in their 2012 US National Library of Medicine National Institutes of Health article *The neural circuits and synaptic mechanisms underlying motor initiation in C. elegans*:

> *Scientists also found a dual-mode of motor initiation (i.e., equipped with both command neurons and disinhibitor neurons to control motor neurons) within the C. elegans nervous system that has also been identified in mammals, suggesting that morphologically distinct nervous systems from extremely distant yet related organisms, may adopt similar strategies to motor control.*

> *[The neural circuits and synaptic mechanisms underlying motor initiation in C. elegans, 2012 Nov 11, Beverly J. Piggott, Jie Liu, Zhaoyang Feng, Seth A. Wescott, X.Z. Shawn Xu, US National Library of Medicine National Institutes of Health]*

And to paraphrase Doctors Lin and Rankin in their 2010 article *Nematode Learning and Memory: Neuroethology*:

> *C. elegans demonstrates highly plastic behavior (i.e., strong learning capabilities), including associative learning (e.g., classical conditioning [Pavlov], operant conditioning [reward and punishment]), non-associative learning (i.e., habituation [desensitizing through repetition], sensitization [sensitizing through repetition]), and memory and learning that leverages mechanical, thermal, and chemical stimuli (e.g., glutamate, dopamine, serotonin, and neuroendocrine signaling).*

> *[Nematode Learning and Memory: Neuroethology, 2010, C.H. Lin Ph.D., C.H. Rankin Ph.D., University of British Columbia, Vancouver, BC, Canada]*

The significance of *C. elegans* to our journey is related to the surprising inventory of capabilities possible with just a few neurons.

Nerve Cord Consciousness has a total of 302 neurons comprised of a small number of neuron types with four sensory neurons, a small collection of interneurons in the first two layers, a small collection of command neurons, a ventral cord of motor neurons, and early types of *neuroglia* (a.k.a. glia, glial cells) before the evolution of a neural bundle (a.k.a. polyganglionic) or brain (a.k.a. predominately a highly layered nervous system).

> *As we shall discuss later, neuroglia cells become an essential factor, having many types that function at many levels.*

> *For example, astrocytes control the growth and maintenance of the central nervous system (CNS); peripheral glia link communication between the CNS and other cell types; enteric glia are essential for every function of gastrointestinal function; glia control synaptic creation and pruning; myelinating glia maintain neuronal structural integrity; glia regulate ion, neurotransmitter, and neuro-hormone concentrations; glia store energy in the form of glycogen for neurons; and glia provide defense for neural tissue.*

The Buddha would have likely posited that the four sensory neurons of *C. elegans* correlate to the first aggregate of form (i.e., 'rupa') for experiencing the physical world, followed by the second aggregate of sensation (i.e., 'vedana') to categorize the form as pleasant, unpleasant, or indifferent, allowing *C. elegans* to make choices of where to move physically.

As *C. elegans* can distinctly perceive various stimuli within its environment, the Buddha would likely have pointed to the third aggregate of perception (i.e., 'samjna') being able to associate with a particular experience and conceptualize it into an idea distinct from other ideas and their experiences.

C. elegans has interneurons that process signals from decision-making sensory neurons that are routed to motor neurons down the length of the organism, demonstrating memory and multiple types of learning.

The Buddha would have pointed to the fourth aggregate of mental formation (i.e., *'caitasika'*) for the ability to choose an action or inaction when it comes to learning, influenced by prior experience.

At this point in evolution, the subcellular components (e.g., cytoskeletal microtubules) available to all eukaryote cells combined with a neuronal nerve cord consisting of sensory, intermediate, and motor neurons in a ventral cord, provide the foundation for nerve types, nerve formations, and the development of *neuroglia* (a.k.a. glia, glial cells) as in nematodes.

Early *neuroglia* cells may also make it possible to support the emergence of the fifth aggregate of consciousness (i.e., *'chetna'*) as an early form of experience (a.k.a. qualia). However, many more *neuroglial* cell types and configurations are yet to emerge.

FIFTH LEVEL OF CONSCIOUSNESS (NEURAL BUNDLE)

The evolutionary step of *Neural Bundle Consciousness* is particularly noteworthy for a variety of reasons, one of which being that it coincides with the emergence of complex social behavior as well as the emergence of new intellectual capabilities, such as possessing a sense of location, duration of time, and object-use.

The term 'object-use' is distinct from 'tool-use' in that an object is used as-is, and a tool is an object that has had its design modified to support a particular purpose.

From the consciousness perspective, there is a significant difference between 'object-use' and 'tool-use' since tool-use includes a conceptualization of a design change and then a problem-solving step to determine how to affect that design change.

Tools themselves may be categorized differently and, as a result, have been assigned scientific terminology.

As examples of this terminology, a 'proto-tool' is a tool not to be held by the user, such as bait left to attract prey; a 'meta-tool' is a tool used to help make another tool, such as a sharpened stone used to fashion points on the end of sticks.

The neural structures of this level belong to the phylum *Arthropoda* (e.g., insects, arachnids, myriapods, and crustaceans). These neural structures demonstrate the first known instance of object use, where insects (e.g., ants of the species *Conomyrma bicolor*) illustrate the behavior of picking up small stones and other objects with their mandibles and drop them down the vertical entrances of rival colonies to thwart them in competing for food. Different species of ants (e.g., *Aphaenogaster*) use leaves as a portable container to transport the water droplets resting on them to their nest.

To paraphrase Lorinczi, Quinquis, Modra, Bovet, Call, and d'Ettorne in their 2017 Animal Behavior article *Tool selection during foraging in two species of funnel ants*:

> *A study in 2017 documented two ant species that were given choices between natural and artificial materials for transporting water and chose the synthetic materials that had a better soaking capacity, indicating plasticity in their object-use behavior.*

> *["Tool selection during foraging in two species of funnel ants," Jan 2017, Istvan Maák, Gabor Lőrinczi, Pauline Le Quinquis, Gabor Módra, Dalila Bovet, Josep Call, and Patrizia d'Ettorre, Animal Behavior Volume 123]*

And to paraphrase Loukola, Perry, Coscos, and Chittka in their 2017 article, *Bumblebees show cognitive flexibility by improving on an observed complex behavior*:

> *Another study in 2017 demonstrated that insects could learn object use, where a species of bumblebee, Bombus terrestris, learned to move a tiny wooden ball to a specific area to receive a quantity of sucrose.*

> *["Bumblebees show cognitive flexibility by improving on an observed complex behavior," Feb 2017, Olli J. Loukola, Clint J. Perry, Louie Coscos, Lars Chittka, Department of Biological and Experimental Psychology, School of Biological and Chemical Sciences, Queen Mary University of London, UK, Science]*

GENUS APIS (HONEYBEE)

The organism chosen for demonstrating *Neural Bundle Consciousness* is the genus *Apis* (a.k.a. honeybee), with seven identified from among the 20,000 species of bees.

The evolutionary path of pre-brain development is marked here by the fusing of neural ganglia to form neural bundles. As part of the insect's central nervous system (CNS), the neural bundle is sufficiently advanced to be organized into three regions: a *protocerebrum*, *deutocerebrum*, and *tritocerebrum*.

The honeybee, one of the many insects equipped with three regions in its neural bundle, exhibits an array of new capabilities, including our next level of consciousness.

While not all bees are social, the honeybee lives in complex societies considered '*eusocial,*' which is an extreme form of social behavior found among a relatively small number of species of insects, crustaceans, and mammals.

> *Eusociality involves the presence of multiple generations cohabitating and exhibiting cooperative brood care, including a method for dividing labor into reproductive and non-reproductive groups.*

Before the emergence of *Neural Bundle Consciousness*, there were few examples of organisms communicating with other individuals at any level. However, this evolutionary step of consciousness expands communication from simply occurring between the cells of the same organism to active communication with other individual members to form a cooperative network across individual members.

Cooperation requires the emergence of a basic language to communicate to achieve coordinated social behavior. The language of the honeybee primarily consists of pheromones that rely upon a sense of smell, but their language also extends to physical movements and signals.

Each honeybee belongs to one of three categories: one queen, female workers, and male drones. The queen and worker are identical genetically as female members. The queen generally remains in the hive while the female worker leaves to forage for food.

To avoid getting lost in the food search, the workers keep track of their physical location relative to the hive and sun and store this information in their memory, which they use to navigate back to the hive.

Bees have five eyes that send stimuli into their sensory neurons. On the top of their heads, honeybees have three black dots that are eyes that only detect light intensity, not shapes.

On either side of its head, the honeybee has a compound eye (i.e., producing images comprised of pixel-like dots) with setae (i.e., fine hairs) growing out of them, which scientists believe detect wind speed and direction to help the bee stay on course in windy conditions.

Bees can see polarized light (i.e., light that has traveled through a filter), making it possible for them to know the sun's location even when shielded by heavy clouds and wavelengths of ultraviolet light, making flowers stand out brightly in the environment.

Bees can also distinguish some colors, such as yellow, blue-green, violet, ultraviolet, and a color known as 'bee's purple,' a mixture of yellow and ultraviolet, though they are blind to red.

Bees have olfactory sensors on antennas on the top of their head equipped with 170 chemoreceptors, which is at the high end for insects, used to detect pollen, flowers, and the presence of other bees and insects.

To paraphrase Galizia and Sachse in their 2010 article, *The Neurobiology of Olfaction*:

> *The olfactory systems of insects and vertebrates have numerous similarities.*

> *[The Neurobiology of Olfaction, 2010, CRC Press/Taylor & Francis, C. Giovanni Galizia, Silke Sachse]*

Also, to paraphrase a 2010 article from the University of Arizona, Honey Bee Senses:

Worker bees have a probiscus (i.e., straw-like tongue) equipped with taste buds that distinguish between sweet, sour, bitter, and salt. Their flavor spectrum is similar to humans, though humans have a comparatively heightened sense of bitterness, and the taste buds of bees are more sensitive to salts.

[Honey Bee Senses, 2010, University of Arizona]

And to paraphrase my 2002 book, <u>*Sensitive by Nature: Understanding Intelligence and the Mind*</u>:

When the female worker bee locates a food source, it navigates its way back to the hive with its memory of the flight path between it and the food source. Upon returning to the hive, the worker honeybee communicates these flight instructions through a language of dance movements, repeating the dance steps until the other female worker bees learn the dance and can repeat it themselves. Then, the female worker honeybees who have memorized the dance translate the dance movements into the flight instructions to the food source to assist in transporting food supplies back to the hive for processing.

For honeybees to communicate, their language must have a vocabulary. While this vocabulary is hard-wired and cannot grow, interneurons of their predominately polyganglionic neurons must convert patterns of visual stimuli from their various eyes into a language of dance movements, thereby conceptualizing the visual stimuli into a sequence of body movements that other workers can observe, imitate, and learn. Scientists believe that the honeybee's memory of this known information persists within the female worker honeybee for up to three days; for comparison purposes only, Dionea muscipula (a.k.a. sensitive plant) retains its memory typically for a month or longer.

Of insects that have evolved neural bundles, the genus Apis is among the most advanced.

Hymenoptera is a large order of insects consisting of bees, wasps, ants, and sawflies, all equipped with neural bundles. The wasp shares a common ancestor with bees, and ants have many hard-wired behavioral routines to perform.

When scientists experiment with wasps and bees by resetting the conditions of one of their hard-wired routines back to its beginning, the wasp will repeat the task repeatedly, potentially until even death; in comparison, the honeybee will repeat the activity for a limited duration of approximately ten minutes before moving on to its following action without regard to the task being complete.

[Sensitive by Nature: Understanding Intelligence and the Mind, 2002, J Luisi, 1ˢᵗ Books Library Publishers]

It is essential to point out that this is the upper limit to which the honeybee can communicate. For example, one honeybee cannot communicate with another honeybee anything other than flying instructions to find food, such as whether the flowers on the other side of the hill are fewer but have more nectar.

While it is unclear as to whether the honeybee can hear sounds, they do respond to vibrations, and they sense the physical world with sight, scent, taste, and touch, consistent with the first aggregate of 'form' (i.e., *'rupa*) for experiencing the physical world.

Concerning the second aggregate of sensation (i.e., *'vedana'*), *Apis* (a.k.a. honeybee) can categorize these sensations as pleasant, unpleasant, or indifferent, allowing *Apis* to choose where to go and what to do.

If he were aware of our modern scientific knowledge of insect object use and the behaviors of the genus *Apis* (a.k.a. honeybee), the Buddha would have pointed to the third aggregate of perception (i.e., 'samjna'). It associates a particular experience and conceptualizes it into an idea distinct from other ideas and their related experiences, such as the ability to perceive gusts of wind to adjust to maintain a straight flight path.

The Buddha may have also acknowledged *Apis* (a.k.a. honeybee) as possessing the fourth aggregate of mental formation (i.e., 'caitasika') for choosing an action or inaction when learning from prior experience.

The examples cited include objects insects use to transport water and the honeybee demonstrating an ability to conceptualize flight instructions into dance movements. It would also involve teaching other female worker bees the dance and then those female workers conceptualizing the dance into flight instructions.

Building upon the previous four levels of consciousness, *Neural Bundle Consciousness* has an array of new sensory equipment, an increased number of interneurons, and an increased number of specialized *neuroglia* cell types that move us closer to the beginnings of the fifth aggregate of consciousness where a basic form of *qualia* may emerge.

Although many parallels continue between the Buddhist framework of consciousness and a scientific one, from here on out, we will leave the Buddhist framework of consciousness behind as our journey focuses on a growing number of scientific disciplines.

SIXTH LEVEL OF CONSCIOUSNESS (PRIMITIVE BRAIN)

Our next level of consciousness, *Primitive Brain Consciousness* (i.e., a predominantly layered neural system), continues to build upon our previous levels.

This configuration of neuronal structures first evolved in the marine invertebrate phyla *Echinodermata*, which is a large phylum including starfish, sea urchins, and sea cucumbers, and *Hemichordata*, which is a minor phylum of acorn worms.

Later, to thrive on land, these neuronal structures become fully organized in the vertebrate phylum *Chordata*, subphylum *Vertebrata*, which are chordates with backbones numbering about 69,300 species.

REPTILIA

The diversity of *Chordata Vertebrata* provides us with an ample continuum of layered neural systems within which the class *Reptilia* can help us illustrate the evolutionary features of *Primitive Brain Consciousness* significantly predating the first mammalian brain.

As such, we will focus next on the primitive brain of the class *Reptilia*.

Our use of the term 'brain' is to align as closely as possible with the biological definition, which is an organ that coordinates animal nervous system functions.

In contrast, an organ is a group of tissues adapted to perform a functional capability. With their specialized functions, organs become grouped into cooperating systems, such as the digestive system's various organs.

We saw the fusing of polyganglionic neurons divided into protocerebrum, deutocerebrum, and tritocerebrum.

In Reptilia, we see many early structures present in the mammalian brain involving the formation of specialized tissues, such that it visually appears analogous to the mammalian brain.

Though the mammalian brain did not evolve from *Reptilia*, they share an extinct amniote ancestor called synapsids, *also known as Theropsids.* This common ancestor lent *Reptilia* many of the same brain tissues found among mammals.

Amniotes refer to animals that begin development with a membrane surrounding the fetus, shared among all tetrapod vertebrates comprising reptiles, birds, and mammals. Tetrapod refers to four limbs consisting of pairs of legs, arms, or wings.

Amniotes lay their eggs on land or carry the fertilized egg within the female, making them distinct from anamniotes (e.g., fishes, amphibians) that are not tetrapods and usually lay their eggs in water.

Basal amniotes, resembling small lizards, were the first amniotes evolving from Reptiliamorpha 312 million years ago in the Carboniferous geologic period.

Basal amniote eggs were the first to survive out of the water, allowing amniotes to branch out into drier environments; this was possible because their eggs could breathe and eliminate wastes through their protective layers. This adaptation allowed amniotes to rapidly emerge as the dominant chordates with backbones on land (i.e., Pangea).

Also, with *Primitive Brain Consciousness,* we see the emergence of the first type of dreaming (a.k.a. regular dreaming) as *Reptilia* experience REM sleep.

To quote James Maynard in his 2016 article, *Do Reptiles Dream? New Study Suggests That Animals Experience REM Sleep*: Quote.

"Humans typically experience REM sleep four to five times each night. Electrodes placed inside the brains of the lizards revealed Pogona vitticeps experienced the effect around 350 times during each period of sleep. These stages lasted an average of just 80 seconds each time."

"This discovery suggests that sleep patterns in humans and birds evolved 100 million years earlier than previously believed. Researchers believe the behavior likely first evolved in amniotes, a distant common ancestor of lizards, birds, and mammals, who lived between 300 million and 320 million years before our own time." End Quote.

["Do Reptiles Dream? New Study Suggests That Animals Experience REM Sleep", April 28, 2016, James Maynard – science writer, Tech Times- Science]

Since reptilian and mammalian brains share a variety of brain regions, circuits, and cell types, it makes it convenient to compare the capabilities across *Primitive Brain Consciousness* and *Mammalian Consciousness.* Interestingly, all general brain regions found in *Mammalia* have homologies in *Reptilia.*

The regions that form the large-scale architecture of Reptilian and Mammalian brains include the pallium, medial pallium, dorsal pallium, striatum, pallidum, subpallium, hypothalamus, thalamus, cerebral nuclei, cerebral cortex, diencephalon, midbrain, tectum, hindbrain, cerebellum, and spinal cord.

These brain tissues cooperate in a layered neuron-based system of functions.

For example, chemical sensors send signals into the olfactory bulb routed to the pallium region. In contrast, signals from the retina enter the pallium, routed to the tectum and thalamus regions.

Reptilia has a wide range of senses.

These include:

Vision - with both a flexible lens that enables focusing on images at various distances and photoreceptors that can detect some colors into the higher wavelengths of the UV range.

Infrared detection - using sensory pits.

Hearing - many species within *Reptilia* hear a range of sound frequencies reasonably well, including low-frequency vibrations.

Smell - using an olfactory system and chemical receptors that facilitate location triangulation of the source in the air.

Taste - common to vertebrates are degrees of an ability to detect sweet, sour, bitter, salty, and umami (i.e., a meaty or savory taste produced by several amino acids and nucleotides, such as glutamate and aspartate).

Tactile senses – that includes touch, temperature, humidity, and sunlight, and the

Vomeronasal organ - specifically to detect pheromones.

To paraphrase Stoyanov, Moneva, Sapundzhiev, and Tonchev in their 2016 article in The Journal of Laryngology and Otology, *The vomeronasal organ - incidence in a Bulgarian population*:

The vomeronasal organ (VO) detects chemical messengers (i.e., pheromones) that carry information between individuals of the same species and sometimes may also provide a sense of smell underwater.

In most mammals, the vomeronasal organ is present in early primate fetal development but often disappears in later fetal development.

The VO is present in a percentage of the Homo sapiens population (e.g., 26.83% of the Bulgarian population) though it is inactive across all Homo sapiens.

["The vomeronasal organ - incidence in a Bulgarian population," April 2016, Stoyanov G., Moneva K., Sapundzhiev N., Tonchev A.B., The Journal of Laryngology and Otology]

To paraphrase Nauman, Ondracek, Reiter, Shein-Idelson, Tosches, Yamawaki, and Laurent in the US National Library of Medicine National Institutes of Health article "The Reptilian Brain":

Reptilia demonstrates a variety of behaviors. These include defensive behaviors that reduce their metabolism, allowing them to blend into the environment, and group defense and alarm signaling with territorial defense as a standard feature of intra-species behavior.

Some species of Reptilia are foragers, while other species are hunters. When food resources are plentiful, some species relax their defensiveness and share food, including the same carcass.

[The Reptilian Brain, 2015, Robert K. Naumann, Janie M. Ondracek, Samuel Reiter, Mark Shein-Idelson, Maria Antonietta Tosches, Tracy M. Yamawaki, Gilles Laurent, US National Library of Medicine National Institutes of Health, Elsevier Publishers]

Some *Reptilia* demonstrate an ability to learn to the extent that they can learn to navigate mazes like many birds and mammals. Like earlier forms of consciousness, *Reptilia* also shows object use, where crocodiles collect sticks to use as bait to capture birds.

A 2013 Science News article from the University of Tennessee at Knoxville explains that:

> *Crocodilians wait for a bird to claim the stick for nesting to spring the trap as the bird approaches while balancing sticks on their heads. This behavior is the first known case of a predator employing an object's use as a lure in coordination with the seasonal behavior of its prey.*

> *["Crocodiles are cleverer than previously thought: Some crocodiles use lures for hunting their prey," Dec 4, 2013, the University of Tennessee at Knoxville, Science News], ["Crocodiles and their ilk may be smarter than they look," Dec 9, 2013, Jason G. Goldman Ph.D. psychology, The Washington Post, Health and Science]*

Reptiles can become domesticated to the extent that they recognize their human owner, though most can never be fully tamed.

Reptilia responds with a much broader set of behaviors than just the proverbial fight or flight response, including actively hiding, blending into the environment, mimicking death, self-inflation, and vocalization to frighten off a potential threat.

The first evidence of primitive emotions also occurs when consciousness achieves *Primitive Brain Consciousness*. Before this level of consciousness, organisms appear limited to simple categories of pleasant, unpleasant, or indifferent feelings.

In *Reptilia,* emotions include sexual attraction, fear, aggressiveness, and social status, where social status manifests itself in ways such as sun-basking placement, breeding, and forming family units, sometimes exhibiting long-term monogamy among mates.

Sexually motivated combat for mates in *Reptilia* also emerges, where the winner earns the right to mate, and the subordinate animal must temporarily or permanently leave the group.

The seven senses are present in the class *Reptilia* (e.g., vision, hearing, smell, taste, tactile, infrared, and vomeronasal). They support the ability to experience the physical world in various ways, and those experiences are enhanced with primitive emotions, such as sexual attraction, fear, aggressiveness, and social emotions, that help the organism decide where to move and how to behave.

Reptiles can perceive a wide array of stimuli within their environment. They can also conceptualize them into an idea distinct from other ideas and their experiences, such as an intra-species invasion of territory. Moreover, the *Reptilian* behavior involving object use is a reasonable indicator of having the ability to associate a particular experience and then conceptualize it into an idea.

Reptiles have brain regions that process signals in an assembly line from sensory neurons to make decisions routed to motor neurons of the organism, demonstrating memory and multiple types of learning.

Therefore, it can choose an action or inaction when it comes to learning as influenced by prior experience, such as being able to recognize its human pet owner so as not to become alarmed.

The *Reptilian* behavior of employing twigs as a lure to trap prey during the appropriate season also indicates an ability to choose an action to capture prey.

Building upon the previous five levels of consciousness, *Primitive Brain Consciousness* has an array of sensory equipment, a vastly increased number of interneurons, brain regions that are homologous to the mammalian brain, and an increased number of specialized *neuroglia* cell types that support early forms of *qualia*.

There is much more to learn about *Reptilia* and perhaps its predecessor, as this is our first glimpse into the first brain that resembles the major brain regions of mammals, primates, and *Homo sapiens*.

SEVENTH LEVEL OF CONSCIOUSNESS (MAMMALIAN)

An extinct amniote ancestor (i.e., *synapsids,* a.k.a. *theropsids*) that lent *Reptilia* its brain tissues provided the foundation for the mammalian brain. Upon doing so, evolutionary forces continued to develop distinct mammalian features.

However, let's pause momentarily and ask, "What might have been at least one of those forces?".

First, this would require a force that could alter genes at a molecular level. More specifically, it would require modifying the nucleotide sequences of the genome in question.

Such changes can result from the imperfect copying of genetic molecules during replication, or they can result from damage caused by chemicals or radiation (e.g., ultraviolet, gamma) before or during replication.

> *Mutation rates due to imperfect copying or damaged nucleotide sequences are highest, involving sexual reproduction predominantly caused by the male partner.*
>
> *One significant reason males are more likely to produce genetic defects is that defects increase with age, and males continue to produce genetic material daily during their lifetime.*
>
> *In contrast, the female produces their lifetime supply of eggs within 20 weeks of gestation while still in the womb before they are born.*

However, while defects during the production of sperm may be a contributing factor, evolutionary forces would appear to advance more rapidly than these factors could reasonably explain, particularly concerning the evolutionary rate of the mammalian brain.

One force that could propel evolution faster for all areas of life is a factor known as a retrovirus.

RETROVIRUS

Several million different viruses roam within the environment shared by mammals. Most think of a virus as a simple strand of genetic material that enters a living cell only to take over its reproductive mechanisms to replicate more of itself, eventually destroying the cell and releasing a few hundred replicas to repeat the process.

Aside from the type of virus that replicates itself, another kind of virus inserts itself into the genetic material of cells, called a *retrovirus*.

Many viruses are known as either DNA, RNA, or reverse-transcribing viruses.

Reverse transcribing viruses include retroviruses and para-retroviruses.

A retrovirus takes its RNA and uses a DNA intermediate to replicate, whereas a para-retrovirus takes its DNA and uses an RNA intermediate to replicate. It always borrows one or the other to replicate.

A retrovirus is a type of RNA virus (a.k.a. single-stranded positive-sense RNA virus) that inserts a copy of its genome into the DNA molecule of a host cell to result in a modified and rather extended version of the host cell's DNA molecule.

*It is referred to as '**retro**' because it first uses its reverse transcriptase enzyme to produce DNA from its RNA genome, which is the opposite of what is considered the usual procedure employed by viruses, hence the term '**retro**.' Hence, it works backwards to first create DNA before using it.*

Until recently, tracing the origins of viruses was impossible, as viruses leave no fossils. With scientific advancements in the mapping of nucleotide sequences and computer analysis, it is now possible to identify new and older viruses present in the genome of numerous older organisms, and it is becoming possible to determine the effect of these altered genomes.

For example, the fact that several recently discovered viruses are in a limited number of species suggests that these viruses are relatively new.

Genetic strands that comprise viruses may have developed in many ways, first emerging among pre-life chemicals and then bacteria, early plants, or primitive insects millions of years ago. From the beginning, these genetic strands may have participated in the payload of all genetic material.

Once a retrovirus has become inserted into the genome of a species, it propagates as part of that species' genetic material, making it an '*endogenous retrovirus* (ERV).'

Retroviruses and their strands of nucleotide sequences began developing before the formation of life itself. Previously, scientists believed prokaryotes to be the ancestor of all known life.

Endogenous retroviruses span the entire phylum of *Chordata* (i.e., vertebrates). Approximately ten percent of the DNA of simple mammals, such as mice, match those of known *endogenous retroviruses*. As more nucleotide strands are studied, it is becoming increasingly apparent that retroviruses have played a key role in rapidly propelling evolution.

Endogenous retroviruses also influence cells by triggering the expression of other genes in the DNA. While it is understandable that physicians look at viruses as parasites, in the larger context, they are nucleotide editors that roam, reproduce, and insert strands of nucleotides into other strands of nucleotides, where they become a permanent part of the genome.

One example of how retroviral gene modifications have become critical to mammalian life is the following.

To quote Doctor Elizabeth Mitchell in her 2015 article, *Endogenous Retroviruses: Key to Mammalian Brain Development?*: Quote.

> *"In recent years, scientists have learned that the ability of the trophoblastic cells to fuse, forming the placenta, comes from certain retroviral genes in the mammalian genome. The specific genes differ from species to species, but an expression of these genes is essential to the placental formation and, therefore, to mammalian reproduction."* End Quote.

> *[Endogenous Retroviruses: Key to Mammalian Brain Development? Feb 21, 2015, Dr. Elizabeth Mitchell, Answers in Genesis, Answers in Depth]*

Overall, *retroviruses* are one of the factors that help explain the accelerated rate of evolutionary advancement within the mammalian brain as opposed to it being propelled solely by random copy errors and mutations.

The impact of each genetic edit on the cell, organism, or species will either be favorable, unfavorable, or indifferent, determined immediately, near-term, or long-term in the form of extinction, survival, or evolutionary advancement, such as to mammals.

EMERGENCE OF MAMMALS

Biology defines mammals as vertebrates characterized by the presence of mammary glands with which females produce milk for feeding their newborns.

The first mammals were soft-shell egg-laying organisms that evolved approximately 225 million years ago (mya). Then, at about 160 mya, a marsupial branch emerged from one of the early marsupial branches, creating placental mammals.

Placental mammals diverged into four major branches, constituting over 90 percent of mammalian species.

To quote Bob Strauss in his 2018 article in ThoughtCo, *The Evolution of the First Mammals*: Quote.

> *"Recently, paleontologists discovered conclusive fossil evidence for the first important split in the mammal family tree, the one between placental and marsupial mammals."*

> *"Technically, the first marsupial-like mammals of the late Triassic period are known as metatherians. From these evolved the eutherians, which later branched off into placental mammals."*

> *"The type specimen of Juramaia, the "Jurassic mother," dates to about 160 million years ago, and demonstrates that the metatherian/eutherian split occurred at least 35 million years before scientists had previously estimated." End Quote.*

> *[The Evolution of the First Mammals, Oct 10, 2018, Bob Strauss - science author, ThoughtCo]*

The brain tissue of early mammals enjoys several advantages over the brain of *Reptilia*, including a significant increase in neural layering, now numbering between fifteen to twenty specialized cortical areas.

To paraphrase Jon H. Kaas, Department of Psychology, Vanderbilt University in his 2014 article, *The Evolution of Brains from early mammals to Humans*:

> *For example, Reptilia's lateral and median cortical regions are now significantly enlarged with many more neurons and renamed to the piriform cortex and hippocampus. What was the dorsal cortex in Reptilia is now a much thicker neocortex subdivided into six layers with different functional roles.*

> *[The Evolution of Brains from early mammals to Humans, Jan 1, 2014, Jon H. Kaas, Department of Psychology, Vanderbilt University]*

The emergence of mammals introduced a variety of more advanced features, including mammary glands, a middle ear bone (i.e., mammals have two bones for hearing that all other amniotes use for eating), a different jaw joint, different shapes of teeth, a boney secondary palate, fur or hair, more erect limbs (forelimbs and hindlimbs), a muscular diaphragm for breathing, a four-chambered heart to separate oxygenated and deoxygenated blood, warm-bloodedness to support a more efficient and powerful metabolism, and a larger more advanced brain with a larger brain mass relative to body mass consisting of a significant increase in both the number of neurons and *neuroglial* cells and their types.

A larger brain mass is typically metabolically costly to maintain, taking longer developmental time to become sufficiently functional to support the organism; in response, mammals developed systems to help their higher metabolic rates and modified their behaviors to nurture their offspring for the longer duration needed to ensure their survival.

By the time mouse-like mammals evolved, the environment and the challenges of predators drove the behaviors of early mammals.

For example, dinosaurs evolved simultaneously with the first mammals, rapidly becoming the dominant terrestrial animal until their extinction was just 65 mya.

To quote Bob Strauss again from his article, *The Evolution of the First Mammals*: Quote

> *"Very few early mammals were larger than mice, for a simple reason: dinosaurs had already become the dominant terrestrial animals on earth."*

> *"The only ecological niches open to the first mammals entailed a) feeding on plants, insects, and small lizards, b) hunting at night (when predatory dinosaurs were less active), and c) living high up in trees or underground, in burrows."* End Quote.

> *[The Evolution of the First Mammals, Oct 10, 2018, Bob Strauss - science author, ThoughtCo]*

Then, with the extinction of the dominant dinosaur species, 65 mya mammals were free to adapt to the many ecological niches abandoned by dinosaurs, in many cases adopting a similar body plan and lifestyle to that of dinosaur species.

Bob Strauss writes, quote:

> *"Giraffes, as you may have noticed, are eerily similar in body plan to ancient sauropods like Brachiosaurus, and other mammalian megafauna pursued similar evolutionary paths."* End Quote.

> *[The Evolution of the First Mammals, Oct 10, 2018, Bob Strauss - science author, ThoughtCo]*

GENUS *RATTUS*

To illustrate features of consciousness that emerged among early mammals, we have chosen the genus *Rattus*, one of the largest genera of mammals comprised of approximately seventy species equipped with a primitive mammalian brain.

Members of the genus *Rattus* demonstrate a high awareness of their environment, primarily due to their curiosity and general penchant for exploration.

For example, with no prior experience or training with levers, most members of Rattus will press levers multiple times over a relatively short duration.

As well as being more proficient than *Reptilia* at learning a maze, the genus *Rattus* also demonstrates more robust learning capabilities than *Reptilia* involving both direct causal learning (i.e., a click indicating the presence of food) and common causal learning (i.e., first learning that light causes a sound tone, which in turn indicates food, and then concluding that food co-exists with light).

Unlike *Reptilia*, *Rattus* also demonstrates an understanding of the causal relationship between their actions and outcomes, which points to a neural architecture that is associatively connected.

To quote Associate Professor Aaron P. Blaisdell of the UCLA Brain Research Center in his 2010 article, *Rational Behavior in Rats*: Quote.

"... rats show the ability to draw rational inferences about their novel actions before any experience with that action and its effects." End Quote.

[Rational Behavior in Rats, Jan 2010, Aaron P. Blaisdell – Associate Professor of Psychology, University of California, Los Angeles, UCLA Brain Research Center Institute member, Psychological Science Agenda]

According to brain study sciences, prospective memory is the ability to take action in the future. Prospective memory is demonstrated in mammals, such as those found in studies of the genus *Rattus,* and in *corvids* (i.e., crow family), such as ravens, crows, jays, and magpies.

Delayed gratification is one of the specific abilities for scientists to test. When measuring the limits of delayed gratification, dogs can think into the future for a few minutes, children can think into the future for a range from minutes, hours, and days, and adult humans can think into the future the longest, decades or without limitation.

To paraphrase Professor Jonathon D. Crystal Ph.D. Indiana University in his 2012 article, *Remembering the past and planning for the future in rats*:

Individuals must be able to use past information to construct simulations about future events to demonstrate prospective memory (e.g., episodic simulation, planning, prediction, and remembering intentions).

The genus Rattus demonstrates memory of past events, whether or not it expects a future need for the information, and can correctly anticipate food availability in trained trials.

In the mammalian brain, the areas required for prospective memory appear to coincide with the brain areas used to remember the past (e.g., medial prefrontal regions, posterior regions in the medial and lateral parietal cortex, the lateral temporal cortex, the medial temporal lobe, and hippocampus).

[Remembering the past and planning for the future in rats, Dec 7, 2012, Professor Jonathon D. Crystal Ph.D., Department of Psychological & Brain Sciences, Indiana University, Bloomington, IN, PMC US National Library of Medicine National Institutes of Health, Author manuscript]

Prospective memory either developed in parallel among corvids and mammals or emerged earlier in amniotes, the common ancestor to birds, reptiles, and mammals. It became strengthened later in birds and mammals.

Although REM sleep emerged with the common ancestor to *Reptilia* and *Mammalia* (i.e., amniotes), it is not until *Mammalian Consciousness* that the complete dreaming pattern (a.k.a. regular dreaming) emerges, where genus *Rattus* experiences the same stages of NREM (e.g., light sleep, deep sleep) and REM sleep as *Homo sapiens*.

In comparisons of Rattus' brain activity while navigating a maze and sleeping, their brain patterns are claimed even to indicate their location in the maze.

Not all mammals share the same features of dreaming, such as dolphins and seals. While in the water, mammals only allow one hemisphere of their brain the opportunity to perform anything resembling sleep.

To quote Dr. Jean-Pierre Legros M.D. Rheumatology of Stanislas College, in his 2018 article, *Do dolphins dream with only half their brain? How do they separate dreams from the real world?: Quote.*

"Dolphins take out of conscious integration only one of their brain hemispheres at a time. The physiological functions and the environment required for them a minimum of permanent attention. They cannot dream as humans do. The recordings of their brain activity show that they have no REM-sleep, where dreams are concentrated. The resting of a hemisphere nonetheless brings an alternating state of consciousness that may resemble a lucid dream or simply a torpor with bizarre ideas. Conscious integration has not disappeared; it is only reduced."

"It is interesting to note that seals, who sleep in the water but also on land, enter REM-sleep only on land. They dream only on dry land. As much for the dreamlike reputation of the 'big blue'" End Quote.

['Do dolphins dream with only half their brain? How do they separate dreams from the real world, Aug 27, 2018, Jean-Pierre Legros, M.D. Rheumatology, philosopher and writer, Stanislas College, Quora]

Concerning emotions, *Rattus* is also more advanced than *Reptilia* in experiments that have demonstrated empathy-driven behavior where members of *Rattus* will choose to free a captive companion rather than feast on a chocolate stash they could have had for themselves.

Another noteworthy feature of the *Rattus* brain is its problem-solving capabilities.

To quote Professor Marc Bkoff, Professor emeritus of Ecology and Evolutionary Biology, in his 2011 article, *Empathetic Rats and Ravishing Ravens*:

> *Inbal Ben-Ami Bartal noted. "These rats are learning because they are motivated by something internal. We're not showing them how to open the door, they don't get any previous exposure on opening the door, and it's hard to open the door. But they keep trying and trying, and it eventually works."*

> *[Empathetic Rats and Ravishing Ravens, Dec 8, 2011, Marc Bkoff Ph.D. Professor emeritus of Ecology and Evolutionary Biology, University of Colorado, Boulder, Colorado, Psychological Today, author of Animal Emotions]*

To paraphrase Lea Winerman in the 2005 article of American Psychological Association, *The mind's mirror*:

> *Neurologists point out that empathy-driven behavior may be supported by mirror neurons that evoke the same emotions in an observer of another individual and may help explain how individuals learn through mimicry.*

> *[The mind's mirror, Oct 2005, Lea Winerman, American Psychological Association]*

To quote Christian Jarrett Ph.D. psychology, in the Psychology Today article, Mirror Neurons: The Most Hyped Concept in Neuroscience?: Quote.

> *"Back in the 1990s, neuroscientists at the University of Parma identified cells in the premotor cortex of monkeys that had an unusual response pattern. They were activated when the monkeys performed a given action and, mirror-like, when they saw another individual perform that same movement." End Quote.*

> *[Mirror Neurons: The Most Hyped Concept in Neuroscience?, Dec 10, 2012, Christian Jarrett Ph.D. psychologist, Psychological Today]*

Genus *Rattus* also demonstrates significantly improved abilities over *Reptilia* in teaching themselves object-use and object-use as the result of training, as they are eager to explore the potential use and effect of any environmental objects (e.g., chains, levers, and buttons).

EIGHTH LEVEL OF CONSCIOUSNESS (PRIMATE)

Continuing our journey to the next advancement in consciousness, our next form of consciousness is *Primate Consciousness*.

Primates are a highly diversified order, consisting of 14 families and over 350 species varying in size between the 40-gram mouse lemur and the 200 kg gorilla, with the first *Primates* emerging around 82 million years ago before branching again around 65 million years ago (dinosaur extinction) into *strepsirrhine* (e.g., lemurs, lorises, and galagoes) and *haplorrhine* branches (e.g., *tarsiers* and *simians*).

Following the evolution of *simians* (a.k.a. *anthropoid*), around 35 million years ago, groups of *simians* colonized South America to become what we now call 'New World monkeys' (Americas), where the remaining *simians* (a.k.a. 'Old World monkeys') eventually split into apes in regions of Africa and Asia around 25 million years ago.

The evolutionary branch from apes also includes our closest common ancestor, 'chimpanzee - human last common ancestor' (CHLCA), or 'most recent common ancestor' (MRCA), which may have emerged just thirteen million years ago according to the science of dating mutations.

Although there are numerous variations across early *Primates*, the brain of these early *Primates* is distinct from their mammalian ancestors in four crucial ways.

To paraphrase Jon H Kaas, Department of Psychology, Vanderbilt University in his 2014 article, *The Evolution of Brains from early mammals to Humans*:

> *First, there is a significant increase in the brain-to-body mass ratios; second, there are several additional neuronal tissue layers; third, there are several distinct processing modules and subdivisions facilitating greater functional specialization; and fourth, neuron densities have significantly increased (three to five times greater) resulting in many more neurons in Primates than the equivalent brain tissue mass of their mammalian relatives.*

> *[The Evolution of Brains from early mammals to Humans, Jan 1, 2014, Jon H. Kaas, Department of Psychology, Vanderbilt University]*

Today, there are four extant (i.e., still alive today) genera of hominids, also known as great apes.

- genus *Pan* with its two extant species of *bonobo* and *common chimpanzee*
- genus *Gorilla* and its two extant species of '*Gorilla Gorilla*' (a.k.a. Western Gorilla) and '*Gorilla Beringer*' (a.k.a. Eastern Gorilla)
- genus *Pongo* with its three extant species of *Pongo pygmaeus* (a.k.a. Bornean orangutan), *Pongo abelii* (a.k.a. Sumatran orangutan), and *Pongo tapanuliensis* (a.k.a. Tapanuli orangutan) and
- genus *Homo* and its one extant species *Homo sapiens*

Primate Consciousness demonstrates a variety of advancements over *Mammalian Consciousness*, especially regarding social behaviors within which communication and language skills play an essential role.

At this point, we need to differentiate between communication and language, as clearly, many organisms communicate with one another using various techniques. However, few successfully cross that boundary into language basics beyond rudimentary communication.

Doctor Lisa Fosbender, Ph.D. writes in Psychology:

> *For our purposes, we define language as symbols represented in the form of vocal sounds or visual images and gestures, with rules for combining them to share ideas with other individuals.*
>
> *While various forms of communication may be instinctive, a language is learned and is passed from member to member as a learned skill.*
>
> *Languages have four design components, the first consisting of a feature requiring them to be symbolic to represent ideas or concepts.*
>
> *For example, the word "CAT" and the sound created by pronouncing the word "cat" are symbolic representations of an idea or concept.*
>
> *The second feature of a language, semantics, is that symbols must have a meaning. The symbol 'cat' means an animal we understand as different than other types of animals.*
>
> *The third design feature of a language, generativity, is using a relatively finite number of symbols to represent more ideas.*
>
> *For example, one may use the sequence of words 'metal,' 'cup,' and 'drink' to represent the idea of 'thermos.'*
>
> *The fourth design feature of a language, structure, is that when using combinations of symbols with one another, they are not sequenced randomly but instead must follow the rules, known as grammar, affecting the meaning. For example, 'man bites cat' has a different meaning than 'cat bites man.'*
>
> *[Lisa Fosbender, Ph.D., Psychology]*

Today, most humans learn an existing language instead of inventing a language. If we all had to develop a language before its use, many of us would be severely disadvantaged.

Each of the four extant hominid genera has demonstrated learning at least three of the four design components of language. However, the genera *Pan*, *Gorilla*, and *Pongo* require a tremendous coaching effort compared to *Homo sapiens*.

At their peak, these other hominids can achieve a language competency equivalent to that of a three-year-old *Homo sapiens* child, with little or no understanding of grammar.

To paraphrase Glasersfeld, Rumbaugh, and Savage-Rumbaugh of the Yerkes National Primate Research Center, Emory University, Georgia State article:

Common chimpanzees, bonobos, gorillas, and orangutans have demonstrated the ability to communicate with humans and with each other using sign language, physical tokens, and lexigrams (i.e., keyboards whose keys represent symbols corresponding to objects or ideas comprised of three panels totaling 384 keys.

[Ernst von Glasersfeld, Duane Rumbaugh, Sue Savage-Rumbaugh, Yerkes National Primate Research Center, Emory University, Georgia State University, Atlanta, Georgia]

To paraphrase Allen and Beatrice Gardner, and Van Cantfort in their 1989 article, *Teaching Sign Language to Chimpanzees*:

Washoe (Sept 1965 – Oct 30, 2007), a female common chimpanzee, was the first non-human to communicate using American Sign Language (ASL). She learned approximately 350 signs of ASL and, unassisted, taught her adopted son Loulis some signs.

[Teaching Sign Language to Chimpanzees, 1989, R. Allen Gardner, Beatrix T. Gardner, Thomas E. Van Cantfort, State University of New York, State University of New York Press]

[The Study of Signed Languages, 2002, David F. Armstrong, Michael A. Karchmer, John Vickrey Can Cleve, Gallaudet University Press, Washington, D.C.]

[Attitudes to Animals, 1999, Francine L. Dolins, Cambridge University Press, Cambridge, UK]

To quote Hillix and Runbaugh, University of Chicago, in their 2003 article, *Animal Bodies, Human Minds: Ape, Dolphin, and Parrot Language Skills*: Quote.

"For researchers to consider that Washoe had learned a sign, she had to use it spontaneously and appropriately for 14 consecutive days." End Quote.

[Animal Bodies, Human Minds: Ape, Dolphin, and Parrot Language Skills, 2003, W. A. Hillix, Duane Runbaugh, University of Chicago, Chicago, IL]

To again quote Allen and Beatrice Gardner in the 1984 article in the Journal of Comparative Psychology, *A vocabulary test for chimpanzees*: Quote.

"Also, Double-blind sign language and controlled vocabulary tests with independent observers agreed were necessary to accurately demonstrate generalization (e.g., the sign DOG could refer to any dog, FLOWER to any flower, SHOE to any shoe)." End Quote

[A vocabulary test for chimpanzees, 1984, R. Allen Gardner, Beatrix T. Gardner, Journal of Comparative Psychology, American Psychological Association]

And to paraphrase Francine Patterson, Ph.D. Psychology, Stanford University, Stanford, CA:

> *Regarding Koko (July 4, 1971 – June 19, 2018), Dr. Francine Patterson reported that a female Western lowland gorilla learned approximately 1,000 symbols in Gorilla Sign language (GSL), which is like American Sign Language (ASL) and demonstrated an understanding of about 2,000 English words.*

> *[Francine Patterson Ph.D. psychology, Stanford University, Stanford, CA]*

And to paraphrase Sue Savage-Rumbaugh Ph.D. psychology and primatology, University of Oklahoma:

> *A male bonobo, Kanzi (Oct 28, 1980) learned more human language than any other from non-humans while observing keyboard lessons given to his adoptive mother, Matata, by researcher Sue Savage-Rumbaugh.*

> *[Sue Savage-Rumbaugh Ph.D. psychology and primatology, University of Oklahoma, OK]*

Then, aside from language itself, there are various language applications.

When it comes to the ability to deceive individuals using communication for selfish goals, *Primate Consciousness* demonstrates a high degree of proficiency to mislead each other as a common practice. In response, individual primates are typically on guard against falling victim to deception themselves.

To quote Frans B. M. de Waal, Associate Professor of Psychology and Research Professor, Emory University, Atlanta, Yerkes Regional Primate Research Center, Atlanta, GA, in his 1992 article, *Intentional deception in primates*: Quote.

> *"The accumulated evidence is quite suggestive, implying sophisticated cognitive mechanisms, particularly in the great apes."*

> *"Primates not only suppress or hide certain signals, but also project false images or seem to react to non-existing external events to redirect another's attention." End Quote.*

> *[Intentional deception in primates, 1992, Frans B. M. de Waal Associate Professor of Psychology and Research Professor, Emory University, Atlanta, Yerkes Regional Primate Research Center, Atlanta, GA]*

To paraphrase Professor John McWhorter Ph.D., Stanford University, Columbia University, in his 2010 course lecture, *The Story of Human Language*:

> *Although the communication skills of primates seem impressive, the other three genera of primates have never progressed to the level where they can communicate anything like, "After ate berries near swamp yesterday stomach hurt," even when their vocabulary could support such an idea.*

Instead, their communications are short, like "that banana," "want a banana," and "me you out" to communicate, let's go outside.

Perhaps the most impressive observed event, though isolated, occurred upon Washoe seeing a swan. Washoe spontaneously initiated communication by pointing to the swan and signing "water" and "bird."

[The Story of Human Language, Professor John McWhorter Ph.D., Stanford University, Columbia University, March 17, 2010, The Great Courses]

Another significant capability of *Primate Consciousness* over *Mammalian Consciousness* is the ability of the individual to recognize themselves as being themselves in a mirror.

Self-recognition is a trait that pertains to the Great Apes: *pan, pongo, and homo*, though *gorilla* only passes the self-recognition test if the test conditions are modified and when the *gorilla* matures in captivity with extensive human interaction. The reason attributed to this is that being raised in captivity permits the individual to suppress their tendency to react aggressively.

To paraphrase Gordon G. Gallup Jr., Psychology Department, Tulane University, New Orleans, Louisiana in his 1970 article, *Chimpanzees: Self-Recognition*:

The mirror self-recognition test (MSR), developed by psychologist Gordon Gallup Jr. in 1970, was a method for determining whether species other than Homo sapiens demonstrated self-recognition. This MSR test is also known as the 'mark test,' 'red spot,' or 'rouge test.'

In the classic MSR test, an animal is anesthetized and marked on an area of their body that is not generally within its field of vision except when exposed to a mirror. If the animal notices the spot by investigating or touching it, then that behavior indicates that the animal perceives the reflection as an image of itself.

Approximately 75% of young adult common chimpanzees pass the mirror test, with percentages decreasing in younger and older members.

[Chimpanzees: Self-Recognition, Jan 1970, Gordon G. Gallup Jr., Psychology Department, Tulane University, New Orleans, Louisiana]

According to Amanda Pachniewska, founder and editor of Animal Cognition, Animal Cognition, in her 1970 article, *List of Animals That Have Passed the Mirror Test*:

Though research is ongoing, the few examples of other species presently demonstrating the evident ability to recognize themselves include the large brain mammals of Asian elephants, bottlenose dolphins, orca whales, and the only non-mammals, the Eurasian magpie.

[List of Animals That Have Passed the Mirror Test, Jan 1970, Amanda Pachniewska, founder and editor of Animal Cognition, Animal Cognition]

In contrast, although they do not pass the mirror self-recognition test, many lesser 'primates' and 'mammals' (e.g., manta rays) show interest in their reflections. Most species tested show no interest in their 'visual reflection,' though the logistics of performing this test is challenging to apply to many species, and such a test may have several flaws, such as individuals of a species simply not caring in the least whether they happen to have a red dot on their face.

Yet another significant advancement in primate consciousness relates to lucid dreaming. The discipline of neuroscience has revealed that lucid dreaming emerges with *Primate Consciousness.*

The article *Neural Correlates of Dream Lucidity Obtained from Contrasting Lucid versus Non-Lucid REM Sleep: A Combined EEG/fMRI Case Study, Sleep* in Science Daily says:

Lucid dreaming is distinct from regular dreaming in that individuals become aware of themselves within the dream. Brain activity in regular dreaming and lucid dreaming are essentially the same, except when the lucid state-specific regions of the cerebral cortex become highly active within seconds.

[Neural Correlates of Dream Lucidity Obtained from Contrasting Lucid versus Non-Lucid REM Sleep: A Combined EEG/fMRI Case Study, Sleep, Max-Planck-Gesellschaft, Science News, Science Daily]

PAN TROGLODYTES (COMMON CHIMPANZEE)

Lucky for us, there is a vast body of primate research.

To illustrate the features of *Primate Consciousness,* we have chosen the species *Pan troglodytes* (a.k.a. *'common chimpanzee'*) of the genus *Pan,* whose only other extant species is the closely related *bonobo* (a.k.a. *'pygmy chimpanzee').*

The genus *Pan* demonstrates additional complex social behaviors, including the emergence of tool use, a significant advancement over the various forms of object use that our earlier levels of consciousness supported.

Lawrence E. Johnson, Cambridge University Press, in his 1991 book, <u>*A Morally Deep World*</u>, writes:

The genus Pan (i.e., bonobos and common chimpanzees) make sponge-like materials using leaves and moss to soak water for use in grooming, trimming sticks for grooming under fingernails and toenails, and making use of stone tools and sticks for fishing insects out of tight spaces.

[A Morally Deep World, 1991, Lawrence E. Johnson, Cambridge University Press]

And Paul Raffaele writes in his 2011 book, <u>Among the Great Apes: Adventures on the Trail of our Closest Relatives</u>:

Common chimpanzees sharpen sticks to use as weapons to kill sleeping bushbabies in tree hollows.

[Among the Great Apes: Adventures on the Trail of our Closest Relatives, 2011, Paul Raffaele, Harper]

Matt Walker writes in his 2009 Earth News article, *Chimps use cleavers and anvils as tools to chop food*:

Chimpanzees in the Nimba Mountains of Guinea, Africa, use stone and wooden cleavers and stone anvils to chop up and reduce Treculia fruits into smaller bite-sized portions. These fruits can be the size of a volleyball, weigh up to 8.5 kg, and are hard and fibrous. But, despite lacking a hard outer shell, they are too large for a chimpanzee to get its jaws around and bite.

Instead, the chimpanzees use various tools to chop them into smaller pieces. Observations chopping food is the first account of chimpanzees using a pounding tool technology to break down large food items into bite-sized chunks rather than just extracting it from other unobtainable sources such as baobab nuts.

It is also the first time we see wild chimpanzees use two distinct types of percussive technology, i.e., movable cleavers against a non-movable anvil, to achieve the same goal. Neighboring chimpanzees in the nearby region of Seringbara do not process their food this way, indicating how apes learn tool use.

[Chimps use cleavers and anvils as tools to chop food, Dec. 24, 2009, Matt Walker- Editor, Earth News]

Regarding the development of the physical brain, *Primates* continue developing more subregions, neuronal layers, neural circuits, neuronal cell types, and *neuroglial* cell types.

The final physical enhancement to the brain is our next level of consciousness, *Homo Consciousness*.

NINTH LEVEL OF CONSCIOUSNESS (HOMO)

The ninth level of consciousness, *Homo Consciousness*, represents the last physical (i.e., hardware-based) evolutionary advancement.

This hardware improvement has a significantly greater brain mass, where 80% is the neocortex, with more neuronal tissue layers, distinct subdivisions with over 200 areas in the neocortex, many more neuronal circuits, higher neuron density, and a significant increase in the types of neuronal cells and *neuroglial* cells.

After this level of consciousness, all further advancements involve advancements that pertain to human software supported by the physical brain discussed in this section, representing its final hardware upgrade as provided by evolution.

The genus *Homo* includes the following ten species, and their brain volume ranges from fossil records when it is known.

- *Homo habilis* (550 to 687 cubic centimeters),

- *Homo rudolfensis*,

- *Homo ergaster*,

- *Homo erectus* (900 to 1251 cubic centimeters),

- *Homo antecessor*,

- *Homo floresiensis*,

- *Homo heidelbergensis* (1230 cubic centimeters),

- *Homo naledi*,

- *Homo sapiens neanderthalensis* (1300 to 1736 cubic centimeters), and

- *Homo sapiens sapiens* (900 to 2100 cubic centimeters)

Among these, *Homo habilis* emerged two and a half mya, demonstrating tool use involving sophisticated stone tools.

The first to leave Africa was *Homo erectus* two million years ago.

About 500,000 years ago, *Homo heidelbergensis* migrated out of Africa and is the likely ancestor of *Homo neanderthalensis*. Therefore, *Homo neanderthalensis* was already in Asia and Europe before the speciation of *Homo sapiens* just 300,000 years ago.

Although some groups of *Homo sapiens* may have ventured out much earlier, the only clear evidence of *Homo sapiens* migrating out of Africa was just 60,000 to 70,000 years ago (referred to as the Southern Dispersal).

Although the two species existed over the same for 25,000 years, the two species co-existed in overlapping regions for only about 5,500 years, and then *Homo Neanderthalensis* populations declined into extinction around 40 thousand years ago with numerous competing theories to explain the cause.

Most *Homo sapiens* have about 2.5% *Neanderthalensis* DNA, with some individuals having a higher proportion. Shared ancestry was more likely than interbreeding, though modern science with DNA sequencing points to some degree of interbreeding.

Although first-generation interbred offspring resulting in males (XY) might be sterile from the effects of genetic drift between the species being too great, females (XX) would not have had the drifted Y chromosome to affect them, which could make them viable for continued reproduction.

Michael Slezal writes in his 2014 article, *Thoroughly modern humans interbred with Neanderthals*:

> *While sub-Saharan Africans have no Neanderthal DNA, Europeans have about two percent, and Asian populations have more.*

> *[Thoroughly modern humans interbred with Neanderthals, Oct 22nd, 2014, Michael Slezak, NewScientist]*

Rebecca Turner writes in her 2018 World of Lucid Dreaming article, *10 Animals with Self-Awareness*:

> *A significant behavioral trait of extant species, Homo sapiens exhibits a finer self-awareness by age three than Primate Consciousness in recognizing that their image can exist in a photograph or video.*

> *And Homo sapiens can also develop rapidly changing consciousness states, such as being highly conscious in front of an audience of other individuals, in a state of disassociation immersed in a story, falling asleep, or engaged in regular dreaming or lucid dreaming.*

> *[10 Animals with Self-Awareness, 2018, Rebecca Turner BSc Zoology, Massey University, Auckland, New Zealand, founder World of Lucid Dreaming]*

And, according to the Science Daily News article, *Neural Correlates of Dream Lucidity Obtained from Contrasting Lucid versus Non-Lucid REM Sleep: A Combined EEG/fMRI Case Study, Sleep*:

> *With the help of neuroscience, scientific detection of self-awareness is possible during moments of self-awareness because the precuneus region of the brain becomes particularly active, which is a part of the brain linked with self-perception.*

> *[Neural Correlates of Dream Lucidity Obtained from Contrasting Lucid versus Non-Lucid REM Sleep: A Combined EEG/fMRI Case Study, Sleep, Max-Planck-Gesellschaft, Science News, Science Daily]*

Regarding communication, *Homo sapiens* can learn all four design components of language: symbolic, semantic, generativity, and structure. Language, however, is neither the vehicle of thought nor the foundation upon which conceptual information occurs within the mind.

So, what is language, and what is its role in consciousness?

First and foremost, language is a learned social construct used within the confines of a social group that shares the same social customs. Initially spoken, languages have become formalized as systems consisting of vocabularies and grammatical rules that constantly evolve for as long as they remain in general use.

As to what languages cannot do, we begin with the fact that all languages suffer from a pervasive ambiguity of words and phrases expressing multiple meanings that only context and correct inference could hope to represent.

In contrast, ideas 'in thought,' separate from language, accurately represent ideas crisply distinctly with no ambiguity.

During spoken or written language exchanges, speakers invent words, borrow from other languages, place emphasis accordingly, and devise similes and metaphors that sequentially communicate ideas they try to represent.

At the same time, listeners actively make corrections and approximations of the meanings expressed by words and phrases.

Ambiguity would not be possible if language were the vehicle of actual thought. Hence, relying on language for knowledge representation only undermines the precise conceptual meanings that language purports to represent.

However, languages lacking words for ideas do not restrict individuals from experiencing perceptions not expressed as words. Other forms of communication, relying on gestures or stories, can often find a way to communicate an idea through a shared experience.

- - -

This statement reminds me of a good friend in San Diego who introduced me to an aerospace company's team of engineers, all of whom had a Ph.D. in Mathematics.

Jim's friend, "Everyone, this is Jim. He is from New York, but don't let that fool you. Jim is smart, and he has an extensive repertoire of words. It's just that he pronounces them all the same."

Jim shakes his head in the affirmative and says, "Yup, yup, and yup."

- - -

As to what languages can do exceptionally well, having a well-formed taxonomy for concepts and objects allows for efficient communication of those concepts or objects. However, the science of language is quite deep, not just where language influences linguistic cognition but also where it affects nonlinguistic cognition.

As an example, Gleitman and Papafragou write in the 2013 chapter, *Relations Between Language and Thought*, in The Oxford Handbook of Cognitive Psychology edited by Daniel Reisberg:

Findings had been reported earlier by Brown and Lenneberg (1954), who found that colors that have simple verbal labels are identified more quickly than complexly named ones in a visual search task (e.g., color chips called "blue" are, on average, found faster among a set of colors than chips called "purplish-blue," etc.), suggesting that aspects of taxonomy do influence cognition.

[Relations Between Language and Thought, Lila Gleitman, Anna Papafragou, Mar 2013, The Oxford Handbook of Cognitive Psychology - edited by Daniel Reisberg]

As one might surmise, compared to one another, some communicate thoughts and concepts better than others.

For example, ask someone with a doctorate in mathematics to do basic long multiplication or division using Roman numerals. Creating new taxonomy within specialized areas, such as business, science, or the arts, is a means to express specific thoughts more efficiently and exactingly.

To quote Lila Gleitman and Anna Papafragou in *Relations Between Language and Thought,* in The Oxford Handbook of Cognitive Psychology edited by Daniel Reisberg: Quote.

"Languages differ in their vocabulary and structural patterns, impacting the procedures by which forms resolve to their meanings. But in nonlinguistic tasks, individuals with different linguistic backgrounds are found to respond in terms of the same conceptual categories." End Quote.

[Relations Between Language and Thought, Mar 2013, Lila Gleitman, Anna Papafragou, The Oxford Handbook of Cognitive Psychology - edited by Daniel Reisberg]

Aside from facilitating communication with other individuals, language can also help us communicate with ourselves to help shape ideas in both the tangible and intangible world.

Language, at times, can act as an additional layer above the mental layer with which we can communicate with ourselves. Each of us can listen to the various voices of both linguistic and nonlinguistic modes of representation within, and occasionally, we choose to speak back and converse with those voices using either our linguistic or nonlinguistic methods.

Interestingly, as unavoidable as it is for language to underspecify thought, when thinking in linguistic terms to ourselves, we know precisely the meaning associated with our linguistic thoughts as we automatically fully augment our linguistic thoughts with fully specified thoughts within ourselves.

Internally, we also know the precise meaning of what we intend to convey linguistically to others. However, we frequently cannot transfer our fully specified thoughts.

Language is a discipline with many subdisciplines. Language experts tend to fall into one of three categories of thought:

- *'Lingualism' claims that in the absence of language, there can be no thought*

- *'Language of thought' theory claims that language and thinking are independent*

- *'Independent' theory, founded by Noam Chomsky, asserts that 'thought' and 'linguistic thought' both exist and interact rather fluidly with one another where at times 'thought' is primary and 'linguistic thought' secondary, where occasionally the reverse is true, as each represents their aspect of cognition among a larger population of cognitive systems.*

According to Noam Chomsky, the earliest languages of *Homo sapiens* emerged around 100,000 years ago.

However, modern human society beyond that of the basic hunter-gatherer did not occur until agriculture and animal domestication emerged 11,000 years ago.

Agriculture and animal domestication arguably led to the emergence of the first ancient civilizations around 5,700 years ago (e.g., Mesopotamia 3,700 BCE; Egypt 3,150 BCE; India 2,900 BCE; and China 1,850 BCE), with independently developed written languages emerging 5,400 years ago (e.g., Mesopotamian pictographic writing in 3,400 BCE; Egyptian pictographic writing in 3,100 BCE; Chinese pictographic writing in 1,200 BCE) and the first pure alphabets (i.e., a standard set of letters that strictly represent the phenomes of a spoken language used in written form) emerging around 3,800 years ago (e.g., Egypt 1,800 BCE).

The next strides in language-based reasoning occurred about 3,600 years ago in Egypt, with the first empirical method of science (i.e., the precursor to the scientific method) appearing in an Egyptian medical textbook in 1,600 BCE.

Language-based reasoning, as well as other logical forms of reasoning, were gaining momentum with the emergence of philosophy 3,000 years ago (e.g., Hindu philosophies 1,000 BCE) and with the Buddha and Pre-Socratic thinkers emerging simultaneously 2,600 years ago (e.g., 6th century BCE) in Nepal and Greece respectively.

> *Arguably, Siddhartha Gautama, the Buddha, is the first to be identified by name for advancing 'conscious reasoning.' His teachings inspired royal patronage, crediting him with advancing literature, morality, equality across gender and caste systems, and (degrees of) 'free will' achievable through techniques found within meditative practices.*

By the 5th century BCE, a scientific tradition started gaining momentum.

By the 4th century BCE, Socrates and Plato (e.g., The Republic) made significant contributions. Aristotle developed an inductive-deductive method of reasoning with a wealth of taxonomies across many disciplines.

To paraphrase Hugh G. Gauch and Hugh G. Gauch Jr. in their 2003 book, *Scientific Method in Practice*:

> *Aristotle's method used inductive reasoning from observations to infer general principles and then applied deductive reasoning to the general principles to confirm further observations to establish knowledge.*

> *[Scientific Method in Practice, Hugh G. Gauch, Hugh G. Gauch Jr., 2003, Cambridge University Press]*

The scientific method and scientific experimentation experienced a series of advancements over the past 3,600 years, of which just a partial list includes:

— *Following Aristotle, Epicurus is attributed to the scientific method in the 3rd century BCE, positing that all matter was composed of atoms.*

— *Experimental science was developed by the Arab physicist Hasan Ibn al-Haytham in 1021, conducting verifiable experiments to test a formulated hypothesis.*

— *Experimental science was further advanced by the Persian scientist Abu Rayhan al-Biruni around 1020, mainly in mineralogy.*

— *The Persian philosopher and scientist Avicenna circa 1025 is credited with advancing the scientific method in medicine with medical devices.*

— *The new scientific method was attributed to the English philosopher and scientist Robert Grosseteste around 1100 for an improved sequence of steps defining the scientific method.*

— *The English physician Roger Bacon, circa 1256, advocated scientific methods of learning and is credited with predicting the invention of the submarine, the automobile, and the airplane.*

— *Around 1600, the English philosopher Sir Francis Bacon established the application of inductive reasoning, forming generalizations from observations.*

— *The French philosopher Rene Descartes, around 1640, introduced the notion of skepticism as an essential part of the scientific method.*

— *Around 1640, Galileo Galilei (Italian mathematician and astronomer) was furthering the understanding of planetary movements.*

- *In Circa 1687, Isaac Newton (English mathematician and physicist) was furthering the understanding of gravitational effects in astronomy involving the mass of objects.*

- *The American philosopher and mathematician Charles Sanders Pierce 1877, dealt with fallibilism in science.*

- *The Austrian-British philosopher Karl Popper 1934, introduced the empirical approach that can never be proven but only disproven.*

- *The American physicist and philosopher Thomas Kuhn 1962, who coined the term 'paradigm shift,' allowed alternative methods for viewing scientific observation.*

Even though all species except ours within the genus *Homo* are long extinct, by studying the archeological record, it is apparent that their level of consciousness was well above *Primate Consciousness.* This high level of consciousness is particularly true of *Homo neanderthalensis,* which coexisted and interacted with *Homo sapiens.*

If Noam Chomsky is correct and language developed 100,000 years ago in *Homo sapiens,* since *Homo neanderthalensis* was extant up to 40,000 years ago, there was a 60,000-year period in which *Homo sapiens* language overlapped with the then extant species of *Homo neanderthalensis.*

If we accept the premise that these two species interacted for at least 5,500 years, language can be responsible for the extinction of *Homo neanderthalensis.*

> *Homo neanderthalensis had a large brain, and assumedly they could comprehend language, much like Koko, though they may not have developed the ability to produce language.*

> *Suppose language developed 45,000 or more years ago. In that case, it is plausible that language played a pivotal role in the extinction of Neanderthalensis as females may have had to choose between offspring with the ability to produce language (i.e., a Homo sapiens male parent) and offspring that could not produce language (i.e., a Neanderthalensis male parent).*

> *It would not require a large percentage of eligible females of Homo neanderthalensis to eliminate the species within relatively few generations since, in those periods, life expectancy was what it was.*

Following the emergence of language, agriculture and animal domestication emerged around 11,000 years ago, which would have significantly improved nutrition and health for larger groups of individuals, culminating in the emergence of civilizations, governments, written languages, and advancements in philosophy and science.

It facilitated the emergence of various philosophies, which propelled advancements advocating reasoning in an environment of knowledge accumulation further fueled by an increase in educated individuals.

Some scientists ponder whether we had a significantly higher IQ than our recent *Homo sapiens* ancestors just a few thousand years ago.

Some scientists cite recent trends that demonstrated IQ tests that indicate a rapid increase in intelligence in the United States between the 19th and 20th centuries; this phenomenon is called the Flynn effect.

However, over decades, the Flynn effect has been seen to occur in either an upward or downward direction within the geographic locations measured.

The scientific community now believes that a change in IQ among populations is much more likely due to changes in nutrition or other environmental factors other than any evolutionary process in such a minimal time increment. Evolutionary forces, at least at a physical hardware level, take significantly more extended periods to develop and spread through populations than just a few thousand years.

When it comes to evolutionary forces, it is reasonable to expect different evolutionary rates for other components of the mind. The primary component upon which science has focused is the 'hardware' component, consisting of various sensory organs, neurons, *neuroglia*, and their configurations into layers, expressways, and paths comprising the central nervous system (CNS). This branch of science is known as **neurophysics**, which studies the physical structures involved in cognition.

The evolutionary rate for the 'hardware' component of the mind was likely the most rapid in the early development of the mind, to be overtaken by pace by the following type of component, 'software.'

As one might expect, the evolutionary rate of software-based capabilities can occur at a completely different pace than that of the evolutionary progress of the physical brain.

But how do software-based capabilities evolve?

People program software on computers. They conceptualize capabilities, design them, program them, and then run the programs.

In contrast, software-based brain capabilities are analogous to how early sorters were programmed before there were programming languages and machine languages for computers.

The early sorters were programmed using wiring boards with a plug-hole matrix over the board's surface. To program a sorter, the programmer would slide the board out of its harness and plug cables into the holes connecting them in a pattern that told the sorter how to sort the decks of computer cards placed into the intake mechanism.

Likewise, connections between nearby neurons are unplugged from one or more neurons and then plugged into one or more other neurons to program the brain.

As for the programmer, the other difference is that *neuroglia* cells act as the programmer, choosing which connections to disconnect and which new ones to connect. The process appears to operate using probabilistic decision-making as the programming is often performed correctly and sometimes not.

While it is relatively easy for physicians to determine the correct rewiring of neurons when it involves motor neurons, the rewiring of the brain to support intellectual activities is far more complex to monitor and understand.

As for the rate at which programming occurs to support intellectual activities, nature and the forces of nature can be experimenting with the evolution of software at various speeds across populations of physically identical individuals driven by differing natural pressures for survival.

The branch of science for 'intellectual software' doesn't yet exist, but I believe it will, and it will be known as *neuro-software*. Neuro-software would be a multi-discipline branch of science that investigates the software architecture of the brain leveraging neuroscience, artificial intelligence, and mathematics.

In 'computer science,' software and information architecture define the software and the data. Similarly, in neuro-science, I would expect the next branch of science to be *neuro-data* to study the information collected for use by the brain.

After all, computers use software programs to act upon data. In the brain, cell cytoskeletal structures store the data, and the function of the eukaryotic cell determines the type of data stored, such as the amplitude or pitch of a sound.

As new types of cells evolve, new types of data emerge. If these new cell types and their data are helpful, then there is a chance that the individual organism has a better chance of survival than individuals lacking that type of data.

In this sense, the capability for organisms to process vibrations perceived as sounds and tones comes from cells that have specialized in storing data about sounds and tones of specific frequencies and frequency ranges.

For example, if the brain encountered a new source of stimuli, say the ability to detect magnetic fields, the brain of some individuals would rapidly use its *neuroglia* and neuronal cells to process the recent stream of stimuli with *neuro-software* and *neuro-data*.

The most important feature of the ninth level of consciousness is that the physical brain has sufficiently evolved to support *neuro-software* and *neuro-data* to take us through a variety of software-based levels of consciousness.

Once our *neuro-data* included the vocabulary and grammar of spoken and written language, the information available to the *neuro-software* of the brain accelerated at an incredible pace, amassing quantities of knowledge shareable with other individuals.

Initially, information traveled verbally at a moment in time among the individuals present at that time. Written language changed that, providing a medium transcending time and space, persisting through generations.

The advent of sailing vessels improved the reach of shareable knowledge significantly. It was just 1860 when the first pony express carried letters via horse and rider at the limits of horse-driven technology. In 1869, the first transcontinental railroad became open for business. The widespread adoption of the telegraph occurred in the 1870s. The widespread adoption of the telephone only happened in the early 1900s.

In the late 1960's the Internet was invented. However, it didn't emerge outside the military until the 1980s and didn't achieve widespread adoption until two decades later, with Google launching as a company in 1998. As of June 2018, 55% of the world's population had some form of access to the Internet.

Today, Internet access is available at the tap of a finger or a voice command, such as Hey Google, thus making a wealth of information available on demand. We then assimilate that data into our minds and use it to inform us and teach us new things, or it can help identify an expert on a topic we may wish to reach out to.

Why is the acceleration of knowledge transfer so significant?

There are two reasons.

The apparent reason is the one that many have written about.

Accelerating the transfer of knowledge accelerates scientific discovery and modernization. Modernization is the rate at which findings have been found practical and actionable and subsequently applied to the toolset of society. These included the advancements propelling us into the Bronze Age and the Iron Age. It also provided for discovering electricity, nuclear power, and beyond.

The second reason is not so apparent.

Accelerating the transfer of knowledge also accelerates the rate at which the brain's software evolves.

When individuals develop new software capabilities for understanding the world around them, such as a new philosophy or way of thinking, various tools are available to share them around the globe. Moreover, tools such as the Internet help like-minded individuals find one another to refine their ideas as a collective like never before.

As we shall see, for many of the software-based levels of consciousness to become widespread, individuals must learn them, as they do not automatically come with the brain's hardware.

There are several implications for this.

First, this means that the rate at which consciousness evolves will continue to accelerate. Perhaps more importantly, new *neuro-software* programs are being developed that process *neuro-data* in new ways, creating new insights.

These new insights typically give individuals competitive advantages but can also be disadvantageous. Though this would be a separate book, there is much to say about neuro-software programs that can and do emerge.

For now, let's state that most software-based levels of consciousness require reinvention or learning to become widespread. Unfortunately, this means that humanity would revert to its hardware-based levels of consciousness in a complete societal collapse.

Continuing to our next level, we will continue our journey traversing the stepping stones of consciousness associated with the software of the mind, which are advancements in how we think.

As these forms of software are all learnable, this places a high value on quality education, though a few are learnable only through direct experience.

Even though the strictly hardware-dependent world of consciousness is perhaps not as fascinating as the software-dependent world of consciousness, the levels of consciousness provided by the hardware are essential to support the entire realm of software-based consciousness.

As such, the software supporting consciousness is invisible within the fossilized skull of an organism, lobes, layers of tissues, or seen with magnetic resonance imaging, yet as we shall see, it is critical to advancements in consciousness even before the emergence of philosophy and science.

TENTH LEVEL OF CONSCIOUSNESS (MEDITATIVE)

Imagine you have purchased and downloaded a classic film you heard much about and were looking forward to enjoying. You arrange the time to enjoy the movie, and upon starting the film, it begins with a dialog among many people who are expressing their opinions about each event.

At first, you believe that this will happen at the beginning to set the stage for the film and that soon you will be able to hear the dialog and enjoy the movie. But then you realize that this discussion will continue throughout the film.

The commentary ruins your film experience, so you become relatively discontent with your latest download.

The commentary is much like how we experience life, with voices in our heads rendering opinions about everything we hear and experience as each event unfolds. We fail to fully appreciate the experiences that life has to offer by creating a dialog that distracts us from the whole experience, even potentially distorting it to something completely different than what we could have experienced.

As Professor Mark W. Muesse, Ph.D. explains in his 2013 course, *Practicing Mindfulness: An Introduction to Meditation*:

> *In Buddhism, experiencing any phenomenon without any focus is called mindlessness.*
>
> *[Practicing Mindfulness: An Introduction to Meditation, Professor Mark W. Muesse, Ph.D. Director of Asian Studies Program at Rhodes College, Memphis TN, July 18, 2013, The Great Courses]*

The opposite of mindlessness is mindfulness. Mindfulness is all about focus and is the first objective for the serious meditation practitioner, which is the specific countermeasure for mindlessness. Hence, mindfulness begins with establishing an awareness of your mind's focus.

Therefore, if you focus on something, such as a particular image or sound, and then your mind drifts away, and you are aware that you have done so, this is mindfulness. In this sense, you have spun up a program to monitor your focus. The more an individual practices this, the better the program becomes.

In comparison, a more advanced capability of remaining focused on something and not drifting away from that something is called 'one-pointedness.'

A meditation practitioner need not achieve one-pointedness to attain mindfulness. All that is necessary is for the practitioner to know that the mind has drifted.

To achieve mindfulness is to become a passive observer of one's thoughts without any judgment about those thoughts. It is not mindfulness to evaluate the merit or pertinence of any idea, as that would be a return to mindlessness.

As a result, the practitioner learns to create an additional layer sitting above their thoughts as an impartial observer, not as a judge or jury. It takes a regular meditation practitioner to attain proficiency in mindfulness.

Meditation, beginning with mindfulness, is one of the best methods for controlling and programming one's mind. Although the underlying hardware of the mind ultimately supports these programs, the programs you strive to create need not be aware of any aspect of the hardware.

In computer technology, there is hardware, software, and data, with software usually compartmentalized into layers starting with an 'operating system' at the foundational layer sitting directly on top of the hardware, with additional software programs laid upon the operating system.

Likewise, in the framework of computer programs, the programs that the programmer creates sitting on top of the operating system need not be aware of any aspect of the computer hardware.

The role of an 'operating system,' which is a software program itself, is to provide an environment within which other software programs can operate. When these other programs need services from the hardware, it is the operating system's job to accept requests for these services to act as a broker to acquire these services from the hardware.

All programs, including the operating system, are unquestionably dependent upon the hardware, yet only operating systems, including specific system drivers, must deal directly with the hardware.

Such a layered approach allows software that sits on top of the 'operating system' to be hardware independent, not from the perspective of not needing hardware but from the standpoint of not having to know the many details necessary to interface with the hardware.

The critical thing to remember is that although software programs need hardware to operate, they neither need to know anything about the hardware nor even that it exists.

The extensive system that exists to transport signals between sensory organs and the CNS, and between the CNS and muscles through motor neurons, are all dealt with as part of the operating system. The hardware moves the signals from point A to point B, and the operating system interacts with the hardware to access those signals.

From before birth, signals flow through the CNS through a myriad of hardware circuits, starting when the brain starts developing and only ceasing when the organism reaches the end of its life when the brain and supporting CNS become permanently dead as the hardware gets destroyed.

However, during its development, the hardware of the CNS and its operating system evolves thanks to a combination of pre-wired genetics and learning at unconscious levels that help complete the operating system as various sensory cells become active and the system gains programs.

IN-BOUND SIGNALS

Sensory stimuli received from sensory organs are not the only source of sensory stimuli. Sometimes augmented by specialized *neuroglia* and neuronal cells, the CNS also receives signal data that may have once originated from sensory cells but now comes from *neuroglia* and neuronal cells.

Together, these signals move along a neuronal expressway to regions in the brain. The circuits within the physical hardware of these regions then process the sensory stimuli through various steps.

Many steps are hardware-supported using software that cannot change. In some cases, *neuroglia* will alter neuron connections, effectively reprogramming the software. However, this occurs unconsciously, which we will discuss later.

Neuroscientists can measure the heavy activity of significant brain regions, though they cannot detect most signals traversing few neurons, and they cannot discern the software within the brain any more than an engineer can observe a television program by measuring the signal strength of one's Internet service.

One noteworthy aspect of monitoring the brain is to detect *qualia*. *Qualia* is the mind's sensation when it experiences either signal data from the senses, such as experiencing the aroma of freshly baked bread or recalling that same experience from memory. In both circumstances, the central nervous system sends signal data to the appropriate brain hardware that ultimately generates the given sensation.

Neuroscience can neither determine the aroma nor sense a smell within the brain. If an experience is enjoyable, then neuroscience can detect when the brain's pleasure center is stimulated. However, whether it is due to an actual aroma or a pleasant memory it invokes is unknown.

At the earliest levels of consciousness, *qualia* would have had to exist in some rudimentary form where the first determination of like, dislike, or indifference occurs. *Qualia* may begin within the individual eukaryotic cells that first detect an environmental factor with sensory organs. They then relay these signals to the cytoskeletal structures within the cell.

In the presence of a physical brain, whether a stream of stimuli came from a sensory organ or was generated internally within the brain from the recollection of a memory or other cause, it most likely involves the cytoskeletal structures of various cells at various levels of consciousness within the organism.

When from external sources, the cytoskeletal components involved begin with the cells that comprise the sensory organs. They then continue by engaging the cells that form the neural expressway to the brain. It would also include the cells within the layers of neurons in the brain where the signals are delivered and within the cells surrounding concentrations of *neuroglial* cells that encase the layers of neurons.

However, it is reasonable to believe that the cytoskeletal structures of all cells participating in the detection, generation, transmission, and processing of each stimulus generate *qualia,* each play their part in generating the various aspects of experience.

OUT-BOUND SIGNALS

In the other direction, the CNS sends signals through motor neurons to activate the contraction of muscles. The amount of contraction largely depends upon the number of muscle fibers stimulated. Controlling the strength and frequency of the signals transported by motor neurons is referred to in computer science as a *control system*-related capability.

> *Recall that a 'control system' is a software system that automates the operation of physical machinery guided by streams of signal data emanating from sensors, as opposed to an 'information system' that strictly automates information processing.*

In contrast, the software realm of consciousness that comprises our framework in computer science is an *information system*, which in turn communicates with one or more *control systems*.

OUR CHOSEN TYPE OF SOFTWARE

To understand the tenth level of consciousness we must momentarily return to early Buddhism for meditation to create our first layer of software that sits on top of our standard operating system.

Meditative Consciousness is the first software level of consciousness due to its importance as the first that allows an individual organism to control its destiny in an active, self-directed manner. Unlike the hardware-based levels of consciousness, the software-based levels are optional. However, there are also some levels of consciousness built upon *Meditative Consciousness*.

Until now, all previous levels of consciousness provided each organism with a choice determined by a combination of factors.

For example, some chemical processes that influence decision-making become overridden by the influence of learning and are further overridden by what the organism wants. After the emergence of primitive, mammalian, and *Homo sapiens* brains became further overridden by the default programming of the brain's operating system, particularly involving emotions.

The tenth level of consciousness, *Meditative Consciousness*, represents the emergence of an ability to consciously gain access to the brain's operating system to override the previous factors that typically influence how we react.

In other words, the tenth level of consciousness marks where *Homo sapiens* begin to choose new behaviors other than what they instinctually do, have learned, or want at various levels of their consciousness to separate themselves from the combination of their genetics and the tides and currents of life's events.

HISTORY OF MEDITATION

The historical precursor to meditation was prayer.

> *Prayer is an invocation or act of spiritual communication to give praise or thanks, state devotion, or as an illustration of worship toward a spirit or deity that may potentially be associated with meteorological or astronomical events, charms or idols, spells or incantations, offerings or celebrations, hymns, dance, and or a variety of ceremonial practices.*

Built on the shoulders of prayer, meditation originated 5,700 years ago, two thousand years before the emergence of civilization (e.g., Mesopotamia 3,700 BCE). It emerged as a practice restricted to the realm of spiritual leaders, medicine men, monks, and priests within various ancient spiritual traditions.

Before the birth of Buddhism (i.e., 2,600 years ago), meditation was typically included within education for the upper classes and nobility to prepare their male children for leadership roles.

The Buddha was born into nobility with a father and mother who were King and Queen of a territory named Kosala, located in what is now considered northern India. Here, the Buddha received training commensurate with someone expected to become a king, which included practicing basic meditation.

The Buddha built upon the practice of simple meditation to form an extended journey that ultimately can lead to *nirvana*, a transcendent state of mind in which there is neither suffering, desire, nor a sense of self. It is considered the ultimate goal of ancient Buddhists.

Religious aspects of Buddhism can come into play when *nirvana* additionally represents the mechanism by which the practitioner frees themselves from the effects of *karma* and the cycle of death and rebirth.

The state of mind that we focus on for this level of consciousness is *Meditative Consciousness*, which is the secular practice.

To define *Meditative Consciousness,* let's briefly explain meditation and what it means to meditate, though it is fair to point out that there are many styles and techniques from which to choose.

First, meditation is an altered state of consciousness between awake and asleep.

To prepare for the process of meditating, the individual may wish to set a duration for which to meditate using a timer, or they may choose to rely upon another individual who will act as the timekeeper.

Additionally, the individual should place themselves in a comfortable posture where they can reasonably relax, slowing down their physical and mental selves.

Without training, the mind will tend to race through various thoughts. The endless onslaught of thoughts is the natural state for all individuals equipped with the physical brain supporting *Homo Consciousness* and its standard operating system.

The first objective of meditation is to disconnect oneself from the onslaught of the many thoughts and emotions that naturally occur so that they can begin to take on the role of an observer of those thoughts and feelings.

Although this sounds easy, it requires a regular practice regimen to increase the duration of control so the practitioner can achieve this gradually. Once completed, the practitioner can observe their thoughts as a separate observer.

Typically the ability to observe one's thoughts will naturally dissipate, and the practitioner will immerse themselves in their thoughts instead of observing them. But with effort, the practitioner can use their will to extract themselves from the stream of thoughts to be above it again as an observer.

This step and the ones that follow may each take significant practice, but success comes with practice, generally consuming less time to achieve the desired outcome with increased practice.

When an individual becomes proficient at detaching themselves to observe their thoughts instead of being immersed in them, the following exercise can further build up one's strength or ability to focus.

To do this, the individual may choose anything upon which to focus. The target of one's focus may be an individual stimulus, such as a single sound, image, scent, taste, or feeling.

The desired target of one's focus may also be a combination of stimuli from various senses. The challenge, however, is to focus the mind on only the chosen target, overcome the mind's tendency to introduce thoughts other than the desired focus, and overcome the mind's tendency to engage the individual in extraneous thoughts instead of being an observer of them.

An undisciplined mind will constantly lose focus, change focus, wander off, and introduce a myriad of thoughts outside those chosen. However, with much patience and practice, the practitioner will pull the focus back to the desired focus and control the disruption caused by intruding thoughts.

To paraphrase Professor Rick Repetti, Ph.D. Philosophy in his 2019 book, *Buddhism, Meditation, and Free Will: A Theory of Mental Freedom:*

For a glimpse into some of the skills that a practiced meditator can develop, they include:

1. *Immediate awareness when one's attention strays away from the intended point of focus*

2. *Rapidly reacquiring the intended point of focus*

3. *Gaining awareness of competing thoughts and perceptions and allowing them to dissipate*

4. *Detecting and observing emotional responses while remaining detached from them*

Some skills that expert practitioners can develop include:

1. *The ability to have thoughts of one's choosing*

2. *The ability to have the mental state of one's choosing*

3. *The ability to experience the emotions of one's choosing*

4. *A strong ability to resist external manipulation*

[Buddhism, Meditation, and Free Will: A Theory of Mental Freedom, 2019, Rick Repetti Ph.D. Philosophy, Professor of Philosophy CUNY New York City, USA, Routledge Critical Studies in Buddhism, Routledge Taylor & Francis Group]

The benefits derived from meditation can align with the individual's objectives and the corresponding amount of effort they apply. It could be as simple as using meditation as a technique to achieve relaxation and improved mental health or as ambitious as exploring the extent to which the individual may be able to achieve mental freedoms in their lives away from the default states of their operating system, or even Buddhist *nirvana.*

At this point, we have just enough of an understanding of what meditation is to define *Meditative Consciousness.*

In its simplest form, *Meditative Consciousness* is the recognition of the tools available to reprogram one's mind and the ability to use those tools to any extent.

It represents the first step in taking control of one's mind by learning how to become an observer to attain a degree of mindfulness. It includes the ability to occasionally extricate oneself from being emersed in the uncontrolled stream of thoughts. Although it takes practice, it is the only way to program one's mind directly.

Aside from meditation, there are indirect means of programming one's mind, such as actively managing which books to read versus those to put aside, which friends to engage in, sharing time versus ones to disengage, and films and other content to view versus to avoid.

It also includes conversations in which one chooses to participate versus those avoided and subject matter to research, weigh, and write about versus those to pass on. The things we choose to focus our attention on are all ways of indirectly programming one's mind.

The degree of attention we apply to these choices determines the influence we can exercise over our consciousness by informing, exploring, directing, and redirecting the focus of our internal voices to equip them with the desired supporting knowledge.

Without *Meditative Consciousness,* emotions drive our thought processes and behavior. As discussed in future chapters, emotions are valuable for making rapid decisions. However, everything has its limitations.

The influence of emotion tends to inhibit logical reasoning. However, assuming that feelings will always result in the wrong decision and logical reasoning for the correct decision is incorrect. Sometimes, forms of decision-making result in a bad decision. Occasionally, logical reasoning gets it wrong, and there are times when emotions get it wrong. Which to choose largely depends on the type of decision and its potential long-term effect.

Choosing a career because of one's passion is usually the best decision to be driven by one's emotions, whereas determining how best to land a damaged aircraft safely is usually best in the hands of someone void of emotion with a calm focus on logic and reasoning.

To paraphrase Donald Robertson a cognitive-behavioral psychotherapist in his 2010 book, *The Philosophy of Cognitive-behavioral Therapy (CBT): Stoic Philosophy as Rational and Cognitive Psychotherapy*:

> *According to cognitive therapy, founded by Aaron T. Beck, emotions and behavior intertwine, and irrational thoughts commonly cause feelings. In cognitive-behavioral therapy (CBT), individuals learn to challenge and refute their ideas.*
>
> *Though the process of reasoning is an essential element, the first phase is gaining degrees of control over the mind to allow the individual to identify and question the beliefs that underlie the emotional states that drive them.*
>
> *[The Philosophy of Cognitive-behavioral Therapy (CBT): Stoic Philosophy as Rational and Cognitive Psychotherapy, 2010, Donald Robertson a cognitive-behavioral psychotherapist, Karnac Books, London, UK]*

Ancient philosophical traditions have helped influence the basis of cognitive therapy, such as Stoicism, founded by Zeno of Athens 2,300 years ago (i.e., 3rd century BCE).

Stoicism teaches the wisdom of maintaining composure in the face of either criticism or praise. These teachings focus on using one's will (i.e., volition or choice) to rationally choose how to react to impressions by repeatedly catching oneself from making snap emotional decisions.

Hence, there are possible blends and combinations of direct and indirect forms of programming in one's mind. However, only direct programming, *Meditative Consciousness*, has been shown to reprogram the brain most directly.

As for scientific evidence, scientific studies reveal that practicing the altered mental state of meditation as a tool to explore one's mind measurably affects the brain in various ways.

To quote Professor Rick Repetti Ph.D. in his 2019 book, *Buddhism, Meditation, and Free Will: A Theory of Mental Freedom*: Quote.

> *"One classical example of many such studies concerns one particularly advanced árya [Sanskrit for Buddhist spiritual warrior or hero], a Tibetan yogi named Mingyur Rinpoche (Goleman and Davidson 2017, pp 216-28), the study of whose brain activity during his monitored meditations (Lutz et al. 2004) "has been cited over 1,100 times in the world's scientific literature" (Goleman and Davidson 2017, p.220). Goleman and Davidson summarize some of the traits – well-stabilized brain-and-behavioral dispositions – demonstrated by the most advanced*

meditation virtuosos in the lab:"

"Finally, there are the yogis at the 'Olympic' level, who have an average of 27,000 lifetime hours of meditation. They show clear signs of altered traits, such as large gamma waves in synchrony among far-flung brain regions - a brain pattern not seen before in anyone – and which also occurs in rest among these yogis who have done the most hours of practice. ...Also, yogis' brains seem to age more slowly compared to the brains of other people of their age."

"Other signs ... include stopping and starting meditative states in seconds, and effortlessness in meditation. ... [They exhibit] little signs of anticipatory excitement, a short but intense reaction during the pain itself, and then a rapid recovery. During compassion meditation, yogis' brains and hearts couple in ways not seen in other people. Most significant, the yogis' brain states at rest resemble the brain states of others while they meditate – the state has become a habit. (Goleman and Davidson 2017, p. 274)" End Quote.

[Buddhism, Meditation, and Free Will: A Theory of Mental Freedom, 2019, Rick Repetti Ph.D. Philosophy, Professor of Philosophy CUNY New York City, USA, Routledge Critical Studies in Buddhism, Routledge Taylor & Francis Group, p. 158-59]

ELEVENTH LEVEL OF CONSCIOUSNESS (REASON-DRIVEN)

Decisions based on emotions and how one feels are the default mechanisms that animals equipped with brains employ. In contrast, more simple forms of animals make decisions based on a simple determination of favorable, unfavorable, or indifference.

The most fundamental of these feelings may include basic feelings of hunger, thirst, anger, and fear of feelings as sophisticated as an intertwined effect of mood, temperament, personality, disposition, and motivation.

Among *Homo sapiens,* this form of decision-making often comes with the illusion of reasoning, as individuals are eager to list logical explanations that justify decisions based on emotions. However, logically explaining after the fact only acts as confirmation bias to bolster emotional choices. Although this may feel like reasoning to the practitioner, this is not reasoning.

Making decisions based on one's feelings is effectively a shortcut that bypasses true reason-driven consciousness. It is a highly efficient form of decision-making in terms of time and energy and is extremely practical for most decisions individuals render daily.

The reason for its practicality is that this form of decision-making leverages prior experiences and beliefs, which, depending on the quality of those earlier experiences and the accuracy of one's beliefs, typically have some probability of being near-optimal decisions.

The downside to emotion-based decision-making is that acting upon emotions can lead to poor and unintended outcomes. When individuals use emotions as the basis of decision-making, the role of reason is to rationalize emotion-based decisions.

In contrast, first learning to act as an observer (i.e., *Meditative Consciousness*) of one's thoughts and emotions before making any decisions can help achieve degrees of *Reason-Driven Consciousness*.

As such, *Meditative Consciousness* can serve as a stepping stone to developing *Reason-Driven Consciousness*, facilitating a higher degree of control over one's decisions and behaviors that carefully consider outcomes and consequences that may be difficult or impossible to roll back.

However, even without *Meditative Consciousness,* one can still develop basic controls to keep emotional responses in check.

> *A basic example of Reason-Driven Consciousness would be to withhold a response to an emotionally charged event and withhold one's conclusions about what you think about that event.*

> *Such a delay provides an opportunity to detect the emotions, understand why those emotions exist, and inquire how those emotions may be creating a bias. These measures are handy when emotional bias works against the individual's interests.*

That said, *Reason-Driven Consciousness* is a skill that one must learn as it is not part of the standard operating system of the brain. The learned ability to withhold a response to an event and the ability to withhold drawing conclusions both take conscious effort and repeated practice to achieve.

Beyond the basic level, an individual may learn various forms of reasoning.

Reason-Driven Consciousness has a history that traces back at least to the ancient Greeks.

> *'Non-classical logic' emerged 2,000 years ago in the time of Plato and Aristotle. These formal systems employ neither propositional nor predicate logic, often involving philosophical statements about necessity and possibility. In contrast, 'classical logic' was developed in the 19th century.*

> *'Propositional logic' is as simple as cause-and-effect statements, such as 'eating more food causes an increase in weight,' which may be true or false as eating only celery will cause extreme weight loss.*

'Predicate logic' uses quantifiers (e.g., 'for all,' 'there exists') and variables (e.g., 'X,' 'Y') and is the standard for mathematical systems.

As we can see, different disciplines may be most appropriate for reasoning depending upon the circumstances.

Among the most common are deductive reasoning, inductive reasoning, abductive reasoning, reductive reasoning, hypothetico-deductive reasoning, analogical reasoning, metaphorical reasoning, creative reasoning, holistic reasoning, reductionist reasoning, categorization reasoning, generalized reasoning, and logically fallacious reasoning.

Deductive reasoning - reasoning using a sequence of two or more premises linked to reaching a logically inevitable conclusion that is similarly linked (e.g., all men are mortal (1st premise), Socrates is a man (2nd premise), Socrates is mortal (conclusion))

Inductive reasoning - reasoning using a set of observations that has an explanation with some probability of being accurate (e.g., every swan I have seen is white; therefore, all swans are white)

Abductive reasoning - reasoning using a sequence of two or more premises that link to reach a logically probabilistic conclusion that is similarly linked (e.g., cookies are in the cookie jar (1st premise), the toddler has a cookie (2nd premise), the toddler has been in the cookie jar (conclusion))

Reductive reasoning (a.k.a. reduction ad absurdum) - reasoning to assert that something is true by showing that an absurd result follows by its denial (e.g., prisons need to be managed by professionals; the inmates should run the prison system)

Hypothetico-deductive reasoning (a.k.a. scientific method) - reasoning where the first step is that observations form a hypothesis, and then tests are devised by making reasonable predictions based on the hypothesis being true, where inaccurate predictions invalidate the hypothesis (e.g., water constantly freezes at zero degrees centigrade (hypothesis); experiments show that water freezes at different temperatures as atmospheric pressure is increased or decreased (invalidating the hypothesis))

Analogical reasoning - reasoning by applying the rules of one situation having a known solution to the analogous solution in another that appears similar (e.g., a wild bear is charging me; when a strange dog charged at me, it was helpful for me to stand my ground and yell at him to sit)

Metaphorical reasoning - reasoning by applying the rules of one situation having a known solution to a metaphorical perspective in another case that does not appear to be similar (e.g., the newly designed synthetic paintbrush with smooth bristles paints in streaks (situation); a type of pump employs fibrous strands having irregular surfaces to propel liquids in a forward direction (metaphorical case); synthetic paintbrushes need rough surfaces to pump paint to flow forward (metaphorical solution))

Creative reasoning - reasoning using perspectives derived from either a process of trial and error or from viewing a problem from other paradigms to identify potential solutions (e.g., a man is hanging from the ceiling in an empty vault locked from the inside (situation); the man stood on a block of dry ice to hang himself (possible solution); the killer escaped through an air vent (possible solution); the floor of the vault dropped a couple of feet (possible solution); the ceiling of the vault raised a couple of feet (possible solution); the inside of the vault had been temporarily in a state of zero gravity (possible solution))

Holistic reasoning - reasoning that incorporates the interconnectedness of the various elements that comprise the larger system (e.g., measuring the output of the entire system best determines the performance of an engine while it is operating

Reductionist reasoning - reasoning that attempts to understand a domain from its constituent parts (e.g., product counterfeiting is often best performed by taking something apart to see how it works)

Categorization reasoning - reasoning that organizes individual items as being members of a conceptual group (e.g., poodles and collies are types of dogs)

Generalized reasoning - reasoning that generalizes all instances of an item together (e.g., when driving, I should generalize stop signs into one class and stop at instances of stop signs that I have not previously encountered)

Logically fallacious reasoning - reasoning that is logically flawed, falling into any of the hundreds of logical fallacies that exist (e.g., when critics attack individuals for a position that they don't believe by distorting, exaggerating, or misrepresenting the position of an argument (straw man logical fallacy))

Although *Reason-Driven Consciousness* at times is significantly more reliable than emotion-based decisions, it has a degree of susceptibility to defects contributed to by a handful of factors, such as inaccurate beliefs and assumptions, misleading information, missing information, insufficient experience, flawed analogies, ambiguities in meaning, logical fallacies, and or employing either the wrong type of reasoning or potentially the wrong paradigm.

For example, Quote. "... given the problem, 'What is one plus one?' Although the assumed paradigm or system of rules would have us conclude that the answer is "Two," the correct answer for other paradigms or systems may not be "Two."

Such is the case with "one cloud plus another cloud creates one cloud" or "one drop of water added to another drop of water results in one drop of water." End Quote.

[Sensitive by Nature: Understanding Intelligence and the Mind, 2002, J Luisi, 1ˢᵗ Books Library Publishers]

A reliable technique for detecting flaws is the ability to see and acknowledge any contradictions, large or small, that may be present in the conclusion of the reasoning process, regardless of whether they confirm or refute one's emotional bias. Quote.

"Detecting contradictions is critical to logic and reasoning since they indicate flaws in the reasoning process. When contradictions occur, any information involved in the reasoning process can be incorrect." End Quote.

[Sensitive by Nature: Understanding Intelligence and the Mind, 2002, J Luisi, 1ˢᵗ Books Library Publishers]

In summary, *Reason-Driven Consciousness* is a learned skill crucial for particular decisions, though not at all practical for the myriad of trivial decisions an individual may make during the day.

Decisions that can alter the course of one's life require the most reliable form of reasoning that may be available. Many of the world's greatest decision-makers postpone decisions they face to allow them to gather additional information that may become available later.

TWELFTH LEVEL OF CONSCIOUSNESS (PERSONA)

The next software-based level of consciousness is *Persona Consciousness.*

The notion of animal societal groups with roles for individual members first emerged with neural bundles in insects. Then, the idea of one individual playing more than one role appears with primitive brains in Reptilia with the maternal instincts of Pythons.

[Python Moms Care for Their Young, Surprising Experts, South Africa Study Finds (nationalgeographic.com), National Geographic, March 15, 2018]

The notion of one individual playing more than one role is further expanded upon and strengthened in the mammalian brain, where individuals may add to their natural family-based roles with the role of herd, pack, or pride leader.

Primates take the notion of roles one step further with a broader set of roles that support complex social and military hierarchies within and among tribes of individuals.

Fast forwarding to *Homo sapiens,* by the time civilization emerged, the concept of playing societal roles extended well beyond instinctual functions as societies invented a myriad of roles within governmental, military, and economic systems, thus allowing individuals to add as many roles to their repertoire as necessary.

Furthermore, accompanying each role was a set of desired and allowable behaviors sometimes learned early.

To quote Kendra Cherry in her 2018 article, *The 4 Major Jungian Archetypes:* Quote.

> *"Over the course of development, children learn that they must behave in certain ways in order to fit in with society's expectations and norms. The persona develops as a social mask to contain all of the primitive urges, impulses, and emotions that are not considered socially acceptable. The persona archetype allows people to adapt to the world around them and fit in with the society in which they live." End Quote.*

> *[The 4 Major Jungian Archetypes, Dec 01, 2018, Kendra Cherry Master of Science, BA Educational Psychology from Boise State University, BS Psychology from Idaho State University, author and educator, VeryWellMind.com – Personality Psychology]*

However, engaging in a role is not limited to enacting desired and allowable behaviors. It also affects the perceptions of the individual while participating in a role.

There is a discipline called *personality psychology,* a branch of psychology that investigates the individual psychological differences and similarities that influence cognition, motivation, and emotion. It also encompasses the phenomenon of *personas.*

One method to detect the presence of *personality psychology* as being in effect is for individuals who are experts in those roles to be able to predict the behavior of the role player when confronted with various circumstances.

The degree to which the role player's perceptions match up to each circumstance and the decisions they make should be able to differentiate between an individual who has embodied the *persona* versus someone who is acting the role from a different *persona.*

Hence, we define *Persona Consciousness* in our framework as a learned identity that an individual portrays while tailoring their perceptions to be consistent with the *persona,* sometimes with a specialized vocabulary that acts as a shorthand to communicate to other individuals in the same or related role.

In contrast, an actor attempting to impersonate a *persona* must consciously behave consistent with the correct perceptions of the individual who embodies the *persona.* They must simultaneously repress any behaviors that may interfere with the projected image that would reveal that they are an imposter, trainee, or actor.

The construction of a *persona* stems from what an individual believes is the appropriate behavior associated with the *persona*. Optionally, the individual may employ a role model to act as their guide in determining their behavior. When the individual does not embody the given *persona*, they must rely upon their imagination to help guide them to appropriate behavior and how the target audience will perceive them.

When the individual embodies the *persona*, their perceptions and the rules that govern their behaviors will automatically act as their guide. In simple terms, the difference is like someone being a policeman versus someone not a policeman, just putting on the uniform.

The notion of a *persona* is distinct from the idea of being empathetic. Empathy involves placing yourself in the other person's shoes so that you feel what they are feeling. In contrast, a *persona* goes beyond being empathetic to create a different way of perceiving stimuli and generating behaviors that are appropriate to fulfill the responsibilities of the *persona*.

A *persona* in our model is an individual operating within a single paradigm. But let's consider the persona operating within more than one paradigm. Our idea of *persona,* in this case, includes the ability to design and craft a *persona* to meet its objectives instead of copying the *persona* of a role model.

> *Personas span various professional disciplines, such as politics, business, military, religion, sports, and entertainment. Many successful people invent their own persona that they then project to the world.*
>
> *Individuals who invented their public personas include Freddie Mercury, Elton John, and Michael Jackson. During their lives, they have created and evolved their public personas to meet their requirements specifically.*

To summarize *Persona Consciousness,* a fully developed concept of *personas* emerges in *Homo sapiens.* Here, individuals can add or invent an endless array of new *personas* that support the many new societal roles or simply one's creative needs.

THIRTEENTH LEVEL OF CONSCIOUSNESS (COMPARTMENTALIZED)

Our next software-based level of consciousness is *Compartmentalized Consciousness.*

To begin, the science of psychology defines compartmentalization as a subconscious psychological defense mechanism used to avoid cognitive dissonance involving incompatible systems of thought, such as conflicting beliefs, value systems, emotions, or ideas.

To paraphrase Professor Mark R. Leary, Ph.D. Psychology in his 2005 handbook, *Handbook of Self and Identity*:

> *In this manner, compartmentalization allows conflicting thoughts that would cause cognitive dissonance to co-exist by inhibiting direct or explicit acknowledgment and interaction between the compartmentalized self-states.*

> *[Handbook of Self and Identity, July 13, 2005, Mark R. Leary, Ph.D. Professor of Psychology at Wake Forest University, June Price Tangney, Ph.D. Professor of Psychology at George Mason University, Guilford Publications]*

For our purposes, however, this definition is incomplete in that compartmentalization encompasses so much more. As a level of consciousness within our framework, *Compartmentalized Consciousness* also includes consciously compartmentalizing systems of thought as an intellectual tool.

In this manner, compartmentalization is also a choice we willfully and freely make. A simple example would be when one consciously tries to balance one's life between work and personal life by compartmentalizing them.

> *Stress counseling is helpful to individuals who obsess about their workday.*

> *To quote Maria Bararra, Ph.D. in her 2013 article in Psychology Today, Compartmentalizing: A tool for achieving a balance between work and home: Quote.*

> *"What's worse is spending the evening thinking about what transpired during the workday and thinking about what needs to be done tomorrow and never experiencing a break. Utilizing the tool of compartmentalizing can help establish a break from work and learn to set that boundary." End Quote.*

> *[Compartmentalizing: A tool for achieving a balance between work and home, July 13, 2013, Maria Bararra Ph.D. L.C.S.W., Psychology Today]*

Another way to understand *Compartmentalized Consciousness* is to consider those situations in which compartmentalization is explicitly part of the job description.

In various industries, one's job could involve working on projects the government has classified as highly confidential or top secret (e.g., criminal investigators, pharmaceutical researchers, and government defense engineers). In a position like this, the employee must adapt their behavior to avoid discussing any aspect of their workplace and work tasks with anyone who does not have the appropriate clearance or situations where you cannot confirm whether they have the proper clearance.

When employees such as these find themselves outside the confines of a secure work area, they must compartmentalize everything they might think and speak about. In other words, they must quarantine thoughts about sensitive projects as only being in scope when working within a secure area explicitly involving those projects and only interacting with other individuals with the credentials that have given them access to the same secure areas.

These individuals compartmentalize their thinking so that they are operating inside the compartment, able to engage in the subject matter of the compartment, or they are operating outside the compartment, concealing their knowledge about the subject matter, potentially concealing that the subject matter even exists.

An example of a secure work area is a 'sensitive compartmented information facility (SCIF)' dedicated to that specific project in the US and Britain.

A SCIF is a secure enclosed work area requiring special access keys to enter where the entire SCIF would have electromagnetic shielding to prevent cell phone signals from entering or leaving the SCIF.

Inside the SCIF, individuals store work materials in combination safes. Individuals with access to those work materials must memorize the combinations to each safe and are not allowed to record the combination of any safe onto any substance or device.

Perhaps the most common use of *Compartmentalized Consciousness* is to help an individual manage the personal and work priorities that compete for their time and attention. Without compartmentalization, one's focus can wander off into pressing concerns to generate cycles of unmanageable distracting thoughts.

An example would be Ryan Blair, who was learning how to make progress with his son's autism while also engaging the court system to release his ailing mother from life support while also acting as an active partner and executive in a company that was adding hundreds of jobs to its growing employee base every month.

To quote Ryan Blair in his 2012 article, *5 Steps of Compartmentalization: The Secret Behind Successful Entrepreneurs*: Quote.

"One of the key reasons I had such a successful year, despite the private and professional paradox, is that I accepted the fact that I had several fulltime focuses, but only a limited amount of emotional and mental energy to devote to each one."

"Normally, entrepreneurs think about their businesses all day long and therefore focus on nothing else. In the past, I would have worked on a long list of projects. Instead, I had all these other things that were demanding attention from my mind and heart, and there were only a few events or priorities I was humanly capable of focusing on per day."

"I learned prioritizing is saying "no" and focusing on only the few things that matter most."

"So, to sum it up, here is a five-step system for dealing with adversity and extreme challenges while running a business:

1. *Compartmentalize it. Isolate the issue from all the other challenges you have.*

2. *Apply extreme focus on each compartment, but only for a short time.*

3. *Move forward in incremental steps. And once you see progress,*

4. *Close the compartment and open the next one.*

5. *Say "no" to things that don't deserve a compartment." End Quote.*

[5 Steps of Compartmentalization: The Secret Behind Successful Entrepreneurs, June 26, 2012, Ryan Blair contributor, Forbes]

In addition to the conscious phenomenon of *Compartmentalized Consciousness*, the subconscious form also illustrates a subconscious psychological defense mechanism that psychology defines as *compartmentalization.*

Some real-life examples of subconscious compartmentalization would be:

- A police officer, fireman, or rescue worker must enter a life-threatening situation to save a child after promising their spouse they would return home safe and sound.

- A soldier returning to civilian life must block out the many traumas and reflexes of combat.

- A devoutly religious parent must lovingly nurture and protect their homosexual child.

- A young person acting on a dare from their peers does something they know violates their parents' value system.

As stated in the definition of *Compartmentalized Consciousness*, the subconscious form of compartmentalization, as defined in psychology, occurs automatically as a mechanism to avoid cognitive dissonance involving incompatible systems of thought (e.g., incompatible beliefs, value systems, emotions, or ideas).

In contrast, the conscious forms of compartmentalization we have discussed are freely willed choices that the individual chooses to focus on and away from.

However, when unconscious compartmentalization breaks down, the individual will exhibit problems coping with the cognitive dissonance that results from the disparate systems of thought interacting with one another. When this form of compartmentalization breaks down, it can potentially bring the individual to a state of collapse, leaving them unable to perform their tasks.

Whereas, when conscious compartmentalization breaks down, it deteriorates the effectiveness of the individual in their ability to perform the roles that require compartmentalization. When this form of compartmentalization breaks down, the effect is often momentary until the individual reestablishes the focus of their attention.

FOURTEENTH LEVEL OF CONSCIOUSNESS (IN-THE-MOMENT)

Although we will define these terms more thoroughly later, let's start defining a few that will be useful now.

In psychology, the term *subconscious* is the part of the mind that is not currently in one's awareness. However, unlike the unconscious part of the mind, the subconscious sits just below the surface and, with some effort, can potentially be in one's awareness.

In contrast, the term *unconscious* is the part of the mind that is deeper, on the other side of the subconscious, and is not available for introspection regardless of the effort applied.

In medicine, the autonomic nervous system refers to the part of the nervous system responsible for controlling bodily functions generally not consciously directed, such as breathing, heartbeat, and digestive processes.

The *autonomic nervous system* has three branches. The *sympathetic nervous system* accelerates the heart rate, constricts blood vessels, and raises blood pressure. The *parasympathetic nervous system* slows the heart rate, increases intestinal and gland activity, and relaxes sphincter muscles. The *enteric nervous system* (*ENS*) is a substantial grouping of neurons outside the central nervous system that form the circuits responsible for autonomous reflex activity.

Recall the ' polyvagal theory ' regarding the sympathetic and parasympathetic nervous system.

To paraphrase John E. Hall, in his 2011 textbook, *General Principles of Gastrointestinal Function*:

> *The tenth cranial nerve (a.k.a. vagus nerve) has two neural fibers that connect numerous primary organs to the brain.*

> *One neural strand, large and coarse, originates in primitive lizard anatomy and is part of a defensive mechanism that helps the organism to be dormant and blend into the environment. Fine and smooth, the other strand only emerges in mammalian anatomy and operates the fight and flight response and most facial muscles.*

> *The enteric nervous system is essentially a mesh-like system of some 500 million neurons that can independently govern the function of the*

gastrointestinal tract. The enteric nervous system is in the lining of the gastrointestinal system beginning in the esophagus and extending to the anus.

[General Principles of Gastrointestinal Function, 2011, John E. Hall, Guyton and Hal Textbook of Medical Physiology 12th edition, Saunders Elsevier Publishers]

And to paraphrase Michael D. Gershon:

The enteric nervous system operates independently of the brain and spinal cord.

[Transplanting the enteric nervous system: a step closer to treatment for aganglionosis, April 2007, Michael D. Gershon - Professor of Pathology and Cell Biology, Columbia University College of Physicians and Surgeons, NY, NY, BMJ Journals, Gut]

But what do these different parts do, and how do they interact?

The *unconscious* and *subconscious* mind are constantly at work supporting activities here and now. In contrast, the *conscious* mind can be focused on the past, dwelling on memories of events that have happened, consisting of good memories, bad memories, or lost opportunities.

Some individuals spend most of their brain cycles stuck somewhere in the past; these individuals wear attire from the past and groom themselves as if they were still in that period, often their high school years.

Just as *conscious* thought may dwell on the past, it can also concentrate on the future, focusing on what could happen, whether it is a certainty, a likelihood, or a remote possibility. Some individuals spend most of their time thinking about the future, trying to imagine what it will be like when they attain their aspirations.

This next level of consciousness in our framework, *In-the-moment Consciousness*, is also a software-driven form of consciousness, as it focuses on being present at the moment instead of being in the past or future where our default operating system often roams.

When the entire focus of conscious thought is in-the-moment, we are engaging with others using our full attention on what and how they are doing it. When in-the-moment we are not only alert to a more significant portion of everything happening here and now, but we also provide a significantly richer experience for others, with them experiencing our complete focus on them.

Focusing on the past or future automatically directs our brain's processing cycles to support these activities. The simple fact is that the more we allow our focus to wander around on the past or future, the less we can focus our limited processing cycles on the present here and now.

In-the-moment Consciousness is one of the best ways to improve one's life as the resulting focus improves experiences for oneself and those who experience the focus of your attention upon them. In contrast, being in-the-moment, fosters better new memories for oneself and the individuals one interacts with, thereby fostering better relationships.

In Buddhist terminology, this is called *mindfulness*. Beyond anything, Zen Buddhism teaches us the importance of living in the present.

To quote Tim Lott in his 2012 book, *Off-beat Zen: Alan Watts, the Western Buddhist who healed my mind*: Quote.

> *"The emphasis on the present moment is perhaps Zen's most distinctive characteristic. In our western relationship with time, in which we compulsively pick over the past to learn lessons from it, and then project into a hypothetical future in which those lessons can be applied, the present moment has been compressed to a tiny sliver on the clock face between a vast past and an infinite future. Zen, more than anything else, is about reclaiming and expanding the present moment."*
>
> *"It tries to have you understand, without arguing the point, that there is no purpose in getting anywhere if, when you get there, all you do is think about getting to some other future moment. Life exists in the present, or nowhere at all, and if you cannot grasp that, you are simply living a fantasy."*
>
> *"For all Zen writers, life is, as it was for Shakespeare, akin to a dream – transitory and insubstantial. There is no "rock of ages cleft for me." There is no security. Looking for security, Watts said, is like jumping off a cliff while holding on to a rock for safety – an absurd illusion. Everything passes, and you must die. Don't waste your time thinking otherwise. Neither Buddha nor his Zen followers had time for any notion of an afterlife. The doctrine of reincarnation can be more accurately thought about as a constant rebirth, of death throughout life, and the continual coming and going of universal energy, of which we are all part, before and after death."* End Quote.
>
> *[Off-beat Zen: Alan Watts, the Western Buddhist who healed my mind, Sept 21, 2012, Tim Lott, Aeon edited by Lizzie Kirkwood]*

As we would expect, one of the most helpful prerequisite skills to assist *In-the-moment Consciousness* is *Meditative Consciousness*, where the individual trains the mind to return their focus from the past or future to this moment, which, instead of fantasizing about the future, lays the actual foundation for one's future.

FIFTEENTH LEVEL OF CONSCIOUSNESS (LEVEL ZERO PARADIGMATIC)

We begin paradigmatic consciousness at the lowest level, *Level Zero Paradigmatic Consciousness.*

In medical terms, *Level Zero Paradigmatic Consciousness* is also sometimes referred to as 'acute stress disorder,' which can occur as a natural response in the victims of kidnappings, hostage instances, domestic abuse, child abuse, human trafficking, incest, prisoners of war, political terrorism, cult indoctrination, slavery, prostitution, or captivity of any kind. It is also known as Stockholm syndrome.

Individuals in this level of paradigmatic consciousness are trapped intellectually within this level of consciousness and generally cannot escape without external assistance. They exercise altered behaviors from their norm.

Most notably, they dispense with their typical concern for their safety, needs, and interests. Instead, they form a paradoxical emotional bond with their captor, abuser, or cult leader regarding the interests of their abuser over their self-interests.

Hence, instead of having an ordinary sense of self, individuals forfeit their sense of self in substitution of their abuser's self-interests.

The term 'Level Zero' is because the individual possesses zero paradigms that pertain to themselves.

Although we will discuss what paradigms are more thoroughly in the next section, for now, a paradigm is the system of concepts that define an individual's reality, complete with all the rules that depict how the world works.

According to scientific data, the likelihood of an individual moving away from a paradigm of self into a paradigm of no self varies from under a ten percent chance to a near certainty depending upon a few psychological factors, such as in hostage-taking circumstances.

To paraphrase G. Dwayne Fuselier, Ph.D., in his 1999 article, *Placing the Stockholm Syndrome in Perspective*:

A Federal Bureau of Investigation (FBI) study of over 1200 hostage-taking incidents determined that 8% of the hostages developed Stockholm syndrome. FBI researchers interviewed flight attendants taken hostage during airplane hijackings and identified three factors as necessary for the syndrome to develop:

a. The hostage situation must last for several days or more.

b. The hostage-takers remain co-located with the hostages.

c. Hostage takers show some kindness toward the hostages or at least refrain from harming them.

In contrast, hostages that captors abuse may develop anger toward them and then, as a result, do not tend to develop the syndrome.

[Placing the Stockholm Syndrome in Perspective, July 1999, G. Dwayne Fuselier Ph.D., http://www.au.af.mil/au/awc/awcgate/fbi/stockholm_syndrome.pdf, FBI Law Enforcement Bulletin 68: 22.]

At the other end of the continuum of hostage situations are cult members. Cult leaders carefully select and groom these victims in a setting that permits the targeted victim to opt out or escape.

As a result, the likelihood of cult members becoming trapped in *Level Zero Paradigmatic Consciousness* that have elected to join the cult is close to 100% certainty.

In the middle of these two probabilities, 8% for *Stockholm syndrome* and 100% for cult members, are the other forms of victimhood, such as domestic abuse victims. In this middle range, the victim has freedoms unavailable to a hostage, but they elect to remain in the relationship out of fear and a lack of self-worth.

Again, the paradigm of the victim places little or no importance on protecting their interests because their paradigm focuses solely on the interests of their captor, cult leader, or abuser.

SIXTEENTH LEVEL OF CONSCIOUSNESS (LEVEL ONE PARADIGMATIC)

"When we first begin to believe anything, what we believe is not a single proposition, it is a whole system of propositions. (Light dawns gradually over the whole.)."

[Ludwig Josef Johann Wittgenstein, 1889-1951]

Our next software-based level of consciousness is *Level One Paradigmatic Consciousness.*

Science and philosophy define a 'paradigm' as a distinct set of concepts or thought patterns that pertain to a scientific or philosophical discipline. Although correct, this definition provides just a glimpse into the depth and detail of *Paradigmatic Consciousness.* Quote.

"Similar to the context of information and behavior, a paradigm provides meaning to everything that is within the framework of the paradigm."

"The difference between the context and a paradigm, however, is that the 'context' of something originates from the outside world and enters into the brain as stimuli from sensory organs, whereas a paradigm originates from within the brain and becomes projected to the outside world." End Quote.

[Sensitive by Nature: Understanding Intelligence and the Mind, 2002, J Luisi, 1st Books Library Publishers]

The understanding of one's world that any paradigm determines is profound.

First and foremost, one's paradigm determines how an individual interprets the stimuli from the world around them.

Second, one's paradigm largely determines the events an individual may perceive. In this manner, it often filters one's awareness, only allowing the individual to be aware of particular events within one's environment to which the individual's paradigm can relate.

As a teenager, I took the opportunity to participate in market research exercises conducted on groups of random people in the local shopping mall.

Either together or separately, the individuals selected viewed the same film clip and were provided a standard list of questions afterward. These questions asked about what they had just witnessed, their emotions, and whether it made them curious about what would happen next.

Although the events the individuals viewed were identical, their documented experiences varied greatly, including what they recalled seeing, their interpretations of what it meant, and how it made them feel.

The exercise highlighted that although the *context* of an individual's experience may be identical, including the process for signing up for the experiment where each received the same sales pitch, shared the seating in exact surroundings, viewed the same images, and experienced the same sounds. The only variable was the individual's paradigm.

Therefore, our definition of the term *paradigm* for us to begin our journey into *Level One Paradigmatic Consciousness* is that a *paradigm* is a system of ideas that determines how an individual arrives at a particular understanding of the world and events around them.

A given paradigm comprises a filter system that selects what stimuli an individual becomes aware of and which they do not.

The sensory organs bring the information into the given region of the brain so that the data is present. However, a given paradigm will determine whether the data's presence is acknowledged or acknowledged but lacking importance.

Upon filtering out events and stimuli, the paradigm must determine what the remaining events and stimuli mean.

In this step, the given paradigm uses what it believes about the world to interpret the events within its field of awareness. The resulting interpretation stems from a system of rules that determines the importance of each event and how these events ultimately relate to one another.

As the interpretation unfolds within the individual's mind, the individual experiences the emotions corresponding to that interpretation.

Unless meticulously trained to do so, very few individuals can recall the events they observed as they genuinely occurred without adding the bias of their paradigm.

This effect not only brings into question which individual's paradigm is accurate but also whether any paradigm is accurate and whether any paradigm can be valid.

Due to the differences in the filtering of stimuli and differences in the emphasis placed on them, our paradigms can lead us to a wide range of interpretations of the same events.

Hence, individuals who grow up in the same culture are bound to have paradigms that result in similar interpretations, while different cultures can lead to vast differences. Those differences in meaning are just as real and justified for each cultural group.

Therefore, how an individual interprets the world is primarily influenced by the cultural groups they associate with and identify. However, one's paradigm might vary depending upon the group of people they are associating with at any given moment.

The given meaning can vary depending on an individual's base *paradigm* for functioning as a member of their cultural group or for the different groups they are members of, such as scientific groups, religious groups, clubs, organizations, or one's professional vocation.

Of course, when groups of individuals having different paradigms interact, it gives rise to their paradigms to conflict and collide. When *paradigms* collide, the result is often outrage, as the reflex of most individuals is to defend their *paradigm*.

To illustrate how a paradigm can distort an individual's perceptions and interpretation of stimuli, let's consider the following story of the doctor and the nurse. Quote.

"A doctor is kneeling beside a patient lying unconscious on the floor."

"The doctor yells at a nurse, 'Get my bag!'"

"When the nurse returns with the doctor's bag, she is angry that she is not getting the proper respect."

"The doctor then yells to the nurse, 'Don't just stand there. Find this patient's chart, quickly!'"

"Now the nurse becomes hostile toward the physician. She snarls at him and hurries down the hall in a rage. Upon returning, she fights the urge to throw the chart at the doctor." End Quote.

[Sensitive by Nature: Understanding Intelligence and the Mind, 2002, J Luisi, 1ˢᵗ Books Library Publishers]

The reality behind the story is that the physician's behavior stems from the physician's reality that he is both confused and scared about what is happening.

In contrast, the nurse is operating from a *paradigm* that she knows she is more competent as a medical professional than many of the physicians in this hospital, and the lack of respect received is because she doesn't have the same medical degree.

In this story, however, the nurse fails to recognize the proper context of the situation. Even though the nurse had previously heard that the patient was a long-time friend of the physician whose children had attended the same school in their early grades, she failed to place appropriate importance on the fact that the parents had become acquainted through their children and became close friends.

In this story, the nurse's paradigm caused her to misinterpret the physician's behavior as disrespect for her not having the same medical degree. Her paradigm failed to consider the possibility of another interpretation that could be more applicable and consistent with the facts. Yet, this is her reality.

More accurately, the physician is afraid and panicking because he doesn't know what is happening to his close friend.

Meanwhile, the patient in the story, who is immobile, hears everything happening around him. He can tell that his long-time friend does not know what is wrong with him, and knowing his friend so very well, the patient correctly perceives the fear and panic in his physician friend's voice.

The patient also recognizes the nurse's tone from previous conversations and correctly identifies her emotional state of feeling ordered around due to her perceived subservient professional status.

The patient lying on the floor, unable to communicate, is caught between the paradigm of his friend and the nurse and quickly realizes that he may be in real trouble and, as a result, is potentially screwed.

I have a personal friendship with my physician, and I know that if found in similar circumstances, my friend would say, "Jim, if you hear me, I have no idea what is wrong with you, and because we are good friends, I have to tell you, I think you are screwed."

Upon hearing these solemnly spoken words, Jim would then use his last ounce of strength to wave goodbye to his close friend, mustering the strength to only wave but one finger.

Humans begin their lives unconsciously from childhood, building the base *paradigm* with which they interpret the world. An individual's *paradigm* relies on the foundation of the value systems primarily from one's culture, generally followed by various other sources, such as family, peers, education, neighborhood, and the many personal choices one makes involving friends, music, film, and reading materials.

Genes also influence one's paradigm.

However, when individuals become aware that they have a paradigm, they can sometimes override and consciously reshape it. Quote.

"While paradigms often manage the individual, individuals with superior perceptive abilities are often able to manage their paradigms. [Likewise] They also tend to demonstrate a greater level of sophistication in understanding the paradigms of others." End Quote.

[Sensitive by Nature: Understanding Intelligence and the Mind, 2002, J Luisi, 1st Books Library Publishers]

Many individuals may never inquire into their minds as to whether they have a *paradigm*. However, they become more likely to expand beyond *Level One Paradigmatic Consciousness* once they do.

In summarizing *Level One Paradigmatic Consciousness*, let's consider one of the fundamental Buddhist principles referred to as the "two truths."

To quote Chokyi Nyima Rinpoche in his 2018 book, *Sadness, Love Openness: The Buddhist Path of Joy*: Quote.

"The two truths refer to ultimate truth and relative truth. The ultimate is the nature of reality, the way things are, while the relative is the way things appear to us, the way they seem to be." End Quote.

[Sadness, Love Openness: The Buddhist Path of Joy, pg. 10, 2018, Chokyi Nyima Rinpoche, Shambhala Publications]

As such, *Level One Paradigmatic Consciousness* individuals only perceive one truth, conflating the way things appear with the way things are.

SEVENTEENTH LEVEL OF CONSCIOUSNESS (LEVEL TWO PARADIGMATIC)

Level Two Paradigmatic Consciousness is the next level of consciousness in our journey. Achieving this level of consciousness means that the individual has gained an awareness of the paradigms of others with an understanding of how to relate to the other's paradigm and potentially influence it.

For convenience, we will refer to individuals with *Level One Paradigmatic Consciousness* as *"Level Ones"* and *Level Two Paradigmatic Consciousness* as *"Level Twos."*

While *Level Ones* are not necessarily aware of their paradigm, even though they may have a good sense that other individuals have their ways of interpreting the world, their paradigm is the person they know themselves to be and the things they believe.

But how do *Level Ones* become *Level Twos*?

From early childhood, we start as *Level Ones*. As children, we see the world from the perspective of ourselves and what we want. It usually takes a degree of training to learn how to share with others when we know that the world is not all about ourselves.

As life experiences accumulate, the brain automatically attempts to make sense of the world by integrating new information into one's base paradigm. The collage of data and the relationships that result builds our *Level One* reality; whether that information consists of superstitious ideas, religious doctrine, belief in science, or tangible observation, the *paradigm* forms a unified view of the world from which to interpret all events.

As a *Level One*, any piece of information that conflicts with one's paradigm is an opportunity that will be resolved either by rejecting the new information, correcting the old information, or compartmentalizing the two sets of information into separate compartments so that they do not collide.

Quote.

> *"Being categorized as a Level One only refers to the fact that the individual thinks solidly within one paradigm at a time, rather than perceiving many. Such individuals span the full continuum of academic, professional, and intellectual achievements. It is neither good nor bad, nor is it a determination of one's intelligence."*

> *"The only characteristic that all Level Ones have in common is that they only experience a single paradigm at a time. Whether it is because the brain centers chose the first paradigm that made sense or the brain only encounters a single paradigm, Level Ones remain firmly rooted in their present paradigm and sense of reality."* End Quote.

> *[Sensitive by Nature: Understanding Intelligence and the Mind, 2002, J Luisi, 1st Books Library Publishers]*

Level One individuals interpret information rather consistently from a single paradigm. Their views tend to remain unchanged as the *Level One* paradigm automatically and unconsciously protects itself by filtering data and interpreting the filtered information with the rules of their paradigm.

Therefore, the core of each community's cultural values derives stability from how *Level One* individuals protect their paradigm. As soon as cognitive dissonance occurs, the conflicting information is either filtered out by the paradigm or is compartmentalized to prevent cognitive dissonance from disrupting the *Level One* individual's paradigm.

Occasionally, however, a portion of the *Level One* population becomes aware of the conflicting paradigms as forms of logical inconsistencies.

When logical inconsistencies occur that *Level One* individuals cannot ignore, it may not be possible to envision another paradigm where the logical inconsistencies do not exist, allowing them to shift their universe of understanding to the new paradigm.

Surprisingly, when this shift occurs, the *Level One* individual usually has no memory of their former paradigm, completely forgetting their differences. When pressed, the *Level One* individual will completely deny that their old paradigm existed as they can only conceive of their one paradigm.

Though an individual shifting from one base paradigm to another will be a topic for later discussion, it is essential to note here that some individuals successfully attain awareness of paradigms upon detecting these shifts in other *Level Ones*. The individual who becomes aware of these paradigm shifts in others is what we refer to as the emergence of *Level Two Paradigmatic Consciousness*.

The conscious improvement of a *Level Two* over a *Level One* individual is that the *Level* Two individual recognizes their ability to perceive some paradigms of other individuals. However, they do not necessarily recognize the implications of their paradigm.

Once the beginner *Level Two* perceives another individual's paradigms, they notice paradigm shifts within themselves. Importantly, recognizing that paradigms can shift in others makes the *Level Two* individual intuitively aware that this may be a valuable intellectual tool, after which the *Level Two* individual then begins to recognize opportunities to use this fact.

At this point, the development of *Level Two* individuals is determined predominantly by personality. As one can imagine, individuals can choose to do many things with skills involving *paradigms*.

PRODUCTIVE *LEVEL TWOS*

One such path is that they can be productive members of society, earning a living in the community using their abilities to be more effective in their jobs and other *personas*. We refer to these individuals as 'productive' *Level Twos*.

When being 'productive,' *Level Twos* play some of the most essential roles in society. These individuals can help shape the paradigms of others in productive ways.

One may frequently find productive *Level Twos* developing new skills to become outstanding executives, negotiators, attorneys, and judges. They use their abilities to perceive paradigms to develop amazing plays, comedies, and dramas within the entertainment industry. For the most part, productive *Level Twos* excel at roles heavily dependent upon understanding and relating to people who think differently than themselves.

Productive *Level Two* behavior is vital for selecting highly effective managers and leaders.

For example, when a 'productive' Level Two encounters high quality and ethical values in an individual, they tend to assist that individual and promote them to benefit the organization.

EGOISTIC *LEVEL TWOS*

Another path the *Level Two* individual can choose is to focus their skills to accumulate power, money, possessions, or simply attention by manipulating other individuals in potentially deceptive ways, basically tricking and cheating others to achieve their objective. We refer to these rather edacious types as 'egoistic' *Level Twos*.

Having 'egoistic' tendencies, even strong ones, does not necessitate that 'egoistic' *Level Twos* are sinful or criminal, as they may crave power, money, or attention. Such individuals are often brilliant and driven and can be highly effective when harnessing their strengths when there are ample protections to manage their potentially damaging 'egoistic' characteristics.

For an 'egoistic' *Level Two* to be highly effective, they must be extremely effective at hiding their 'egoistic' tendencies, or else they make themselves easy targets by those that oppose them, often those willing to use any means at their disposal.

PROBLEMATIC *LEVEL TWOS*

These individuals see themselves as well-meaning people who believe that the ends justify the means. Problematic *Level Twos* see no problem knowingly perpetrating falsehoods to manipulate their intended audience.

When they become adept at using *Level Two* skills, they can be rather formidable petty tyrants, cult leaders, scam artists, pretenders, cheaters, and manipulators who are often difficult to identify, not to mention overcome.

Problematic *Level Twos* play some of the worst societal roles, often responsible for a wide array of societal and organizational dysfunctions, often manifesting as petty tyrants who tend to be remarkably well-hidden within large organizations and groups.

To quote Carlos Castaneda in his 1991 book, *Fire from Within: The Teachings of Don Juan #7*:

> *"A petty tyrant is a (self-important) person who causes distress by imposing his/her will on others using psychological pressure rather than physical force.*
>
> *The warrior who stumbles on a petty tyrant is a lucky one. You're fortunate if you come upon one in your path because if you don't, you [would] have to go out and look for one."*

[Fire from Within: The Teachings of Don Juan #7, Jan 01, 1991, Carlos Castaneda, Washington Square Press]

They may attack unwitting individuals to advance their agenda, be motivated out of jealousy, or be encouraged due to being prejudiced against an individual or what they represent.

For example, if a 'problematic' *Level Two* feels threatened by the quality of another individual, the 'problematic' *Level Two* will choose their moment to engage in psychological warfare.

Management may have difficulty identifying a 'problematic' *Level Two* because 'problematic' *Level Twos* are particularly good at making themselves appear as valuable team players because they manage upwardly quite well. In contrast, the victims of petty tyrants may include anyone not above them.

As an example of one countermeasure, the wiser organizations institute regular personnel surveys to clamp down on bad actors, such as 'problematic' *Level Twos* or any individual with some form of organizational dysfunction.

EVIL *LEVEL TWOS*

At the far end of the spectrum, *Level Twos* that willfully commit sinful or criminal acts have the skills to be formidable characters to thwart investigators and law enforcement. These we refer to as 'evil' *Level Twos*.

Here, we have the most formidable bad actors, including terrorists, cartel leaders, crime bosses, and tyrants, and state bad actors that conduct and fund activities to harm their competitors.

Generally, when encountering 'problematic' or 'evil' *Level Twos,* the best defense is to acquire the aid of 'productive' and 'egoistic' *Level Twos* as they are most likely to have the understanding and skill set to assist.

As you can imagine, it is possible to dedicate an entire book to the various types of *Level Twos* and the best approaches to identifying and interacting with them.

In summarizing *Level Two Paradigmatic Consciousness*, individuals generally move from one group of *Level Twos* to another. However, to advance to the next level of consciousness within our framework, I believe 'productive' *Level Twos* primarily make the next transition.

Returning to the fundamental Buddhist concept of the "two truths," *Level Two Paradigmatic Consciousness* individuals can perceive more than one truth. However, these *truths* may each represent another way the truth may appear to us.

As we learn more about *paradigms,* these ways can be how things seem or, more likely, how things could seem. However, they never seem to be how things are in objective reality.

EIGHTEENTH LEVEL OF CONSCIOUSNESS (LEVEL THREE PARADIGMATIC)

Level Three Paradigmatic Consciousness is the next level for our journey into software-based consciousness.

By my rough estimation, *Level One* individuals represent the most considerable portion of the population at around 80% of all individuals. Level Two individuals follow them, representing nearly the entire difference of almost 20%. In contrast, *Level Three* individuals represent only a few percent. However, this may be because *Level Threes* must first become *Level Twos* before becoming positioned to transition to the next level.

Every individual's paradigm is unique. Given even subtle differences in our experiences, we each have no choice but to end up with our different realities. The degree of difference between these realities may begin with minor differences in our respective experiences, though those differences become increasingly significant as we experience different cultures and subcultures.

The ability to bridge the gap between individuals having disparate *paradigms* is well within the skill set of a skilled *Level Two*. *Level Twos* possess the skill set to understand disparate realities. They can often find ways to assist *Level One* individuals, not to filter out stimuli necessary to address some differences among individuals with disparate *paradigms*.

To accomplish this, a *Level Two* individual must build trust by demonstrating that they understand and can explain the root cause of the differences. Once completed, the next step is to garner trust by presenting the root cause of differences in earnest to the person with the opposing reality in simple terms so that they can come to understand the distinct *paradigm*.

As discussed previously, *Level Twos* can be 'productive,' 'egoistic,' 'problematic,' or 'evil' using their paradigmatic insights. As one can imagine, the intended outcomes of *Level Two* involvement can vary significantly.

It is important here to highlight the difference among 'productive,' 'egoistic,' 'problematic,' or 'evil' *Level Twos* simply because it is infrequent for an 'egoistic,' 'problematic,' or 'evil' *Level Two* to transform to *Level Three*, which we will eventually see why.

Now that we have laid the groundwork for *Level Three Paradigmatic Consciousness,* let's consider the following story where an individual enters the process of attaining *Level Three* status. Interestingly, the process usually occurs relatively early in life.

Dan is a young and successful Level Two executive in a Fortune 50 company, thanks mainly to his productive Level Two skill set. Recently married, Dan is a good earner and an attractive partner for many women at work.

One particularly assertive young lady, also Dan's manager, enjoys working with Dan primarily because conversations with Dan demonstrate his rare understanding similar to hers.

On a business trip, after several cocktails, they each make the rather big mistake of crossing the professional boundary by becoming personally intimate. When Dan attempts to break off the personal aspect of their relationship, his manager prefers not to cooperate.

Dan attempts to find another position in the firm, separating himself from his manager, but finds that other people are beginning to behave differently toward him and realizes that he has no idea who he may be able to confide in. Also, given this situation, he has no one he can confide in at home. Additionally, Dan has no friends outside work because his work consumes his entire life at this point in his career.

Dan finds himself isolated, and the job that consumes his life is no longer viable. Dan's paradigms collapse without compartmentalization, and he finds that he can neither function at work nor home.

One's paradigm rests on a combination of potential anchors, beginning with the primary groups in which the individual is a member, such as one's immediate family, extended family, friends, co-workers, neighbors, religious groups, and clubs or societies.

Suppose the workplace represents the dominant cultural group of the individual. In that case, it only takes severe cognitive dissonance within that one domain for the individual to lose touch with their reality. If the dominant cultural groups are both work and home, then it takes disruptive cognitive dissonance within those two domains for the individual to lose touch with reality.

When the individual realizes that, in addition to their cognitive dissonance, they have no idea whom they can trust even to have a conversation, *paradigmatic* collapse is inevitable and swift.

As a popular reference, a paradigm crash is much like the last scene for the character Javert, played by Russell Crowe, in the motion picture Les Misérables.

Javert is a French police inspector who initially met Jean Valjean when Valjean was a prisoner for stealing a loaf of bread. After Valjean's release, Valjean breaks his parole and becomes a successful businessman. The French inspector Javert reemerges again and again throughout Valjean's life, constantly threatening to expose Valjean's identity and cause his downfall. Javert believes in authority and obedience to the law above all else. The law is so sacred to him that he cannot envision any other system of morality or justice.

Eventually, Javert faces a series of undeniable contradictions as to the goodness of character of Valjean. His choices are to either continue to support his belief in the law to expose Valjean or to believe Valjean represents even a higher level of morality than the law. Quote.

> *"And must I now begin to doubt.*
> *Who never doubted all these years?*
> *My heart is stone and still it trembles.*
> *The world I have known is lost in shadow." End Quote.*

Unable to reconcile the contradiction of his purpose in life, Javert then issues his final words leading up to his tragic suicide. Quote.

> *"I'll escape now from that world*
> *From the world of Jean Valjean*
> *There is nowhere I can turn*
> *There is no way to go on!" End Quote.*

The *Level Two* individual does not realize that at this point, given their new psychological condition, they have become a *Level Three* candidate, though admittance is far from guaranteed.

Previously, we mentioned that it is rare for the 'egoistic,' 'problematic,' and 'evil' *Level Two* to transform themselves into *Level Three* individuals, and several reasons are worth illustrating.

First and foremost, the 'egoistic,' 'problematic,' and 'evil' *Level Two* are highly resistant to a *paradigmatic* collapse simply because their ego is such that they are more likely to justify their behavior and protect their damaged *paradigm*.

It is the very nature of these *Level Twos* not to need or want any counsel from other individuals. These *Level Twos* feel they are more intelligent than everybody else, so since they know themselves better, why should they seek advice from a trusted source when they only truly trust themselves?

The next question is whether a *Level Two* individual can attain *Level Three Paradigmatic Consciousness* using their imagination and intellectual facilities.

The answer here is also no.

Becoming a *Level Three* requires a journey of great uncertainty that typically takes weeks, months, or years. In hindsight, it is uncannily like the Buddhist equivalent of being able to attain enlightenment without taking the journey. Hence, there are times when the journey is necessary.

Chokyi Nyima Rinpoche, one of our time's leading Buddhist scholars and writers, points out the following, and I quote:

> *"If we are searching for freedom and awakening, treating topics such as impermanence and suffering, love and compassion, or insight into the nature of the mind as abstract concepts are not sufficient."*

"The only way to truly understand these crucial points is through direct experience." End Quote.

[Sadness, Love Openness: The Buddhist Path of Joy, 2018, Chokyi Nyima Rinpoche, Shambhala Publications]

To continue our story from the inside of the paradigmatic collapse.

Dan now feels completely disoriented and is unable to function. He attempts to reassess every person he knows to determine if he can trust them.

He makes a list, and all he can come up with on his frighteningly small list is mom, dad, and his pet dog, which died earlier in his youth. What's even worse is that it occurs to Dan that he cannot even place himself on the list, as he knows he cannot even trust himself to think straight.

What the *Level Three* candidate must do at this point is to rebuild their base *paradigm* to allow them to function within their work and home environment, even if it will enable them to operate only at a minimal level, much like booting up your laptop in 'Safe Mode' after it crashes uncontrollably as the individual struggles even to think.

If the individual can get their brain's software running again in 'Safe Mode,' then they may be able to operate sufficiently to enable them to begin piecing together a way to interpret personal interactions into a *paradigm* that works, one that can reconcile, or at least compartmentalize the conflicting interpretations.

This stage of the Level Two individual's journey out of a paradigm crash is precarious.

If the Level Two individual succeeds at proceeding through the steps necessary to emerge as a Level Three, they will be significantly better for the experience.

However, suppose the individual finds they can only draw inward into themselves. In that case, they will likely find themselves in a psychiatric ward with a nervous breakdown or, worse, as a potential suicide victim.

To explain the levels of consciousness, we will continue the journey of a *Level Two* individual that emerges as a Level Three, from where Dan is still in a *paradigmatic* collapse. The side paths that lead to a long-term nervous breakdown are a different journey that would take precious space to explore.

Continuing with Dan, he begins to realize some of the building blocks of paradigms and starts assembling them. Dan succeeds in placing the first few building blocks together as parts of his new foundation, only to experience that they collapse again.

After numerous attempts, Dan achieves an increasingly complete system of building blocks before they collapse. After much effort, Dan eventually assembles a structure of building blocks that might allow him to function, although that version of reality also collapses.

Dan is encouraged when he realizes that new versions of reality can be reassembled faster with each attempt and that each attempt results in a slightly more stable paradigm.

When Dan eventually achieves a paradigm stable enough with which to function in the real world, he thinks of a series of steps that he must take to address some of the interpretations that create the most dissonance.

He phones his manager, who coincidentally happens to be going through the same process, and they agree to collaborate. They both agree that their intimate relationship must end if they are to be able to function.

At this point, the most unpredictable segment of the journey is over.

Once the *Level Three* candidate can assemble the building blocks that form paradigms consciously, it is a matter of time before they construct a stable and operational paradigm. The alternative of remaining trapped inside a collapsed *paradigm*, trying to get to 'Safe Mode' or becoming entangled in 'Safe Mode,' has been averted.

We can now continue the journey of an emerging *Level Three*.

Establishing a stable working *paradigm* after a *paradigmatic* collapse is essential to achieving *Level Three Paradigmatic Consciousness*. But by this point, the *Level Three* candidate has collected some crucial clues they need to put together. So, let's now return to Dan and his journey.

Dan now breathes a sigh of relief with the painful memories of panic and fear behind him.

In the aftermath, however, it soon dawns on Dan that he can assemble other working paradigms, and, as he quickly realizes, now that he has practiced rebuilding paradigms, it becomes apparent that he can build paradigms at will.

True to form, Dan starts assembling many paradigms.

He creates multiple paradigms to explain his observations and paradigms to explain the behavior of others.

At this point, Dan can now look through the lens of many realities on demand, and he can do so with little effort.

He now can see any number of paradigms simultaneously, some reasonable, some not so much.

At this point, however, Dan has just attained Level Three Paradigmatic Consciousness.

The journey through a paradigmatic collapse is necessary. Intellectually imagining the journey is not a substitute that experience provides.

While the journey itself is not without grave perils, it is not exactly a journey upon which one ever chooses to embark. Instead, it is a journey that results when the forces that act upon one's *paradigm* overcome that paradigm and the usual methods for grappling with those disruptive forces.

Aside from the occasional 'productive' *Level Two* finding themselves on this journey, let's take a moment to consider whether a *Level One* could make the same journey without first becoming a *Level Two*.

If we recall, *Level Ones* see the world from a single *paradigm* that defines them.

The first question is whether a *Level One* can experience a collapse of their *paradigm*.

Here, the answer is yes. Although it does not occur easily, the events in one's life can be sufficiently severe to cause their paradigm to collapse.

The problem at this point is that without prior knowledge of the existence of *paradigms* and how they work, a *Level One* is severely disadvantaged in completing that journey. Ultimately, when *Level One* individuals find themselves amid a paradigmatic collapse, they lack the sense of paradigms that might equip them to deal with the obstacles they will face.

Even equipped with *Level Two* knowledge of *paradigms*, a 'productive' *Level Two* still finds it challenging to complete the arduous journey back to psychological stability. Additionally, the *Level Two* individuals who are predominately 'egoistic,' 'problematic,' or 'evil' are not likely to embark on the journey.

Yes, there are many brilliant *Level One* individuals, some with extremely high IQs and emotional intelligence. However, attaining *Level Three Paradigmatic Consciousness* is neither a question of emotional intelligence nor IQ.

Interestingly, individuals who attain *Level Three Paradigmatic Consciousness* are keenly aware of their capabilities. They may not be familiar with its taxonomy or realize how they became *Level Three*, but when discussed with them, they still retain a recollection of the journey.

But assuming that most people are unaware of our taxonomy or that someone thinks they are a *Level Three* but are not. How can a *Level Three* be detected?

A simple test can identify someone who can create and see many *paradigms*. The same simple test can identify a *Level One*, *Level Two*, or *Level Three* with the following puzzle.

Here are the puzzle rules.

Puzzle Rules – You find yourself seated in a triangle facing two other people ('A' and 'B'), and all three individuals are wearing a blindfold and a hat, including you.

Everyone hears that there are only three white and two black hats in the total inventory of hats and that one is on the head of each.

The only movement permitted is eye movement, to look at the hats of the two individuals participating with you.

Everyone also knows that each of the three individuals is highly intelligent.

When everyone is unblindfolded, you see a white hat on the head of each of the other contestants, though you do not know what color hat you have resting on your head.

Then, the participants learn that the winner will be the first to answer the question with the correct answer and explanation.

You, the reader, should check the exact time, including the hour, minute, and second, to see how quickly you can solve the puzzle.

Puzzle Question – What is the color of the hat on your head, and how do you know?

The length of time that it takes you to solve the puzzle with a clear explanation will reveal much about your paradigmatic consciousness. Take the time now to solve the puzzle, and when you are confident that you have completed it, pick up again from here.

Upon hearing the question, *Level Threes* will have the correct answer with total confidence in their corresponding explanation within two to three seconds.

Level Twos will solve the puzzle, though they will take at least one to ten minutes.

Level Ones will take some longer, though some will never get the answer no matter how much time they devote to it. Stranger still is that some *Level Ones* will not understand the correct answer even once explained. The inability to understand the answer is surprising, especially concerning someone highly intelligent.

So, let's walk through the puzzle together.

First, without trying to do so, *Level Three* has had more than sufficient time to prepare four *paradigms*, one for each seated individual (i.e., 'A,' 'B,' 'you,' and 'a higher you').

Upon hearing the question, a *Level Three* would simultaneously experience the thought process corresponding to each of the four paradigms as their versions of reality unfolded. It is like overhearing the internal conversation inside each person's head.

It would go something like the following:

[Time: 0 Seconds] The Voice of You, as heard by the higher You – I see two white hats.

[Time: 0.5 Seconds] The Voices of You, A, and B, as heard by the higher You – A and B are confused because neither see two black hats.

[Time: 1.0 Seconds] The Voices of You, A, and B, as heard by the higher You – If I saw one black hat, I know that A or B could deduce that they had a white hat if they saw me with a black hat.

[Time: 1.5 Seconds] The Voices of You, A, and B, as heard by the higher You – If I had a black hat, A and B would have been able to deduce that they had on a white hat from the confusion of the other.

[Time: 2.0 Seconds]

Level Three's answer is, "My hat is white because if I had a black hat, the other contestants would have been able to quickly deduce that they had on a white hat from the confusion of the others, so they are looking at two white hats just like me."

The above is the first winning answer with an explanation that would only come from a *Level Three* individual and in two to three seconds by seeing the four paradigms simultaneously.

Let's now look at ourselves as *Level Two* contestants as we begin to logically deduce the puzzle verbally in our mind using sentences for reasoning it out logically.

Here, the *Level Two* individual has some ability to see the perspective of A and B, with most of their attention focused on oneself, and with some effort, they can envision a higher level of themselves.

[Time: 0 Seconds] The Voice of You – I see two white hats.

[Time: 5 Seconds] The Voice of You as A – I see one white hat and a hat of an unknown color.

[Time: 10 Seconds] The Voice of You as B – I see one white hat and a hat of an unknown color.

[Time: 15 Seconds] The Voice of You – I see two white hats, but let's assume for a moment that I hypothetically have a black hat on my head.

[Time: 20 Seconds] The Voice of You as A – I see one white and a black hat.

[Time: 25 Seconds] The Voice of You as B – I see one white hat and a black hat.

[Time: 30 Seconds] The Voice of You as A – I cannot tell myself because I do not see two black hats.

[Time: 35 Seconds] The Voice of You as B – I cannot tell myself because I do not see two black hats.

[Time: 40 Seconds] The Voice of You – I cannot tell myself because I do not see two black hats.

[Time: 45 Seconds] The Voice of You – If I saw one black hat, I know they could deduce that they had a white hat if they saw me with a black hat.

[Time: 55 Seconds] The Voice of You as A – If I saw one black hat, I know they could deduce that they had a white hat if they saw me with a black hat.

[Time: 65 Seconds] The Voice of You as B – If I saw one black hat, I know then they could deduce that they had a white hat if they saw me with a black hat.

[Time: 75 Seconds] The Voice of You – If I had a black hat, the other contestants would have been able to deduce that they had on a white hat because they are intelligent.

[Time: 85 Seconds] The Voice of You as A – If I had a black hat, the other contestants would have been able to deduce that they had on a white hat.

[Time: 95 Seconds] The Voice of You as B – If I had a black hat, the other contestants would have been able to deduce that they had a white hat because they are intelligent.

[Time: 105 Seconds or much later] The Level Two's answer is, my hat is white because if I had a black hat, the other contestants would have been able to deduce that they had on a white hat, so they must be looking at two white hats like me.

The second correct answer would only come from someone with proficient *Level Two* skills for this prolonged duration by simultaneously seeing two paradigms.

Finally, let's look at you as a *Level One* contestant as you begin to deduce the puzzle verbally using sentences for reasoning it out logically before drawing the problem out with paper and pencil.

After spending a reasonable amount of time on the diagram, the *Level One* individual will figure it out, or they will conclude that there was insufficient information to determine the answer as they can only perceive one paradigm at a time. With assistance, sometimes they can momentarily see part of another individual's paradigm to deduce the solution.

When the *Level One* individual hears the explanation, they may argue that the description cannot be the correct answer.

One might conclude that having *Level Three* skills only comes with intellectual advantages. However, they also experience disadvantages.

It seems that *Level Threes* benefit from perceiving numerous paradigms simultaneously, giving them access to many systems of interpretation simultaneously. However, consider the following story involving an expensive private school.

> *A fourth-grade teacher designs a test for her classroom of nine-year-old students. After the test is administered and graded, the only student who failed it takes it home to be signed by their parents as confirmation to the teacher that the parents saw the test results.*

> *Dad goes to school the next day with his daughter and suggests to the teacher that the test she designed had additional correct answers that the teacher did not recognize.*

> *The Level One teacher condescendingly explained that there was only one correct answer for each question and that the student just got it all wrong.*

> *Dad asks the teacher if the three of them could review the test so that his child could understand why her responses were incorrect, and to the teacher's credit, she eagerly agrees.*

> *The first test question marked as wrongly answered asked the student to circle the items that might not bounce. Among the things was a ball. The teacher said that a ball bounces, so the answer is incorrect.*

> *Dad asked his daughter to explain, and the child said that some balls are bean bags you can toss around, but they don't bounce.*

> *The teacher said, okay, I'll give credit for that one, but then eagerly wanted to go on to the next question.*

> *The next test question asked how many times a day a broken clock could tell the correct time. The teacher said the only correct answer was two, once for AM and once for PM, and the child wrote at least twenty-four.*

> *Dad asked his child to explain, and the child said that a broken clock had to be correct at least once in every time zone, and there were at least twenty-four of them.*

> *At the end of the meeting, the dad thanked the teacher for his child's perfect score.*

Level Threes generally experience difficulty taking multiple-choice exams as they see interpretations from alternate paradigms and perspectives that confuse the test taker. Interestingly, only carefully designed tests that had already undergone statistically monitored results should be considered reliable.

Professional organizations (e.g., Educational Testing Service (ETS)) carefully analyze tests for alternate interpretations. Before going live with test items, ETS researchers first test their test items by embedding them in tests just for analysis purposes, as they exclude them when calculating a test taker's score.

If responses are statistically less accurate in specific cultural groups, the question is analyzed more closely for how that cultural group interprets it.

The types of anomalies that are exposed are things like a question's reference to the color of a given citrus fruit, which may be typically a different color within a particular geographic region, a fact that the test item designer was likely unaware of.

One skill that *Level Threes* excel at is detecting when individuals in a conversation are inadvertently speaking past one another. Talking past one another can occur when two individuals use words that mean one thing from one person's paradigm while meaning something quite different from another.

Level Three individuals can perceive the disparate *paradigms* employed by each speaker. They can insert themselves into the conversation to convey what each person means when they speak.

Unchecked, the two individuals would typically walk away from each other believing they had an agreement, only to feel that the other party deceived them when their subsequent actions did not align with their agreed-upon result. When both individuals act in good faith, the reality is that each spoke past the other without necessarily realizing it.

The disadvantage of seeing many paradigms can also be an advantage. Instead of being confused by many paradigms, one lesson that one learns from Buddhism is to apply valuable selection criteria when choosing a paradigm to act upon.

Realizing that no one paradigm is necessarily the only possible truth, the Buddhist scholar learns to adopt the interpretation that does the most good, giving deference to the most constructive *paradigm.*

Selecting the most empowering and constructive interpretation or paradigm is the noblest choice by far, and it is the way *Level Threes* and Buddhist monks learn to see the world.

NINETEENTH LEVEL OF CONSCIOUSNESS (LEVEL FOUR PARADIGMATIC)

This level of consciousness is present in a significant percentage of the population.

Level Four Paradigmatic Consciousness departs from the *paradigms* of individuals and moves toward a greater sense of spirituality and *paradigms* of diminished self-importance. It is distinct from religion and the notion of becoming religious. Spirituality and a *paradigm* of diminished self-importance means that the individual appreciates that they are part of a greater whole that supports them, namely the entire biosphere.

Even though *Level Four Paradigmatic Consciousness* may be agnostic to religion, this level of consciousness is specific to the types of *qualia* associated with spiritual experience, whether with a belief-based or a spiritual mindset.

ME-DEFINERS

From a scientific perspective, spiritual experiences involve a specialized type of *qualia* that neuroscientists have linked to decreased 'right' parietal lobe activity, an area of the brain mainly focused on self-awareness and self-focus. The right parietal lobe influences what scientists call a 'me factor.'

To quote Robin Nixon in the 2008 article, *Spirituality Spot Found in Brain*: Quote.

> *"The area in question — the right parietal lobe — is responsible for defining "Me," said researcher Brick Johnstone of Missouri University."*

> *"People with less active Me-Definers are more likely to lead spiritual lives, reports the study in the current issue of the journal Zygon."*

> *"Spiritual outlooks have long been associated with better mental and physical health. These benefits, Johnstone speculated, may stem from being focused less on oneself and more on others — a natural consequence of turning down the volume on the Me-Definer."*

> *"In addition to religious practices, other behaviors and experiences are known to hush the Definer of Me. Appreciation of art or nature can quiet it, Johnstone said, pointing out that people talk of "losing themselves" in a particularly beautiful song. Love, and even charity work, can also soften the boundaries of "Me," he said."*

> *"The greatest silencing of the Me-Definer likely happens in the deepest states of meditation or prayer, said Johnstone, when practitioners describe feeling seamless with the entire universe. That is, the highest point of spiritual experience occurs when "Me" completely loses its definition."* End Quote.

> *[Spirituality Spot Found in Brain, Dec 24th, 2008, Robin Nixon — B.A. biology and psychology Columbia University, Live Science]*

The factor that reinforces this effect is that experiential sensations associated with spirituality are perceived as highly pleasurable, creating an affinity to repeat the experience.

To quote Lynne Blumberg in the 2014 article in Health, *What Happens to the Brain During Spiritual Experience?*: Quote.

"(Neuroscientist Dr. Andre)] Newberg suggests in his new book that mystical [or spiritual] experiences are described as blissful or ecstatic because they share many of the same neural pathways in the parietal and frontal lobes that are involved in sexual arousal." End Quote.

['What Happens to the Brain During Spiritual Experience?': The field of neurology uses science to try to understand religion and visa-versa., June 5th, 2014, Lynne Blumberg, Health]

A noteworthy practice that helps quiet the *Me-Definer* is '*Metta Meditation*' for its more spiritual prayer-like qualities.

METTA MEDITATION

Metta meditation (a.k.a. *metta*, a Pali word) can also be translated from Pali as "loving-kindness," though that translation alone cannot convey the entire concept.

According to Thanissaro Bhikku, a San Diego, California Buddhist monk, 'metta' is not necessarily about a feeling of love or kindness but more about sincerely wishing well for others.

The Pali word 'metta' shares roots with the Pali words corresponding to gentleness and friendliness.

As such, One Mind Dharma defines the word 'metta' more precisely as caring for and desiring the well-being of others, which includes responding with a gentle and aware heart when interacting with others.

To help us understand this more fully, let's look at the practice and teachings of *metta meditation* and the allegory of its origin, with the Buddha aptly seizing the opportunity for a teaching moment, as he was often known to do.

The Buddha sent a group of monks into the forest to meditate. The monks returned to explain that they had abandoned their meditation because the ghosts and tree spirits in the forest were hostile and frightened them.

Upon hearing their story, the Buddha explained to them the practice of 'metta,' in which they needed to return to the woods to meditate while offering the ghosts and tree spirits goodwill, kindness, and peace.

The monks went back into the forest to meditate. Upon completing their meditation, they returned noting that wishing the ghosts and tree spirits goodwill, kindness, and peace changed everything.

Instead of the spirits haunting the monks and scaring them off as they did the first time, the spirits stopped taunting the monks and eventually grew to extend goodwill in return and gave them protection as their guests.

The practice of *metta* ranges from offering a simple utterance of a phrase wishing goodwill, kindness, and peace to the recital of a thorough and formal chant. The intended recipient of the *metta* can be any sentient being, whether tangible or intangible.

The words are short phrases to meet the occasion, wishing any stranger a modicum of health and happiness or any other message of kindness as a lengthy and formal discourse, such as the *Karaniya Metta Sutta*.

The Karaniya Metta Sutta, as translated from Pali by the Amaravati Sangha, is: Quote.

> *"This is what should be done*
> *By one who is skilled in goodness,*
> *And who knows the path of peace:*
> *Let them be able and upright,*
> *Straightforward and gentle in speech,*
> *Humble and not conceited,*
> *Contented and easily satisfied,*
> *Unburdened with duties and frugal in their ways.*
> *Peaceful and calm and wise and skillful,*
> *Not proud or demanding in nature.*
> *Let them not do the slightest thing*
> *That the wise would later reprove.*
> *Wishing: In gladness and in safety,*
> *May all beings be at ease.*
> *Whatever living beings there may be;*
> *Whether they are weak or strong, omitting none,*
> *The great or the mighty, medium, short or small,*
> *The seen and the unseen,*
> *Those living near and far away,*
> *Those born and to be born —*
> *May all beings be at ease!"*

> *"Let none deceive another,*
> *Or despise any being in any state.*
> *Let none through anger or ill-will*
> *Wish harm upon another.*
> *Even as a mother protects with her life*
> *Her child, her only child,*
> *So with a boundless heart*
> *Should one cherish all living beings"* End Quote.

[What is Metta? – Metta Practice, Meditations, and Explanation, One Mind Dharma, https://oneminddharma.com/what-is-metta/]

Of course, depending upon the disposition of the individual offering a *metta*, one may view this simple act as disingenuous. Those who practice *metta* sometimes report that the action was initially disingenuous. However, over time, it became sincere and offered a surprising benefit to the practitioner of the *metta*.

Practitioners of *metta* indicate that they have realized that *metta* has a worthwhile benefit to their internal peace and calmness, much like the monks in the forest.

Likewise, depending upon the disposition of the individual receiving a *metta*, the recipient may also view the act as disingenuous or heartfelt. If the recipient's interpretation is that the *metta* was genuine, it will likely have a favorable effect, much like the spirits in the forest.

SUMMARY

In summary, *Level Four Paradigmatic Consciousness* is a level of consciousness that taps into a spiritual realm of consciousness. Although this level of consciousness belongs to one of the levels associated with the mind's software, it affects the brain's hardware in ways that neuroscience can physically detect.

In contrast to our earlier levels of paradigmatic consciousness, this level focuses on relaxing the individual's standard operating system that emphasizes the self.

In Buddhism, this is *selflessness*, which is the opposite of 'selfishness.' The Buddhist sense of *selflessness* is a significant concept, which we will consider with a quote of wisdom from the Tibetan poet Shantideva.

To quote Noah Rasheta in his 2016 podcast, *True Selflessness*: Quote.

> *"Whatever joy there is in the world arises from wishing for others happiness."*

> *"Whatever suffering there is in the world arises from wishing your own happiness."* End Quote.

> *[True Selflessness, March 15, 2016, Noah Rasheta, Buddhism podcast published by Secular Buddhism Podcast,* https://secularbuddhism.com/true-selflessness/*]*

To paraphrase Noah Rasheta in his podcast, *True Selflessness*:

In Buddhism, the notion of *self* cannot exist without everything else, as the concept we refer to as "self" is the total of all other people and things; the profundity of this statement is multi-fold, worthy of a moment to unpack the idea.

- Consider that the body we refer to as the "self" is the culmination of our parents and the long line of their parents before them.

- Consider that others almost entirely produced the food the "self" consumes.

- Consider that others almost entirely produced the clothing worn by the "self."

- Consider that others almost entirely produced the shelter that shelters the "self."

- Consider that others nearly entirely produced all possessions of the "self."

As a result, there cannot exist a "self" that exists entirely apart from others.

[True Selflessness, March 15, 2016, Noah Rasheta, Buddhism podcast published by Secular Buddhism Podcast, https://secularbuddhism.com/true-selflessness/*]*

Realizing that the true self is selfless helps us tame the "Me" factor that typically dominates our perspective. As a result, the Buddhist teachings of *selflessness* are a spiritual, yet secular, way to help us relax the sole emphasis on the self, where its benefit is that it shows us a path to inner peace.

In other words, once we learn to emphasize the well-being of others, such as all 'sentient beings,' they, in turn, will tend to look out for our well-being as well.

From the opposite perspective, *Level Four Paradigmatic Consciousness* can also mean that the act of hatred generates a response of hatred. Instead, the only possible approach to ending any cycle of hatred is to extend meaningful and sincere sentiments of goodwill to the other.

The practice of exercising *metta* meditation, even a simple *metta,* before encountering someone you may dislike often makes it more challenging to extend ill feelings toward another individual.

When anyone detects a decrease in ill feelings directed towards them, it makes it more difficult for them to maintain ill feelings in return. Hence, *metta* is often the first step in de-escalating tensions.

Another noteworthy benefit of *Level Four Paradigmatic Consciousness* is that expert meditation practitioners claim that practicing *metta* moments before meditation is an effective way to accelerate calming the mind in preparation for meditation.

TWENTIETH LEVEL OF CONSCIOUSNESS (BUDDHIST CONSCIOUSNESS)

Buddhist Consciousness is our next level of consciousness. This level of consciousness represents the culmination of the journey into Buddhist consciousness.

Though relatively few experts achieve this level of consciousness, it is reportedly the closest our species can ever get to experiencing actual reality. As such, it should not be left unmentioned from a comprehensive consciousness framework. Also, in the interests of full disclosure, this one is the most difficult to comprehend of all the levels of consciousness we will discuss.

We refer to this level as *Buddhist Consciousness* in honor of the Buddha and the principles that he put forth to learn the truth regarding the ultimate nature of reality. In contrast to our taxonomy, experts in Buddhism refer to this state of consciousness as 'thought-free wakefulness,' which will only make sense after we explore its meaning.

Meditative Consciousness is a necessary precursor to prepare oneself for *Buddhist Consciousness*, though oddly, this level of consciousness does not involve meditation. If this sounds confusing, let's see if we can explain it more easily.

Buddhist Consciousness is fascinating because the practitioner must develop their meditation skills as the vehicle to transport them for nearly the entire journey. However, to make the final leg of the journey, what was previously essential must be discarded.

The Buddha described it to his monks in the following way.

You must use my teachings as if I were teaching you how to build a raft. When you get to the river, you will use these skills to make the raft and then use the raft to get to the other side of the river.

But once you arrive on the opposite side, you do not carry the raft for the remaining part of the journey. Instead, you leave it behind and discard it, for it has already performed the task it was supposed to serve.

Like *Level Three Paradigmatic Consciousness*, *Buddhist Consciousness* is grasped only through experience. One cannot achieve it by using the imagination or understanding its description in words. Buddhists consider this state of consciousness as literally unthinkable.

Yet, distinct from all levels of software-based consciousness, *Buddhist Consciousness* is the only level void of paradigms and interpretation of stimuli.

That said, we will make the best attempt possible to define this level of consciousness and the characteristics that expert practitioners have described.

As a state of consciousness, it is free from the stream of stimuli that flow through the mind. In this context, all our senses and feelings are merely an artificial representation or interpretation of reality that one must forfeit to experience reality.

Strangely, it is also free from the various altered states of consciousness achievable with expert meditation. It is a state of consciousness that some Buddhist experts describe with the term *'primordial wakefulness.'*

To quote Chokyi Nyima Rinpoche in his 2018 book, *Sadness, Love Openness: The Buddhist Path of Joy:* Quote.

"According to the leading practitioners of Buddhism, on the one hand, to understand the true nature of the mind, one must achieve thought-free wakefulness. On the other hand, it is impossible to convey a description using words that can accurately depict it within one's imagination."

"Realizing primordial wakefulness is a matter of recognizing thought-free wakefulness. When we hear that, we might get the impression that we just have to make sure not to have any thoughts. But just having no thoughts is surely not the same as actualizing thought-free wakefulness. Thought-free wakefulness is bright, sharp, vivid, and direct. It has to unfold like that if we want the recognition of thought-free wakefulness to be our practice. In other words, it is crucial that we see things as they are." End Quote.

[Sadness, Love Openness: The Buddhist Path of Joy, pg. 96, 2018, Chokyi Nyima Rinpoche, Shambhala Publications]

Buddhist Consciousness is the last stop along the Buddhist journey, which, according to the Buddha, is where one may finally experience the real world for what it is. This reality is free from thought, free from a stream of consciousness, and free from any distraction associated with our sensory organs.

From a secular perspective, the journey consists of principles, ideas, and experiences that one should assimilate in a particular sequence and merge with one's intellectual discoveries of knowledge and experiences encountered during the journey.

As such, Buddhism is not a disciplined system of thought that passes knowledge from teacher to student but is a system of teachings to help prepare the student for a journey and a map to help guide the student along the path of a virtuous and fulfilling life.

The journey builds upon a foundation of teachings that offer a way to choose various freedoms, such as *freedom of will,* which is having the volition one wants, which we will discuss later. The teachings consist of diverse thought-provoking perspectives, such as how to view the self and one's desires. These principles are practices to gain control over one's mind to tame, manage, and then redirect the mind.

Regarding our consciousness framework, *Buddhist Consciousness's* destination is only attainable by programming the mind's software to the extent that it dismantles the standard programming that we are born with. The goal is for a pure form of reality to emerge once our conscious stream's noise, distractions, and judgments are fully compartmentalized away from the usual influences of conscious thought.

Let's introduce a few fundamental principles for use as tools along the journey to *Buddhist Consciousness.*

FIRST KEY TEACHING: DEPENDENT ORIGIN

First, understanding the essential principle of dependent origination is an excellent place to start.

Dependent origination is a rather encompassing concept that lies at the core of Buddhist teaching. We should begin by not conflating the principle of *dependent origination* with the modern Western concept of *hard determinism,* which points to the fact that every event, no matter how large or small, has mechanically occurred based on following the laws of physics starting from the moment of the big bang.

A more thorough discussion of these frameworks will eventually follow.

Although there is much debate about what the Buddha thought about *free will,* the Buddha dismissed the notion that our decisions depend on fate. Thus, if we use Buddhism as our philosophical guide as we explore levels of consciousness, we can bypass the argument of *hard determinism,* and using similar reasoning, we can disarm the idea of *hard indeterminism* as well.

In contrast, the Buddhist principle of *dependent origination* states that everything is interconnected and affects everything else. What is happening now is part of what happened previously and what will happen next. As a result, no organism or phenomenon can exist independently from other organisms and phenomena.

During his lifetime, the Buddha was quiet on the origin issue.

To quote Barbara Hoetsu O'Brien in her 2018 book, *The Principle of Dependent Origination in Buddhism*: Quote.

> *"In Buddhism, unlike other religious philosophies, there is no teaching of a First Cause. How all this arising and ceasing began—or even if it had a beginning—is not discussed, contemplated, or explained. The Buddha emphasized understanding the nature of things as they are rather than speculating on what might have happened in the past or what might happen in the future."*

> *"Things are the way they are because they are conditioned by other things. You are conditioned by other people and phenomena. Other people and phenomena are conditioned by you."*

> *"As the Buddha explained,*

> *When this is, that is.*

> *This arising, that arises.*

> *When this is not, that is not.*

> *This ceasing, that ceases." End Quote.*

> *[The Principle of Dependent Origination in Buddhism, April*

5[th]2018, Barbara Hoetsu O'Brien – Bachelor of Journalism degree, University of Missouri, student Zen Mountain Monastery, Mount Tremper, New York, ThoughtCo. Humanities > Religion & Spirituality]

From one perspective, the Buddhist principle of dependent origination is simply and reasonably accurate when we consider that every organism entirely depends upon its parent or ancestors that preceded it.

From another perspective, when we consider the complex chain of dependencies that plant, animal, bacterial, and viral organisms have upon other organisms, it is also accurate, and science agrees that *dependent origination* is applicable in many more ways than we have yet been able to discover.

From another perspective, the notion of dependent origination is also accurate when we consider the many chains of events that unfold in the wake of humans exploring, building civilizations, consuming resources, negotiating alliances, creating financial systems, and establishing economic trade.

SECOND KEY TEACHING: KARMA

Our second essential teaching for the journey into *Buddhist Consciousness* involves the Buddhist notion of karma or *kamma-vipaka*. In *kamma-vipaka*, *kamma* means 'action,' and *vipaka* means 'effect,' though it is more commonly known as the expression we recognize as "we reap what we sow."

The term *karma* is in everyday use across more than fifty languages. However, the Buddhist meaning of the word is somewhat different from its common usage.

To quote Matthew Sockolov in his 2017 manuscript, *What is Karma? – Definition, Explanation, and Investigation*: Quote.

> *"The common misunderstanding is that karma is incredibly direct and linear. You may hear someone say that it is their karma when something bad happens to them. The conventional understanding seems to be that if I cut people off in traffic a lot, my karma is that I'm going to get cut off in traffic a lot. Although this may happen to be true for other reasons, this is not how karma works in the Buddhist understanding."*

> *"Many of us take karma as a tit-for-tat principle. If we do something to someone, someone else will do it to us. One of my favorite examples is lying. If I lie to you about something, karma isn't that somebody else is going to lie to me necessarily. There are many effects to this action, but here are a few I see."*

> *"First, I'm cultivating a mind inclined toward dishonesty. When I lie, it may make it easier to lie in the future. When I lie to you, I'm also cultivating a relationship that is not open and honest."*

> *"Finally, I have to sleep with myself. I may deal with guilt, aversion, or another form of suffering. There are also more concrete effects that may*

arise. I may end up having to make amends for lying or cover up with more lies."

"Karma may be complex, but the basic principle is relatively simple. When we action intentionally, we are creating our options for the future."

"At this moment, you have a choice of how you are going to act. Your choices at this moment are influenced by your past choices and present choices." End Quote.

['What is Karma? – Definition, Explanation, and Investigation', Aug 27th 2017, Matthew Sockolov, Buddhist meditation teacher and author, Spirit Rock Meditation Center, One Mind Dharma]

In other words, every decision we make at a fork in the road leads us down a path to another set of possible forks in the road. Since one can never go back in time to choose a different path, we have closed off other possibilities.

Furthermore, *kamma-vipaka* represents a 'cyclical process.' The 'process' portion involves every action one makes, no matter how insignificant. It has to do with how one behaves down to the most subtle factors, such as the tone of voice one uses, influencing both the present and future.

As for the 'cyclical' portion, it is much like the movie, 'Groundhog Day,' where one is doomed to repeat the cycle until one earns the right to escape the process by making good choices, even subtle ones, to achieve liberation for advancement.

THIRD KEY TEACHING: IMPERMANENCE

Our third essential Buddhist tool to use in one's journey to *Buddhist Consciousness* is the principle of *impermanence.*

To understand the Buddhist principle of *impermanence,* we should begin with the realization that we are formed from the Earth, which will eventually return to the Earth.

All conscious beings are made up primarily of water and various quantities and types of carbon molecules and minerals. Perhaps the most eloquent rendition of this fact is from the British-born poet Robert William Service's poem titled 'Mud.' Quote.

"Mud is Beauty in the making,

Mud is melody awaking;

Laughter, leafy whisperings,

Butterflies with rainbow wings;

Baby babble, lover's sighs,

Bobolink in lucent skies;

Ardours of heroic blood

All stem back to Matrix Mud."

"Mud is mankind in the molding,

Heaven's mystery unfolding;

Miracles of mighty men,

Raphael's brush and Shakespear's pen;

Sculpture, music, all we owe

Mozart, Michael Angelo;

Wonder, worship, dreaming spire,

Issue out of the primal mire."

"In the raw, red womb of Time

Man evolved from cosmic slime;

And our thaumaturgic day

Had its source in ooze and clay . . .

But I have not power to seeSuch stupendous alchemy:

And in the star-bright lily bud

Lo! I worship Mother Mud." End Quote.

[Mud, circa 1930, Robert William Service]

Buddhist teachings of *impermanence* stem from the realization that every being is temporary, as nothing is permanent.

Our possessions are temporary, as we merely borrow them briefly. Every relationship is brief, as we share them for a short time.

Yet we cling to things and people as if they are permanent.

Each of our pleasures is temporary, as we experience them momentarily, and then they are gone. Likewise, our pains are temporary, as these too shall pass.

Whether the individual is a child or adult, the less one clings and grasps, the more prepared that individual will be to face whatever awaits them.

When students understand *impermanence*, they can move forward by letting go of all the petty things upon which they expend energy. Only then can the student cease to experience the useless wild swings of joy and sadness from gaining worldly things and then losing them.

Thus, a deep understanding of principles, such as *dependent origin, karma, impermanence,* and others, become part of the inspiration for taking the next steps of the journey to attain *Buddhist Consciousness.*

Whether *Buddhist Consciousness* is the closest humans can ever achieve in learning the truth regarding the ultimate nature of reality, I do not know. I know that there is so much more to reality than what our extremely limited senses can tell us.

Now we understand that we have at least some of the parts for building a raft, though we do not know what it will take to complete it and get to the other side, and we have no idea what awaits us on the other side. All we know is that whatever we must face, we must face it alone.

To borrow a few phrases of wisdom from the Buddhist master, Chokyi Nyima Rinpoche, and I quote:

> *"In this context, there are three levels of experience: the deluded experience of sentient beings, the meditative experience of yogis, and the pure experience of buddhas."*

> *"At the final stage of nonmeditation, all types of habitual tendencies and convictions need to be dissolved, left behind. There is nothing more to cultivate, nothing more to reach. One has arrived at the end of the path. All that needs to be purified has been purified. Karma disturbing emotions, and the habitual tendencies, have all been cleared up so that nothing is left."*

> *"Thinking is thought. Thinking is not a thought-free state. It is the identity of that which thinks that is thought-free." End Quote.*

> *[Mahamudra and Dzogchen: Thought-Free Wakefulness, Nov 1st, 2002, Chokyi Nyima Rinpoche, Lion's Roar: Buddhist Wisdom for Our Time]*

TWENTY-FIRST LEVEL OF CONSCIOUSNESS (UNCONSCIOUS)

The following three levels of consciousness will deal with the unconscious, subconscious, and conscious levels.

While it is evident that *Homo Consciousness* represents the hardware-based level upon which the *unconscious, subconscious,* and *conscious* layers reside, we must separate these subdivisions to identify their distinct roles.

Let's begin with the assertion that the *unconscious* mind is at the lowest level, which serves as the foundation to deal with the myriad of stimuli that enter the body. Resting immediately on top of the *unconscious* mind is our *subconscious,* which we will discuss later. And on top of the *subconscious* mind is our *consciousness,* which we will discuss at its level.

The *unconscious* mind is the layer of the central nervous system (CNS) closest to the physical systems of the physical body. These include hard-wired circuits that manifest as reflexes and the many other circuits within the CNS that are the first to process sensory signals from sensory organs.

In this *unconscious* layer, we will also include the many neural expressways that transport signals around the body from sensory organs (i.e., sensory neurons) and back to muscles (i.e., motor neurons).

Although the precise boundary between the *unconscious* and the *subconscious* mind has many unknowns, it is apparent that the portion of the mind that is entirely inaccessible to the *conscious* mind belongs to the unconscious mind. That said, the definition of 'inaccessible,' however, can be somewhat ambiguous and controversial.

It is relatively safe to conclude that anything the mind is aware of is part of the *conscious* mind. This awareness includes awareness of our thoughts, whether those thoughts pertain to the intangible world, such as an idea, or whether they pertain to the tangible world of matter and or energy.

It is also relatively safe to conclude that anything the mind is unaware of is either part of the *subconscious* or the *unconscious*. The challenge then becomes how to allocate a capability of the mind as belonging to the *subconscious* or the *unconscious* mind.

One way to determine whether a capability of the mind belongs to the *subconscious* or *unconscious* mind is to create some essential criteria that we can agree upon.

Considering information stored in the *subconscious* mind, we know it can be accessible to the *conscious* mind using techniques such as hypnosis. Therefore, we can begin by stating that if something is potentially accessible to the *conscious* mind, it must belong to the *subconscious* mind. Otherwise, if it is never accessible, it belongs to the *unconscious* mind.

Likewise, if something can potentially be controlled or influenced by the *conscious* mind, then it must also belong to the *subconscious* mind. Otherwise, if it cannot ever be controlled or influenced, it belongs to the *unconscious* mind.

Therefore, to refine the meaning of the term 'inaccessible,' it means that our *conscious* mind can never achieve awareness of it, control it, or have influence over it, either directly or indirectly.

Using this as our criteria, let's look at controlling the heartbeat.

> *Medical journals state that although one cannot control heartbeat directly using our conscious mind to control it voluntarily, the rate of one's heartbeat can be decreased by either carefully regulating breathing (given that the individual's sinus arrhythmia may be strong enough) or by trying to force a bowel movement (i.e., vagal maneuvers).*
>
> *Focusing the mind on certain emotions can accelerate one's heartbeat, such as anxiety or fear.*
>
> *Given this criterion, the heartbeat belongs to the subconscious rather than the conscious or unconscious mind.*

In contrast, the conscious mind can't influence a reflex. Therefore, it resides solidly within the unconscious level.

If we look at the tasks performed by the unconscious mind, it absorbs thousands of sensory signals in any given second and processes them to make only a subset of these signals known to the *subconscious* mind.

From the perspective of artificial intelligence, millions of stimuli enter the *unconscious* mind from across every sensory organ and every nerve ending of the body daily. The volume of stimuli is so great that it could easily overwhelm both the *subconscious* and *conscious* mind. However, the neuronal circuits comprising the unconscious mind also process these signals.

What types of processes are these?

Within the unconscious mind, various stimuli undergo the early steps of pattern recognition, such as streams of stimuli from visual sensory organs, detecting changes in the primary lines and angles, and generating a set of less complex stimuli that will pass into the subconscious mind.

While there are functions in the unconscious mind that leverage forms of memory supported at the cellular level, information learned by the conscious mind is not available for use by the hard-wired functions that have evolved to support vision.

The primary role of the *unconscious* mind is two-fold, one for each direction.

First, regarding inbound stimuli, the *unconscious* mind acts to pre-process impulses from sensory organs and the myriad of nerve endings. Thus, it filters out the higher volume of raw signal data that would otherwise overwhelm the subconscious layer.

Second, regarding stimuli being sent from the central nervous system to control the various parts of the body, the *unconscious* mind is the only interface able to communicate with the different muscles of the physical body.

In other words, the *unconscious* mind acts as an information system to pre-process raw inbound stimuli and acts as the base operating system for the control system aspects of the individual.

Recall that a 'control system' is a software system that automates the operation of physical machinery guided by streams of signal data emanating from sensors instead of information systems that automate information processing.

A series of muscle actions may originate from within the unconscious mind, as with a reflex or hard-wired circuit; the subconscious mind, as with a reaction of increasing the pulse and blood pressure if frightened; or the conscious mind, as with a response to hold the hand of your child when crossing the street.

In all three circumstances, the unconscious mind dispatches the necessary signals through the unconscious mind, which communicates directly to the motor neurons to control the muscles.

In summary, a helpful way to view *Unconscious Consciousness* is to imagine you are the CEO of an organization with many employees, consultants, outsourced services, outsourced vendors, and partner companies. In that circumstance, all of them may try phoning, emailing, wiring, and mailing communications all at the same time.

In contrast, when you have layers of personnel dealing with the myriad of messages, such as the phone system, the email system, and the mail room in each building, the CEO only deals with the small subset that rises to the level of importance that warrants their attention.

TWENTY-SECOND LEVEL OF CONSCIOUSNESS (SUBCONSCIOUS)

Any organization has a substantive layer of middle management with thousands of employees, consultants, outsourced services, vendors, and partner companies.

Immediately below this significant layer of middle management is a substantial array of supervisors and their staff, and immediately above is the executive team.

Similarly, our *subconscious* (a.k.a. middle management) and *conscious* levels (a.k.a. executive management) have no awareness of stimuli detected by sensory organs as they enter the *unconscious* level of the CNS.

For stimuli to become known to the *subconscious* mind, they must have sufficient importance to be 'bubbled up' from the *unconscious* mind to the *subconscious* mind. At this point, as individuals, we still lack *conscious* awareness of these stimuli. However, the *subconscious* mind is busy processing it to determine if it should be 'bubbled up' to the *subconscious* level.

The hierarchy within large organizations is where information is 'bubbled up' after simplified information, passing only the essential facts while excluding impertinent detail. Noteworthy is that the *unconscious* mind will not 'bubble up' anything that fails to pass a certain threshold of importance, such as those items the mailroom would recognize as obvious junk mail.

Like a one-person business, simple organisms lack an *unconscious* or *subconscious* level, as they only have a *conscious* level.

A simple organism does not have sufficient sensory organs and nerve endings to benefit from an *unconscious* and *subconscious* level. Only more complex organisms need the 'support staff' to deal with a myriad of sensory organs and stimuli they receive.

Although many believe such primitive organisms must lack a conscious level. Instead, they lack unconscious and subconscious levels.

The central nervous system of insects does not receive vast quantities of stimuli that would require a vast array of functions to process them. Hence, they need only a conscious level that informs them about their environment in relatively simple terms.

In contrast, more advanced organisms equipped with an incredible array of sensory organs receive many stimuli that could easily overwhelm the *conscious* level. Quote.

"When additional levels are introduced into the brain, additional sets of capabilities follow. The single-level brain cannot achieve much more than the hard-wired functions, which provide basic survival abilities. However, a brain with more than one level can cope with sensory organs that are significantly more sophisticated, which generates many complex neural messages. But how do we know that the brain has multiple levels?"

"A simple way to demonstrate that humans have more than one level of consciousness is with the use of subliminal stimuli. Subliminal stimuli can be shown to operate below the conscious level of the brain, demonstrating a measurable impact on the behavior of an individual. Although rapidly flashed messages hidden in motion pictures have been proved as ineffective, one of the most common forms of subliminal stimuli that are found to be effective is used in print advertisements to enhance the sale of merchandise." End Quote.

[Sensitive by Nature: Understanding Intelligence and the Mind, 2002, J Luisi, 1ˢᵗ Books Library Publishers]

Once the *unconscious* level determines the importance of stimuli, the *subconscious* level receives it.

To define *Subconscious Consciousness* (i.e., the *subconscious* mind), let's consider where it finds itself within the mind and some of the critical tasks it needs to perform.

The *subconscious* mind is the central nervous system (CNS) layer between the unconscious and conscious minds. It is responsible for communicating stimuli that are 'important' between those levels.

The transmission of stimuli to higher levels is a 'bubbling up' process. These stimuli arrive from outside the body to arrive at sensory organs, or they are generated internally and 'bubbled up.'

In contrast, stimuli sent rather than received convey motor commands to muscle tissue and travel in the opposite direction to the *unconscious* level to eventually travel through motor neurons for use by muscle tissue.

Motor command stimuli may originate from within any of the three levels of consciousness.

The *conscious* mind may originate motor commands by enacting a conscious volition requested by the *conscious* mind.

In contrast, the *subconscious* mind may originate previously learned actions or responses to be requested automatically without *conscious* decision-making. These requests may be automatic responses, such as a response of fear or surprise, or learned through repetition.

Finally, the *unconscious* mind may originate hard-wired actions or responses, such as reflexes involving hard-wired paths that the *conscious* or *subconscious* mind cannot control.

Although the *conscious* mind can never achieve control, influence, or awareness of the *unconscious* mind two levels down, the *conscious* mind can gain degrees of influence and awareness of the *subconscious* mind directly below. However, accomplishing access or influence is primarily a matter of technique, effort, and training.

> *As examples,*
>
> *Meditative Consciousness is a level of consciousness that interacts with the conscious and subconscious mind. At an expert level of Meditative Consciousness, it can partially program both the conscious and unconscious mind to manage the stream of consciousness automatically and direct their focus.*
>
> *Level Three Paradigmatic Consciousness is yet another level of consciousness that leverages the subconscious mind to help create awareness of paradigms that are potentially applicable to the circumstances and events associated with the focus of one's attention.*
>
> *Though highly speculative for most, Buddhist Consciousness is a level of consciousness that potentially drives deep into the subconscious mind to quiet its processes to experience reality absent sensory inputs and streams of consciousness.*

From the perspective of 'artificial intelligence (AI),' the *subconscious* performs many intellectual functions.

From a 'psychological' perspective, a primary function of the *subconscious* mind is to guide the individual's thought process and emotional responses to adhere to the genetically determined programming of the *subconscious*.

Re-programming one's *subconscious* may be through meditation or simply with the repetitive practice of some physical response, like in a sport, such as practicing a particular return in tennis.

The overwhelming majority of our programming is genetically determined. Our genes and epigenetics decide on our initial programming.

Let's also include the 'Buddhist' perspective. To do this properly, we must introduce the Buddhist term *saṃskārā* in the following passage as an '*embodied cognitive schema.*'

In this context, embodied cognitive schema refers to the behavioral responses we tend to repeat such that they become second nature.

In our discussion earlier in this section, we mentioned that there are ways to program the *subconscious* mind, such as meditation or the repetition of some behavior. Technically, epigenetic forces also influence our genes due to the experiences of our close ancestors.

If we look more deeply at programming by repetition, there are different forms of this programming. One form may be the product of consciously directing one's will to get better at a desired skill, while our body chemistry drives the other for behaviors that stimulate the brain's pleasure centers.

Hence, it is often the pleasurable effect that causes an individual to repeat something until engrained as an *embodied cognitive schema (saṃskārā)*, which the framework asserts is stored in the *subconsciousness*, potentially rising to the level of addiction.

To quote Professor William S. Waldron in his 2017 book, *A Buddhist Theory of Unconscious Mind (ālaya-vijñāna)*: Quote.

> *"This body is not yours, nor does it belong to others," the Buddha declared, "it should be seen as [the product of] past karma, generated and fashioned by volition, and something to be felt" (S II 64). The way these come about, according to the Buddha, is through the feedback relationship between our embodied cognitive schemas (saṃskārā), the forms of consciousness (vijñāna) and feeling they facilitate, the emotional responses these evoke, and the actions (karma) these instigate—which in turn reinforce the very saṃskārās that influenced them in the first place."*

> *"This pattern is seen in something we all know well: habit-formation. When we do something enjoyable, like drinking tea or eating sweets, it affects our bodies and minds in certain, mostly pleasurable ways. These experiences create and/or reinforce specific neural pathways in the brain and body which conduce to their being used again, just as rainwater erodes away the earth, attracting yet further rainwater until, with time and repetition, a constant stream may develop (Milinda, 1969, 79f; I. vii. 57). Similarly, we come to experience physiological and psychological cravings (S. tṛṣṇā; P. taṇha) for the sensations that these actions provide, and thus tend to repeat them over and over again. In this way, actions gradually reinforce the conditions that conduce to their own repetition, resulting in the psycho-physiological complexes called dispositions, in Pāli, anusaya (S. anuśaya), underlying tendencies." End Quote.*

[A Buddhist Theory of Unconscious Mind (ālaya-vijñāna), 2000-2017, William S. Waldron – Professor at Middlebury College, Glens Falls, New York, USA, Middlebury College, p. 9]

In summary, the fact that the *subconscious* mind may be, to an extent, programmable by conscious choice beyond the forces of genetics and epigenetics is a powerful realization.

If the *conscious* mind realizes that it too can influence the programming of the *subconscious* mind, then depending upon the degree of one's focus and will over a protracted duration, a new layer of custom programming can develop and take shape.

To accomplish this effectively, one must consider the desired outcome and the program design necessary to achieve that outcome. Determining that design, however, can only be achieved by using the *conscious* mind.

TWENTY-THIRD LEVEL OF CONSCIOUSNESS (CONSCIOUS)

The philosopher and physician John Locke proffered the first modern definition of consciousness, *"as the perception of what passes in a man's mind."*

[Essay Concerning Human Understanding: In Four Books, 1690, John Locke, London, England]

The complete thesis of John Locke consists of four books.

The first book asserted the blank slate theory, claiming that children did not bring ideas into the world.

The second book stated that all ideas are derived from experience directly through sensation or indirectly through reflection.

The third book addressed symbolic ideas represented by building words into a language.

The fourth book stated that thought was the sum of ideas and perceptions and the limitations of knowledge as to determining whether knowledge was accurate or truthful.

Many, like Locke, have come to believe in the blank slate theory that humans do not bring ideas into the world, though three hundred years after Locke, there is evidence to the contrary.

For example, Steven Pinker, a professor of psychology at Harvard University and formerly a chair professor of psychology at MIT, makes the case that human beings have an inherited universal structure shaped by the demands made upon the species for survival, albeit with plenty of room for cultural and individual variation.

Furthermore, it is plausible that humans start life at their time of birth with a rudimentary paradigm.

[The Blank Slate: The Modern Denial of Human Nature, Sept 30th, 2002, Professor Steven Pinker, professor of psychology at MIT, Viking Press]

To go back to the earliest writings about consciousness, early Buddhists expressed *consciousness* as a *'process.'* In their view, events within the mind occurred as an outcome of this ongoing process, as opposed to the notion of an *'object'* that acts.

The notion of a process as opposed to an object is much in line with the Buddhist idea that *consciousness* is like a stream, ever-changing as water flows past each point of the stream. As such, the stream consists of different instances of matter, such as the flow of water molecules, silt, leaves, and twigs, slowing or quickening, never the same from moment to moment.

In contrast, a stone (i.e., *representing an object*) rests in its place. Plants may grow on it, insects may crawl beneath it, and it may slowly wear with time, though the matter that comprises the stone is fundamentally the same day after day.

This view of consciousness is beneficial for understanding the underlying Buddhist meaning when concluding that the mind is absent an 'agent,' where 'agent' is an *object* that 'acts' instead of a process that experiences events. From the Buddhist perspective, an *object* 'watches,' whereas a *process* experiences 'seeing.'

To quote Professor William S. Waldron in his 2017 book, *A Buddhist Theory of Unconscious Mind (ālaya-vijñāna)*: Quote.

"For if cognitive awareness is not an act which one does but an event which occurs, then there is no need, indeed no place in cognition for an active agent or a substantive subject."

"In this respect, Buddhist and scientific analyses of consciousness share a certain formal similarity. They both ask how things occur, not what they are—a question that is answered by causes and conditions, not by essences or entities. They, therefore, both dismiss the idea of a substantive self (ātman) and for much the same reason: their modes of analysis preclude a causal role for unchanging entities on methodological grounds. How, after all, could something that does not itself change cause something else to change? An unmoving billiard ball does not make another ball move. Similarly, a truly unchanging self could neither act nor experience the result of actions (i.e. karma), since both actions and experience are specific, discrete temporal events." End Quote.

[A Buddhist Theory of Unconscious Mind (ālaya-vijñāna), 2000-2017, William S. Waldron – Professor at Middlebury College, Glens Falls, New York, USA, Middlebury College, p. 7]

The Buddhist concept of *process* versus *object* is the source of much debate among philosophers in that many argue that if the mind is not an *agent,* then it cannot possess *agency.*

The claim that 'something that is not an *agent* cannot possess *agency*' may initially seem unimportant, but two significant problems arise.

The first problem is that some philosophers are eager to conclude that we have no *free will.* They leverage this claim to arrive at the following: If the mind is not an *agent,* then it cannot possess *agency,* and if it cannot have *agency,* then it cannot possess *free will.*

The second problem is that *agents* and *agency* as concepts are quite distinct, even though they may sound alike in the ear.

> *The powerful counterargument proffered by Professor Rick Repetti of CUNY is the plausibility of 'agentless agency'; one need not be an agent to possess agency as they (i.e., agent and agency) are distinct concepts.*

> *[Buddhism, Meditation, and Free Will: A Theory of Mental Freedom, 2019, Rick Repetti Ph.D. Philosophy, Professor of Philosophy CUNY New York City, USA, Routledge Critical Studies in Buddhism, Routledge Taylor & Francis Group]*

The third problem, and a more comical one, is that the philosophers who adopt the line of thought that *free will* does not exist are saying that they had no choice but to arrive at this conclusion as they lacked *free will* to do otherwise. The notion proves that some will go to any extent to manufacture an argument.

Philosophy defines *consciousness* as the following concepts: a) *knowledge* (i.e., epistemology), which are the things and facts we believe; b) *intentionality,* which is the power of a mind to be about or to stand for ideas and principles; c) *introspection,* which is the process of generating thoughts; and d) *phenomenal experience,* which are the sensations one experiences from the senses.

One definition of *consciousness* from the discipline of psychology is as follows: Quote.

> *"Consciousness is the sensation that human beings claim to encounter, inclusive of cognitive details spanning from somatic and sensory interpretation to cognitive speech, intentions to take action, recollections, dreams, semantics, delusions, fringe or emotionally entwined feelings, and facet of motor and mental control." End Quote.*

> *[Consciousness, April 7, 2013, N., Pam M.S. Child Psychology, Psychology Dictionary Professional Reference]*

As a general definition, science defines *consciousness* as being the state or quality of awareness or of being aware of an external object or something within oneself.

OUR PERSPECTIVE

As is apparent in the definitions that stem from various modern disciplines, these definitions are all different. However, one aspect they share is that they introduce a human bias by including feelings, thoughts, and or ideas.

However, as we see from the framework, *consciousness* is not restricted to the domain of *Homo sapiens* and is built upon a foundation that begins with *Unicellular Consciousness.*

Science is closest to a working definition we can use as a starting place.

For our purposes, we will define the term *'consciousness'* in the following manner:

> *Consciousness concerns an individual organism (or entity) that possesses any degree of awareness of any quantity of matter and or energy within one's local physical environment, whether inside or outside the confines of the body of the organism.*

> *Suppose an organism can demonstrate the ability to choose any different reaction based on its prior experience of awareness. In that case, an ability exists to choose otherwise, and then that organism can be said to have demonstrated consciousness.*

> *Suppose an organism can demonstrate the ability to choose a reaction based on its prior experience of awareness but never demonstrates it. In that case, it can be said not to have consciousness.*

> *Suppose the organism cannot demonstrate the ability to choose a reaction based on its prior experience of awareness. In that case, that organism may have consciousness as it may lack a mechanism to react to demonstrate its consciousness.*

Note the insertion of the qualification that *'If an organism can demonstrate the ability to choose any different reaction based upon its prior experience of awareness, then there exists an ability to choose otherwise.'*

One reason for the qualification is to avoid misapplying the term *consciousness* to encompass simple human-made machines, such as an ordinary household thermostat or robotic vacuum cleaner.

Note that even early forms of consciousness can demonstrate an ability to choose otherwise not found in these machines, as these machines cannot freely choose.

Readers aware of the philosophical arguments that reference household thermostats as meeting the criteria of most definitions of the term 'consciousness,' notably within academia, will likely appreciate this seemingly subtle yet important qualification.

That said, let's consider the basic thermostat.

Given this definition of *consciousness*, let's revisit *Dionea muscipula* (a.k.a. the Venus flytrap) and *Mimosa pudica* (a.k.a. the sensitive plant).

If we recall, the behavior of *Mimosa pudica* (a.k.a. the sensitive plant) demonstrates the ability to choose a reaction based on its prior experience while also demonstrating an ability to choose otherwise. Quote.

> *"If an organism can demonstrate the ability to choose any different reaction based upon its prior experience of awareness, then there exists an ability to choose otherwise, and then that organism can be said to have demonstrated consciousness." End Quote.*

In contrast, *Dionea muscipula* (a.k.a. The Venus flytrap) could not choose a reaction based on its prior experience and could not demonstrate an ability to choose otherwise. It always reacted mechanically and could not confirm the ability to choose otherwise. Quote.

> *"If the organism cannot demonstrate the ability to choose a reaction based upon its prior experience of awareness, then that organism can be said to potentially have consciousness as the organism may lack a mechanism to react to demonstrate its consciousness." End Quote.*

Therefore, since *Dionea muscipula* (a.k.a. the Venus flytrap) could not demonstrate to *Homo sapiens* that it could choose a reaction based upon prior experience, the Venus flytrap can be said to potentially have consciousness. After all, just because a cell cannot move does not mean it cannot perceive anything about its immediate environment.

> *One can envision a person unable to move while being conscious of everything around them, such as perceiving people speaking in the room.*

So how do we determine whether the Venus flytrap will likely have consciousness, though it cannot demonstrate it, versus the determination that it does not possess the capacity for consciousness?

The answer is that the inner workings of the Venus flytrap and the sensitive plant eukaryotic cells are identical. These cells contain equivalent cytoskeletal structures. However, one has an overall design that can demonstrate to humans that it is aware of its environment when observing its actions, including showing that it could choose otherwise, while the other does not.

The overall difference between the internals of the respective cells of these two plants is somewhat indistinguishable except for the DNA. Hence, it is not unreasonable to classify all living things equipped with similar internals as likely to have a level of consciousness equivalent to *Unicellular Consciousness*.

In sharp contrast, no example of any thermostat demonstrates *"the ability to choose any different reaction based upon its prior experience of awareness."*

Thermostats cannot choose otherwise. Every thermostat behaves the same mechanical way as all devices with similar designs and internal structures.

Yes, one may imagine manufacturing a thermostat that produces random behavior. Still, random behavior fails to demonstrate the ability to choose a reaction based on its prior experience of awareness with the ability to choose otherwise.

Many readers may be wondering why this issue is essential. Let me say that some philosophy professors would argue that thermostats meet the criteria of possessing consciousness if they could, and now they cannot.

Now that we have established a working definition of *consciousness*, we are now prepared to address the purpose of *Conscious Consciousness*.

One essential difference here is that *Conscious Consciousness* pertains to individual organisms equipped with a brain possessing a distinct *unconscious* and *subconscious* that collaborate as a team.

For our purposes, we view *Conscious Consciousness* in the following manner: Quote.

"Conscious Consciousness pertains to any individual organism (or entity) equipped with a brain that has developed an unconscious and subconscious in support of consciousness."

"While Conscious Consciousness may be able to access, control, or influence the resources of the subconscious level, it cannot access, control, or influence any of the resources of the unconscious level."

"Conscious Consciousness depends entirely on the nine hardware-related levels of consciousness and allows for the co-existence of any combination of software-based levels of consciousness. " End Quote.

Conscious Consciousness is a high bandwidth enterprise consisting of numerous processes that collaborate on multiple levels while consuming significant amounts of energy to support calculations that direct and transport stimuli, the retrieval of *qualia*, the generation of the psychological effects associated with *qualia*, as well as to support the various software-related levels of consciousness that follow.

To quote Professor John R. Searle, Ph.D. in his 2005 book, *Consciousness: What We Still Don't Know*: Quote.

"Perception…does not create consciousness but modifies a preexisting conscious field…. the field was there before you had the perceptions. You had to be already conscious before you had the perceptual experience." End Quote.

[Consciousness: What We Still Don't Know, Jan 13, 2005, John R. Searle Ph.D. philosophy, Slusser Professor of Philosophy at the University of California, Berkeley, The New York Review of Books]

While most thoughts and feelings originate from lower levels, thoughts also originate from within the *Conscious level*.

Another way to state this is that this level of *consciousness* cannot operate in isolation away from the capabilities provided by the *unconscious* and *subconscious* mind, which themselves cannot support the survival of an organism in isolation away from the capabilities provided by the various other levels of *consciousness*.

Although no analogy is perfect, let's consider the following analogy to convey a thought.

> *One may argue that a CEO is not directing their company because most decisions come from lower management.*

> *The underlings do not share the decisions or the information used to make those decisions with the CEO.*

> *What the CEO sees is usually the impact of those decisions on the financial and operational metrics that are available.*

> *Regardless of how involved a CEO may wish to become in the operation of their organization, the CEO probably is only ever aware of making the most significant decisions since almost everything happens without the knowledge of its CEO. To do otherwise would incapacitate any large organization.*

> *That said, every capable CEO requires select information and makes decisions as they deem appropriate to suit their management approach.*

> *In this manner, the CEO exists as a distinct entity with a litany of capabilities involving areas such as management, finance, operations, and communications and may imagine and initiate a new organizational direction or new priority at any time.*

> *Those priorities will be either well-coordinated, competing, conflicting, or disjoint, just as are many of the priorities within an individual's mind.*

> *But without the rest of the organization, the CEO can do nothing.*

While it is apparent that *Conscious Consciousness* necessarily relies upon the capabilities of *subconscious* and *unconscious* levels, all of these, in turn, are entirely dependent upon the many hardware-related levels of consciousness.

TWENTY-FOURTH LEVEL OF CONSCIOUSNESS (GROUP CONSCIOUSNESS)

Our final level of consciousness is *Group Consciousness*.

This level of consciousness is unique from previous levels because although it operates within an individual, it manifests itself by driving the behavior of individuals in the form of coordinated 'group-think' involving many individuals.

Interestingly, it is a collective behavior that operates long-term at the biological level of the organism, as opposed to a short-term emotionally based collective behavior.

To help understand *Group Consciousness,* we will consider three distinct theories that illustrate behaviors of individuals serving to form a coordinated 'group-think' at a biological level.

We will then contrast *Group Consciousness* to another form of 'group-think' that can be triggered by a form of communication consisting of either spoken or written words, memes, gestures, images, or other form of initiation that results in the short-term effect more commonly known as 'mob psychology theory.'

THEORY #1

Our first illustration of *Group Consciousness* is a form of long-term 'groupthink' influenced at our biological level involving potentially large populations of individuals. It is commonly known as the *'r/K Selection Theory.'*

> *As for the name 'r/K Selection Theory,' the letter 'r' refers to the maximum reproduction rate due to abundant resources, and the letter 'K' refers to the carrying capacity of the local environment when resources are scarce.*

'r/K Selection Theory' was initially developed by Robert MacArthur and E.O. Wilson in 1967 in their work on island biogeography, which became integrated into a more encompassing 'Life History Theory' that incorporates various strategies employed by living organisms to optimize their overall reproduction and survival as a species.

In basic terms, there are 'r' selected individuals and 'K' selected individuals, where 'r' selected refers to individuals who focus on maximizing population size. This biological approach to survival emphasizes quantity over quality to take maximum advantage of an abundance of resources while also improving the chances of introducing much-needed variation in the resulting gene pool.

The primary benefit of maximizing population size when resources are plentiful is that a larger population will contain a higher variability of traits. It can prove extremely valuable to the survival of a species in the event of a disaster, such as a plague, where only a tiny percentage of the population may be either resistant or immune.

In contrast, 'K' selected individuals refers to a population with a low reproduction rate, thereby emphasizing quality over quantity. 'K' selected individuals have offspring that receive a more considerable investment in preparedness to be stronger and more intelligent to survive in either a highly competitive or even hostile environment.

Such environments can only offer a scarcity of resources, an abundance of predators, or adverse conditions, such as excessive temperatures, inclement weather, or poor availability of suitable shelter.

The advantages these two strategies provide a species for long-term survival are profound. Notably, 'r' selected individuals will tend to expand until depleting the resources, leading to a population crash associated with a massive loss of life.

On the other hand, relying solely upon smaller populations of 'K' selected individuals makes a species much more susceptible to mass extinction in any natural disaster or plague.

An accurate perception that resources are abundant indeed serves to help a species by expanding its numbers to better survive a plague or other unforeseen disaster. However, a false perception that resources are plentiful can easily lead a population of 'r' cycle individuals to an otherwise avoidable collapse that will invariably occur when the reality of resource scarcity manifests itself.

Organisms that have developed these two strategies alternate in times of resource abundance and scarcity to significantly improve their chances for survival over prolonged periods through times of natural disasters or plagues.

In human society, 'r' selected individuals align themselves as being liberals (with a small 'L'), and 'K' selected individuals to align themselves as conservatives, with each needing the other for their respective strengths to avoid either the 'r' cycle collapse or 'K' cycle susceptibility to extinction. The irony is that neither side realizes they need the other to optimally ensure the species' survival.

> *Extending the theme of 'r/K Selection Theory' further into political and ideological affiliations and factions, as some tend to do, is generally an overextension and oversimplification that only creates further division and is best avoided.*

Populations that align with 'r/K Selection Theory' represent a form of coordinated 'group-think' at the biological level, influencing individuals' long-term collective behavior.

THEORY #2

In our second illustration of *Group Consciousness*, we will consider a form of long-term 'group-think' at a biological level for potentially large populations of individuals called '*Affluence Theory*.'

'*Affluence Theory*' is best illustrated by the British historian Sir John Bagot Glubb in 'The Fate of Empires and Search for Survival.'

As a student of history born in 1897, Sir John Bagot Glubb noted that history, as taught in university, was largely propaganda focused on one's nation, as opposed to being focused on the history of humanity.

According to Sir John, sorely missing were the well-balanced investigations that would teach the stages involving the repeated rise and fall of empires and the dependencies that each had on prior empires, including the empires of Assyria, Persia, Greece, Rome, Arabia, Mameluke, Ottoman, Spain, Romanov Russia, and Britain.

According to Sir John Bagot Glubb, the repeating stages of empire are:

- *The Age of Pioneers*
- *The Age of Conquests*
- *The Age of Commerce*
- *The Age of Affluence*
- *The Age of Intellect*
- *The Age of Decadence*

The fall of an empire, as marked by decadence, has easily identifiable characteristics.

To quote Sir John Bagot Glubb in his 1976 book, *The Fate of Empires and Search for Survival*: Quote.

> *"Decadence is marked by defensiveness, pessimism, materialism, frivolity, an influx of foreigners, the welfare state, a weakening of religion."*

> *"Decadence is due to too long a period of wealth and power, Selfishness, Love of Money, [and] The loss of a sense of duty." End Quote.*

> *[The Fate of Empires and Search for Survival, 1976, Sir John Bagot Glubb, William Blackwood & Sons Ltd., Edinburgh, Scotland]*

Most important, however, according to Sir John, is the turning point of an empire that leads to its intractable decline, which he refers to as '*The Age of Affluence.*'

To quote again Sir John Bagot Glubb in his 1976 book, *The Fate of Empires and Search for Survival*: Quote.

> *"There does not appear to be any doubt that money is the agent which causes the decline of this strong, brave, and self-confident people. The decline in courage, enterprise, and a sense of duty are, however, gradual."*

> *"The first direction in which wealth injures the nation is a moral one. Money replaces honor and adventure as the objective of the best young men. Moreover, men do not normally seek to make money for their country or their community, but themselves. Gradually, and almost imperceptibly, the Age of Affluence silences the voice of duty. The object of the young and the ambitious is no longer fame, honor or service, but cash."*

"Education undergoes the same gradual transformation. No longer do schools aim at producing brave patriots ready to serve their country. Parents and students alike seek educational qualifications, which will command the highest salaries. The Arab moralist, Ghazali (1058-1111), complains in these very same words of the lowering of objectives in the declining Arab world of his time. Students, he says, no longer attend college to acquire learning and virtue, but to obtain those qualifications which will enable them to grow rich. The same situation is everywhere evident among us in the West today." End Quote.

[The Fate of Empires and Search for Survival, 1976, Sir John Bagot Glubb, William Blackwood & Sons Ltd., Edinburgh, Scotland]

What is essential for us to note in '*Affluence Theory*' is that it also appears to represent a form of coordinated 'group-think' at the biological level, instantiating the long-term collective behavior of a population.

Not coincidentally, '*r/K Selection Theory*' and '*Affluence Theory*' share analogous elements, such as the effect of scarcity and abundance.

THEORY #3

Our third illustration of *Group Consciousness*, another form of long-term 'group-think' at a biological level for potentially large populations of individuals, is the '*Coddling Theory*.'

'*Coddling Theory*' is best illustrated by an outstanding book entitled, 'The Coddling of the American Mind: How Good Intentions and Bad Ideas are Setting Up a Generation for Failure,' written by Greg Lukianoff and Professor Jonathan Haidt.

To help illustrate the phenomenon of '*Coddling Theory*,' Jonathan Haidt points out that American parenting changed in the 1990s and usually asks the segment of the audience currently over forty how old they were when they were allowed to go outside to play with friends in the absence of adult supervision.

The responses are always between five and eight years of age. Naturally, when unsupervised, the children would get into arguments, but they would also play games and do things to earn money and learn responsibility. In other words, unsupervised children learn to become independent in these early years.

Upon establishing that fact, Professor Haidt asks the part of his audience now under twenty-five years of age how old they were when they were allowed to go outside to play with their friends without adult supervision.

Here, the responses are always between twelve and sixteen years of age.

In sharp contrast, instead of practicing to become independent at an earlier age, children were not allowed to practice independence until just before it was time to go to college.

As a result, these adolescents attend college with insufficient practice in being independent and are unprepared to cope with conflict.

In a bizarre twist, these adolescents are not learning to deal with conflict themselves. Instead, they ask adults for protection from what they perceive as social threats to their safety, asking adults to enforce principles of fairness on their behalf.

> *[The Coddling of the American Mind: How Good Intentions and Bad Ideas are Setting Up a Generation for Failure, Sept 4, 2018, Greg Lukianoff – attorney president of the Foundation for Individual Rights in Education (FIRE); and Professor Jonathan Haidt Ph.D. social psychology University of Pennsylvania 1992, currently the Thomas Cooley Professor of Ethical Leadership at New York University's Stern School of Business, Penguin Random House Publishing, U.S.]*

> *Coddling Theory, therefore, has an interesting double-edged sword.*

On the one hand, poor kids are generally not coddled, but with even a modest degree of affluence comes a greater likelihood of coddling.

On the other hand, it is the coddling process that accustoms children to mistakenly believe that they don't need to earn money and learn responsibility because mom and dad will provide for them instead of them having to go out and experience what it means to be independent.

Again, we see how an experience cannot be substituted with either spoken or written words. Explaining to coddled children that they do not need a safe zone will only cause emotional upset and panic.

Also, not an accidental coincidence, *r/K Selection Theory, Affluence Theory,* and *Coddling Theory* all share analogous elements, such as learning to adapt and fend for oneself at an early age versus being granted a relatively care-free environment.

SUMMARY OF THEORIES

The collective behaviors that belong to *Group Consciousness* appear to be triggered by resource availability and lifestyle in a more pronounced way during formative years.

Upon establishing independence and self-reliance in the formative years, 'r' select tendencies become mitigated. However, if they persist past the formative years, they become more ingrained into how the world is expected to work.

Also interesting is that an 'r' selected tendency, or the effect of coddling, whichever one prefers, cannot be reversed through communication or isolation from the group. It becomes a long-term effect that seems tied to one's biology and development.

As we shall see, the behaviors of *Group Consciousness* are inconsistent with *deindividuation theory* (i.e., individuals acting in anonymity). Instead, they are a system of values that stem from the individual's formative years due to the absence or abundance of resources, affluence, or parental coddling.

Mob Psychology Theory

Let's consider the differences between this long-term collective behavior we call *Group Consciousness* and the collective behavior we will refer to as 'mob psychology theory.'

Mob psychology theory is a 'collective behavior' based on the psychological state of individuals who choose to participate.

Mob psychology is a branch of social psychology that includes behaviors associated with riots, panics, crazes, and emotionally driven stampedes, typically from fear, anger, or rage. Once in this state, participating individuals accept the most improbable statements as statements of fact.

While there is no shortage of theories, let's briefly summarize the views more frequently mentioned in sociology curriculums.

Deindividuation Theory - Individuals in crowds act in anonymity, group unity, and arousal while suppressing emotions such as guilt, shame, and self-consciousness. This crowd behavior, however, is limited only to individuals who already possess a degree of aggressive tendencies that would otherwise not materialize.

This state of mind reduces rational forethought among individuals which would otherwise help them maintain normal social behavior.

Gustave Le Bon's Theory - Individuals act as if not individually conscious of their acts, coining the term 'group mind,' thinking and acting based on emotions, appeals, suggestions, and slogans in anonymity.

In this state of mind, they behave significantly differently than one would as an individual outside the influence of others.

McDougall's Theory — It is easy to influence individuals when triggered in groups with common emotions that become reflected and amplified.

In this state of mind, individuals act lower intellectually, suspending self-consciousness, self-respect, and any sense of responsibility.

Freud's Theory - Individuals in a collective are held together with emotions and motivated by repressed drives.

In this state of mind, the restraints of the 'superego' become suspended, and the customarily suppressed impulses of the 'id' surface.

Allport's Theory - Individuals become ready to do the same things in response to a shared stimulus, and when so prepared, the sight of one executing that response heightens and releases that response in the other.

A common theme among these theories is that they describe temporary conditions that are all relatively short-term, where individuals with motivations possess an acute sense of heightened emotionality, which rapidly dissipates when isolated from the group.

For our framework, these modes of collective behaviors do not meet our criteria for *Group Consciousness* primarily because they are short-term psychological behaviors.

Instead, they are driven by a temporary heightened emotional state that is short-term and triggered by communication with whom the individuals identify as the equivalent of their 'herd' leader.

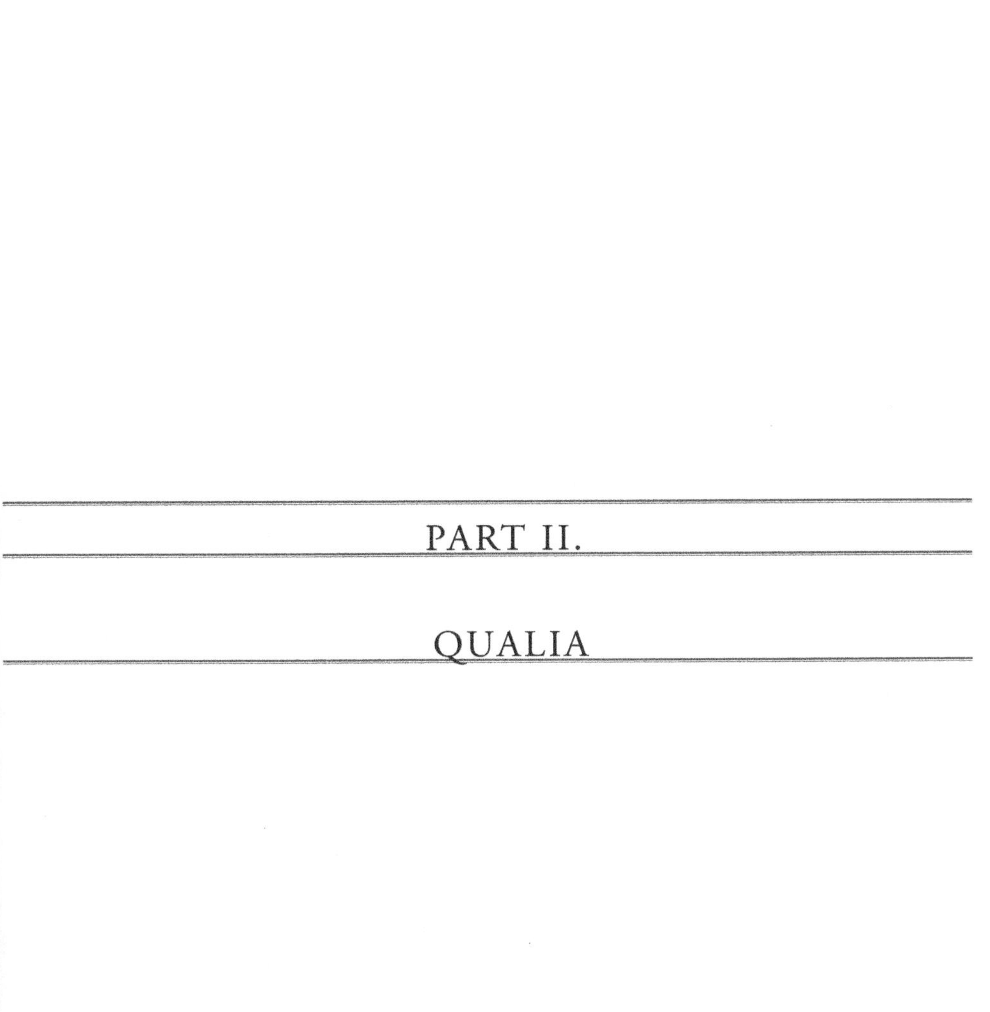

PART II.

QUALIA

QUALIA

Now that we have a comprehensive consciousness framework, we can continue our journey by preparing for a test drive to understand where it can take us, what we can see, and what it can help us do.

The physical evidence indicates that *Homo sapiens* didn't appear fully formed on this planet. Instead, there was an evolutionary process and a history of life and humanity that historians, archaeologists, and biblical scholars have been piecing together.

[King Manasseh and Child Sacrifice: Biblical Distortions of Historical Realities, 2004, Professor Francesca Stavrakopoulou Ph.D. - Ancient Religion, Oxford University, UK, De Gruyter]

[The Bible's Buried Secrets, 2011, Professor Francesca Stavrakopoulou Ph.D., BBC – TV, UK]

The point is not to criticize those who believe in divine creation. The point is that it is simply easier to analyze something as complex as *consciousness* by following its path of development from the beginning, which is severely lacking in today's literature.

Some of the best content on this subject is among the interviews of one particular specialty series, *'Closer to Truth.'* The PBS television series, *'Closer to Truth,'* was produced, written, and narrated by Robert Lawrence Kuhn.

Robert Kuhn aptly pulls together myriad opinions in interviews with professors and researchers of various disciplines to touch upon one or more aspects of consciousness.

The series 'Closer to Truth' has an impressive list of contributors: philosophers, researchers, scientists, neuroscientists, physicists, and biologists from many of the world's top universities.

Some of the most recognizable contributors include John Searle, Ned Block, Deepak Chopra, Peter van Inwagen, Galen Strawson, Stuart Hameroff, Sir Colin Brian Blakemore, Paul Davies, Jared Diamond, Sir Roger Penrose, Neil deGrasse Tyson, David Elieser Deutsch, Baroness Susan Adele Greenfield, Ray Kurzweil, David Finkelstein, David Chalmers, Daniel Dennett, and Marvin Minsky.

It helps to analyze the developmental stages of any unknown from its inception, which is why our journey approaches consciousness in the steps of its evolutionary path.

Now that we have a consciousness framework let's take that test drive and see what we can do to tackle some of the most significant issues involving consciousness.

A TEST DRIVE INTO QUALIA

After our journey through the evolution of consciousness, there will be those who will be quick to point out that none of the levels of *consciousness* ever explained *qualia*.

So, let's look at what is meant by the term *qualia*.

Qualia refers to the 'experience' portion of our consciousness. At its most basic level, the term refers to how an organism experiences a sensory stimulus or a sequence of stimuli.

If we had previously experienced a sensory stimulus, we could imagine with reasonable reliability what it would be like to experience it again. However, if we had never experienced that type of sensory stimulus, it would not be possible to imagine how our minds would experience it reasonably.

For example, someone color blind could read the world's books on what it is like to see the color red. However, without ever experiencing it for themselves, they could not reasonably imagine what it is like to experience seeing the color red.

Some confuse this type of experience with activities like riding a unicycle. They say that someone can read the world's books on how to ride a unicycle, though without experiencing it, they could never know how to ride it.

However, analogies are rarely perfect. This analogy is not fitting because learning how to ride a unicycle creates new neural pathways that accelerate the necessary reaction to small changes in one's balance, allowing the individual to compensate for imbalance more rapidly.

It is much like the process involved in learning how to play tennis, where the expert player learns how to predict where the ball is going based on their opponent's movements before the tennis racquet strikes the ball. Repeated experience is required to train the subconscious mind as to what to expect just as much as it trains the conscious mind, and this training involves the rewiring of neurons to improve the programming of the mind.

However, the experience of *qualia* is different.

The experience of *qualia* is neither learned nor learnable. A color-blind individual cannot learn how to experience the color 'red' no matter how long and often they practice. Neither can a tone-deaf individual develop perfect pitch, no matter how long and often they practice hearing middle 'C.'

Notwithstanding, all *qualia* are comprised entirely of signals in that their substrate is merely the flow of electrical signal data and its subsequent interpretation.

Whether it is a gentle caress on one's palm or a spike driven through one's palm, streams of stimuli will travel to the central nervous system as signal data. The central nervous system transports the signals to the brain, where they get radically different interpretations and sensations. This resulting sensation, *qualia*, is how the signal data gets interpreted.

In either the caress or the severe injury, psychological effects emanate by releasing various hormones that help generate the overall experience. While the specific hormones released differ in each case, the resulting experience is purely signal-driven in the form of electrical and chemical signals communicated to various brain centers for interpretation.

One thing for sure is that the emergence of *qualia* was an essential step in the evolution of life. When signals from sensory organs emerged, organisms did not have the intellectual capacity to sit there and ponder the meaning of a given sequence of signals. In contrast, an instant interpretation of signals was necessary to assess the event as favorable, unfavorable, or indifferent without lengthy deliberation.

Think of it like the rewiring of the brain to generate a more rapid response, much like the rewiring of neural circuits needed to compete in a professional tennis match, but at an evolutionary level.

As a result, unicellular and multicellular organisms, such as our *Paramecium* and *Mimosa Pudica,* respectively, can rapidly determine whether signals emanating from their sensory organs are favorable, unfavorable, or indifferent, all without the presence of any neurons or neuron-like structures.

The only structures supporting this pattern-matching function are the cytoskeletal structures within their eukaryotic cells. While this does not rise to the level of *qualia* experienced in our *Homo sapiens* minds, it is an essential first step.

For a deeper dive into *qualia*, let's start somewhere everyone can relate.

Several types of *qualia* likely occur at different levels of consciousness and within different collections of cells (e.g., individual eukaryotic cells, sensory organs, neurons, and *neuroglia*). So, to delve into this more deeply, let's begin where the sensory signal originates.

In *Homo sapiens*, there are millions of sensory nerve endings with different chemoreceptors for detecting taste in the mouth versus odors in the air. There are different mechanoreceptors for detecting pressure on the skin's surface, impacts on the body, and stretching of muscles. Different types of thermoreceptors sense changes in relative temperature or overheating. Different nociceptors (i.e., specialized for pain) also sense pain caused by heat, pressure, chemicals, and hot spices. Additionally, there are photoreceptors for detecting light, color, and the various parts of shapes. And finally, there are specialized mechanoreceptors for detecting sound frequencies and amplitude.

However, the path these signals take along this expressway of neurons is not a simple broadcast to all neurons. Instead, each neuron is responsible for determining which nearby neurons should receive each signal as the signal travels to where it should go for processing.

In contrast, within a single cell *Paramecium,* each signal is not passed to any other cell. As with all eukaryotic cells, the signal is processed locally within the only possible components capable of processing the signal, namely the cytoskeletal structures, which comprise a complex structure of microfilaments, microtubules, and intermediate fibers.

In eukaryotic cells, these signals likely establish the first level of consciousness (e.g., Unicellular Consciousness), starting in the sensory organ cells where the signal originates. In more complex organisms, each signal continues through the hardware levels of the framework, which comprise the first nine levels of consciousness and then selected software levels that may exist.

Of the numerous signals received into the *Unconscious Consciousness* layer, comparatively, few will make it to the layer of *Subconscious Consciousness,* where few of those will ever reach *Conscious Consciousness.*

The fact that our *Conscious Consciousness* receives such a small percentage of the massive array of inbound stimuli, and hence can be said to ignore most of what goes on around us, does not mean, however, that *qualia* were not occurring at each step of the process below *Conscious Consciousness.*

There are bound to be primitive forms of *qualia* in the lower levels as signals traversed from cell to cell, sensory organ cell to neuron, neuron to neuron, neuron to *neuroglia, neuroglia* to neuron, returning to neuron to neuron.

Considering the many details that we regularly ignore in our visual landscape, auditory landscape, taste, olfactory landscape, as well as our tactile, temperature, and pressure landscapes, it begins to dawn on us that very little of the world around us ever enters *Conscious Consciousness.*

Of these signals that may never reach *Conscious Consciousness,* the lower levels of hardware-based levels of consciousness most assuredly are experiencing primitive forms of *qualia,* even if it is simply to categorize a given segment of stimuli as pleasant, unpleasant, or indifferent.

TYPE ONE QUALIA
(UNICELLULAR QUALIA)

Upon encountering our first level of consciousness, *Unicellular Consciousness,* the single-cell organism *Paramecium* demonstrates the most basic form of *qualia.* Within its sub-cellular structure of microfilaments, microtubules, and intermediate fibers that recognize the stimuli pattern of a predator is rendered as a negative experience to influence the *Paramecium* to move away, while the stimuli pattern of food as a positive experience to influence the *Paramecium* to move toward it.

The organism's interpretation of the stimuli as being pleasant, unpleasant, or indifferent is what we call *Unicellular Consciousness Qualia. Paramecium* must be equipped with a rudimentary form of pattern recognition to differentiate from the relatively small number of environmental factors it can detect.

Next comes an important issue. Upon rendering its *qualia*, what happens next is a decision that, once enacted, reveals the volition the organism wants. In the case of *Paramecia*, this means that it had *freedom of attention, freedom of will,* and *freedom of action.*

The intellectual activities that lead to a decision must also encompass what the organism has learned on top of what knowledge the *Paramecium* already possessed genetically.

> *As Professor Stuart Hameroff cites, when Paramecia are in a capillary tube, such as an eye dropper, they escape more rapidly each time.*

> *This likely means that Paramecia can remember and identify the circumstances in which they find themselves and recall what volitions were adequate to escape.*

For *Paramecium*, the deciding factor for choosing the volition one wants must consider the combination of the *qualia* it senses plus its accumulated knowledge (i.e., genetic and learned) for choosing a volition. Ultimately, the volition would be to choose locomotion in a particular direction at a particular rate of movement.

But let's take a moment to ask, is *qualia* necessary to have the volition one wants? Interestingly, the answer appears to be no.

Let's consider the following relatively simple thought experiment.

> *Imagine you, the reader, suddenly have an allergic reaction to something you've ingested that causes sudden and total visual blindness. Although your experience of qualia diminishes by losing your visual senses, you would consider yourself no less conscious than when you had your sight.*

> *You are no less conscious when placed in a room of total darkness than when you find yourself outdoors in total sunlight.*

> *If your auditory nerves are also affected by the same allergic reaction causing total loss of hearing, you will no longer hear any sounds, including the sound of your heartbeat. Although your experience of qualia diminishes further yet again, you would still consider yourself no less conscious than when you had your hearing.*

> *More importantly, would you consider yourself any less conscious if you still had some sense of vision, such that you were aware of what was in front of you but did not experience any qualia whatsoever?*

> *Likewise, would you consider yourself any less conscious if you still had*

some sense of hearing, such that you were aware of vibrations around you but did not experience any qualia whatsoever?

If an organism is aware of what is around it, either with the capacity to experience qualia or without, its capacity for consciousness, defined within any of our twenty-four levels of consciousness, is not materially affected. That organism will retain the same freedoms, such as their freedom of attention, will, and action, as well as any other freedoms they previously had.

Although *qualia* are not essential for consciousness, they play a valuable role.

For example, later, we will see how *qualia* may help perform a variety of essential tasks based on the role of the cell, such as whether it has a direct connection to the central nervous system or participates directly in the flow of signals within the central nervous system.

It is also worth noting here, for single-celled organisms that do not have a form of locomotion, that just because a cell may be trapped physically among a collection of cells without the ability to exercise locomotion on its own, it does not necessarily mean that that it cannot experience this primitive form of qualia.

TYPE TWO QUALIA (MULTICELLULAR QUALIA)

In *Multicellular Consciousness*, we learned how adjacent cells trigger one another, such as the triggering mechanism of the hair-like structure that rapidly closes a leaf in the Venus flytrap to trap prey or the closing and opening of leaflets in *Mimosa pudica* to protect its leaves from predators.

Upon triggering these mechanosensors, these plants have chemoreceptors that detect ions released to communicate their signal, forming a wave traversing through a series of adjacent cells.

All plants are eukaryotes and, therefore, have cytoskeletal structures, as do all eukaryotes, such as *Paramecium*. Given this common foundation that all eukaryotic cells share with similar cytoskeletal structures, it is reasonable to assert that *Multicellular Consciousness* may support similar *qualia* and decision-making capabilities as *Paramecium*.

In the case of *Mimosa pudica,* when the mechanosensors of the plant detect movement, the sensor creates a signal that the cytoskeletal structures communicate to other cells. The cytoskeletal structure categorizes stimuli as pleasant, unpleasant, or indifferent. If the stimuli are unpleasant, it signals adjacent cells to close the plant's leaves.

In addition to what *Mimosa pudica* already knows genetically, we also need to consider the knowledge that the *Mimosa pudica* has accumulated from learned experience. The cytoskeletal structures use this combined knowledge to determine the volitions they want before freely choosing to enact them by triggering the mechanism to communicate a signal to adjacent cells to close their leaves.

For *Mimosa pudica*, as for *Paramecium*, the deciding factor is the *qualia* that result from stimuli created by the mechanosensors combined with its accumulated knowledge (i.e., genetic and learned).

We refer to the experience across multiple cells as *Multicellular Qualia* as a potentially shared experience. The *hypothesis* is that a collection of cells, such as the collection of cells of any multicellular organism, may experience *qualia* as a collection as their microfilaments and microtubules react and communicate with adjacent cells.

One idea to consider is how collections of cells may specialize in their *qualia*-generating capabilities by the type of sensor and combinations of sensors, whether chemical, mechanical, or photoreceptive, which we will explore later.

Following *Multicellular Qualia*, the next advancement in *qualia* occurs when the collection of cells has a direct interface with a high-speed communication network, such as a central nervous system.

TYPE THREE QUALIA
(NEURONAL QUALIA)

The emergence of neurons in the consciousness framework is an essential advancement for *qualia* for many reasons.

Previously, neurons found within simple organisms, such as the species *C. elegans* of the phylum *Nematoda*, created single one-lane expressways to transport stimuli rapidly over longer distances within an organism. This expressway allowed the organism to coordinate movement along the entire length of the worm. However, with one lane and no other connecting expressways, the only decision was to choose an exit along the expressway and, if so, which one.

Soon after the single one-lane unidirectional expressway succeeded, a network of expressways emerged from the main expressway with multiple lanes supporting traffic in both directions with both on and off ramps. This enhancement allowed the organism to transport an increased variety of stimuli from many physical locations, both on the surface of and within the organism. Essential for improved movement, it allowed stimuli to travel from dispersed sensory organs and to the different muscle tissues of the organism.

After advancing through the levels of consciousness to *Homo Consciousness*, there are many decisions to make regarding routing signals. In *Homo sapiens*, billions of routing decisions are made every second, with some individual neurons having up to ten thousand connections with other neurons from which to choose.

Current estimates show that the typical *Homo sapiens* body contains a hundred billion neurons, eighty-five billion belonging to the brain. Each eukaryotic neuronal cell has cytoskeletal structures consisting of specialized microfilaments and microtubules.

It means that the cytoskeletal structures of a hundred billion neurons are making routing decisions at any given moment, determining which direction in which to route each signal.

Recall that there are many types of neurons, and depending upon their type and location, their connections may include other neurons of the same type or different and may also communicate with a variety of other cell types, such as sensory organs, muscle fibers, and or *neuroglia*.

These decision-making neurons determine the routing of stimuli using their cytoskeletal structures, and it is this aspect of the cytoskeletal brain that we refer to as *Neuronal Qualia* as a group. The *hypothesis* here is that *Neuronal Qualia* is specialized to primarily support signal routing using simple calculations.

Note that each neuron does not spread the signals it receives to every connection, as this would require significant energy expenditures and create an unmanageable avalanche of signal transmissions.

Instead, neurons calculate which other neurons or other cell types to route signals using their freedom of attention, will, and *action*.

TYPE FOUR QUALIA
(NEUROGLIA QUALIA)

To paraphrase D.J. Solecki in his 2004 article, *Neurons inch along*:

Approximately one hundred billion neurons in Homo sapiens have an equal number of unevenly distributed neuroglia surrounding them. It turns out that the brain regions associated with regions comprised of layered architectures of neurons, which are our most advanced brain regions, are surrounded by four times as many glial cells as compared to glia among more ancient brain regions.

[Neurons inch along, Solecki, D.J. et al. Nov 2004. Nat Neurosci. Doi:10.1038/nn1332., Research Roundup, jcb.rupress.org]

For some years, scientists have been concluding that the primary role of *neuroglia* is to attenuate physical and chemical effects upon neurons and to help determine what synaptic connections nearby neurons should establish with one another.

Again, it points to the fact that programming is occurring, this time being performed by *neuroglia* constantly making programming adjustments within the brain. However, their physical locations and concentrations are evidence of a potentially more significant role in consciousness.

To quote, William A. Wells, in his 1997 article, *'Lowly glial cells strengthen brain connections'*: Quote.

> *"The brain is the only tissue in the body where we don't know the function of the major cell type," said Barres. ... Some glia wrap [themselves] around nerve cells and insulates them with a protein called myelin. Glia at synapses acts both as a physical barrier that prevents crossed wires and as a disposal unit that mops up extra messenger molecules released by nerve cells."*

> *"In the presence of glia or the glial factor, nerve cells made more connections among themselves, but this effect alone could not fully account for the increased transfer of messages," Barres said. The more significant change occurred inside each nerve cell, transmitting the message to its neighbors. For some reason, the glial factor made the transmitting nerve cell release its chemical messengers more readily in response to an electrical signal." End Quote.*

> *[Lowly glial cells strengthen brain connections, Sept 24, 1997, William A. Wells, Stanford University, Stanford Report]*

However, neurons are not just communicating with other neurons, sensory organs, and muscle fibers. They are also communicating with certain types of glia without the use of their synaptic mechanism that neurons use to communicate with other neurons.

To quote R. Douglas Fields and Beth Stevens-Graham in their 2002 article, *New Insights into Neuron-Glia Communication*: Quote.

> *"The signals between neurons and glia include ion fluxes, neurotransmitters, cell adhesion molecules, and specialized signaling molecules released from synaptic and nonsynaptic regions of the neuron. In contrast to the serial flow of information along chains of neurons, glia communicates with other glial cells through intracellular waves of calcium and via intercellular diffusion of chemical messengers. By releasing neurotransmitters and other extracellular signaling molecules, glia can affect neuronal excitability and synaptic transmission and perhaps coordinate activity across networks of neurons." End Quote.*

[New Insights into Neuron-Glia Communication, Oct 18, 2002, R. Douglas Fields and Beth Stevens-Graham, US National Library of Medicine National Institutes of Health, PMC1226318, https://www. ncbi.nlm.nih.gov/pmc/articles/PMC1226318/]

Neuroglial cells share many of the same cell parts of neurons, though they lack the membrane to fire an action potential. Instead, they communicate back and forth with neurons chemically.

Continuing to quote R. Douglas Fields and Beth Stevens-Graham in their 2002 article, *New Insights into Neuron-Glia Communication*: Quote.

> *"Although many of the same voltage-sensitive ion channels and neurotransmitter receptors of neurons are found in glia, glial cells lack the membrane properties required to fire action potentials. Nevertheless, these ion channels and electrogenic membrane transporters allow glia to sense the level of neuronal activity indirectly by monitoring activity-dependent changes in the chemical environment shared by these two cell types." End Quote.*

[New Insights into Neuron-Glia Communication, Oct 18, 2002, R. Douglas Fields and Beth Stevens-Graham, US National Library of Medicine National Institutes of Health, PMC1226318, https://www. ncbi.nlm.nih.gov/pmc/articles/PMC1226318/]

Glial cells also communicate among themselves using a variety of signaling systems. Some of these signaling systems specialize in glial-glial signaling. Still, since they are chemically based, it becomes clear why glial cells are concentrated physically around more advanced layers of neurons.

Again, continuing to quote R. Douglas Fields and Beth Stevens-Graham: Quote.

> *"Advanced imaging methods, which allow observation of changes in intracellular and extracellular signaling molecules in real-time, show that glia communicates with one another and with neurons primarily through chemical signals rather than electrical signals. Many of these signaling systems overlap with the neurotransmitter signaling systems of neurons, but some are specialized for glial-glial and neuron-glial communication." End Quote.*

[New Insights into Neuron-Glia Communication, Oct 18, 2002, R. Douglas Fields and Beth Stevens-Graham, US National Library of Medicine National Institutes of Health, PMC1226318, https://www. ncbi.nlm.nih.gov/pmc/articles/PMC1226318/]

There are six types of glia. The central nervous system (CNS) comprises four types: astrocytes, olidgodendrocytes, microglia, and ependymal cells. The peripheral nervous system (PNS) has two types: satellite and Schwann cells.

The peripheral nervous system (PNS) is all the neurons outside the brain and spinal column. Schwann cells myelinate neurons in the PNS, while olidgodendrocytes myelinate neurons in the CNS.

It may be that all glial cell types participate in generating the effects of *qualia*, though it may be that astrocytes are likely the primary mechanism. As far as glia go, astrocytes are highly specialized cells concentrated in brain regions associated with layered architectures of neuronal tissue, which are physically adjacent to the most advanced areas of the brain.

The assertion is that the microfilaments and microtubules of astrocyte cytoskeletal structures facilitate a far greater range of experience than simply as pleasant, unpleasant, or indifferent as their reach allows them to communicate with *neuroglia* among various locations around advanced neural layers.

In addition, given the variety of *neuroglia* and degree of specialization, *neuroglia* cells may even be specialized for experiencing each sensory type (e.g., visual, auditory, olfactory, and taste) or combination of sensory types.

Therefore, *Neuroglia Qualia* is at the heart of understanding the mystery of *qualia* operating in local clusters and networked by specialized astrocytes that span relatively large distances that can facilitate chemically controlled psychological sensations.

TYPE FIVE QUALIA
(COLLECTIVE NEUROGLIA NEURONAL QUALIA)

Collective Neuroglia Neuronal Qualia occurs when integrating the various *Neuroglia Qualia* into a broader unified experience.

We left off with *Neuroglia Qualia* in generating *qualia* through psychological states and sensations and leveraging specialized glia, such as astrocytes, to communicate with other distant concentrations of glial cells that form around our more advanced layers of neuronal tissues.

However, *neuroglia* cells can network more effectively by leveraging the network of neurons that extend throughout the body to reach better both other concentrations of *neuroglia* and glands that release hormones.

Together, *neuroglia* and neurons can reach more cells that can create psychological states and effects by leveraging every chemical mechanism available to the body.

An essential factor in *qualia* is that astrocytes appear to compartmentalize regions of the brain that form memories. Different types of memories may relate to specialized cytoskeletal structures of a given specialized astrocyte for a particular sensory type, such as music, taste, or smell.

To quote R. Douglas Fields and Beth Stevens-Graham in their 2002 article, *New Insights into Neuron-Glia Communication*: Quote.

> *Thus, parts of the brain (such as the hippocampus where memories form) are divided by astrocytes into separate compartments, each the sole domain of an individual astrocyte. End Quote.*

> *[New Insights into Neuron-Glia Communication, Oct 18, 2002, R. Douglas Fields and Beth Stevens-Graham, US National Library of Medicine National Institutes of Health, PMC1226318, https://www. ncbi.nlm.nih.gov/pmc/articles/PMC1226318/]*

These astrocytes represent a mechanism by which individual astrocytes can invoke related memories of their experience with other brain parts to support associations of one experience triggering another.

Compartments of *neuroglia* organized and managed by astrocytes are potentially how combinations of sensations are realized, thus allowing taste and smell to trigger one another with the sensations of memories associated with patterns of stimuli that match or resemble one another.

This experience would manifest within the *neuroglia* at conscious, subconscious, and unconscious levels. As this occurs, they release a combination of chemicals corresponding to related stimuli streams that reside in glial cytoskeletal structures.

Essentially, the cytoskeletal structure of neurons may store many of the facts associated with memories, but glial cells store the experiential data of what it feels like. These glial cells combine chemicals to recreate that experiential effect when adequately triggered.

These actions create a feedback mechanism that repeats the cycle of facts and feelings coursing through our biological systems, interpreting these effects as a view of the world, memories, dreams, and fantasies.

We have dual mechanisms for transporting stimuli responsible for our experiential phenomenon.

One is that astrocyte cells are much larger than previously thought, so many signals do not have to be transported by the neuronal expressway but instead traverse the body of an expansive astrocyte that reaches as a network into various other physical areas of the brain. These expansive astrocytes allow communication within compartments of *neuroglia* concentrations.

To paraphrase R. Douglas Fields and Beth Stevens-Graham in their 2002 article, *New Insights into Neuron-Glia Communication*:

> *Based on histology, the prevailing view has been that astrocyte stellate processes form a tightly intermingled web throughout the brain. Still, now it seems that these cells are much larger than previously thought, and the processes of adjacent astrocytes do not overlap extensively.*

[New Insights into Neuron-Glia Communication, Oct 18, 2002, R. Douglas Fields and Beth Stevens-Graham, US National Library of Medicine National Institutes of Health, PMC1226318, https://www. ncbi.nlm.nih.gov/pmc/articles/PMC1226318/]

The second mechanism is that neurons transport stimuli responsible for our experiential phenomenon to distant *neuroglia* at high speed, reaching various glands that can secrete hormones.

The *hypothesis* here is that *Collective Neuroglia Neuronal Qualia* operates at the subconscious and conscious levels, where integrated forms of *qualia* support dreams and memory recall with the correct corresponding experiential effect created by the combination of hormones, ions, chemical messengers, neurotransmitters, and other extracellular signaling molecules.

Many motivations and reactions may directly result from *Collective Neuroglia Neuronal Qualia* that manifest in the subconscious layer relatively instantaneously and just outside the purview of our awareness.

QUALIA AND GENETICS

Let's pause to put the subject of *qualia* in perspective using our five types of qualia and our consciousness framework.

Within the disciplines of science and neuroscience, *qualia* are poorly defined and understood. One of the reasons for this is that neuroscientists have been looking for *qualia* in neurons in the same way that they've been looking for consciousness in neurons. The adage that if all you have is a hammer, then every problem looks like a nail is alive and well.

Neurons in and of themselves are no more responsible for *qualia* and consciousness than the infrastructure of the telephone company can be held responsible for the content of the conversations over them. However, their cytoskeletal structures do listen in.

Neurons deliver and route messages but read the recipient's address like the postal service. They may calculate how best to get it there, much like network servers do with Internet traffic. Still, as anyone knows, neither the postal service nor the Internet are responsible for the content of the data they transport.

Neurons are essential for many reasons. Their ability to route signals of specific types to specific locations is essential. Their ability to perform rapid calculations is critical. Their ability to be programmable by glia and conscious effort is indispensable for effecting restoration of capabilities from injury and supporting advancements into new learned and or evolved capabilities.

We also know that consciousness emerged well before neurons, much like messages traveled well before the Internet. That said, it is still unclear how these simple organisms experience *qualia*.

Does this mean we know nothing about how the experience of *qualia* feels in organisms outside ourselves?

All living cells equipped with cytoskeletal structures are eukaryotes that evolved from prokaryotes. There are differences among the microfilaments and microtubules in different eukaryotic cells, but there are also similarities.

Hence, there is at least a possibility that different organisms experience some primitive forms of stimuli (e.g., saline concentrations, electrical impulses, light) in similar ways, and the more that individual organisms share structural similarities, the more likely it is that they will experience stimuli in similar ways.

This phenomenon may be especially true of organisms that share a direct line of ancestry in their evolutionary journey.

TASTE AND OLFACTORY SENSES

As such, the way we experience the taste of salt or sugar and how other primates or mammals equipped with similar sensory apparatus experience salt or sugar may be reasonably similar. There are more reasons for the resulting experience to be similar than different, at least for something relatively basic like salt or sugar.

More complex flavors, however, may require more sophisticated astrocytes to experience the numerous sensations of a wine's mouthfeel, nose, and taste, which a rodent may not fully appreciate.

However, it is also clear that individuals of the same species can have a different affinity for a given flavor and a different sensation. Some individuals have an affinity for hot, spicy foods, while others strongly dislike them. But perhaps our experiences are also controlled by genetics.

> *For example, consider individuals who experience the flavor of the coriander leaves (a.k.a. cilantro) as a pleasant flavor for enhancing a variety of dishes. In sharp contrast, somewhere between 10 and 14% of the human population that has tried cilantro smells and tastes the characteristics of soap.*

> *This difference in the sensory experience of cilantro is due to at least three subtle differences in their genome, demonstrating that how we experience qualia can vary with genetic variation.*

> *There are also a variety of chemicals that segments of the human population cannot smell or taste, while others do taste them. There are also different types of bitter flavors, and these differences are due to subtle differences in the genome.*

> *What is important here is that these differences in the genome may result in subtle differences in the cytoskeletal structures of all eukaryotic cells, such as neuroglia.*

VISUAL SENSES

We also know that males and females do not experience color identically or share the same preferences for colors.

To paraphrase Doctors Anya Hurlbert and Yazhu Ling in their 2007 article, *Male Vs. Female Color Perceptions and Preferences*:

> *Human females are significantly better at detecting distinctions among wavelengths of visible light. Where males may detect purple, females detect maroon, plum, eggplant, grape, orchid, and lavender.*

> *[Male Vs. Female Color Perceptions and Preferences, 2007, Drs. Anya Hurlbert and Yazhu Ling, Digital Synopsis,* https://digitalsynopsis.com/design/male-vs-female-color-perceptions-preferences/*]*

How humans experience color varies measurably, particularly by gender in various aspects.

To quote a 2012 article in SciTechDaily, *Females Distinguish Colors Better While Men Excel at Tracking Fast Moving Objects*: Quote.

> *"Males require a slightly longer wavelength than females to experience the same hue. Longer wavelengths are associated with warmer colors, implying that colors like orange might appear redder to a man than a woman. Likewise, green appears a bit yellower to men than women."*

> *"Men are also less adept at distinguishing among the shades in the center of the color spectrum, like blues, greens, and yellows."*

> *"Men could detect quick-changing details from afar, and could track thinner, faster-flashing bars within a bank of blinking lights."*

> *"The team associates this evolutionary advantage down to neuron development in the visual cortex, which is boosted by male hormones. Testosterone means that males are born with 25% more neurons in [the visual cortex] brain region than women." End Quote.*

> *[Females Distinguish Colors Better While Men Excel at Tracking Fast Moving Objects, Oct 2nd, 2012, SciTechDaily,* https://scitechdaily.com/females-distinguish-colors-better-while-men-excel-at-tracking-fast-moving-objects/*]*

AUDITORY SENSES

Absolute pitch (AP), commonly called perfect pitch, is the ability to identify musical notes without another tone to use as a point of reference.

The trait of absolute pitch (AP) can arise from a combination of genetic and nongenetic influences, with a nongenetic influence being music training.

To quote Baharloo, Johnson, Service, Gitschier, and Freimer in their 1988 article in the American Journal of Human Genetics, *Absolute Pitch: An Approach for Identification of Genetic and Nongenetic Components*: Quote.

> *"Forty percent of musicians who had begun training at ≤ 4 years of age reported AP, whereas only 3% of those who had initiated training at > 9 years of age did so."*

> *"Recently, [Profita and Bidder (1988)], presented pedigrees with a high prevalence of AP. They suggested that, in these families, AP was inherited as an autosomal dominant trait with incomplete penetrance. There also is persuasive evidence that an environmental influence, in the form of very early musical training, contributes to the development of AP, [Sergeant (1969), Miyazaki (1988a), Takeuchi (1989)]. Such studies suggest the existence of a so-called critical period for the genesis of AP; it is known that the development of certain neural circuits depends on the presence of sensory stimuli during such critical periods [Goodman and Shatz (1993)]. This proposed critical period for the development of AP may parallel the period during which children's speech perception becomes specialized for the sounds of their native language [Takeuchi and Hulse (1993)]." End Quote.*

> *[Absolute Pitch: An Approach for Identification of Genetic and Nongenetic Components, Feb 1, 1988, Siamak Baharloo, Paul A. Johnson, Susan K. Service, Jane Gitschier, Nelson B. Freimer, American Journal of Human Genetics, Volume 62, Issue 2]*

However, absolute pitch is not exclusive to *Homo sapiens*.

To quote Kathryn Brown in her 1999 article in New Scientist, *Striking the Right Note*:

> *"it [absolute pitch] has also demonstrated in animals, such as bats, wolves, gerbils, and birds, for whom specific pitches facilitate identification of mates or meals." End Quote.*

> *[Striking the Right Note, December 4th, 1999, Kathryn Brown, New Scientist]*

It does not necessarily mean that bats, wolves, gerbils, and birds experience those pitches exactly as humans, though they may be similar. The point here is that genetic factors can also play a role in the auditory senses of individuals.

SENSES SUMMARIZED

Shared cytoskeletal structures and genetics are likely to influence the experience of *qualia* to be similar across individuals. At the same time, differences in genetic factors cause individuals in some circumstances to experience identical stimuli differently.

Although we currently do not know if other animals experience *qualia* like ourselves, organisms of similar evolutionary lineage are likely to share the way they experience stimuli the more rudimentary the stimuli, such as how it feels to experience extreme temperatures, the flavor sensation of salt, or the primary colors perceived in vision.

When we leverage the framework to determine whether neurons influence the experience of *qualia*, the answer would generally be no. Although neurons may be responsible for delivering stimuli to the correct physical locations, there is currently a lack of evidence to conclude that they create the experience of *qualia*.

Instead, the role of neurons is primarily the transportation of signals and sometimes to perform calculations to facilitate routing decisions. Once signals arrive at the appropriate *neuroglia*, neurons transport stimuli recalled from the cytoskeletal memories of *neuroglia* to more distant glands and other specialized *neuroglia* to help facilitate prolonged psychological effects.

Glial cells operate at a chemical level. *Neuroglia*, as specialized eukaryotic cells of various types, are the least understood by neuroscientists because they do not emit waves of electrical potentials that neuroscientists can measure. Instead, they study neurons because they have equipment sufficiently sensitive to measure the significant traversal of ions within a significant mass of neurons.

CYTOSKELETON
(THE CENTRAL NERVOUS SYSTEM OF A CELL)

Within all eukaryotic cells, the cytoskeleton is a network of microfilaments and microtubules that traverse throughout the cell's cytoplasm, networking all cellular structures together except for the cell's nucleus.

Prokaryotes (a.k.a. ancestor of eukaryotes) are comparatively primitive. In prokaryotes, the cytoskeleton is barely present, essentially amounting to a small collection of parts that reside in a small clump of scaffolding inside the cell.

Additionally, prokaryotes have neither a distinct nucleus with a membrane nor any specialized organelles.

To paraphrase Erfei Bi, Joe Lutkenhaus in the 1991 article in Nature, *FtsZ ring structure associated with division in Escherichia coli*:

> *Prokaryotic cells were long thought not to have cytoskeleton until advances in structural visualization technology led to the discovery of microfilaments in the early 1990s.*

> *[FtsZ ring structure associated with division in Escherichia coli, Nov 14th 1991, Erfei Bi, Joe Lutkenhaus, Department of Microbiology, Molecular Genetics & Immunology, University of Kansas, Nature 354 1991]*

The cytoskeleton underwent a significant transformation in the evolutionary transition from a prokaryote to a eukaryote.

In eukaryotes, the cytoskeleton determines the shape of each cell and its degree of flexibility. Cytoskeletal structures also determine the location of organelles that tether into positions within the cell. Within the remaining space, the cytoskeleton shuttles molecules through the cell's cytoplasmic liquid to and from organelles.

Occasionally, the cytoskeletal structures extend outside the cell membrane as cilia to provide mobility for the cell.

The cytoskeleton also acts as the central nervous system for the eukaryotic cell in that it communicates signals to the different parts of the cell. Most significant for our journey into consciousness, the eukaryotic cytoskeleton supports memory and learning, evaluates stimuli as pleasant, unpleasant, or indifferent, and is also responsible for decision-making.

Another significant difference in eukaryotes is that the cytoskeleton actively participates in cell division.

> *Cell division in prokaryotes (i.e., simple one-cell organisms having one membrane, no division internally, and no true nucleus) involves simple cell binary fission (a.k.a. splitting).*

> *In eukaryotes, cell division involves mitosis for asexual reproduction and meiosis for sexual reproduction involving two donors, each providing only half of the required genetic material.*

Though cytoskeleton structures exist in all cells, their proteins can vary significantly between organisms. The eukaryotic cytoskeleton has three types of elongated chains of proteins that form physically identifiable structures known as *microtubules, intermediate filaments,* and *microfilaments* (a.k.a. actin filaments).

Microtubules are the thickest fibers of the cytoskeleton, shaped as hollow tubes measuring approximately twenty-three nanometers in diameter and comprised of the protein tubulin (e.g., alpha and beta-tubulin). These are complex components whose functions are only partially understood.

> *On the cell's exterior, these components form flagella and cilia, the tails and filaments in cells that support cell mobility.*

> *Most of the cytoskeletal structures within the cell consist of microtubules numbering in the thousands, centrally organized from an organelle called the centrosome, known as the microtubule-organizing center (MTOC).*

> *These microtubules form the spindle apparatus (a.k.a. mitotic spindle), separating sister chromatids so that a copy may move into each daughter cell during cell division.*

Intermediate filaments are an essential part of the cytoskeleton found numbering in the thousands, ranging between eight and twelve nanometers thick.

Intermediate filaments are composed of a variety of proteins, such as keratin, a durable protein found in hair, nails, scales, horns, and hooves; desmin, a protein involved in stabilizing muscle tissue structures; lamin, a fibrous protein; and vimentin, a resilient and flexible protein.

Microfilaments are the thinnest filaments of the cytoskeleton, again numbering in the thousands that support material movement within the cell.

Microfilaments consist of two strands of actin protein wound in a spiral just seven nanometers thick and support the movement of various cell components, including cytoplasmic streaming, which is the flowing of cytosol (i.e., the liquid matter of the cytoplasm).

Three movement proteins perform the movement of microfilaments (e.g., kinesin, dynesin, and myosin), which receive their energy from adenosine triphosphate (ATP) within the mitochondria (a.k.a. the power supply of all life within the cell).

To quote Deborah Fields in her 2018 article, *What is a Cytoskeleton?*: Quote.

"Kinesin, fueled by ATP, moves the microtubules filaments; dynesin, a motor protein in cells, changes energy from ATP into movement; and myosin, another type of motor protein, contributes to essential movement in muscles and other activities with the energy from ATP." End Quote.

[What is a Cytoskeleton?, Aug 23rd, 2018, Deborah Fields B.Sc. Chemistry - the University of Birmingham and Journalism Postgraduate Diploma - Cardiff University, www.news-medical.net/life-sciences]

The significance of actin is that the proteins actin and myosin are the primary components of muscle tissue and most all eukaryote cytoskeletal structures that facilitate contraction.

To quote Deborah Fields in her 2019 article, *What is the Actin Cytoskeleton?*: Quote.

"The actin cytoskeleton was originally isolated as a component of the actomyosin complex in muscle cells and was later identified as a component of all eukaryotic cells."

"...the actin cytoskeleton can easily alter the morphology of a cell simply by reorganizing itself. This flexibility in the organization enables cells to adopt a wide range of shapes easily altered. The shape and motility of cells are determined by the orientational cellular distribution of actin filaments, which vary greatly in length and form imperfect mesh-works."

"Focal adhesions also serve as sites for signal transduction and induce signaling pathways when adhesion occurs." End Quote.

[What is the Actin Cytoskeleton?, Feb 26^{th,} 2019, Deborah Fields B.Sc. Biomedical Science – Greenwich University, BioMed Center, www.news-medical.net/life-sciences]

As we see, the cytoskeletal structures of cells perform various functions. Since transportation plays an essential role in the cytoskeleton, let's look at what it is transporting and using as containers.

CYTOSKELETON AND VESICLES

Cytoskeletal structures use a variety of containers to transport specialized material to various locations within the cell. These containers are known as *vesicles*.

The term *vesicle* is from the Latin word *vesicula*, meaning small bladder. Lipid molecules comprise these bladders where each lipid molecule (a.k.a. phospholipid) is hydrophilic on one end and hydrophobic on the other, with proteins tossed in to provide some needed variety.

The hydrophilic heads aggregate with other hydrophilic heads, and the hydrophobic tails aggregate with other hydrophobic tails, lining up the molecules to form the first layer. When two layers combine with their hydrophilic heads coming together with their respective hydrophobic tails facing outward to both the inner and outer surfaces of the bladder, the result is a membrane (a.k.a. lipid bilayer) that creates a barrier between two bodies of water.

This lipid bilayer is the basis for the cellular membrane, organelle membrane, and nuclear membrane of most organisms; however, it is never purely comprised of lipids as some proteins are also present.

The proteins added to the membrane determine the functions of the vesicle in that the proteins determine the types of molecules that are allowed and not allowed to pass through the lipid membrane.

The following thought experiment illustrates the importance of these membranes.

Let's consider a single-celled organism exists in a freshwater lake and another in a saltwater ocean.

First, osmosis is a process by which the molecules of a solvent tend to pass through a selectively permeable membrane, generally from a less concentrated solution to a more concentrated one.

Osmosis continues until the forces that draw the water molecules become equalized, only causing water molecules to flow in and out at the same rate.

In osmosis, the solutes in a concentrated solution exert a force that draws and retains water molecules. Different solutes exert different degrees of force depending upon their physical chemistry. This attractive/retentive force is 'osmotic pressure' or 'osmotic gradient.'

A single cell in the freshwater lake will experience a net inbound water flow as it attracts the solvent (e.g., water) to the higher concentration of solutes inside the cell, eventually rupturing the membrane.

In contrast, a single cell in a saltwater body of water will experience a net outbound flow of solvent (e.g., water) to the higher concentration of solutes (e.g., salt) outside the cell, eventually collapsing.

It is only through the expenditure of energy (e.g., adenosine triphosphate (ATP)) by proteins built into the membrane that actively pump (via ion pumps, ion channels, or aquaporins) either unwanted molecules out of the cell or wanted molecules into the cell, facilitating the ability of cells to maintain an ideal range of equilibrium that allow them to function.

Among the materials transported into and out of a cell through the cell membrane are small bladders that act as shipping containers. These microscopic bilipid containers are *vesicles*.

Vesicles may contain engulfed food molecules and bubbles of gasses to control cell buoyancy, or they can be hormones that create physiological and psychological effects.

As one can easily guess, since the payload of these containers can vary significantly, the result is that there are various ways in which *vesicles* specialize to better adapt to their role.

The *vesicles* of most significant interest to our framework contain hormones and neurotransmitters, known as *synaptic or neurotransmitter vesicles*.

Vesicles operate within the cell to transport material to different parts of the cell (i.e., intracellular *vesicles*), some specializing in breaking down complex molecules into smaller components beneficial to the cell. At the same time, some secrete enzymes, co-factors, peptides, mucus, and hormones.

When signaled to do so, vesicles that secrete hormones internally within cells help form the mechanism that facilitates what we referred to in an earlier section on *Unicellular Qualia*.

These hormones are at least one of the mechanisms that cause cells to have a particular message that informs the rest of the organelles sharing the same cytoplasm of that message.

Single-cell organisms that are free to move about, such as *Paramecium*, would result in an experience restricted to the interior of the *Paramecium*, whereby it may activate its microfilaments to cause the organism to move away or towards the source of external stimulation.

CYTOSKELETON AND EXOSOMES

Other types of *vesicles* called *exomes* occur outside the cell membrane (i.e., extracellular *vesicles*), traveling within extracellular fluids (i.e., fluids that exist outside the cells of an organism) sealed in by body cavities, such as those formed by membranes and tissues throughout the organism to encounter other cells in the immediate physical area.

> *The primary cavities of most Chordata, including Homo sapiens, are the dorsal body cavity, comprised of the cranial and spinal cavities, and the ventral body cavity, comprised of the thoracic and abdominopelvic cavities.*

> *For our purposes, the essential cavities are the cranial cavity, comprised of numerous cranial membranes that compartmentalize regions of the brain, and the many cavities formed by the circulatory system, which traverse the entire body in the form of arteries, veins, and capillaries.*

Once an extracellular *vesicle* has reached the cell membrane of another cell, the proteins of that cell membrane will determine whether it is of an appropriate type to allow it to travel through its membrane.

> *During the process known as endocytosis, the microfilaments pull vesicles as portable containers within the cell.*

> *Many different types of vesicles have many roles. Vesicles have two layers of lipids known as a lipid bilayer, safely separating the molecules inside the vesicle from the cytoplasm, typically transported into vacuoles for future use.*

> *Vacuoles are organelles maintained by the cytoskeleton specially designed to act as a warehouse of various molecules in various states of matter (i.e., solid, liquid, or gas).*

Once ingested, the vesicle's contents can perform its biological function.

Vesicles transporting hormones and chemicals with signal-bearing properties are then able to help form a mechanism that facilitates *qualia* triggered by exomes within a collection of nearby cells equipped with proteins to accept and ingest the *vesicles*.

CYTOSKELETON AND LOW-SPEED REMOTE SIGNALING

The most effective mechanism for transporting hormones over more significant distances is via the circulatory system, using a chemical messengering system of hormone-producing glands known as the endocrine system.

One hormone that acts on almost every tissue of the body is adrenaline (a.k.a. epinephrine), acting directly or through the expression of adrenergic receptors. The adrenal glands and certain types of neurons secrete adrenaline.

As Knut Schmidt-Nielsen Ph.D. – Professor Emeritus at Duke University explains in his 1997 book, *Animal Physiology: Adaptation and Environment*:

> *Adrenaline production emerges early in animal evolution and occurs in many animals, including some single-cell organisms.*

> *[Animal Physiology: Adaptation and Environment, 5th Edition, 1997, Knut Schmidt-Nielsen Ph.D. – Professor Emeritus at Duke University, Cambridge University Press]*

Some hormones cannot directly reach the tissues they affect through the circulatory system of some organisms. Instead, these hormones must go through additional steps and intermediary hormones.

These intermediate steps act as a checkpoint preventing the original message's passing. The translation of the original message occurs at the checkpoint, and then the translation continues its journey on the other side.

To paraphrase James L. McGaugh in his 2012 article, *Memory Modulation*:

> *Adrenaline does not flow through the blood-brain barrier. So, it relies upon adrenergic receptors, specifically β adrenoceptors, at the periphery of the brain to be expressed on the other side of the barrier.*

> *[Memory Modulation, Dec 1st, 2012, Benno Roozendaal – Department of Neuroscience, University of Groningen, Netherlands, James L. McGaugh – Department of Neurobiology and Behavior, University of California, CA, PMC US National Library of Medicine, National Institutes of Health, PMC3236701]*

To paraphrase Toth, Ziegler, Sun, Gresack, and Risbrough in their 2014 NIH article, *Impaired conditioned fear response and startle reactivity in epinephrine deficient mice*:

> *Adrenaline emerged early as a mechanism to deal specifically with the emotional response of fear. It does not involve emotion other than fear (e.g., anger or amusement).*

> *[Impaired conditioned fear response and startle reactivity in epinephrine deficient mice, Feb 1st 2014, Mate Toth, Michael Ziegler, Ping Sun, Jodi Gresack, Victoria Risbrough, PMC US National Library of Medicine, National Institutes of Health, PMC3558035]*

Vesicles carrying hormones through the circulatory system represent a low-speed, long-range, wide-distribution mechanism for chemical stimuli.

The recipient cell membrane requires proteins to accept and shuttle the *vesicle* through the membrane into the interior of the cell's cytoplasm to receive the hormone. *Vesicles* that do not encounter the appropriate proteins on cell membranes continue their journey through the circulatory system.

Once transported through the cell membrane into the interior of the cell, specialized proteins either release the contents of the *vesicle* into the cytoplasm or ingest the contents of the *vesicle,* thereby altering it before releasing it into their cytoplasm.

Once released, the hormone communicates its effect to the cytoskeleton that facilitates *qualia* triggered by these hormones delivered by the circulatory system.

To paraphrase Larry Cahill and Michael T. Alkire in their 2002 book, *Neurobiology of Learning and Memory: Epinephrine enhancement of human memory consolidation: interaction with arousal at encoding:*

> *It is important to note that adrenaline, or a modified form that results from β adrenoceptors, plays an essential role in long-term memory, both in recalling memories and determining the strength with which new memories occur.*
>
> *[Neurobiology of Learning and Memory: Epinephrine enhancement of human memory consolidation: interaction with arousal at encoding, Dec 27th, 2002, Larry Cahill - Department of Neurobiology and Behavior and Center for the Neurobiology of Learning and Memory, University of California at Irvine, Irvine, CA, Michael T. Alkire - Department of Anesthesiology, University of California at Irvine, Irvine, CA, Science Direct, Elsevier Publishers]*

In summary, *vesicles* transporting hormones through the circulatory system represent a low-speed, long-range, wide distribution mechanism for transporting chemical stimuli, where their journey may traverse through checkpoints that translate one hormone into another before continuing its journey.

Also, adrenaline, or its modified form that results from β adrenoceptors, is among the chemicals that significantly affect cytoskeletal structures at the core of memory, learning, and *qualia* that have received their stimuli through the circulatory system.

CYTOSKELETON AND MEDIUM-SPEED REMOTE SIGNALING

Having established that the circulatory system is a low-speed, long-range, wide-distribution mechanism for transporting chemical stimuli, potentially utilizing a checkpoint to translate one hormone into another, let's consider the next fastest method of communicating stimuli.

The next fastest means of signal transfer occurs when the hormones traveling through the local streets of the circulatory system have access to the on-ramp to the neuron expressway.

Here, *synaptic or neurotransmitter vesicles* play a significant role. Within the cells of neurons nearest the synapses, *synaptic vesicles* house various neurotransmitters released outside the cell into the synapse.

A voltage-dependent calcium channel controls the release, including the amount of release. Neurons are constantly regenerating the neurotransmitters and the *synaptic vesicles* that transport these neurotransmitters.

The overall nervous system of Homo sapiens has three main parts: the first two are physical, and the third one is logical. They are the central nervous system (CNS), peripheral nervous system (PNS), and autonomic nervous system (ANS), which we will decompose further.

The autonomic nervous system (ANS) comprises the sympathetic and parasympathetic systems.

The sympathetic nervous system is responsible for the response commonly referred to as the 'fight or flight' response. In contrast, the parasympathetic nervous system is responsible for the response commonly referred to as the 'rest and digest' response.

What is essential to understand is that the CNS and PNS refer to actual physical nerves, while the ANS does not. The ANS is a logical system that relies upon the CNS and PNS. The ANS refers to emotional states of being excited (a.k.a. sympathetic) versus quiesced (a.k.a. parasympathetic).

Although the initial phase of the signal's journey travels at the speed of the circulatory system, which is about thirty centimeters per second (i.e., approximately a third of a meter every second), the second phase travels at the speed of the neurons.

For those of us on the English system, a meter equals 1.09 yards, 3.28 feet, or 39.37 inches.

The signal speed of neurons without a myelin-sheath is approximately one meter per second, while neurons with myelin-sheath segments along their axon conduct an electrical impulse at rates of two orders of magnitude faster (100 times faster) than neurons lacking myelin-sheath segments, approximately one hundred and twenty meters per second.

To paraphrase Doctor James L. Salzer MD, Ph.D in his 2016 article in Current Biology, *Myelination*:

Myelin is a substance composed primarily of lipids.

In the central nervous system, myelin emerges from glial cells named oligodendrocytes. In the peripheral nervous system, glial cells, called Schwann cells, form myelin. Schwann cells are another type of glial cell, also called neurilemma or neurolemmocytes.

Schwann cells get their name from the German physiologist Theodor Schwann, who discovered them in the 19th century.

Myelin significantly accelerates the transmission of electrical impulses, referred to as action potentials, along myelinated axons by reducing the magnitude of the forces that would otherwise slow down the movement of positively charged sodium ions.

The presence of myelin first emerges with jawed vertebrates, facilitating faster signal transmission rates within their descendant species.

[Myelination, Oct 24th 2016, James L. Salzer MD, Ph.D. – NYU School of Medicine, Neuroscience Institute, Current Biology Vol 26 Issue 20]

In summary, *vesicles* transporting hormones through the circulatory system to trigger the neurotransmitters of neurons act as the entrance ramp, which operates at a medium speed as it reaches the expressway.

CYTOSKELETON AND HIGH-SPEED REMOTE SIGNALING

Having established that the on-ramps provide a medium-speed, long-range, wide-distribution mechanism for transporting stimuli, let's now consider the fastest communication method.

Without question, the fastest method for signals to reach their destinations, including ones that can rapidly trigger memories and *qualia* within the cytoskeletal structures of *neuroglia*, are the electrical stimuli traversing the Central Nervous System (CNS) or Peripheral Nervous System (PNS) expressway.

The role of the Peripheral Nervous System is primarily to connect the Central Nervous System to the various organs, limbs, muscles, and glands.

As an extension of the Central Nervous System, limited to the brain and spinal cord, the Peripheral Nervous System extends to the rest of the body and is not protected by the blood-brain barrier.

The effects of exomes, the circulatory system, the neurochemicals of neurons, and the ion flow of neurons naturally combine to support various internal communication rates. As such, let's consider a journey within the mind and body consistent with the framework that put this together.

A JOURNEY WITHIN THE MIND

Let's begin our journey into the mind with something commonly found within our environment that we encounter daily.

Even though we typically refer to it as sound, within the physical world, sound is a vibration that travels through the air. Furthermore, let's stipulate that these vibrations are within a range of vibrational frequency that humans can hear and are of sufficient amplitude (a.k.a. volume) for humans to hear.

These vibrations now move through the air in a space shared by a typical average human not wearing headphones or earbuds.

The vibrations enter both ears through the body part referred to as the outer ear, also called the *pinnae* or *auricle*.

OUTER EAR

A sufficient portion of these vibrations now travels through the ear canal with some assistance provided by the shape of the *pinnae* (a.k.a. outer ear), which is part of the outer ear. These vibrations travel to the *eardrum*, where the outer ear's boundary ends and the boundary of the middle ear begins.

MIDDLE EAR

The *eardrum* is a thin tympanic membrane about half the size of a dime attached to a tiny bone called the malleus, the first part of a tiny three-bone assembly of decreasing size, referred to as the *ossicles*.

The *ossicles* are comprised of the *malleus*, which is attached to a smaller bone called the *incus*, and the *incus*, in turn, is attached to the smallest of the three, called the *stapes*.

The vibrations that reach the *eardrum* cause the membrane of the *eardrum* to vibrate, which in turn causes the *malleus* to vibrate, then causes the *incus* to vibrate, which then finally causes the *stapes* to vibrate.

The sequence of decreasing bone size in the middle ear creates the acoustic effect of amplifying the incoming vibrations as they travel to the *cochlea*, where the boundary of the middle ear ends, and the boundary of the inner ear begins.

INNER EAR

The inner ear converts these mechanical vibrations into electrical signals that leverage neurotransmitters to enter a specific set of CNS neurons.

The significant aspect of this on-ramp to the CNS is the following.

> *The cochlea is a small snail-shaped structure of the inner ear filled with a liquid (endolymph), and inside the liquid is a membrane (basilar membrane) covered in hair cells.*

> *Sitting on top of the hair cells are bundles of cilia (stereocilia) that ride the waves of the endolymph fluid.*

As stereocilia undulate with the waves of endolymph, ions from the top of the stereocilia rush down the hair cells, causing neurotransmitter chemicals to emerge at the bottom of the hair cells.

As these neurotransmitter chemicals bind to the auditory nerve cells, they create an electrical signal transported by the cochlear nerve (a.k.a. auditory nerve) into the CNS.

Different hair cells in the *cochlea* react to different frequencies of vibrations. Then, the stimuli for each hair cell traverse a separate path from the stimuli for other hair cells to retain the information about sound frequency.

The hair cells at the base of the cochlea's large spiral specialize in detecting distinct frequencies. It detects high frequencies, such as from a piccolo, with the hair cells moving up toward the top of the cochlea's smaller spiral, specialized to detect progressively lower frequencies, such as from a trumpet or trombone, with the most petite at the top of the spiral specialized to detect very low sound frequencies, such as from a tuba.

The cochlear nerve transports these signals along 'frequency separated nerve fibers' to the medulla into the cochlear nuclear complex (i.e., dorsal cochlear nucleus (DCN), anteroventral cochlear nucleus (AVCN), and posteroventral cochlear nucleus (PVCN)), which is part of the brain stem located closest to the back of the neck, delivering them to different areas of the medulla while continuing to preserve the frequency information.

These signals travel from the remnants of the primitive brain to the advanced areas of the *Mammalian* brain into the auditory cortex. The various frequencies continue to be delivered separately by separate channels into different locations to preserve frequency information.

It means that distinct primary cortex neurons receive electrical signals corresponding to the specific frequencies initially entering the outer ear.

AUDITORY CORTEX

The auditory cortex itself has three separate parts: the primary (a.k.a. the core), secondary (a.k.a. the belt), and tertiary auditory cortex (a.k.a. the parabelt), which envelop one another with the primary in the center, secondary layered between the primary and tertiary, with the tertiary enveloping the primary and secondary.

PRIMARY AUDITORY CORTEX – PITCH AND AMPLITUDE

The primary auditory cortex receives signals directly from the *cochlear nuclear complex of the medulla* (e.g., DCN, AVCN, and PVCN).

> *The primary auditory cortex specializes in pitch and loudness, containing stripes of neurons activated by the left ear, other stripes of neurons activated by the right ear, and a third set of neuron stripes activated from signals received by both ears.*

The cytoskeletal structures of neurons in the primary auditory cortex communicate chemically with the glia encasing them, which specialize in memorizing and recalling previously experienced pitch and loudness signals.

These recalled signals augment the initial signals and are then chemically communicated back to the neurons that route enriched signals into other *neuroglia* specialized in experiencing these signals as psychological effects that the brain interprets as sounds.

> *The glial cells within the primary auditory cortex specialize in generating many of the psychological effects of musical tones. The degree to which these specialized glial cells develop determines the richness of the tonal experience.*

> *The secondary auditory cortex has less tonotopic organization (i.e., neurons for specific frequencies) than the primary auditory cortex. Still, it plays a vital role in sound localization and analysis of complex sounds regarding the sequence of sounds.*

> *Wernicke's area, critical to language comprehension, is within the secondary auditory cortex.*

The cytoskeletal structures of neurons in the secondary auditory cortex route signals to the layer of *neuroglia* encasing them, which specialize in memorizing and recalling both the sequence and timing of signals and identifying their patterns.

These glial cells then send the recalled signals back into neurons in the form of neurochemicals that route the augmented signals into other *neuroglia* specialized in experiencing these signals as psychological effects that the brain interprets as sequences of tones to establish recognition of speech.

To paraphrase Janata, Birk, Van Horn, Leman, Tillmann, and Bharucha in their 2002 article, *The Cortical Topography of Tonal Structures Underlying Western Music*:

> *There are even neurons for detecting specific tonal arrangements for sounds like vowels outside the auditory cortex in the rostro-medial prefrontal cortex.*

> *[The Cortical Topography of Tonal Structures Underlying Western Music, Nov 1st, 2002, Petr Janata, Jeffery L. Birk, John D. Van Horn, Marc Leman, Barbara Tillmann, Jamshed J. Bharucha, PubMed, PMID 12481131, US National Library of Medicine]*

SECONDARY AUDITORY CORTEX

The *neuroglia* of the secondary auditory cortex and rostro-medial prefrontal cortex generate many psychological effects that support name and word recognition.

Neurons that perform calculations on signals returned from glial cells detect that signals and their sequence identified by the secondary auditory cortex match the signals of a particular name and then recognize that the name most likely refers to an individual likely to be male or female.

TERTIARY AUDITORY CORTEX

The tertiary auditory cortex remains largely a mystery. However, it seems to integrate the signal responses from other neuronal areas. Then, it routes these signals to other neuron collections that create associations with the same patterns, thereby causing other *neuroglia* to augment the signals with yet additional patterns (e.g., visual, olfactory) that neuronal pathways have associated.

These actions, in turn, route additional signals to other neuron pathways that release various types of hormones.

At this point, a girl's name corresponds to a specific young lady, recalling her last name, then some words she spoke, and a litany of other related memories that become activated.

When stimuli of the girl's name reach the occipital lobe, memories of her visual appearance are activated.

> *The occipital lobe is where most visual processing occurs, whereas the parietal lobe is where experiences regarding food taste, texture, and aroma are processed.*
>
> *[What Is the Difference between the Occipital and Parietal Lobes?, http://www.wisegeek.net/what-is-the-difference-between-the-occipital-and-parietal-lobes.htm, wiseGeek]*

Like the auditory cortex, visual signals have topographical maps (i.e., neurons dedicated to specific parts of the field of vision) in the primary visual cortex (a.k.a. striate cortex) and the somatic sensory cortex of their visual sensory array.

But where are these signals aggregated into an integrated and unified experience?

Is there a difference between creating an integrated experience that stems from one's actual experiences versus one's imagination?

Interestingly, we know that the integrated experiences of reality occur in a different location of the brain than the integrated experiences of imagination.

To paraphrase Christopher Wanjek in his 2014 Live Science article, *Imagination and Reality Look Different in the Brain*:

> *It turns out that the collection of signals that stem from 'reality' flows from the brain's occipital lobe down to the parietal lobe. In contrast, signals originating within the 'imagination' flow from the parietal lobe to the occipital lobe.*

> *[Imagination and Reality Look Different in the Brain, December 23, 2014, Christopher Wanjek, Live Science]*

In summary, the details perceived by sensory organs (e.g., sound frequency) persist by routing stimuli that correspond to specific frequencies into specific lanes within the expressway of neurons. Additionally, each lane has separate exit ramps that enter separate locations of the brain organ that is their destination.

Upon arriving at their destination, their signals become re-dispatched to other areas with supporting or related information, such as memories, so that the additional qualia may generate a fuller experience.

The resulting psychological effects are the culmination of specialized glial cells that leverage a combination of chemical hormones and neurotransmitters added into the processing for each type of stimuli (e.g., auditory, visual) and their characteristics (e.g., vibrational frequencies).

At a fundamental level, neurons and their corresponding glial cells are often highly specialized to deal with a particular aspect (e.g., a specific frequency) of a particular type of stimulus (e.g., sound vibrations in air).

This 'incremental' buildup of mechanical, electrical, and chemical signals by sensory organs, bones, tissues, neurons, and glial cells results in an orchestration of hormones and neurotransmitters strategically released in various locations within the brain and body, and the 'integrated' experience that occurs is the culmination of what I term the Integrated Incremental Consciousness Theory.

Whatever the organism and levels of consciousness that organism may be capable of, that organism's ability to experience its environment is the culmination of Integrated Incremental Consciousness.

How cytoskeletal structures generate these psychological effects within our minds from the cytoskeletons of glial cells and neuron bundles is still a mystery. The answer hides in the tiny world of cytoskeletal structures, their thousands of strands, the hormones they control, the related neurons they signal, and so on.

Do glial cells release the psychological effects that our cytoskeletal structures have stored?

Do we automatically react before we realize it?

How much control do we have to detect the world around us, experience the psychological effects, and then react thoughtfully?

In other words, do we hear what we want to hear, do we hear what we expect to hear, or do we truly hear the stimuli received by our sensory organs?

And what gives our perceptions meaning?

And can the meaning associated with the same sequence of stimuli change?

The answer appears to depend upon the levels of consciousness an individual is equipped with or has developed.

We are subject to the phenomenon illustrated in the lyrics of many songs, perhaps this one in particular, in which the country songwriter is unknown. Quote.

"Your Meanings"

(A song, author unknown)

"You put your meanings in my words
Till my words don't mean what they say"

"I don't mean you hear just what you want to hear
No, you hear what you think I would say
And when some of your meanings hurt you
Then you get angry at me"

"And I put my meaning in your bitter tears
And I hate you for hurting at me"

"But I only wanted you to know me
To see me and hear me as I feel me inside
Laughing easy, crying hard, seldom certain,
always wishing we could fly"

"But you put your meaning in my words
While my meanings stumble and fall"

"Our lips are still moving, there is sound in the air
But I don't think we're talking at all"
End Quote.

PART III.
SEVEN FREEDOMS

PHILOSOPHY AND SCIENCE

For centuries, the collaboration between science, philosophy, and sometimes religion propelled thought into the observable and unobservable world.

From the sixth century B.C.E., the time of the Buddha (i.e., Siddhartha Gautama, born 563 B.C.E.), and the fifth century B.C.E., the time of Socrates, Plato, and Aristotle (i.e., Plato, born 427 B.C.E.), the thinkers were both philosophers and scientists.

There was no distinction between scientists and philosophers until the 18th century when a significant divergence emerged. It was at this time that science and philosophy became separate tracks of study within the places of higher education.

Explanations for this separation exist, though the two most reasonable are a) that the sheer volume of material for each discipline made it quite challenging to master both, and b) the utility of science in economic terms compared to the utility of philosophy resulted in separate demands for each.

By the 21st century, philosophy as a study track vanished from most universities. Fewer universities, and as a result, fewer people experienced the rigors of philosophical thought and the lessons it taught more than ever before.

However, some of the world's most challenging problems become more approachable with philosophy's assistance.

To illustrate this briefly, let's revisit the *'r/K Selection Theory'* discussed in our twenty-fourth level of consciousness, *Group Consciousness* with a hypothetical conversation between an 'r' selected individual and a 'K' selected individual that takes place in New York City where both individuals are intelligent and well-read, with both earning a good living.

'r' selected: "I think everyone should have access to free health care as it is a human right to have good health. Also, we should abolish hunger, as there is no reason why anyone worldwide should go hungry."

'K' selected: "Sounds great, but how do you pay for it?"

'r' selected: "There should be a tax on corporations. That would pay for it."

'K' selected: "You realize they will just raise prices on their products and services, so people pay for all taxes in the end?"

'r' selected: "The country is wealthy enough to afford it."

'K' selected: "Can your family afford the health care and food costs for just two more families in this country, not to mention the rest of the world? Do you realize what happens when you increase the resources

for any organism? Just a guess, but I'd say that the population gets even bigger. Can you imagine the increased demands upon freshwater and shelter?"

'r' selected: "We should open our borders and let them in."

'K' selected: "Do you have doors on your house? Do those doors have locks? Do you keep them locked? Why do you think that is?"

'r' selected: "But we are citizens of the world. We have a responsibility."

'K' selected: "Do you realize that your solutions put the cost of all these things on some hypothetical other people who may not agree with you?"

'r' selected: "The government has plenty of money."

'K' selected: "Do you know where governments get their money?"

'r' selected: "Yes, everyone knows they print it."

In this instance, the 'r' selected individual has no practical solution, and the 'K' selected individual appears insensitive to the plight of others.

However, if the 'r' selected individual and the 'K' individual collaborate, there is always a possibility of a relatively good solution.

The challenge, of course, is finding a way to gain the cooperation of 'K' selected individuals. One lesson learned repeatedly is that 'r' and 'K' selected individuals need one another to understand the issues fully and to develop and implement the most effective solution that will work without disastrous consequences.

Let's consider another set of positions for the 'r' and 'K' selected individual, as, throughout history, the 'r' selected individual has proffered the ideas that have significantly improved humanity when they collaborate.

We will choose one significant social issue that existed throughout human history until two hundred years ago.

'r' selected: "Slavery is wrong; it should be illegal."

'K' selected: "How do you pay for it? The plantation owners will all go bankrupt."

'r' selected: "As fellow human beings, it is our responsibility not to allow slavery anywhere in the world."

'r' and 'K' selected: "How do we stop slavery everywhere?"

Upon collaborating, in a relatively short time, it became possible to abolish slavery worldwide. It took a military conflict, much political debate, economic pressure, and negotiations.

England was the first to abolish slavery in 1833 in most colonies. Slavery officially ended in the United States in 1865 with the ratification of the 13th Amendment to the Constitution.

> *The abolition of slavery continued globally for some time after that. For example, slavery was abolished in South Yemen in 1967, Oman in 1970, Mauritania in 1981, and Niger in 2003.*

As one might expect, at the heart of it was a philosophical debate that began centuries ago. The first statement identifying that slavery was wrong is from the 6th century B.C.E.

> *The Buddha said that buying and selling human beings is an invalid livelihood, and he encouraged his monks and nuns never to accept enslaved people as gifts.*

Philosophy, as an intellectual pursuit, is quite challenging. It makes you think about different sides of an issue like no other discipline. It forces you to think about how you think and how others think. And it makes you think about what thought is and how it comes about.

Beginning in ancient times, it makes us think about questions such as what is good and what is justice (e.g., Socrates and Plato), and it also makes us think about how we perceive reality and contemplate our place in the universe (e.g., Buddha).

Philosophy also makes one think about what is essential in life and what is not. What makes us happy, and what kinds of lives do we wish to lead?

At a minimum, philosophy provides insight so that we may begin to understand ourselves better. At a maximum, it can provide an invaluable perspective we can better leverage daily in our life's journey.

As we shall see in our journey into consciousness, it provides a much-needed perspective on some of the issues that define consciousness and its boundaries. It also offers invaluable guidance that helps one avoid the wrong turns and mind traps that may await the less prepared traveler.

CONSCIOUSNESS AND FREE WILL

The subject of *free will* is surprisingly controversial.

However, the controversy is not just over which mechanism better explains *free will* or to the extent to which it exists, but whether *free will* even exists.

It is at least reasonable to begin with the declaration that *free will* is entirely dependent upon *consciousness*.

This statement seems obvious to most, though it has two terms with controversial definitions. So, let's take a moment to assess where we are and what path we need to take to continue our journey.

We have done a relatively thorough job of defining *consciousness* at each of the twenty-four levels in the first part of our journey, though we have not addressed the definition of *free will* as thoroughly.

Like *consciousness*, the debate about whether *free will* exists revolves around how *free will* is defined. And like the scientific definition of *consciousness*, there is also no consensus on the scientific definition of *free will*.

In philosophy, *free will* is the freedom of self-determination and action independent of external causes. It entails the ability to make free choices, where choice is free if it is consistent with an individual's desires and nature.

According to Professor Rick Repetti, Ph.D. CUNY, individuals around the age of five see *free will* as having free range to do anything they please.

However, once children reach around seven years of age, they see *free will* as not being able to behave as they please, such as eating the marshmallow placed in front of them when instructed not to do so or choosing not to consume their portion of broccoli when instructed to do so.

It turns out that one's degree of self-control is particularly significant in a child's development as a reliable indicator for predicting success in one's life. Even trivial forms of self-control correlate strongly to controlling one's immediate or near-term desires to better facilitate one's long-term desires.

As we mature, we come to realize a circular effect.

- The choices we have made determine our life's experiences
- Our experiences influence how we make choices

As a result, we can live a life based upon where the currents and tides of life's events cause us to drift, or we can think about the course we would like our lives to take and swim against the current to get us there.

Is that harder for some as compared to others? Yes, though, anyone in an environment rich with opportunity can succeed.

There are also many possible choices between the two scenarios of drifting or swimming against the tide. Many follow a course in between, though some live adrift lives believing this approach results in less pain and effort. Though initially drifting through life results in less pain and effort, it usually maximizes pain and effort over time.

CONSCIOUSNESS, FREE WILL, AND GENETICS

We must not ignore the genetic effect on *consciousness* and *freedom of will*.

Like how large populations of individuals taste the herb cilantro, either experiencing the flavor of cilantro for its intended flavor in many culinary recipes or detecting the flavor of soap, we have many different tastes and preferences.

As a result, we can see that our consciousness experiences can differ at each level of our consciousness depending upon genetics.

Differences due to genetic factors (a.k.a. nature) can and do significantly influence how we perceive reality beyond how we are nurtured and taught.

We realize a slightly more complex circular effect if we include genetic factors not in our control.

- Genetics influence our conscious and unconscious experiences

- Our conscious and unconscious experiences influence the assessment of our choices

- The choices we make determine our learned experiences and life's path

- Our learned experiences and life's path influence our conscious experiences

- Our conscious and unconscious experiences influence the choices we make

The degree to which we take control of unconscious influences will largely determine the degree of freedom we exercise.

Our ability to exert our freedom can only happen to the extent that we can observe our conscious stream of thoughts as they bubble up from our subconscious. And then, as an observer, we can choose which to accept or ignore, that is, if we try to reprogram ourselves using techniques such as meditation.

The amount of effort we are willing to exert sooner rather than later will undoubtedly influence the outcome. It will determine what we focus on, what we refocus our attention on, and, hence, what we dwell on to help us grow and move in the right direction or what we dwell on to hold us back.

Recall in *Unconscious Consciousness,* the entirety of the unconscious mind is genetically and epigenetically determined, with no access to its programming from the conscious or subconscious mind.

Likewise, regarding *Subconscious Consciousness,* most of the subconscious mind is also genetically and epigenetically determined, with degrees of influence that result from learned experiences.

As a result, our genetics and epigenetics determine our initial preferences, affinities, dislikes, and ambivalences. Genetics and epigenetics may account for individuals' snap decisions, with rare exceptions.

One exception to genetically driven snap decision-making involves thoroughly training as an expert.

The more an individual focuses on a subject, the more expertise they attain.

As familiarity increases, they more readily recognize patterns and approach the thought process using a rigorous methodology that becomes rote after sufficient repetition.

> *However, no one can become an expert in more than very few disciplines, never mind all of them.*

But this does not mean that our genetics and epigenetics determine our reasons, reasoning process, or priorities as determined by our *free will.*

Genetics and epigenetics influence our reasons and reasoning through the emotions they generate. Still, education, experience, and the exercise of our *free will* also influence our reasons and reasoning.

Influences upon our reasoning also stem from a variety of external sources that we internalize.

Our culture and various forms of indoctrination influence us. Our families and friends influence us. Our vocations and training influence us. Our role models influence us. The books we read and the programs we watch influence us. Media outlets influence us.

However, our genetics and epigenetics also influence us. Our circumstances influence us. What we have done in the past influences us. How others perceive us or how we think they might perceive us influences us. Also, others who try to help us or harm us influence us.

From this list, one can see that we will be adrift if we don't take control of our life's direction. But where does one begin?

Luckily, one of the most effective tools at our disposal to take control of our reasons and reasoning is to set goals for ourselves, near and long term. When our goals are known to ourselves, we internalize them and work toward achieving them consciously and subconsciously.

These goals need not be easy or hard or reasonable or unreasonable. They only need to be goals that we set for ourselves. Once we have goals, we work toward achieving them by making choices of all shapes and sizes that move us closer to achieving them.

Ultimately, whatever goals we choose, individuals are free to choose them. Individuals maintain the ability to make a choice simply because it is what they want, regardless of the myriad of influences they have.

In this sense, we each have *agency.* With agency, we are the ultimate cause of our actions. Likewise, we can do otherwise under identical conditions, for a reason or for no reason.

Let's engage in a thought experiment where we take a simple example of making a choice and look for influencing factors that may drive that choice.

> *The teacher asks for a volunteer in the class. The volunteer sits in the front of the room, facing the class.*

> *We request the volunteer to choose between chocolate and vanilla ice cream.*

After choosing a flavor, the instructor asks the reason for that choice. The volunteer invariably responds that the reason was that they prefer the chosen flavor.

The same instructor asks the same volunteer the same question, and the cycle repeats for dozens of rounds with the same outcome.

Eventually, the volunteer chooses the other flavor. After making that choice, the instructor asks what the reason was for making that choice. The volunteer invariably responds with the reason being that they were tired of the other previously chosen flavor.

The instructor asks the volunteer the same question again, and the cycle repeats for dozens of rounds with either of these same outcomes until the volunteer finally says they did not have a reason.

Instead of choosing for a reason, the volunteer says they chose because it was what they wanted.

The point, although subtle, is that there may be many influences and reasons for making a given choice. But ultimately, if we dispense with those influences and reasons, we are eventually left with what we want.

THE FREE WILL DEBATE

As indicated earlier, there are four competing frameworks regarding *free will*. They include *hard determinism, soft determinism, soft indeterminism,* and *hard indeterminism.*

Even though philosophers have framed the debate in this manner, it does not mean that the frame includes all possible ways of looking at the problem.

The frame of the debate has so many flaws that many become inextricably trapped within it. Let's begin with a quick review of the original debate.

HARD DETERMINISM REVISITED –
NEUROSCIENTIST ROBOTS

Individuals could not have chosen otherwise in a world entirely determined by the laws of physics, physical chemistry, and chemistry. This perspective is that 'hard determinism' is a universe in which everyone may think they can do otherwise but cannot.

In a universe that operates according to *hard determinism*, everything that happened, starting from the Big Bang, would play out identically if given identical circumstances. Thus, every choice we make stems from the historical events that led up to each decision.

Hard determinism, also known as "The Consequence Argument," has been adopted by some neuroscientists, many of whom have done so in response to a set of experiments we will discuss in an upcoming section. For now, *hard determinism* is a populist view, claiming that almost no matter how it is defined, free will does not exist.

Oddly, these neuroscientist robots could not choose other than to draw this conclusion.

HARD INDETERMINISM

Next, let's briefly revisit the opposite extreme of the four basic frameworks, '*hard indeterminism.*' This extreme framework is a universe in which everything is 100% random.

In a universe that operates according to *hard indeterminism*, everything that began with the Big Bang would have no chance of playing out the same way if given identical circumstances. Thus, every choice you make is random.

However, since every choice is entirely random, the individual cannot exert any control over any choice.

> *I don't know about your experience in raising a child. Still, when it comes to asking my daughter to eat her vegetables, her responses were not random, as she consistently said "no" as she pushed her vegetables to the far edge of her plate.*
>
> *In doing so, my daughter invalidates the theory that the universe is entirely random.*

At this point, neither '*hard determinism*' nor '*hard indeterminism*' can support *free will*.

SOFT DETERMINISM AND SOFT INDETERMINISM

As one might imagine, *soft determinism* and *soft indeterminism* are defined differently by different philosophers (e.g., Augustine, Spinoza, Hume, Aristotle), all presenting their viewpoints justifying a position between *hard determinism* and *hard indeterminism*.

They either dispense with some degree of hard determinism or hard randomness, but in the final analysis, they remain intractably trapped within the framing of the topic.

> *A simple illustration of framing a topic that traps the victim is asking someone if they have stopped beating their spouse. The trap is that the framing of the question assumes that they have been beating their spouse.*

For a mind trap to be effective, it must not allow any possible explanations outside the framework of the trap.

Another example would be to claim that someone's decision was the result of them either being malicious or incredibly stupid, claiming that whichever it was didn't matter.

However, such a decision has a reasonable probability of resulting from something that is not between the two choices. It is also likely that the decision was arrived at from within a different paradigm.

As paradigms go, the scientific disciplines of the quantum world is a different paradigm, such that it has its unique branch of mathematics and laws of physics.

Too many people mistake quantum mechanics for pure randomness, though more accurately, it is probabilistic.

> *Quantum mechanics, particularly quantum computing, operates as a probabilistic function over time. When programming a quantum computer, the probability of arriving at an optimal solution increases over time.*
>
> *In contrast, the probability of selecting a specific card from a standard playing deck remains one out of fifty-two, regardless of how long one waits. It is one in fifty-two now, in one second, in one minute, and in a billion years from now.*
>
> *On the other hand, a quantum process may have trillions of possible solutions now. Still, in thirty seconds, it may have any one of a handful of near-optimal solutions, and in another thirty seconds, it may have the one optimal solution.*
>
> *Therefore, a quantum computer is neither deterministic nor random. It is outside the frame of the philosopher's argument, as it belongs to a different paradigm.*

A DIFFERENT PARADIGM (Q-SOFT DETERMINISM)

The notion of *Q-Soft determinism* addresses two problems regarding *free will*.

Let's begin by carefully defining our terms, as the meaning of the term 'random' is not necessarily what many consider it to be.

> *In mathematics, a 'random' variable is a quantity that may take any range of values in such a way that there is no reliable way to predict an outcome or pattern. As such, any outcome is purely a matter of 'chance.'*
>
> *The issue then becomes what is meant by the term 'chance,' how 'chance' is measured, and what type of randomness results.*

As one might expect, randomness exists in a continuum, ranging from no randomness to complete randomness, where the degree of entropy determines the position on the continuum.

Entropy is a measure of randomness. Within the discipline of thermodynamics, entropy is the degree to which energy is organized or disorganized in a system. Hence, it is a measure of predictability regarding the possible arrangements of atoms in a system and the corresponding energy of those atoms.

For example, the molecules of a salt crystal are highly predictable, as they do not move about in a fixed solid pattern, resulting in a low entropy system.

In contrast, the arrangement of salt molecules in saltwater is highly unpredictable. Therefore, It is a high entropy system with more randomness and unpredictability.

Zero entropy systems provide complete predictability, whereas maximum entropy results in the least predictability possible, which is entirely random.

Furthermore, as time advances, the universe's entropy continually increases. The fact that entropy only ever increases with time moving forward is the second law of thermodynamics.

However, the fact that entropy always increases in the universe does not make *freedom of will* an impossibility any more than it precludes the possibility that there can be life. As the forces of entropy operate at multiple levels around us, other forces operate as time moves forward.

Even though entropy is continually increasing, there are self-organizing systems around us, including in the biosphere. These self-organizing systems often appear as reversing the tide of entropy; if considered in isolation, they do.

However, when considering these self-organizing systems from the macro perspective of the universe, these pockets of self-organizing effects are greatly outweighed by the expansion of the universe and the continued effects of the explosion that started with the Big Bang.

While it is theoretically possible that the universe will eventually achieve maximum entropy, no hard and fast rule states that it ever will. Likewise, there is no hard and fast rule that entropy limits life or *freedom of will.*

At the micro-level, entropy operates at the subatomic level, known as quantum mechanics. Quantum mechanics, coined initially in German as *Quantenmechanik* by physicists Max Born, Werner Heisenberg, and Wolfgang Pauli (University of Gottingen), has evolved into two disciplines: quantum mechanics and quantum computing.

Although many refer to quantum mechanics and quantum computing as a random function, we will soon see that quantum computing is all about eliminating randomness.

OVERCOMING A RANDOMNESS BIAS (Q-SOFT DETERMINISM AND QUANTUM COMPUTING)

The concepts of quantum computing are relatively easy to understand.

Quantum computing requires a combination of two types of computers: conventional and quantum computers. The conventional computer, such as your laptop, relies on *hard determinism*. In contrast, a quantum computer relies on neither hard determinism nor *indeterminism*.

A conventional computer platform is always involved with a quantum computer because it is necessary to program the mathematical formulas that act as the program in the quantum computer. The conventional computer is needed to communicate the mathematical formula and the data to the quantum computer.

Interestingly, the same mathematical formula could also work using a conventional computer, except that a conventional computer would typically be tied up for many years, potentially millions of years, due to the many possible values the formula's variables can consider.

One can program conventional computers to solve the same problems using other approaches. Some only provide rapid approximations, while others may again continue for unreasonably long periods.

Unlike a conventional computer, once a quantum program begins the computation of its given mathematical formula, the energy state of its variables begins to drop. The optimum answer to the mathematical formula corresponds with the lowest energy state possible within the quantum computer.

Finding the lowest energy state possible for a mathematical formula in a quantum computer is aided by quantum physics, which seeks to rest at the lowest possible energy state. The role of the mathematical formula is to provide structure to the energy levels such that as it approaches the lowest energy state, the values of the variables correspondingly change to the values as the computer reaches lower energy states.

To better understand how quantum computing works, let's look at the basic types of conventional computer systems and the types of problems those and quantum computing are good at solving.

BASIC COMPUTING PARADIGMS

Conventional computing programs can be *information systems* or *control systems*. They are sufficiently different that we can do an entire book on that topic alone.

In simple terms, *information systems* are what most people use when they buy a computer to do their accounting, email correspondence, and online banking. These computer programs take data in and send it out, which is why they are information systems.

On the other hand, control systems are software systems that operate machinery with parts that move, where the computer controls their movement.

The software that operates robotics in a manufacturing plant, flies and guides a missile, operates a modern beverage dispenser, or controls the myriad flaps on a B2-bomber are all control systems. They utilize different sensors that process data streams that help operate the moving parts.

Although *information systems* and *control systems* are examples of different computing paradigms, they are both supported with conventional computing components that are fully deterministic.

In contrast, *quantum computers* are not deterministic, but they are also not random.

A conventional computer is necessary to help manage them and give them their formulas and data. Without conventional computers, programming and running a *quantum computer* is not practical.

The *quantum computing* part is particularly good at solving particular mathematical problems in mere seconds or minutes that would otherwise take the most robust information system computers potentially hundreds or millions of years to solve.

Information system computers can do any computational task, but there is a class of tasks that take far too long for us to wait around to get an answer. In mathematics, these problems are *NP-complete* problems, where NP stands for 'Non-deterministic Polynomial-time,' which laymen often refer to as 'Not Possible to Complete.'

NP-complete problems have two types, specifically those that are NP-hard and those that are not. But whether a problem is *NP-hard* only refers to checking whether the answer is correct.

NP-hard refers to the fact that it can take a *conventional computer* a long time to confirm that an answer given by the *quantum computer* is correct. Problems not NP-hard can be confirmed in a reasonable amount of time using a *conventional computer.*

Another essential difference between conventional and quantum computers is the data units. The units of data form the foundation of a computer's internals.

The smallest information units in a classic computer are called bits, which can only have one of two values. For bits, the possible values can be either '0' or '1', sometimes thought of as on and off or true and false.

In contrast, the tiniest information units in a quantum computer are qubits. Each qubit can have one of four values. For qubits, the possible values can be '-1-1', '+1+1', '-1+1', and '+1-1'.

NP-complete problems are *NP-complete* because there are so many possible values or combinations of values for each variable in the formula to be solved.

One exciting aspect of an NP-complete problem is that, mathematically, only one value for each variable determines an optimal result. Identifying the ideal combination of values is challenging, as the number of wrong combinations of answers can approach infinity.

In contrast, a *quantum computer* can identify the few near-optimal combinations of values or the only combination of values that represents the only optimal answer, typically in under a minute. The period of computation is called the annealing process.

However, unlike a *conventional computer*, the answer you get could be near optimal or the optimal answer, as perhaps the oddest thing about *quantum computing* is you can get and often do get different answers to the same question.

Two features of quantum computing are most interesting.

First, one cannot look at the answer and then let it continue processing. Once you look at the answer, you have irrevocably disrupted the process, and then you must start all over again at the beginning. In physics, this feature is called the observer effect.

The second unexpected feature is that in any given iteration of the annealing process, that yields a result having only a probability of being the one optimal solution.

The determining factor of this probability is simply that the annealing process may not have had sufficient time to determine the optimal answer. In other words, it didn't have enough time to achieve the lowest energy state possible to optimize the variables' values in the formula.

The remedy to this factor is to perform the annealing process three or four times. If the process yields the same result, that answer is considered optimal.

If the result differs, we must perform the calculation again with additional time allocated for the annealing process, perhaps just another five or ten seconds.

When you get the same result a few consecutive times, one may conclude that the quantum computer has had sufficient time to determine the optimal answer.

Another way to look at the quantum probabilistic effect versus a random approach is to consider the odds of pulling the same card out of a million decks shuffled together into one deck.

> *If pulling the optimal card once had a probability of one in fifty-two-trillion-trillion, then the probability of doing that three times in succession is one in fifty-two-trillion-trillion times fifty-two-trillion-trillion times fifty-two-trillion-trillion.*

It is now apparent that quantum physics and quantum computing are not hard determinism, hard indeterminism, soft determinism, or soft indeterminism.

Instead, quantum computing lives outside the frame of the argument against *free will*, as it is something that we will call *Q-Soft probabilistic*, which is a probability that changes over time.

Unlike current quantum computer systems, neurons and *neuroglia* do not operate at temperatures of 20 mK with elaborate thermal insulation and electromagnetic shielding.

Even so, the tiny components comprising cytoskeletal structures of eukaryotic cells appear to support twenty-four levels of consciousness that live outside the frame of *hard determinism*, *hard indeterminism*, *soft determinism*, and *soft indeterminism*.

NEUROSCIENCE ADVANCEMENTS

The science of *consciousness* and *free will* has been undergoing a renaissance.

This renaissance is mainly due to the much-needed re-interpretation of results that neuroscientists had incorrectly generated, such as experiments conducted by Benjamin Libet (University of California, San Francisco, 1983).

> *Ironically, these experiments won the Virtual Nobel Prize in Psychology from the University of Klagenfurt, Austria, which claimed that the brain's 'readiness potential' is scientific proof that neurons determine the outcome of a decision before the individual is conscious of their decisions, thereby demonstrating that free will is simply an illusion.*

Many academics with doctorates still hold fast to the findings of Libet as the smoking gun form of proof that *free will* does not exist.

Luckily, there are still scientists who stay abreast of new findings and create waves of thinking in several new directions supporting *free will*.

To paraphrase Prof Peter Ulric Tse, Ph.D. in his 2014 interview on the *Big Questions in the Free Will Project*:

> *The Libet experiment of the early 1980s claimed that an electrical impulse called the 'readiness potential' preceded conscious decision by about one and a half seconds, such as whether to move a finger.*

> *Many neuroscientists interpreted this as evidence that decisions occur before conscious awareness, providing neurological proof that free will is merely an illusion.*

Thirty years after Libet, the Big Questions in Free Will Project (2014)', a collaboration of leading scientists interested in the question of consciousness and 'free will,' was able to determine largely what the 'readiness potential' is and is not.

A central figure in the 'Big Questions in Free Will Project,' Professor Peter Tse, suggests that conclusions dismissing the existence of 'free will' were premature since no one even knows what the 'readiness potential' really is, so his team at Dartmouth College conducted a series of experiments involving different use cases designed to dissect it carefully.

Use Case 1: This use case involved a decision with no motor act. You get a readiness potential despite the internal decision in this use case.

Use Case 2: This use case involved a movement when cueing the subject to perform a motor act. In this use case, there was no readiness potential.

Use Case 3: This use case involved a movement without conscious willingness, where the subject was programmed to perform a motor act using a post-hypnotic suggestion. In this use case, you get a readiness potential even though the decision was not conscious.

Use Case 4: This use case involved a test to determine if the readiness potential had anything to do with the onset of conscious willingness using an experiment initially designed by Haggard and Eimer by measuring temporal relationships between the moments of readiness potential and awareness. The results at Dartmouth refuted the earlier Haggard and Eimer results.

The conclusion was that the 'readiness potential' is not causal to the willingness to move and is largely irrelevant to the questions regarding consciousness and 'free will.'

Instead, according to Professor Peter Tse, the readiness potential seems more related to an expected event, and it is not related to a conscious decision or act as a significant number of neuroscientists and their followers had prematurely claimed it was.

[Big Questions in Free Will Project (2014) – Peter Tse, Prof Peter Ulric Tse, Ph.D. – Professor of Cognitive Neuroscience, Department of Psychological and Brain Sciences, Dartmouth College, Ph.D. Experimental Psychology Harvard University (1998), https://www. closertotruth.com/interviews/49855]

Thus, the eagerness of many neuroscientists to possess a hardware bias and a bias for *hard determinism* led to the misinterpretation of these experiments for thirty-plus years. Forty years later, opponents of *free will* remain trapped by a poor interpretation of a single series of highly published award-winning experiments. The bigger problem was that many scientists were more than happy to accept that *free will* is nonexistent.

Perhaps The Buddha would have cautioned the scientific community on the philosophical flaws of The Libet Experiments to suggest more reflection before jumping to conclusions about such profound implications.

OVERCOMING HARDWARE BIAS (CONSCIOUSNESS AND FREE WILL)

Before we get to a method of developing artificial consciousness in a later section, one of several topics we need to address is hardware bias.

Automating consciousness has been written about in many science fiction novels and attempted at numerous universities and laboratories in one way or another. Prior efforts to automate consciousness failed because consciousness remained largely undefined.

Yogi Berra was quoted to say, "If you don't know where you are going, you'll end up someplace else." [Yogi Berra]

One attempt was a hardware design involving the equivalent of a hundred billion neurons with tens of trillions of synapses to imitate the brain of *Homo sapiens.*

The thought was that a mass of neuron-like components would figure out how to learn. One problem with this hardware design was that it implied that millions of years of evolution generated a uniform meatloaf of neurons that somehow figured out how to learn and collaborate independently.

Thankfully, thought leaders in artificial intelligence are shifting their focus away from hardware, and now software engineers are focusing on *consciousness* and *free will.*

However, the timeless words of Yogi Berra happened to ring true again.

In Part I, we mentioned the need for a diverse skill set of individuals, including over a dozen disciplines, such as philosophy, psychology, protozoology, and entomology.

Then we mentioned, as Jim Collins advises in his books and seminars, that it is crucial to get the right people on the bus and equally essential to get the wrong people off the bus, keeping only the individuals interested in going on the journey with their fellow passengers. Quote.

"If we get the right people on the bus, the right people in the right seats, and the wrong people off the bus, then we'll figure out how to take it someplace great." End Quote. Jim Collins

For example, with guidance from the right philosophers, one can travel around the biases and mind traps that divert us from our path.

Aside from avoiding biases that naturally occur even among scientific minds, philosophers can provide helpful input regarding perspectives of consciousness, much like science fiction writers have influenced contemporary scientists and inventors.

History is replete with science fiction writers dreaming up unique ideas that capture the imagination of readers while the next generation of scientists turn those dreams into reality.

This analogy is not to say that Buddhist or other philosophers are no more than the conceptual equivalent of science fiction writers, though they require similar talents.

Philosophers conceive of complex ideas and determine how they operate within a consistent framework of predictable causal conditions and logical reasoning, with similar theoretical rigor found among our best science fiction writers.

Science fiction writers conceive of believable futuristic worlds that must be consistent with the laws of physics and theoretical science to remain plausible.

In software engineering, enterprise architects determine a logical framework of components, referred to as a reference architecture, that acts as a plausible future state.

It is then the job of the solution architect to determine the physical solution, choosing specific brands that are ideal to meet the project's objectives.

> *Together, the enterprise and solution architects are like the Army Corp of Engineers with plans and know-how to solve current and anticipated challenges for the army.*

> *One of the most significant competitive advantages of the Mongol Army was its engineers, who knew how to rapidly move equipment to build shelters, ladders, pontoons, and catapults.*

> *It is the job of enterprise architecture to think ahead, anticipate, and prepare for the organization's ever-evolving needs.*

Organizations with a robust enterprise architecture and solution architecture organization lead to better-managed technology costs, leveraging a body of highly skilled personnel in pertinent technologies to best equip the organization with the tools needed to rapidly and efficiently accomplish the direction of the business.

> *The advantages that result are like those offered by the engineering corps of the Mongol Army, rendering unstoppable armies of the Mongol Empire of the 13th and 14th Centuries, which established the largest contiguous land empire in history, with the second largest landmass after the British Empire.*

The engineering corps of the Mongol Army had adopted the best combination of light armor and light weaponry, with the skills to manufacture various materials from the timber of local terrain.

Additional success factors included a rapid long-range mail system that outperformed the Pony Express 600 years later and numerous advancements in science and mathematics.

The overall objective of these specialized units is to be more prepared than your competition for every eventuality your side is most likely to face.

The limitations that the Army Corps of Engineers and the engineering corps of the Mongol Army had to deal with were the availability of materials, the laws of physics, and their imaginations.

In contrast, the world of the software expert is rooted in the world of ideas and imagination with comparatively modest constraints imposed by the laws of physics.

To illustrate the vast difference between disciplines bound by hardware and the laws of physics versus software and the imagination, consider the following.

The best television hardware alone can neither create an episode of 'I Love Lucy' nor 'Game of Thrones.' It streams the content into the hardware as data encoded in analog or digital signals embodying the story and drama of the programs we experience.

In contrast, the story's genius and storytelling are as boundless as the human imagination.

Hence, generating consciousness by imitating hundreds of billions of neurons with tens of trillions of hardware synapses is like developing a futuristic holographic television and then waiting for the television to develop the stories and how to tell them.

That does not mean that we can dispense with hardware experts.

On the contrary, we need various experts who collaborate well as a team. To create and view an episode of 'I Love Lucy' on television, we need hardware and software engineers, broadcasters, writers, performers, directors, producers, a set crew, financiers, managers, and more.

To make this pertinent to consciousness, let's consider a software capability that is an integral part of all levels of consciousness and likely to be a core capability of cytoskeletal structures.

OVERCOMING A SOFTWARE BIAS (NEURAL NETWORKS)

One discipline in artificial intelligence is something called *neural networks*.

There are many books and articles written about neural networks. It is a discipline that is highly mathematical and primarily rooted in mathematics. It even has a specialized language to express ideas and concepts.

> *For example, 'semantic case frame instantiation' is a term unique to neural networks, though at its core, that phrase means moving data into a record.*

First developed in the 1950s, by the 1970s, *neural networks* brought a new level of speed and accuracy to the credit approval process at the well-known credit card company American Express, propelling it into dominance.

> *The concept is as follows.*
>
> *A neural network is a class of technology that can learn and recognize visual images and categorize them. Hence, you can teach this technology to recognize the letter 'A' (e.g., lower case, upper case, printed, script, calligraphy, different fonts, sizes, and orientations).*
>
> *After it has sufficiently learned, you now show it letters to recognize and categorize. In this simple example, you want the neural net to recognize when the letter presented is some form of the letter 'A' and not the letter 'A.'*

Now, let's suppose you are in the credit card business.

Over some years of manually processing credit card applications, you've accumulated a lot of data about which people were reasonable credit risks and those who were not.

Your existing credit approval process requires a large staff to review credit card applications to assess them for creditworthiness. Applications are studied individually for a person to decide which applications to approve for credit and for how much.

The credit approval process (aka underwriting) is inconsistent as each person performs the evaluation somewhat differently than the next. Hence, another may approve an application that one person might decline, and the approved credit limit amounts will likely vary significantly.

Armed with your new neural network, you first convert your historical credit card applications to visual images dependent upon the application's data values.

Your next step is to let your neural network learn the images of credit card applications for the customers that ended up being reasonable credit risks and to learn the images of applications that ended up as bad credit risks.

At this point, one computerized employee can process a new credit card application with unsurpassed accuracy in a fraction of a second with total consistency.

As such, neural networks are great at recognizing and categorizing visual images with many variations. Even though it is rare for any two images to be completely identical, the neural network can determine what it most closely resembles.

For our purposes involving image recognition, does the image most resemble the image of a cat, or does it more closely resemble a stuffed animal toy that looks like a cat or a small dog the size of a cat?

The most important feature is that *neural networks* can learn. They learn from their initial learning set and can continue learning as new information becomes available.

Since neural networks learn and make decisions using what they have learned, could this mean that neural networks demonstrate *consciousness* or *free will*?

THE MODERN LEARNING THERMOSTAT

Recall our thought experiment regarding a thermostat. But now, let's say we equip it with a *neural network*, thereby rendering it the *Modern Learning Thermostat*.

Previously, we stated that "there are no examples of thermostats demonstrating the ability to choose a reaction based upon its prior experience of awareness."

What if equipping our new model thermostat with a *neural network* allows it to demonstrate the ability to choose a reaction based on its prior experience of awareness?

But can our *Modern Learning Thermostat* also demonstrate the ability to choose otherwise?

Categorically, the answer is no.

Our *Modern Learning Thermostat* enhanced with the *neural network* cannot demonstrate the ability to choose otherwise. It will make the same choice every time unless its learning set is updated, making the modern learning thermostat choose mechanically in a new way.

In contrast, organisms, whether equipped with different or identical genes, can choose otherwise, regardless of what they have learned.

If we implemented a million identical neural network computers in American Express, used the same imaging process, and provided them the same learning set and credit card applications to process, they would make identical decisions across one million neural network computers.

As a result, one would have to conclude either that all one million neural network computers could choose otherwise and all did so in unison or, the more reasonable interpretation, that they could not choose otherwise.

As a result, our *Modern Learning Thermostat* equipped with neural networks fails to demonstrate any of the twenty-four forms of *consciousness* in our framework. And since all forms of freedom, including *free will*, are entirely dependent upon *consciousness*, *neural networks* do not help facilitate the emergence of *free will*.

Yet, as we will eventually see, *neural networks* are essential for supporting *consciousness*.

DEFINING FREEDOMS

Not all conscious organisms are alike. One conscious organism can have significantly different degrees of freedom than another. But even though the degrees of freedom may differ, the common element among them is the ability to choose and the ability to choose otherwise.

An organism's choice may involve the freedom to choose one's focus of attention, volition, action, emotion, mental state, thought, or paradigm.

As we have seen, each level of *consciousness* supports an ability to support one or more freedoms and to different degrees. Few *Homo sapiens* possess all twenty-four levels of consciousness, though the potential exists.

Of the seven freedoms supported by various levels of *consciousness*, most *Homo sapiens* only exercise three: *freedom of attention, freedom of will,* and *freedom of action.*

The seven forms of freedom exhibit various dependencies.

- *Freedom of attention* is a foundational freedom upon which all others depend.

- *Freedom of will* is the second level upon which the remaining freedoms depend.

- *Freedom of action* is the third level of freedom upon which the remaining freedoms depend.

- *Freedom of emotion* is the fourth level upon which the remaining freedoms do not depend.

- *Freedom of mind* is the fifth level upon which the remaining freedoms do not depend.

- *Freedom of thought* is the sixth level upon which the remaining freedom do not depends.

- *Freedom of paradigm* is the seventh level of freedom, influencing all other freedoms though without their dependency.

FREEDOM OF ATTENTION

Freedom of attention is the ability to have the focus one wants without constraint from an external source, with the ability to choose otherwise. Also, *freedom of attention* is a primary freedom, the only one that all other forms depend on.

Scientists disagree on the definition of attention or focus across different disciplines of expertise. In the context of our framework, however, attention has two significant elements.

First, there is always a constant flow of stimuli. Single-cell organisms receive stimuli from sensory organelles. In more advanced organisms, segments of stimuli are bubbled up to the conscious mind when they have a sufficient level of importance. In doing so, these stimuli can easily distract the conscious mind with any number of these stimuli as they stream up to the conscious level.

Secondly, competing with the streaming flow of stimuli is the focus that the conscious level currently has or currently wants.

In *Homo sapiens*, the practice of prayer and or meditation can help strengthen an individual's ability to exert their freedom of choice in selecting the segments of stimuli upon which to focus one's attention. In this sense, these practices influence what one wants as one's focus of attention.

Depending upon one's awareness of their conscious focus, the conscious level may become aware that their mind became distracted so that they can reapply their focus to the stimuli the individual wants.

Depending upon one's strength of conscious focus, the conscious level may be able to maintain a particular focus for extended periods before becoming distracted by a stream of stimuli constantly bubbling up.

> *As mentioned, Meditative Consciousness is a practice with which one may learn to become aware of one's attention and its natural drift. The devout meditation practitioner can also become skilled at returning and eventually retaining the focus of their attention for increasingly prolonged durations.*

How *attention* is studied scientifically depends upon the scientific discipline, such as psychology, neuroscience, or cognitive science.

One method of attaining perspective on attention is to start in a place where stimuli originate from various sources. It is like focusing on a particular conversation among many ongoing conversations within earshot or on a particular object within a field of vision.

In this case, it is from the perspective of focusing on one's internal thoughts while oblivious to the many other stimuli one may hear, see, or feel.

> *If one listens to several conversations simultaneously, then one's attention is divided as opposed to being focused on choosing just one. Similarly, the meditation practitioner may focus on several simultaneous or single stimuli.*

> *Either way, it is their conscious decision where to apply their attention.*

Controlling one's attention is mainly about determining the level of importance of what one wants. Choosing to focus gives a higher level of importance to the stimuli that are most desirable to travel up from the subconscious level. In this way, the conscious level is countermanding the subconscious level, at least temporarily, potentially retraining the subconscious level to some degree to focus itself.

Several factors can influence the subconscious, such as mental state, emotions, persona, and paradigm. In this way, several levels of consciousness can collaborate to influence the focus one wants.

FREEDOM OF WILL

Freedom of will is the ability to have the volition one wants without constraint from an external source, again, with the ability to choose otherwise. *Freedom of will* is a secondary freedom upon which all remaining forms depend.

Volition is a cognitive process by which an individual chooses a particular action or inaction. When an individual has the volition one wants, they are said to be making up their mind.

In *Homo sapiens,* stimuli bubbling up from the subconscious level are utilized based upon one's current focus of attention, persona, values, mental state, emotions, paradigm, thoughts, immediate, short, or long-term interests, and the volitions one wants.

However, they may also be determined by what one wants independent of the thoughts or stimuli bubbled up from the subconscious.

But first, let's differentiate the idea of 'volition' and 'motivation.'

> *Motivations are distinct from volitions in that motivations are desires below the threshold that would make it a volition. Although motivations may drive toward a particular volition, they can be overridden or embraced.*

The point at which an individual chooses to exercise their will is when what was one or more motivations previously becomes a volition that may or may not align with one's motivations.

However, conflicting motivations can also exist aside from the potential absence of motivations.

To have the volition one wants, one must focus one's attention on the volition, and one must be able to assess the volition as something they either want or do not want with an ability to choose otherwise.

FREEDOM OF ACTION

Freedom of action is the ability to enact a volition without external constraints that would allow it to do so.

One's *freedom of action* depends upon one's *freedom of attention* to focus on enacting the volition one wants and *freedom of will* to have the volition one wants with the ability to choose otherwise.

Therefore, *freedom of action* is a tertiary form of freedom dependent upon both *freedom of attention* and *freedom of will*, but upon which all remaining freedoms depend.

Freedom of action is distinct from all other freedoms in that it is the only one entirely dependent upon external factors. While we might generally think of external factors as things that inhibit physical movement, they can also be software-based, such as a computer program (possibly in a computer chip) under the control of another agent that artificially inhibits the ability to enact the volition one wants. The program-based constraint creates a theoretical dependency on the four remaining freedoms of emotion, mind, thought, and paradigm.

Individuals with *freedom of will* may choose to have volition, such as departing from a particular room. However, a physical limitation would be if the individual chooses to enact the volition to leave the room and the doors cannot be opened to exit the room, then the individual lacks *freedom of action*.

If, however, the individual chooses to enact the volition to remain in the room, then whether the doors are locked or unlocked is immaterial. In this circumstance, the individual successfully exercised their *freedom of action*.

Therefore, to say an individual acted freely is to say they could carry out the volition they chose to enact.

Philosophers often ask, "If the individual chose as their volition to stay in a room whose doors were locked, was the individual able to exercise freedom of action?"

The answer is yes.

The fact is that the locked doors interfered neither with the individual's freedom of will nor action.

However, does such an individual freely choose otherwise?

The answer is yes.

The individual had the 'freedom of will' to choose. Otherwise, they lacked the freedom of action to exercise that choice if chosen.

If the individual chose freely to remain in the room, the fact that they could not leave the room did not affect their freedom of action in their choosing to remain in the room.

In summary, *freedom of action* is the ability to enact the volition one wants without restraint from an external source, with an ability to freely choose otherwise, though not necessarily with an ability to enact otherwise. It is irrespective of whether the individual had foreknowledge of the ability or inability to enact otherwise.

FREEDOM OF EMOTION

Freedom of emotion is to have the emotion one wants with the ability to choose otherwise freely.

One's *freedom of emotion* depends upon one's *freedom of attention* to focus on enacting the volition one wants, *freedom of will* to have the volition one wants, and *freedom of action* to enact the emotion one wants with an ability to choose otherwise.

Therefore, *freedom of emotion* and the remaining forms of freedom are quaternary forms dependent upon *freedom of attention, freedom of will, and freedom of action.*

The definition of *freedom of emotion* is less discussed and debated among scientists, though it represents an essential level of advancement among meditation practitioners.

Within our framework, *freedom of emotion* represents an awareness of one's emotions and the volition to want and have the emotion one wants.

Emotions operate at least at two levels of consciousness: the *Subconscious Consciousness* and *Conscious Consciousness*.

Within *Conscious Consciousness,* emotions are distinct conscious experiences that are perceived consciously. Experiences result from releasing a combination of hormones, neurotransmitters, ions, and other chemical messengers that render the psychological experiences among the *neuroglia* associated with our conscious experience, which we know as feelings and emotions.

Within *Subconscious Consciousness,* emotions influence motivations as a shortcut to circumvent *Reason-Driven Consciousness.* They result from a combination of hormones, neurotransmitters, ions, and other chemical messengers but operate subconsciously to influence what is vital to bubble up to the conscious level.

The accomplished meditation practitioner can only catch the subconscious emotions when they bubble up to the conscious level. Before that, an alert individual would have to catch themselves by detecting and questioning the physical responses they feel before being aware of an emotion.

Most animals advanced beyond neural bundles appear to have basic emotions, which become more advanced with brain advancements. Emotional awareness of one's own emotions only appears to occur in primates.

However, the ability to choose and have the emotion one wants appears only in *Homo sapiens* and rarely, as it requires considerable practice and discipline to develop. It is necessary to gain some degree of control over the release of hormones in one's body, or one must be able to override the experience that stems from the release of hormones. I have not located the results of experimentation to determine which it is.

Either way, having the emotions one wants is an advanced capability with linkages between one's mental state and paradigm, namely *freedom of mind* and *freedom of paradigm.*

The expert meditation practitioner may be capable of having the emotions one wants potentially at both the subconscious and conscious levels.

> *Buddhist Consciousness, or thought-free wakefulness, may be capable of potentially having the emotions one wants at both the conscious and subconscious levels.*

> *It is only possible at a subconscious level because, with practice, it is possible to influence one's subconscious through techniques such as meditation.*

At a basic level, one may alter their emotions to that of their choosing by thinking thoughts that generate the emotions one wants. In this sense, one may leverage *freedom of thought* and *paradigm* as an indirect alternative to have the emotions one wants.

FREEDOM OF MIND

Freedom of mind is to have the mental state one wants with the ability to choose otherwise freely.

Within our framework, a mental state is one's conglomeration of mental attitudes that influence how an individual interprets experiences and memories from within their paradigm. Often, an individual will have a mental state that reflects one's most recent experience.

For example, cutting someone off in traffic and giving them the bird will often shift the targeted individual into a mental state of angry outrage, elevating one's disagreeable or unfavorable attitude.

In contrast, stopping to extend someone the courtesy of safely merging into traffic may shift the subject into a mental state of gratitude that promotes good feelings, elevating one's agreeable or favorable attitude.

A mental state is primarily a psychological construct comprised of shared assumptions about reality that influence one's framework of attitudes that influence the interpretation of experiences and memories.

As such, mental states are often associated with emotions, cognitions, or perceptions that act as a filter that can either restrain or liberate how an individual interprets their experiences and memories.

Like *freedom of emotion*, one may alter their mental state to that of their choosing by thinking thoughts that generate the mental state one wants. In this sense, using *freedom of thought* and *paradigm* are indirect alternatives to create the mental state one wants, with the ability to choose otherwise.

FREEDOM OF THOUGHT

Freedom of thought is the ability to have the thought one wants without constraints from an external source, with the ability to choose otherwise.

The definition of *freedom of thought* involves the ability to have the thought one wants, which begins with having the ability to choose the thought one wants from a set of candidate thoughts, though ultimately, it also involves the ability to formulate original thoughts that one wants to formulate.

While it may be possible to attempt to interfere with an individual's freedom to have the thoughts they want, technically, there are neither external restrictions nor external limitations on what thoughts an individual can formulate.

However, internal restrictions can be rampant as one's paradigms can severely restrict thoughts. Paradigms also determine the interpretation of stimuli affecting one's perception of reality, also affecting thoughts.

Since our paradigms are the framework within which we interpret all stimuli and attribute meaning, it makes them the most powerful of all aspects of consciousness.

Although *one's paradigms constrain freedom of thought, freedom of thought* can occur within one's paradigm, within the limitations of one's paradigms. For this reason, *freedom of thought* cannot reach its full potential until achieving *freedom of paradigm*.

Recall that most individuals have one paradigm, and individuals who can support more than one paradigm tend to employ their dominant paradigm.

In summary, *freedom of thought* is having the thought one wants without constraints from an external source and the ability to choose otherwise. While it may be true that many new thoughts are variations on the theme of prior thoughts, one can generate a new expanse of thoughts with careful selection or creation of one's paradigms.

FREEDOM OF PARADIGM

Freedom of paradigm is the ability to have the paradigm one wants without restraint from an external source, with the ability to choose otherwise. However, the ability to have the paradigm one wants requires that one has more than one paradigm from which to choose. As a result, this freedom is only available to individuals who have achieved either *Level Two Paradigmatic Consciousness* or *Level Three Paradigmatic Consciousness*.

Although the *Level Two* individual may have two or three paradigms to choose from, it does not mean that those fewer paradigms are any less valid or invalid or any more or less productive than the multitude of paradigms perceived by a *Level Three* individual.

> *As such, one's ability to exercise the freedom to choose is the same whether they have a choice between one door or hundreds. The possible choices may differ, but whether they choose not to pass through a door or a particular one requires the same freedom.*

In comparison, a *Level One* individual would not perceive the possibility of a choice as they cannot see any doors. When it comes to paradigms, they walk the path they are on, making choices about the things they can perceive, having no choice of paradigms.

Recall that as *Level Ones*, whenever we encounter conflicting stimuli, we typically filter it out or reject the conflicting information. We will be less likely to integrate the new information into our existing paradigm by correcting our original one. We work hard to hold steadfast to our beliefs.

If correcting our original paradigm turns out to be overly challenging, we will likely attempt to compartmentalize the conflicting information away from that information with which it conflicts and potentially not even recall having done so.

When these measures fail to resolve conflicting stimuli as a final measure, we may switch paradigms to one where the conflict does not exist while not recalling having done so. Oddly, if someone observes and questions this, the *Level One* individual will remember neither doing so nor the difference of their prior paradigm.

Interestingly, the intent of denials is not to be deceptive but results from the new paradigm being unaware of the prior one. The *Level One* individual lacks the tools to reconcile paradigms they cannot simultaneously perceive.

Therefore, when a *Level One* individual shifts from one paradigm to another, it is not a conscious choice. When the previous paradigm ceases to exist, the interpretations associated with it also cease to exist.

> *To a Level One individual, it is like an invisible door where the door and everything beyond it are invisible no matter what side of the door they are on. If they happen to pass through the door, the prior room ceases to exist.*

> *In contrast, a Level Two sees the door and everything beyond it. If they happen to pass through the door, both rooms remain in existence.*

> *The Level Three individual sees the door and themselves in both rooms, viewing everything in each room, simultaneously experiencing both versions of themselves and the version of themselves watching over themselves from above.*

> *There is no reason to pass through the door because they are already on the other side.*

In summary, *freedom of paradigm* is to have the paradigm one wants without any restraint from an external source. When faced with a choice, and depending on the circumstances, the *productive Level Two* is likelier to choose the most constructive paradigm. In contrast, the *egocentric Level Two* is likelier to choose the paradigm that personally benefits them. However, both are equally free to choose either paradigm they perceive.

LEVELS OF CONSCIOUSNESS AND THEIR FREEDOMS

Let us now inspect each of the twenty-four levels of consciousness that form our foundation of consciousness to determine which levels of consciousness have which type of freedom and the degree to which they do.

UNICELLULAR CONSCIOUSNESS AND FREEDOM

In *Unicellular Consciousness, Paramecia* exhibited behavior demonstrating an ability to detect stimuli, assess, and react to them.

We also learned that not all *Paramecia* react the same way each time.

Why is this important?

One of the essential criteria in thought experiments about *free will* is the ability to exercise an ability to choose otherwise.

If an individual does not possess the ability to choose otherwise, then the individual is acting mechanically like a ball rolling downhill without the ability to do otherwise. It would be like the pachinko machine.

Since we have not figured out how to communicate with *Paramecium*, we have no way of asking an individual *Paramecium* what their intentions were. However, we can observe their *freedom of will* and *action* when they choose a direction to move, and we can only infer their freedoms based on these observations.

It is reasonable to assert that each *Paramecium* could choose other than the action they chose, as sometimes the same individual chose otherwise and enacted a different volition when presented with the same stimuli. Therefore, regardless of their choice, each Paramecium demonstrated that they could choose otherwise under identical circumstances.

We are now prepared to discuss the individual freedoms that *Paramecia* may possess.

Freedom of attention, having the focus one wants, requires a level of consciousness that allows an organism to focus on the stimuli it wants, with the ability to choose otherwise.

Freedom of attention in unicellular organisms may either require an organism to have more than one sensory component for it to choose which to give its attention to or the ability to process more than one source of stimuli from the same sensory component such that it could demonstrate an ability to choose one to focus its attention on over the other.

We know that advanced organisms can discern a specific set of stimuli from a single sensory organ receiving stimuli originating from a myriad of items in its field of awareness, such as the mammalian eye that communicates an array of stimuli from potentially many objects that occupy its field of vision.

While we know that *Paramecium* has multiple sensory organs, the point is that there is an apparent lack of published scientific studies on whether an individual sensory organ of *Paramecium* can support *freedom of attention*.

While it is difficult to determine with any certainty whether *Paramecium* can deal with a choice of focusing on two or more competing stimuli without the proper experimentation, let us turn to a simple thought experiment and then attempt to evaluate it against our framework of consciousness.

> *Recall that a thought experiment is an intellectual exercise using only one's imagination to evaluate or determine the potential real-world consequences of a circumstance or event.*

Let's begin by imagining a circumstance where a *Paramecium* receives simultaneous stimuli for two events that would generate opposite responses, such as physically moving in two different directions, one generating a response towards and away from a particular location.

Going into our thought experiment, we already know from scientific experiments that *Paramecium* possesses both *freedom of will* and *freedom of action* in that it may choose a volition and enact the volition while also having the ability to do otherwise.

A thought experiment:

A Paramecium in search of nutrition receives stimuli indicating the presence of food, and from the same direction, the Paramecium receives additional stimuli indicating the presence of a predator.

We already know that Paramecia are attracted to nutrition and away from predators.

Suppose repeated experimentation demonstrated that all of the Paramecium retreated away from nutrition. In that case, we might conclude that the attention of the Paramecium could only become focused on the predator, indicating that it lacks freedom of attention.

Suppose repeated experimentation demonstrated that all Paramecium moved towards nutrition. In that case, we might conclude that the attention of the Paramecium could only become focused on the food, indicating that it lacks freedom of attention.

If, however, repeated experimentation demonstrated that a portion of Paramecium retreated away from the predator and a portion toward the nutrition, we can conclude that the attention of the Paramecium was free to focus on either or both nutrition and predator.

However, if some Paramecium chose to move neither toward nor away from the source of the stimuli, then we might conclude that Paramecium could not focus on either. But given that other Paramecia demonstrated freedom of attention, there is no good reason to conclude that some Paramecia lacked freedom of attention.

Therefore, it is reasonable to conclude that the ones that moved in neither direction chose a volition to remain motionless.

In contrast, if in repeated experiments, random populations of Paramecia move towards, away, and lay motionless, we might conclude that the attention of the Paramecia became neither focused on the predator nor nutrition or that the responses were purely random.

It turns out that *Paramecium* studies also consider the velocities with which an organism can move, including the velocity of its predators and its prey. One fact seems apparent: the ability of *Paramecium* to demonstrate the focus one wants is present.

In contrast, when we consider *freedom of attention* in *Homo sapiens*, we are at a level of consciousness that involves supporting functions performed by the *unconscious* and *subconscious*.

One reason we focus on the *conscious* level within individuals as a separate capability is that individuals' unconscious and subconscious levels are present to support the incredible volume of incoming stimuli from across the entire organism with their distinct capabilities. The assertion is that consciousness occurs before an *unconscious* and *subconscious* mind emerges.

Even though the *unconscious* and *subconscious* mind is in a support role for *consciousness*, they may also support *freedom of attention*. To provide that support, they rely upon '*importance determination.*'

>*Though related conceptually, freedom of attention and importance determination are not identical.*

Within the unconscious and subconscious, *importance determination* determines which stimuli should bubble up to the next level, making it available to the *conscious* level for *freedom of attention* to operate again at the conscious level. However, we will discuss '*importance determination*' in more detail later.

Simple organisms have only a *conscious* level but must also rely on '*importance determination.*'

Since a *Paramecium* lacks neurons and *neuroglia*, the cell's cytoskeletal structures support '*importance determination*' with its other intellectual functions.

In summary, *Unicellular Consciousness,* as represented by *Paramecium,* demonstrates *freedom of attention* in that it demonstrates the ability to have the focus one wants in that it may choose to focus on either nutrition or predators with the ability to choose otherwise.

In contrast, *freedom of will,* having the volition one wants, requires evidence that an agent can freely choose a volition without external influence and can choose a different volition if one wants.

Paramecium demonstrates *freedom of will* in the experiments cited within the section on *Unicellular Consciousness* by ultimately choosing a direction in which to move while also demonstrating that these organisms could have chosen otherwise.

Since movements of the organism represent the only observable feature that our level of science can detect and measure, we are relying upon the combination of the organism's *freedom of attention, freedom of will,* and *freedom of action,* as we are unable to detect the *will* of the organism separate from its *action.*

However, we also have complete control over the environment in which we study *Paramecium* behavior.

One of our additional discoveries from the initial section expounding upon *Unicellular Consciousness* is that we can observe that *Paramecia* have a memory where they can store and recall information. Using this memory, they demonstrate an ability to learn to modify their behaviors based on new experiences.

This realization is remarkable for several reasons.

First, this shows that single-cell eukaryotes have memory and recall, can learn, and can demonstrate the freedom to choose otherwise without the presence of neurons and *neuroglia,* utilizing only their cytoskeletal structures.

The second involves our *Modern Learning Thermostat*, which, by definition, has memory and recall and can learn, though it can never choose otherwise.

Instead, the mechanical system of a *Modern Learning Thermostat* does not permit it a free choice of what to focus on, what volition to want, or any ability to choose otherwise.

Then there is *freedom of action*.

Freedom of action, having the ability to enact the volition one wants, requires evidence that an agent can freely choose a volition and then enact that volition without external influence while maintaining an ability to choose otherwise.

Paramecia demonstrates *freedom of action* in the experiments cited within the *Unicellular Consciousness* section by choosing the volition to move at a certain rate and in a specific direction.

In further support of this statement, *Paramecia* demonstrate that they could enact the volition they want and that they could have acted otherwise.

Again, *Paramecium* demonstrates *freedom of action* where our *Modern Learning Thermostat* can neither choose the volition it wants nor choose otherwise, and it can neither choose the action it wants nor choose otherwise.

Some will say that we can add a randomizer into the *Modern Learning Thermostat* such that some percentage of the time, it will do something random.

This argument fails to recognize that during the time the randomizer was inactive, the *Modern Learning Thermostat* could not choose otherwise, and during the time the randomizer was active, the *Modern Learning Thermostat* had neither the ability to choose what it wanted nor the ability to choose otherwise as a randomizer is an external constraint.

From our discussion of hard determinism and indeterminism, this means that when the *Modern Learning Thermostat* did not employ a randomizer, it would be fully hard deterministic. When it used the randomizer, it would be fully indeterministic.

Hard determinism and indeterminism do not support freedom of choice, as everything is predetermined or random.

In summary, *Unicellular Consciousness,* as represented by *Paramecium,* demonstrates *freedom of action* in that it demonstrates the ability to enact the volition one wants with an ability to choose otherwise.

Then, we have *freedom of emotion*.

Freedom of emotion, having the emotion one wants, requires evidence that an agent can freely choose and enact that emotion, with the ability to choose a different emotion while maintaining an ability to choose otherwise.

Freedom of emotion requires more than a rudimentary ability to determine whether an experience is favorable, unfavorable, or indifferent.

The ability to support emotions occurs only after the emergence of neurons, facilitating some form of collaboration among a collection of cells.

Emotions do not appear as an observable feature until *Neural Bundle Consciousness* within the genus *Apis* (a.k.a. honeybee), or again more clearly later in the *Primitive Brain Consciousness* of *Reptilia*.

Therefore, a discussion about *freedom of emotion* will have to wait until we reach *Neural Bundle Consciousness*.

Next, we have freedom of mind.

Freedom of mind, having the mental states one wants, first requires supporting evidence that the organism has a mind and that the mind can have mental states.

Second, it requires that the organism become aware of its mental states and can choose one of them and could have chosen otherwise.

Even though the cytoskeletal structures of eukaryotic cells can support at least some of the activities performed by a mind, a mind must be far more sophisticated to attain a mental state, never mind the ability to support more than one mental state from which an individual may choose.

A mental state is a relational attitude between the agency of the organism and something within the environment.

Let's unpack this to make it more understandable.

For example, suppose someone wakens a hibernating North American Grizzly bear. In that case, the bear is likely to have a grumpy attitude, where the specific attitude is in the relation between the agency of the bear and that unlucky someone who disturbed it from its slumber.

The more scientifically advanced definition of mental state is that it also includes propositional attitudes that are relational between the agency of the organism and a thought, concept, or proposition.

Using the same example, whoever woke the bear is likely to have an attitude of panic and fear.

Having the 'mental state' one wants requires having a choice of potential mental states, choosing the mental state one wants, and then enacting the mental state one wants so that they do not attempt to run away from the bear in panic and fear.

As such, the ability to demonstrate *freedom of mind* will also have to wait until we reach *Neural Bundle Consciousness,* where mental states potentially emerge.

Last, we have *freedom of thought* and *freedom of paradigm.*

Freedom of thought is not pertinent until we reach our ninth level of consciousness, *Homo Consciousness.*

Likewise, *freedom of paradigm* is not pertinent until we reach *Paradigmatic Consciousness.*

MULTICELLULAR CONSCIOUSNESS AND FREEDOM

In *Multicellular Consciousness,* we discussed two species of multicellular organisms, *Dionea muscipula* (a.k.a. the Venus flytrap) and *Mimosa pudica* (a.k.a. the sensitive plant).

The Venus flytrap has hair-like structures called mechanosensors that send tiny electrical charges toward the leaf's midrib, causing specialized pores within the outermost layer of cells of the leaf to open. This release of ions allows water to rush from inner to outer cells, creating a change of turgor (i.e., internal cell pressure), finally flipping the lobes of the leaf to snap shut within one twenty-fifth of a second (i.e., 0.04 seconds), thereby surrounding prey of sufficient size no avenue for escape before it can react.

The leaf, having secured its prey, then releases an array of acidic digestive enzymes that dissolve soft tissues, excluding insect exoskeleton or the bones of small amphibians and rodents, to absorb nutrients, such as nitrogen, which are not available in the nutrient-poor soil that it naturally inhabits.

Although there is some collaboration among cells and cell types within the Venus flytrap, the mechanism appears to be entirely mechanical, relying upon rudimentary chemistry and physics with no ability to choose otherwise.

Dionea muscipula (a.k.a. the Venus flytrap) fails to show that it can learn or demonstrate decision-making capabilities.

At this point, we might conclude that the Venus flytrap cannot demonstrate to us as observers its ability to learn or make decisions or that it lacks any ability to learn or make decisions.

However, recall the Sensitive plant (i.e., *Mimosa pudica*). *Mimosa pudica* begins its observable activities in much the same manner as the Venus flytrap, where tactile receptors of the leaf release electrically charged ions that travel through to the base, causing cell membranes to alter their permeability.

This release of ions causes a differential of turgor due to water transit through cell membranes. These differences in turgidity cause the leaflets to fold to the leaf's stem, where they have better protection from predators.

However, we chose the Sensitive plant because it demonstrates learning in controlled experiments when plants fell from a height of 15 cm. After a few successive iterations, the plants no longer trigger the closing of their leaves.

To determine whether leaves were suppressing their leaf-folding reflex from habitual learning instead of energy exhaustion, they were re-shaken, at which point their leaves closed. Upon retesting the same plant, hours, days, weeks, and months after shows that they remembered what they had learned and did not close their leaves when the experience resembled one that was not a threat (i.e., shaking the plant).

We are now prepared to discuss the freedoms multicellular organisms may possess.

As one would expect, there are gaps in scientific experiments, particularly studies on *Mimosa pudica* that test the ability of *Mimosa pudica* to focus on one stimulus over another.

How would the plant respond if we trained individual plants to differentiate a harmless fall from a dangerous predator and then expose those plants to both stimuli?

Again, let's turn to a simple thought experiment and evaluate it against our consciousness framework.

> *Imagine we had many Mimosa pudica plants trained to differentiate a harmless fall from a leaf-eating predator's attack.*

> *At this point, each plant is now exposed simultaneously to both types of stimuli.*

> *Suppose most of the Mimosa pudica close their leaves. In that case, we might conclude that the attention of the Mimosa pudica became focused on the stimuli resembling the attacking leaf-eating predator.*

> *Suppose most times the Mimosa pudica keeps its leaves open. In that case, we might conclude that the attention of the Mimosa pudica became focused on the stimuli resembling the harmless drop of fifteen centimeters.*

> *If the response appeared random, with roughly half of the plants observed keeping their leaves open and half observed closing their leaves, we might conclude that half the plants became focused on the harmless stimuli.*

> *In contrast, the other half became focused on the stimuli of the real threat, or the plants could not discern the difference between the two types of stimuli.*

> *If, on the other hand, all plants keep their leaves open, then we might conclude that the plants focused only on the learned stimuli that were harmless, or they could not detect the stimuli of the real threat when the two stimuli coincide.*

> *However, suppose all plants close their leaves. In that case, we might conclude that the plants focused only on the stimuli of the attacker, or they could not detect the stimuli of the harmless threat when the two stimuli coincide.*

The use cases where all plants act in unison are doubtful, as they involve all plants closing or not closing their leaves. Unlike our *Modern Learning Thermostat*, any significant population of organisms with '*free will*' will demonstrate choosing otherwise.

Most *Mimosa pudica* would likely close their leaves when exposed to both types of stimuli simultaneously. However, even if the result was either the first or second use case with disparate ratios, we might tentatively conclude that *Mimosa pudica* could have the focus one wants.

Another more significant reason that would have us assume that plants could choose between two different types of stimuli is that *Paramecium* and *Mimosa pudica* are both eukaryotes that share similar cytoskeletal structures in every cell.

If new information emerges that causes us to correct this conclusion, we will certainly do so. Still, for now, it appears reasonable to assume that, like *Paramecia*, *Mimosa pudica* would also have *freedom of attention* with the ability to have the focus one wants.

Closing these experimental gaps is one of many reasons why funding for scientists and their research teams is critical.

It is also important to note that any given framework offers no value if that framework renders it impossible to either validate, invalidate, or correct it. For any framework to have value, it must be possible to invalidate it with repeatable experimentation and scientific scrutiny.

However, in the interest of full transparency and full disclosure, this framework is somewhat unique regarding its ability to be invalidated, even though applying corrections is expected and desired.

Notably, only a single example of an organism supports this framework within each level of consciousness. It assumes that many examples of organisms within each framework category cannot support the claims of that particular consciousness and the potential existence of additional examples of organisms that do support its claim.

Most theories and frameworks become invalidated upon presenting one exception. In contrast, our framework becomes validated by identifying a single instance where it is valid.

> For example, the Venus flytrap fails to validate either *freedom of will* or *freedom of action* for Multicellular Consciousness but does not invalidate it.

> On the other hand, *Mimosa pudica* (a.k.a. the sensitive plant) validates both *freedoms of will* and *freedom of action*, and potentially *freedom of attention*, for the entire category of the framework known as Multicellular Consciousness.

The framework was designed with this in mind, as there is perhaps no better approach to illustrate these concepts.

This approach certainly does not invalidate the framework, but it renders its invalidation surprisingly tricky. Recognizing this challenge, we will attempt an approach to invalidate the framework in the coming chapters.

In summary, without controlled experimentation to prove one way or another, we will conclude that *Mimosa pudica* has *freedom of attention* for the following reasons.

- It shares eukaryotic cytoskeletal structures with *Paramecia*.

- It demonstrates the ability to focus on a single stimuli type instead of ignoring it altogether.

- It demonstrates learning, which is challenging to support and explain without *freedom of attention*.

- It demonstrates *freedom of will* and *action*, which depend entirely on *freedom of attention*.

Mimosa pudica (a.k.a. the sensitive plant) demonstrates the ability to have the volition one wants in the experiments cited within the section on *Multicellular Consciousness* by recognizing the difference between threats and non-threats and then wanting and choosing to conserve its energy when stimuli associated with non-threats are perceived.

We also see that *Mimosa pudica* can learn and modify its behavior in response to stimuli, relying upon the skills required for learning, including memory.

I suppose we could attempt to argue that *freedom of will*, having the volition one wants, does not require an ability to learn, but that argument seems to fail.

However, if you can't learn or recall the same situation repeating itself, the result seems mechanical and stuck in a loop. Without a memory of the same situation, the organism seems doomed to repeat the same behavior.

Therefore, we conclude that without learning, having the volition one wants or any of the freedoms is impossible.

Instead, the question that we should raise here is what it means to have the volition one wants, with particular emphasis on using the word "wants." This problem here is more related to humans' bias with associating the trait of "wanting" to a plant.

All eukaryotic cells share similar cytoskeletal structures that support a standard set of intellectual capabilities, whether protozoans, plants, or animals.

On the other hand, a protozoan, namely *Paramecium*, is responding to avoid damage to itself by a carnivorous predator, such as *Didinium*, and has evolved to *want* to expend energy to move away from these predators.

> *Didinium is a genus of unicellular ciliates consisting of at least ten known species: free-living carnivores in freshwater, brackish water, and seawater.*

So, does *Mimosa pudica* (a.k.a. the sensitive plant) have *freedom of will,* having the volition one wants?

In the case of *Mimosa pudica*, the plant is responding to avoid damage to its leaves by a predator. Still, when it learns the subtle differences of the stimuli that do not correspond to a threat, it exercises memorization, pattern recognition, and learning.

At the multi-cellular level, *Mimosa pudica* (a.k.a. the sensitive plant) demonstrates self-interest when it conserves energy by not folding its leaves when stimuli are non-threatening.

As we can see, *freedom of attention, will,* and *action* exist at all levels of eukaryotic life. However, these freedoms facilitate self-interest, meaning eukaryotic life at every level demonstrates self-interest.

Since *Mimosa pudica* (a.k.a. the sensitive plant) demonstrates that it can learn the difference between a genuine threat and the stimuli of a non-threat and then observably chooses not to close its leaves involving stimuli of a non-threat while also demonstrating that it could do otherwise, it meets the criterion of *freedom of will,* to have the volition one wants.

The fact that *Mimosa pudica* learns to do this to protect energy reserves is not the primary issue, though there is a relationship.

One need not digress into a debate as to whether the plant sits there and reasons about ways to conserve energy or not, as the intent is not pertinent. What is pertinent, however, is that exercising *freedom of will* conveys some form of self-interest that may, or in some cases may not, enhance the organism's chances of survival.

As it happens, *Mimosa pudica* acts in its self-interest with no less clarity than *Paramecia*. The main difference is that *Paramecia* has greater freedom to exercise observable motion. In its self-interest, *Paramecia* demonstrates *freedom of attention* and *will* to either approach a source of nutrition, move away from an uncomfortable electric charge, or avoid a carnivorous predator.

The other significant factor that eliminates *Mimosa pudica* acting like a *Modern Learning Thermostat* is that it demonstrates that it could also choose otherwise.

In the experiments, each plant demonstrated that it could either fold its leaves into a closed position to protect them from damage or keep them open to preserve valuable energy stores. Their behavior is not mechanical like the *Modern Learning Thermostat,* which adheres to the laws of hard determinism.

A distinction between *Unicellular Consciousness* and *Multicellular Consciousness* is that the cytoskeletal structures of *Paramecia* operate strictly within an individual cell. In contrast, *Mimosa pudica* operates with the decisions rendered by the cytoskeletal structures across multiple cells.

When a threshold of cells decides to act to close the leaves of the plant, it is because the leaves in at least that general vicinity of collaborating cells will cause the plant to close their leaves.

Hence, when multiple cells are involved, a type of voting determines whether the cytoskeletal structures of the minimum number of individual cells create enough of a consensus to cause a wave of turgidity to close the leaves. In contrast, *Unicellular Consciousness* does not vote but acts unilaterally.

Mimosa pudica demonstrates *freedom of action* to enact the volition one wants, with the ability to do otherwise, however, in a way that is observable by humans.

Again, we have the concept that plants could 'want.' It is easy to be biased against the idea of plants wanting since plants generally are not viewed as acting in their interests. They grow or die wherever their seeds land or runners reach out.

One reason we have this misconception is that plants have cell walls in addition to cell membranes. These cell walls help provide structure and strength to plants but also act as a constraint to movement.

Unlike a cell membrane, a cell wall significantly restricts a plant's ability to demonstrate motion, never mind the roots that tether it to the ground. But does this mean that they lack the focus they want and the volition they want?

Instead, it means that they have constraints that cause them to lack the ability to enact the volitions they want, particularly when it comes to the ability to exercise physical motion.

In the experiments cited within the section on *Multicellular Consciousness,* *Mimosa pudica* demonstrated that it could enact the volition to either fold its leaves into a closed position, to reopen them after an elapse of time, or to not fold them by retaining them in the open position.

In these circumstances, no external influences were exerted on the plants, preventing the leaves from folding or reopening. As a result, the plants were free to enact the volition the plant 'wanted.' In other words, they had freedom of action in this rare circumstance.

When repeatedly presented with the same stimuli, each plant demonstrated the capability to remember and learn from past experiences, given their ability to distinguish between the vibrational stimuli generated by a predator versus those resulting when harmlessly dropped from a height of fifteen centimeters.

Regarding the ability to do otherwise, *Mimosa pudica* demonstrated that each plant could have chosen and acted otherwise.

In contrast, *the Modern Learning Thermostat,* although able to learn, cannot demonstrate any ability to do otherwise even though it also has no external influences exerted upon it to restrict its actions within its design parameters.

Yet, some will argue that the *Modern Learning Thermostat* might have both *freedom of attention* and *freedom of will,* but analogous to cell walls' effect on plants, the *Modern Learning Thermostat* lacks *freedom of action.*

To those who make that argument, if we added an ability to move in different ways, thereby rendering *freedom of action*, it would still lack any ability to do otherwise. Each *Modern Learning Thermostat* does whatever its 'hard deterministic' hardware and software tell it to do such that under identical conditions, its actions can never vary.

Next, we have *freedom of emotion*.

Emotions begin to emerge as an observable feature in *Neural Bundle Consciousness* of the genus *Apis* (a.k.a. honeybee), or more clearly in the *Primitive Brain Consciousness* of *Reptilia* and more pronounced with *Mammalian Consciousness*, *Primate Consciousness*, and *Homo Consciousness*.

Some claim the existence of emotions in multicellular organisms, such as plants. However, scientific evidence does not support the claim.

Freedom of emotion, having the emotion one wants and the ability to choose otherwise, is a significant step above simply having emotions.

In summary, we can conclude that *Mimosa pudica* and *Multicellular Consciousness* lack *freedom of emotion*.

Next, we have *freedom of mind*.

The prerequisite for *freedom of mind* is a mental state. An individual's mental state is the result of hormones and neurochemicals. It most frequently is in the relationship between the agency of the organism and its environment.

Thus far, no scientific evidence indicates that multicellular organisms can support a mental state.

While plants have various senses, they lack the hormones and neurochemicals contributing to a mental state and the *neuroglia* to experience it.

For example, plants do not respond to the sound of classical music. This notion, pardon the pun, stems from a popular myth that traces back to a popular book published in 1973 entitled <u>The Secret Life of Plants</u>.

So again, the ability to demonstrate *freedom of mind* will have to wait until we get to *Neural Bundle Consciousness,* where mental states potentially emerge.

A discussion of *freedom of thought* must wait until we reach our ninth level of consciousness, *Homo Consciousness*.

Also, a discussion of *freedom of paradigm* must wait until we reach our seventeenth level of consciousness, *Level Two Paradigmatic Consciousness*.

NERVE NET CONSCIOUSNESS AND FREEDOM

For *Nerve Net Consciousness*, we chose *Tripedalia cystophora* of the class *Cubozoa*, a species of box jellyfish, for its ability to avoid obstacles while using the tree canopy as a point of reference to navigate.

Nerve Net Consciousness is the first level in our framework that embraces neurons to communicate signals rapidly to targeted locations and, in some cases, perform simple mathematical calculations.

> *Typical jellyfish have about 5,600 neurons, while box jellyfish have evolved between 12,700 and 21,500 neurons.*

A fascinating aspect of this jellyfish is that each of its twenty-four eyes corresponds to a neuron path traversing a particular motor capability. As a result, impairing the ability of an eye impedes the organism's ability to move in a coordinated fashion, even though it would seem that plenty of eyes remain.

As one might surmise from this fact, the jellyfish nervous system is far from an evenly distributed simple structure of neurons. Instead, it shows how neurons begin to form an advanced set of cognitive features.

To quote Takeo Katsuki and Ralph J. Greenspan in their Current Biology article, *Jellyfish nervous systems*: Quote.

> *"Although their nervous system is relatively simple, a common misunderstanding is that all jellyfish have only a diffuse nerve net in which neurons are found homogeneously spread apart. In fact, most jellyfish species show some degree of neuronal condensation that serves as an integrative nervous system." End Quote.*

> *[Jellyfish nervous systems, Takeo Katsuki and Ralph J. Greenspan, Kavli Institute for Brain and Mind, UCSD, La Jolla, California, USA, Current Biology Vol 23 No 14 R592]*

These cognitive features provide the jellyfish with excellent cognitive capabilities as a predator. Together with its venom, it makes them one of the most effective hunters, consuming their prey whole into a large stomach for future digestion when food becomes scarce.

One of the few predators that consume box jellyfish are turtles, protected by their shells and equipped with eye protection.

Freedom of attention is reasonably something that an accomplished predator, such as *Tripedalia cystophora* (i.e., box jellyfish), would have to be equipped with.

Here, we have another gap in scientific knowledge, as we could not identify experiments that tested the ability of *Tripedalia cystophora* (i.e., box jellyfish) ability to focus on one stimulus over another.

However, as we have done for *Unicellular Consciousness* and *Multicellular Consciousness*, again, we will now consider a thought experiment based on a simple fact.

> *Organisms that are hunters possess highly developed capabilities to capture prey, mainly prey equipped with brains having survival mechanisms to evade predators, such as fish, prawns, and other species of jellyfish, though not other species of box jellyfish.*

Given that *Tripedalia cystophora* (i.e., box jellyfish) do not hunt members of their species, it would be reasonable to conclude that *Tripedalia cystophora* can have the focus one wants. They can hunt prey, including other jellyfish, while allowing their species to pass without harm.

If new information emerges to cause us to correct this conclusion, we will certainly do so. Still, for now, it appears reasonable to conclude that, like *Paramecia* and *Mimosa pudica* tentatively, *Tripedalia cystophora* has *freedom of attention* and can have the focus one wants.

Tripedalia cystophora (a.k.a. box jellyfish) demonstrates *freedom of will*, having the volition it wants as a highly effective predator.

Recall the ability to learn emerges with the first eukaryotes well before the emergence of neurons. With *Tripedalia cystophora* (a.k.a. box jellyfish), the types of things it can learn are more advanced.

In paraphrasing Sofie Dam Nielsen, Ph.D. in her 2018 manuscript, *Learning in the Box Jellyfish Tripedalia cystophora*:

> *In carefully controlled scientific experiments, Tripedalia cystophora demonstrates that it can learn and remember changes in the relationship between contrast and distance.*
>
> *[Learning in the Box Jellyfish Tripedalia cystophora, Feb 8, 2018, Sofie Dam Nielsen Ph.D. Marine Biology Section, Biology Department, Copenhagen University, Univisen - Kobenhavns Universitet]*

Although the Copenhagen University study attributes learning and memory skills to neurons, we attribute learning and memory to cytoskeletal structures inside the cells.

In our framework, the neurons may assist in performing calculations, though their primary function is rapidly transporting stimuli from sensory organs to muscle fibers.

In summary, *Tripedalia cystophora* (a.k.a. box jellyfish) demonstrates that it has the volitions one wants and could choose otherwise.

Tripedalia cystophora (i.e., box jellyfish) demonstrates a significant degree of *freedom of action* in its movement.

In experiments cited within the section on *Nerve Net Consciousness, Tripedalia cystophora* (i.e., box jellyfish) modifies its behavior to compensate for visual contrast and physical distance changes when pursuing prey to optimize their capture.

In choosing its volitions, in its natural environment, *Tripedalia cystophora* (i.e., box jellyfish) has no artificial or otherwise constraints that would prevent it from enacting the volitions one wants.

Its learning process demonstrates that each organism can choose otherwise in adopting a different strategy for physical movement over time, where each organism demonstrates the capability to remember experiences and learn based upon those experiences.

The actions it enacts are clearly in the self-interest of the organism, as it maintains the ability to choose otherwise.

In summary, *Tripedalia cystophora* demonstrates *freedom of attention*, *will*, and *action*, with the ability to choose otherwise.

The *freedoms of emotion*, *mind*, *thought*, and *paradigm* do not apply to *Nerve Net Consciousness*.

NERVE CORD CONSCIOUSNESS AND FREEDOM

Recall that *Nerve Cord Consciousness* marked the emergence of bilaterians, propelling the evolutionary design pattern that has since dominated nearly all animal life. This design pattern provides for a neuronal nerve cord traversing from the organism's front to back with a hollow gut cavity running in the same direction from mouth to anus.

The species selected for *Nerve Cord Consciousness* was *Caenorhabditis elegans* (a.k.a. *C. elegans*) within the genus *Caenorhabditis* and phylum *Nematoda*, which is a transparent nematode (i.e., roundworm) about 1 mm in length.

The typical nematode has evolved to include 302 neurons.

Like organisms within our framework before *Nematoda*, the observable behaviors of *C. elegans* pertain to its locomotion in response to stimuli, where a change in direction results in response to stimuli. The worm initiates a forward or backward movement (i.e., reversals).

Perhaps the most essential aspect of its intellectual capabilities is that *C. elegans* features a more advanced neuronal architecture and types of *neuroglia* that demonstrate more advanced forms of learning.

> *More advanced forms of learning are highly plastic behavior, including both associative (i.e., classical conditioning [Pavlovian], operant conditioning [reward and punishment]), non-associative (i.e., habituation [desensitizing through repetition], sensitization [sensitizing through repetition]) learning, and memory using mechanical, thermal, and chemical stimuli (e.g., glutamate, dopamine, serotonin, and neuroendocrine signaling).*

Equipped with a more advanced array of sensory organs and learning capabilities, let us now explore the *freedoms* of *Nematoda*.

Like lower-level organisms, there is a gap in scientific inquiry, as experiments within the studies identified did not test for the ability of *C. elegans* (i.e., nematode) to focus on one stimulus over another, whether involving the same sensory organ or different.

However, as we have done for *Unicellular Consciousness, Multicellular Consciousness,* and *Nerve Net Consciousness,* in the absence of any solid evidence for or against *C. elegans* (i.e., nematode), we will make the reasonable assumption, given its advanced learning capabilities, that *Nerve Cord Consciousness* can choose the focus one wants with an ability to choose otherwise.

Again, if new information emerges to correct this conclusion, we will certainly do so. Still, it appears reasonable to conclude that, like *Paramecium, Mimosa pudica, and Tripedalia cystophora, C. elegans* (i.e., nematode) possess *freedom of attention* with the ability to choose otherwise.

As we progress to this next level of consciousness, *C. elegans* is the most proficient organism thus far at learning. One of the most studied organisms, *C. elegans,* exhibits a non-mechanical form of behavior, demonstrating that it can rapidly adapt its decisions from experience.

C. elegans demonstrates *freedom of will* in the experiments cited in the *Nerve Cord Consciousness* section by choosing the direction it wants to move in response to remembered experiences.

Freedom of will is associated with the ability to learn from one's experiences, demonstrating that the organism can choose the volitions one wants while maintaining an ability to choose otherwise.

As with our prior levels of consciousness, *C. elegans* demonstrates *freedom of action* in the experiments cited in the Nerve Cord Consciousness section by enacting the volitions one wants with no external influences preventing the organism from the action it wanted.

C. elegans also demonstrated that it could have enacted other volitions and hence could choose otherwise.

The *freedoms of emotion, mind, thought,* and *paradigm* do not apply to *Nerve Cord Consciousness.*

NEURAL BUNDLE CONSCIOUSNESS AND FREEDOM

In the review of *Neural Bundle Consciousness,* we chose the genus *Apis* (a.k.a. honeybee), of which there are seven species from among the roughly 20,000 species of bees belonging to different genera.

> *Individuals of the genus Apis have 960,000 neurons, compared to the 21,000 neurons of Tripedalia cystophora (a.k.a. box jellyfish) and the 302 neurons of C. elegans (a.k.a. nematode).*

> *In contrast, the cockroach is equipped with 1,000,000 neurons, while the ant and fruit fly have 250,000 neurons, and the significantly more giant sea lobster (a.k.a. a type of sea insect) has just 100,000 neurons.*

The difference is that the neural bundle offers a significant advancement over *Nerve Cord Consciousness* with the emergence of several new capabilities.

These include a social structure with roles, language, more advanced memory, advanced sensory organs (e.g., 170 chemoreceptors and polarized light sensors allowing them to sense direction better), a sense of time, and a variety of new neural calculating abilities, such as automatically adjusting its flight to compensate for encountered gusts of wind, and the ability to translate dance movements and flight instructions into one another.

We continue to have a gap in the scientific record, as experiments within the studies identified did not test for the ability of the genus *Apis* (a.k.a. honeybee) to focus on one stimulus over another.

However, as we have done previously, one can tentatively conclude without any solid evidence, either for or against, that *Apis* can also choose the focus one wants based on its powerful learning capabilities, which are significantly more advanced than its predecessors.

As stated previously, if newly revealed information causes us to correct this conclusion, we will do so.

For now, it appears reasonable to tentatively conclude that like *Paramecium*, *Mimosa pudica*, *Tripedalia cystophora*, and *C. elegans*, the genus *Apis* (a.k.a. honeybee) also has *freedom of attention* with the ability to have the focus one wants.

The genus *Apis* (a.k.a. honeybee), particularly the female worker bee, is an efficient learner, particularly in support of its foraging tasks utilizing memory of dance movement sequences with the ability to translate those sequences into flight instructions to food sources.

Paraphrasing Professor Tan Ken – Xishuangbanna in the 2018 manuscript, *The Buzz Over Queen Bee Learning and Memory*:

> *The female queen bee also demonstrates strong memory and learning skills involving her olfactory senses.*

> *[The Buzz Over Queen Bee Learning and Memory, July 30, 2018, Professor Tan Ken – Xishuangbanna Tropical Botanical Garden, China, Asian Scientist Newsroom, Asian Scientist]*

I have a dear friend, an avid beekeeper, Malcolm Chisholm, Ph.D., who kept some of his honeybees in my backyard. I now understand that honeybees do what they want instead of what their beekeeper wants, as one summer, an entire hive just left to relocate, never to return.

Although a hard determinist would claim complete mechanical behaviors in all levels of consciousness, consider what happens when you obstruct the flight path of a honeybee.

> *When a honeybee makes a beeline to or from the hive, it is not uncommon for it to bump into you. Most frequently, the individual honeybee will run into you, bounce off, and resume its journey by going*

around you. Exceptionally rarely will the individual honeybee decide to sting you.

If you remove their beehive roof to peer inside, some will come out to look at what you are doing, while others ignore you and go about their business. Depending upon the species within the genus Apis, their relative aggressiveness can vary substantially.

In contrast, if you attacked their hive, the behavioral response would be remarkably different. The point is that the bees as a collective have no difficulty distinguishing between interactions that pose no threat and those that do.

Regarding *freedom of will*, having the volitions one wants, the female worker and queen honeybee learn and adapt their behavior exceptionally well. The assertion here is that *freedom of will* comes with the observed ability to learn from experiences with an ability to choose otherwise.

Genus *Apis* (a.k.a. honeybee) demonstrates *freedom of action* by choosing to become part of the audience to view the dance of the honeybee, memorizing, practicing, and then translating it into flight instructions, which it then can follow, and then embarking on the journey to that location.

Throughout this process, the honeybee can enact its volitions without external constraints while maintaining the ability to do otherwise.

Individual honeybees, depending upon their gender and social cast, have a role to play comprised of some set of tasks, where each worker bee chooses what task to perform and when, selecting which area of food to approach, selecting each flower upon which to land, and whether to respond or not respond to a potential threat.

As for the hard determinist's view of the world, given identical mechanical programs, several hundred mechanical bees would invariably get stuck at the opening of the hive as they all try to get out at the same time with the intent to invariably crush the same dainty flower resting among a vast blanket of flowers covering the gently rolling hills.

We conclude that the genus *Apis* (a.k.a. honeybee) demonstrates *freedom of action* in its many activities, with the ability to choose otherwise.

Next, we have *freedom of emotion*.

Some scientists attribute the *genus Apis and* other insects (e.g., ants and cockroaches) with primitive emotions, such as when they act either calm or agitated, making the emergence of basic emotions in *Neural Bundle Consciousness* somewhat controversial and debatable.

The emergence of mental states and emotions may coincide with *Neural Bundle Consciousness. However,* there is no scientific clarity or agreement on what this means within organisms equipped with a neural bundle.

Regardless, although *Neural Bundle Consciousness* may represent the point at which primitive emotions begin to emerge, it is well beyond the capabilities of an insect to be aware of emotions and to have the freedom to have the emotion one wants.

Jason Castro states that during the last decade, some experiments suggest that insects experience emotional states, perhaps limited to a few states, such as being optimistic, regular, or agitated.

> [*Do Bees Have Feelings? Aug 2, 2011, Jason Castro, Scientific American magazine, https://www.scientificamerican.com/article/do-bees-have-feelings/*]

Although *Neural Bundle Consciousness* may be the level at which some emotions and primitive mental states emerge, again, it is well beyond the capabilities of an insect to be aware of its mental state and to have the freedom to have the mental state one wants.

We can confidently state that *freedoms of emotion, mind, thought,* and *paradigm* do not apply to *Neural Bundle Consciousness.*

PRIMITIVE BRAIN CONSCIOUSNESS AND FREEDOM

In *Primitive Brain Consciousness,* we chose the class *Reptilia,* vertebrate phylum *Chordata,* subphylum *Vertebrata* (e.g., chordates with backbones), numbering about 69,300 species as our representative for analysis.

The mammalian brain did not evolve from *Reptilia.* Still, they share an extinct amniote ancestor (i.e., *synapsids,* a.k.a. *theropsids*) that lent *Reptilia* many of the same brain tissues present among mammals, allowing us to conclude reasonably that reptiles and mammals stemmed from this common extinct amniote ancestor.

Due to the wide range of body sizes, *Reptilia* brains vary significantly. However, determining the relative level of brain advancement using size can be misleading.

> *Due to the extreme variability of neuron counts among the class Reptilia, expressing brain size is more meaningful when considering brain size relative to body size.*

> *A bird has five times as many neurons as a reptile for equivalent body sizes, and a mammal has ten times as many neurons as a reptile.*

> *In contrast, a Nile crocodile native to Africa has 80,500,000 neurons, though it is low on the scale of brain-to-body mass.*

At this stage of evolution, *Reptilia* is significantly more advanced than *Neural Bundle Consciousness. Reptilia* shares several brain structures found among birds and mammals.

To quote Felix Strockens in his 2018 manuscript, *Crocodiles Listen to Classical Music in MRI Scanner*: Quote.

> *"Exposing crocodiles to a variety of auditory and visual stimuli while in an MRI, researchers discover their brain processing patterns resemble that of other mammals and birds. The researchers speculate the fundamental mechanisms of sensory processing were formed at an early evolutionary stage." End Quote.*

> *[Crocodiles Listen to Classical Music in MRI Scanner, May 3, 2018, Neuroscience News.com, source of study: Felix Strockens, Department of Biopsychology at Ruhr University, Universitatsstrasse 150, 44801, Bochum, Germany]*

As a consummate predator capable of deception to lure its prey, *Reptilia* demonstrates that it has the focus one wants and can choose otherwise.

Equipped with a brain structure resembling birds and mammals, *Reptilia* demonstrates significantly improved learning capabilities and can perform a variety of more abstract tasks than *Neural Bundle Consciousness*, such as deception to capture unsuspecting prey.

The example we cited was Crocodilians demonstrating object use by balancing sticks on their heads and waiting for a bird to claim the stick for nesting.

Hence, *Reptilia* demonstrates having the volitions one wants by acting in one's self-interest with an ability to choose otherwise. Again, the assertion here is that *freedom of will* comes with the observed ability to have the volitions one wants while possessing an ability to choose otherwise.

Regarding *freedom of action*, the class *Reptilia* demonstrates that one can enact the volitions one wants as no external constraints prevent it, particularly in its natural environment.

Reptilia demonstrates *freedom of action* by altering its behaviors in response to remembered experiences at the appropriate season when birds nest, learning stealthy tactics observed to catch its prey while maintaining the ability to enact a different volition that one may want.

Next, we have *freedom of emotion*.

Recall that *reptilian* emotions manifest themselves in sexual attraction, fear, aggressiveness, and social status, where social status manifests itself in basking placement and breeding and forming family units, sometimes exhibiting long-term monogamy among mates.

Although the variety of emotions is relatively few compared to more advanced organisms, emotions and their utility for behavioral interactions are present in *Reptilia*.

However, the question regarding freedom of emotion is whether *Reptilia* can have the emotions one wants, as in whether Reptilia can be aware of its emotions and consciously choose from among them.

Here again, we can safely assume that *Primitive Brain Consciousness* does not support *freedom of emotion*, having the emotion one wants, as *Reptilia* is neither aware of its emotions nor capable of choosing from among them.

Similarly, although *Reptilia* can experience more than one mental state, we are safe in assuming that possessing an ability to recognize the possible mental states that one may choose from is well beyond the capabilities of *Primitive Brain Consciousness.*

In summary, the *freedoms of emotion, mind, thought,* and *paradigm* do not apply to *Primitive Brain Consciousness.*

MAMMALIAN CONSCIOUSNESS AND FREEDOM

We chose the genus *Rattus* as our mammalian representative for *Mammalian Consciousness.* Genus *Rattus* is one of the largest genera of mammals, comprising approximately seventy species possessing with a mammalian brain.

> *Brains of mammalian organisms have roughly ten times the number of neurons as Reptilia when compared to an equivalent body size.*

> *As a general reference point, the brown rat (a.k.a. a common rat or Norwegian rat), believed to have originated in northern China and is native to every continent except Antarctica, has approximately 200,000,000 neurons.*

The brains of early mammals have several advantages over the most advanced *Reptilian* brain, most notably an increase in neural layering and fifteen to twenty additional cortical areas not present among *Reptilia.*

However, a larger mammalian brain mass is significantly metabolically more costly. In response, mammals have also had to develop systems to support higher metabolic rates and behaviors to nurture their offspring for the duration needed for their survival.

Regarding intellectual tasks, *Rattus* is far more proficient at learning a maze, demonstrating both improved spatial skills and more substantial learning capabilities than *Reptilia* involving both direct causal learning (i.e., a clicking sound that indicates the presence of food) and common causal learning (i.e., first learning that light causes both a sound tone and food to be present, and then concluding that food co-exists with a sound tone).

Unlike *Reptilia, Rattus* represents the first level of consciousness that demonstrates an understanding of the causal relationship between their actions and outcome, which points to a neural architecture that is associatively connected.

With this background as an introduction, let's investigate the *freedoms Mammalian Consciousness* supports.

With the genus *Rattus,* we see the emergence of the intellectual trait of curiosity in great abundance. Genus *Rattus* makes it their primary occupation to study pretty much everything in their environment, turning their focus on one thing after another to understand what it does and how it works.

To understand curiosity better and its importance, we will briefly discuss how psychology views and analyzes this trait.

According to Professor Kashdan in his 2018 article, *What Are the Five Dimensions of Curiosity?:*

In psychology, the term 'curiosity' describes various behavioral and psychological mechanisms that, when carefully analyzed, may be organized into the following five types.

Joyous exploration ... *"is the recognition and desire to seek out new knowledge and information, with the subsequent joy of learning and growing."*

Deprivation sensitivity is pondering abstract or complex ideas to solve a problem or fill a knowledge gap. However, it is associated more with anxiety and tension than joy.

Stress tolerance ... *"is about the willingness to embrace the doubt, confusion, anxiety, and other forms of distress that arise from exploring new, unexpected, complex, mysterious, or obscure events."*

Social curiosity is the desire to know what others are thinking and doing and use observation or conversation to pursue that knowledge.

Thrill-seeking is "the willingness to take physical, social, and financial risks to acquire varied, complex, and intense experiences."

According to the 2018 article, *The Five-Dimensional Curiosity Scale: Capturing the bandwidth of curiosity and identifying four unique subgroups of curious people,* given these five curiosity types, individuals who demonstrate curiosity may be organized into one of four categories.

The 'fascinated' rank high in all types of curiosity.

The 'problem solvers' rank high on deprivation sensitivity and moderate on other types of curiosity.

The 'empathizers' rank high on social curiosity and moderate on other types of curiosity.

The 'avoiders' rank low across all types of curiosity.

[What Are the Five Dimensions of Curiosity? January 2, 2018, Todd B. Kashdan Ph.D., – professor of psychology and senior scientist at the Center for the Advancement of Well-Being at George Mason University, Psychology Today]

[The Five-Dimensional Curiosity Scale: Capturing the bandwidth of curiosity and identifying four unique subgroups of curious people, December 2017, Todd B. Kashdan, Melissa Stiksma, David Disabato, Patrick McKnight, George Mason University, Fairfax, VA]

When we view the genus *Rattus* from the lens that we borrowed from psychology, the type of curiosity we see is 'joyous exploration' emerging with *Mammalian Consciousness*. In contrast, none of the five types of curiosity apply to *Reptilia* at any discernable level.

The conclusion we can draw from this trait of curiosity and exploration is that *Mammalian Consciousness* demonstrates that it has the focus one wants, with an ability to choose otherwise.

Next, we have *freedom of will*.

Genus *Rattus* demonstrates an ability to determine self-taught and learned object use that stems from eager exploration and experimentation regarding the potential use and effect of environmental objects, such as chains, levers, and buttons.

No external influences compel *Rattus* to explore and learn, as *Rattus* demonstrates that they can act in self-interest and have the volitions one wants.

Again, the assertion is that *freedom of will* comes with the observed ability to have the volitions one wants and the ability to choose otherwise.

As a result, the genus *Rattus* meets the criteria of having the volition one wants.

Next, we have *freedom of action*.

From observations, the genus *Rattus* demonstrates *freedom of action* with its continuous experimentation, observation, and communication.

For example, individual rats that successfully escape traps can influence other individuals to avoid both the specific instance of a trap and the general type of trap, even though the subsequent individual did not observe the original incident.

To quote Mike Henderson in his 2019 article, *How to Catch a Smart Rat.* Quote.

> *"Catching a smart rat requires a thoughtful approach. Rats are quick to learn, and some tests even indicate they have better cognitive learning abilities than humans even if their emotions and thought processes are, far more, simple."*

> *"Rats are very suspicious of new things by nature, and they are intelligent enough to learn. If a rat sees another rat get trapped or has a close encounter with a trap, they will remember. They can even share their knowledge with other rats, and some are clever enough to use an object to set off a trap to claim their reward." End Quote.*

[How to Catch a Smart Rat, 2019, Mike Henderson – pest control expert, City Pests]

We can safely conclude that genus *Rattus* demonstrates *freedom of action* by demonstrating the ability to enact the volitions one wants, with the ability to choose otherwise.

Next, we have *freedom of emotion*.

Regarding emotions, the genus *Rattus* represents a significant advancement over *Reptilia*, where scientists have demonstrated empathy-driven behavior where members of *Rattus* will choose to free a captive companion rather than feast on a chocolate stash that they could have had to themselves.

However, as we know regarding freedom *of emotion*, having the emotions one wants requires the organism to recognize that it has an inventory of emotions from which to choose, can freely choose one, and then experience that emotion.

Although various emotions occur in *Mammalian Consciousness*, there is no question that *Mammalian Consciousness* fails to support the capability of having the emotion one wants.

Next, we have *freedom of mind*.

With such a significant increase in the number of neurons and many new brain structures, the genus *Rattus* possesses a significant increase over *Reptilia* in the variety of mental states it can experience.

Again, experiencing various mental states versus recognizing that one has a particular mental state from among many that one may choose from are different. Regarding an awareness of mental states, the notion of being able to choose one from a selection of options is well beyond the capabilities of *Mammalian Consciousness*.

Therefore, although *Rattus* meets the first prerequisite of having mental states, it lacks *freedom of mind*.

In summary, the *freedoms of emotion, mind, thought,* and *paradigm* do not apply to *Mammalian Consciousness*.

PRIMATE CONSCIOUSNESS AND FREEDOM

The *Primate* brain is distinct from its mammalian ancestors in five significant ways.

First, there is another sharp increase in the brain-to-body mass ratio, where the number of neurons increases by two orders of magnitude.

Second, there is a significant increase in neuronal tissue layers within the brain.

Third, there is an increase in the number of distinct processing modules with more subdivisions facilitating greater functional specialization.

Fourth, there is a significant increase in neuron densities (i.e., three to five times greater), which translates to more neurons in *Primates* than their mammalian relatives' equivalent brain tissue mass.

> *Brain size for Primates is still relative to body size.*

> *However, an example comparing mammal brains to primate brains is that the mammalian brown rat has 200 million neurons compared to a common chimpanzee native to Africa, which has 28 billion neurons.*

Fifth, there is a corresponding increase in the neuroglia surrounding neuronal layers.

Although many improvements emerge in *Primates*, the one that is perhaps most noteworthy is that *Primates* have three of the four features of language (e.g., *symbolic, semantic,* and *generativity*). However, they still lack the fourth feature of language, *structure*, which supports understanding grammar.

However, with intensive training, some primates demonstrate that they may understand some minor aspects of grammar.

Regarding *Primate Consciousness,* recall that we have chosen the species *Pan troglodytes* (a.k.a. 'common chimpanzee') of the genus *Pan,* whose only other surviving species is the *bonobo* (a.k.a. 'pygmy chimpanzee').

Primates operate within complex social groups. They may act in various roles, such as a leader, lieutenant, spouse, or follower.

Primates can make tools, learn three out of the four components of language, play-act, and intentionally engage in deceptive behavior. Like their mammalian ancestors, *primates* also possess a strong sense of curiosity.

Primates have an array of sensory organs, including touch, sight, smell, taste, and hearing. When confronted with various competing stimuli, *Primate Consciousness* demonstrates they have the focus one wants.

As such, *Primate Consciousness* readily supports *freedom of attention.*

Concerning *freedom of will, Primate Consciousness* improves upon *Mammalian Consciousness* in several ways. First, the genus *Pan* goes beyond basic object use with tool use, which alone meets the threshold as observable evidence of volition.

To paraphrase Lawrence E. Johnson in his 1991 book, *A Morally Deep World:*

> *Recall our genus Pan (i.e., bonobos and common chimpanzees) makes sponge-like materials using leaves and moss to soak water for use in grooming, trims down sticks for grooming under fingers and toenails, and makes use of stone tools and sticks for fishing insects.*

[*A Morally Deep World, 1991, Lawrence E. Johnson, Cambridge University Press*]

Again, the assertion here is that *freedom of will* comes with the observed ability to learn with the caveat that it can choose otherwise.

As a result, the genus *Pan* meets the criteria of having the volition one wants.

Regarding *freedom of action*, our chosen species, *Pan troglodytes* (a.k.a. '*common chimpanzee*') of the genus *Pan*, demonstrates that they can enact the volitions one wants (a.k.a. *freedom of action*) in the experiments cited within the section on *Primate Consciousness*.

Using their curiosity to explore and learn through observation, experimentation, and communication, their ability to enact volitions to design and manufacture simple tools is another way that they demonstrate that they can enact the volitions they want while always maintaining an ability to choose otherwise.

As for *freedom of emotion*, *Primates* demonstrate an increased range of emotions over their mammalian ancestors. These emotions provide more valuable responses among members of the same species (a.k.a. conspecific) to better communicate and respond to situations.

Most importantly, the quality and depth of research into the emotions of primates have improved significantly in understanding the cause and significance of emotional expression among a range of primates.

To quote Elisabeth G.I. Nieuwburg, Annemie Ploeger, and Mariska E. Kret in their 2021 research article, *Emotion recognition in nonhuman primates: How experimental research can contribute to a better understanding of underlying mechanisms*: Quote.

> "*We define emotion recognition as the ability to form an internal representation of the emotions of others based on the perception of their emotional expressions. Two possible, non-mutually exclusive mechanisms underlying this ability are emotional contagion and cognitive empathy. Emotional contagion is a relatively low-level bottom-up process in which the state of the perceiver of an emotional signal is automatically matched to the state of the sender. It is defined as the tendency to automatically mimic and synchronize emotional expressions with those of others, resulting in emotional convergence (Hatfield et al., 1994). In other words, emotions of others unconsciously evoke a basic internal representation of the emotion in the perceiver (de Waal and Preston, 2017; Morimoto and Fujita, 2011; Preston and de Waal, 2002).*"

> "*A more cognitively demanding way of recognizing emotions is through cognitive empathy. This is the capacity to understand an emotion's meaning or cause without necessarily experiencing the same*

emotion (de Waal and Preston, 2017; de Waal, 2008; Preston and de Waal, 2002). This process results in a more cognitive representation of the perceived emotion and entails a clear self-other distinction in the observer of the emotion." End Quote.

[Emotion recognition in nonhuman primates: How experimental research can contribute to a better understanding of underlying mechanisms, April 2021, Elisabeth G.I. Nieuwburg – University of Amsterdam, Institute of Interdisciplinary Studies, Amsterdam, The Netherlands, Annemie Ploeger – University of Amsterdam, Faculty of Social and Behavioral Sciences, Program Group Developmental Psychology, Amsterdam, The Netherlands, Mariska E. Kret – Leiden University, Institute of Psychology, Cognitive Psychology Unit, Leiden Institute for Brain and Cognition (LIBC), Leiden, The Netherlands, Neuroscience & Behavioral Reviews Volume 123, Pages 24-47]

Studies such as this help define a path to additional research that investigates the evolutionary origins of the emotional landscape of primates, including humans.

Research has made clear that *Primate Consciousness* meets the first criterion of *primates* demonstrating a richer array of emotions than mammals, and primates demonstrate that they are aware of both their emotions and the emotions of others distinct from their own emotions.

The next question is whether *Primate Consciousness* can choose the emotion one wants, and the answer is partially 'yes' and 'no'.

Primates, such as the gorilla, can consciously choose to play the role of an aggressive and angry dominant individual to instill fear in others, all while maintaining complete control of themselves. However, play-acting an emotion, choosing the emotion one wants, and then experiencing that emotion are significantly distinct concepts.

While *Primate Consciousness* has, to a large extent, awareness of its emotions, the ability to have the emotion one wants is still well beyond the capabilities of *Primate Consciousness*. Therefore, we may safely conclude that primates lack *freedom of emotion.*

Regarding *freedom of mind*, as one would expect, *Primate Consciousness* easily meets the requirement of having more than one mental state. Individual primates may also have some degree of awareness of their mental state, occasionally understanding and expressing their awareness of their current or past mental state.

Apes may behave in a manner exuding anger and ferocity, even though they may be in complete control of themselves, acting for the observer's benefit.

However, having a choice of mental states that one may want with the ability to choose the mental state one wants is outside the capabilities of *Primate Consciousness.*

Therefore, primates lack *freedom of mind.*

The freedom to choose the thoughts one wants and the freedom to choose the paradigm one wants are still well beyond this level of consciousness. Hence, the remaining two freedoms, thought and paradigm, do not apply.

HOMO CONSCIOUSNESS AND FREEDOM

Homo Consciousness represents the last level of consciousness that pertains to the physical aspects of the brain's evolution. These hardware-related advancements lead to significantly enhanced intellectual capabilities that propel consciousness to a new level.

The new larger brain has more neurons, where 80% comprise the neocortex with more neuronal tissue layers and distinct subdivisions numbering over two hundred. At this point, the brain has a massive increase in neuronal circuits, a significantly higher neuron density, and a significant increase in the variety of neuronal and *neuroglia*l cells.

We selected *Homo sapiens* as our only choice for this level of consciousness, as it is the only extant species available.

Homo sapiens have freedom of attention, will, and action as primates.

Next, we have *freedom of emotion.*

Homo sapiens experience a relentless stream of emotions that stem from the various intellectual activities at various levels of consciousness. Though often aware of their emotions, *Homo Consciousness* does not allow the ability to choose the emotions one wants.

Next, we have *freedom of mind.*

Although the hardware is present for *freedom of mind* to develop at this level of consciousness, we will save the actual ability to have the mental states one wants for the level of consciousness that has earned it.

Likewise, *Homo sapiens* often experience many mental states that one might choose from, but selecting a mental state created by the standard machinery of the physical brain is distinct from having the freedom to create a new mental state consciously.

A newly created thought can be a minor modification to an existing or entirely new mental state. Creating new mental state requires a form of creativity that one may develop.

Next, we have *freedom of thought.*

Freedom of thought, the ability to think the thoughts one wants, is a capability of consciousness that emerges only after the emergence of *Homo sapiens* hardware. The thoughts of *Homo sapiens,* by default, are entirely driven by emotions and circumstances.

Breaking away from that default process requires significant training, which requires developing software to operate on *Homo sapiens* hardware in our framework.

We will need to leave the emergence of *freedom of thought* for a higher level of consciousness, namely one that requires the emergence of additional software designed for the task.

The freedom to choose the paradigm one wants is beyond this level of consciousness as *Homo Consciousness* does not support an awareness of one's paradigm, never mind the notion of having multiple paradigms from which to choose.

MEDITATIVE CONSCIOUSNESS AND FREEDOM

Our tenth level of consciousness, *Meditative Consciousness*, is the first to sit atop the hardware we call the central nervous system (CNS). As such, it is considered software within our framework.

From here on out, each level of consciousness manifests as a type of brain programming, such as rewiring circuits and components to achieve new capabilities.

Arguably, *Meditative Consciousness* is the most important of these software-based levels as it is also the first level of consciousness that allows an organism equipped with an unconscious and subconscious an opportunity to consciously influence various processes in the brain.

Significantly, this software-based level facilitates strengthening the agency of the individual.

In other words, meditative practices help to clarify further and assert the identity and capabilities of the agent, which begins by teaching the individual to observe the flow of thoughts as an observer of the thoughts and emotions that naturally bubble up to the conscious level.

In contrast, the undisciplined mind frequently loses focus, allowing thoughts to intrude and detract from the agent's chosen focus target. However, with repeated patience and practice, the meditation practitioner can pull the focus back to the chosen focus target to eliminate intruding thoughts.

Meditation's value typically aligns with the individual's objectives for meditation. Though most practitioners' primary objective of meditation is relaxation and the release of tension, meditation offers many benefits for practitioners at all levels.

Thus far, *freedom of attention* appears in each of the nine hardware-based levels of consciousness. It seems reasonable to assume that as we build software-based levels of consciousness upon the same physical brain, the ability to have the focus one wants will persist in each of the software-based levels.

Though *freedom of attention* is present within all software-based levels, *Meditative Consciousness* is unique among the software-based levels in that it significantly strengthens one's *freedom of attention* in various ways.

The beginner meditation practitioner will detect that their focus will either move to something else, slowly drift away, or morph into something else, causing the practitioner to refocus on the thoughts they want.

Somewhat like exercising a muscle, with repeated practice, the individual's focus will strengthen and remain for more extended periods. Reestablishing one's focus will require a decreasing level of effort as one improves one's level of expertise.

The first step of *Meditative Consciousness* is to learn to separate oneself as an observer of one's stream of stimuli and thoughts. Next is to learn how to focus on one or more specific stimuli or thoughts and to detect when that focus strays so that the observer may return one's attention to the focus the observer wants.

Practicing *Meditative Consciousness* improves one's ability to have the focus one wants for extended periods and have the focus one wants with fewer and fewer distractions.

Of particular significance is the fact that the brain's hardware can support this enhanced *freedom of attention*. However, the brain's hardware cannot do so without developing the software necessary for rewiring portions of the brain's hardware to support the new programming that strengthens one's *freedom of attention*.

As we continue through our remaining levels of software-based consciousness, we will not repeat our mention of *freedom of attention* unless there is a noteworthy aspect to discuss in our journey.

Next, we have *freedom of will*.

Freedom of will has occurred within each of the nine hardware-based levels of consciousness, thereby allowing us to conclude that the ability to have the volitions one wants will persist for the fifteen software-based levels of consciousness that follow.

Noteworthy is that *freedom of will* is necessary to have the volition to practice meditation. Therefore, without *freedom of will*, the level of consciousness we call *Meditative Consciousness* would not be possible, as it can only come about through an intentional act of one's will.

As we proceed, like with *freedom of attention*, we will not speak to *freedom of will* again to each level of software-based consciousness unless there is some noteworthy information to illustrate along our journey.

Next, we have *freedom of action*.

Freedom of action has occurred within each of the nine hardware-based levels of consciousness. It is reasonable to assume that the ability to enact the volitions one wants will persist for the fifteen software-based levels of consciousness.

Noteworthy again is the fact that *freedom of action* is necessary to have the ability to enact the volition one wants to practice meditation. Likewise, without *freedom of action,* the level of consciousness we call *Meditative Consciousness* would not be possible, as it can only come about through an intentional act to enact the volition one wants.

Hence, we will not speak to *freedoms of attention and will* discuss the levels of consciousness that follow unless there is some additional noteworthy information to discuss in our journey.

Next, we have *freedom of emotion.*

At the fully developed level of the physical brain, armed solely with its default programming, humans are not equipped to have the emotions they want. Instead, the agent experiences a stream of emotions that stem from the activities at various levels of consciousness.

Meditative Consciousness provides the meditation practitioner the first foothold to help them gain control over one's default programming. Even so, *freedom of emotion* is about the degree of control an individual can exercise over their emotions to choose and have the emotion one wants.

There are claims that *freedom of emotion* is attainable at expert levels of meditation. However, scientific evidence in this area is difficult to determine and collect.

There appears to be some evidence that expert meditation practitioners can sufficiently alter their default programming so that the resulting differences can be measured by devices available to neuroscience today. The question is whether this can measure one's ability to have the desired emotion for any period.

While *Meditative Consciousness* may be a prerequisite for *freedom of emotion,* again, we will save the actual ability to have the emotions one wants for the level of consciousness that more clearly earns it.

Next, we have *freedom of mind.*

Meditative Consciousness easily meets the first two requirements of having more than one mental state and awareness of mental states. It may also have the volition to want a particular mental state. However, *freedom of mind* requires the individual to be capable of having the mental state one wants.

Once chosen, the individual would be able to have the mental state one wants with the experience of being in that mental state.

However, when choosing the mental state one wants, the task may also require overcoming the effect of hormones and chemicals in the body, which may require a carefully controlled diet.

To quote Jon Yaneff in his 2019 article, *What to Eat Before You Meditate*: Quote.

> *"Yogic tradition suggests a diet that consists of mostly sattvic foods. These are foods that encourage your meditation and promote a peaceful mental attitude. The foods before your meditative practice will include whole grains, fruits, vegetables, legumes, nuts, seeds, herbs, natural sweeteners, and organic dairy." End Quote.*
>
> *[What to Eat Before You Meditate, 2019, Jon Yaneff, Foods For Better Health, foodsforbetterhealth.com]*

It is unclear whether the expert practitioner can overcome the influences of hormones by augmenting their meditative regimen with diet and hormones. However, it is relatively safe to conclude that only the most accomplished meditation practitioners might be able to have the mental state they want.

While *Meditative Consciousness* may be a prerequisite for *freedom of mind*, again, we will save the actual ability to have the mental states one wants for the level of consciousness that has earned it.

Next, we have *freedom of thought*.

Meditative Consciousness is an essential precursor to *freedom of thought* for its ability to strengthen one's *freedom of attention*, *freedom of will*, and *freedom of action*, as well as for its capacity to support the independent observer concept within the mind.

To achieve *freedom of thought*, one must be able to passively observe thoughts, stimuli, and emotions distinct from choosing to engage and react to them.

However, the question is whether *Meditative Consciousness* renders the ability to think the thoughts one wants.

Recall *Homo sapiens* has an inventory of thoughts that one might choose from, but again, selecting a thought created by the standard machinery of the physical body is distinct from the idea of having the freedom to create a thought created as the result of one wanting to think it.

As such, something else is necessary to support *freedom of thought* as we have defined it. Although *Meditative Consciousness* is an essential ingredient, we must leave the emergence of *freedom of thought* for a higher level of consciousness, which requires the emergence of yet additional software and levels of consciousness.

The freedom to choose one's paradigm is beyond this level of consciousness. *Meditative Consciousness* does not even support an awareness of one's paradigm, never mind the notion of having multiple paradigms from which to choose.

REASON-DRIVEN CONSCIOUSNESS AND FREEDOM

Reason-driven consciousness is our second software-based level of consciousness that sits on top of the hardware of the physical brain.

Reason-driven consciousness is a learned skill that generally comes with education, though interestingly, it is impractical for the many trivial daily decisions an individual makes.

Recall, forms of reasoning include deductive reasoning, inductive reasoning, abductive reasoning, reductive reasoning, hypothetico-deductive reasoning, analogical reasoning, metaphorical reasoning, creative reasoning, holistic reasoning, reductionist reasoning, categorization reasoning, generalized reasoning, and logically fallacious reasoning.

Reason-driven consciousness is most appropriate for decisions that are likely to have a significant influence on the direction of one's life, such as relocations, choosing a spouse, having children, selecting a vocation, and perhaps choosing an employer, choosing one's friends, the experiences one chooses, as well as one's choice of what to read and learn.

We mention *freedom of attention, will,* and *action* in *Reason-driven Consciousness* for their importance in influencing the major decisions and direction of one's life.

Many *Homo sapiens* live the life dealt to them, somehow missing that they are agents that can choose a different life and work towards it. When one develops a goal for one's life and a corresponding plan to achieve that goal, reason-driven consciousness can help propel the individual in the desired direction.

Paying attention to the appropriate stimuli and thoughts throughout each day provides many opportunities to help advance an individual toward their goal. These decisions can range between either one's life choices that denote one's choice of cultural groups, possibly as one's choice of clothing and manner of speaking, or the shaping of one's mind, such as one's choice of conversational topics, reading material, and educational activities.

As we explore how freedoms are enhanced and extended in Reason-driven Consciousness, we must acknowledge the value that reason brings to shaping the lives of those individuals who utilize it to its greatest extent. These are the individuals we often recognize as the most accomplished among us.

Reason can also serve to temper the emotions one does not want, and it can determine the ideal emotion in given situations.

In an ironic reversal, *Reason-Driven Consciousness* offers little benefit on its own since reasoning is most often employed to justify the emotions that one has and is experiencing, as opposed to selecting the emotions that would help most in a given circumstance.

Humans generally cannot choose the emotions they want, as most emotions stem from the release of hormones. As a result, *Reason-Driven Consciousness* alone does not render an ability to have the emotions one wants.

When individuals exercise reasoning that creates the appearance of having controlled their emotions, *Reason-Driven Consciousness* is operating to help the individual mask their emotions and control their behavior. *Meditative Consciousness* can play an essential role in separating the agent as simply an observer of the emotions they are experiencing and improving their ability to mask them.

Even so, we will need to postpone *freedom of emotion*, having the emotions one wants, for a higher level of consciousness that requires the emergence of yet additional software.

Next is *freedom of mind.*

One limiting factor is that *Reason-driven Consciousness* is subject to one's mental state during the reasoning process. Reason alone cannot alter the individual's mental state to allow them to have and experience the mental state one wants.

Among the few exceptions would be the circumstance that allows the individual to reason that they should not even be in their current mental state. It could be due to a misinterpretation that can correct the combination of hormones and the resulting mental state.

However, correcting a misinterpretation is quite different from realizing that a different mental state would work to one's advantage and consciously achieving it.

It is essential not to make decisions when an individual is in an inappropriate mental state, even though the ideal situation would require the ability to have the mental state.

The ability to have the mental state one wants may sometimes be achieved in collaboration with a robust meditative practice, though to become reasonably practiced at having the mental state one wants, we will need to leave the emergence of *freedom of mind* for a higher level of consciousness, one that requires the emergence of yet additional software.

Next is *freedom of thought.*

Reason can be an essential tool for rejecting and dispensing with the thoughts that one does not want, as well as for recognizing the thoughts one wants. The rudimentary notion that embodies *freedom of thought* is selecting the thoughts one wants from the relentless flow of thoughts that bubble up from the unconscious and subconscious levels.

More significantly, however, is that *freedom of thought* involves formulating new thoughts one wants. It entails the ability to identify criteria for thoughts and to design and construct those thoughts.

While *Reason-Driven Consciousness* offers an advantage for selecting the thoughts one wants from a stream of thoughts, it does not support the ability to formulate the thoughts one wants, as it merely uses a reasoning process (e.g., deductive, inductive) from the existing inventory of thoughts and ideas that the individual experiences from lower levels of consciousness.

We will need to leave the emergence of *freedom of thought* for a higher level of consciousness, which requires the emergence of yet additional software.

The freedom to choose one's paradigm is beyond this level of consciousness. *Reason-driven Consciousness* does not support an awareness of one's paradigm, never mind the notion of having multiple paradigms from which to choose or the ability to create a new paradigm.

PERSONA CONSCIOUSNESS AND FREEDOM

A *persona* is a behavioral framework representing how one should behave in a given role. It often has a role model and accounts for how one imagines the intended audience will perceive the *persona*.

The emergence of civilization is only possible when the participants can play societal roles that comprise a civilized society. A civilized society consists of an immense variety of roles (e.g., dock worker, doorman, accountant, auditor, politician, fireman, nurse, taxi driver) that extend beyond the instinctual family and tribal roles (e.g., mother, father, medicine man, hunter, farmer, chief), thereby allowing individuals to add as many *personas* to their repertoire as situations may require that can be associated with a variety of necessary vocations and professions necessary to support the civilization.

Hence, a *persona* in our framework is a learned identity that an individual may wish to project depending upon the social or vocational context, much like the mask of an actor that, on the one hand, attempts to portray a particular image while simultaneously repressing any traits that may interfere with the projected image.

We mention *freedom of attention, will,* and *action* for *Persona Consciousness* for its importance in achieving societal and or professional success within the complexities of a civilization.

Having the focus one wants, the volitions one wants, and the ability to enact those volitions are essential tools of *Persona Consciousness* to allow an individual to emulate the combination of behavioral characteristics they deem appropriate to portray the desired *persona*.

Initially, when portraying a *persona*, the individual focuses on seeing themselves. As such, the individual is observing themselves behave in the *persona* according to their belief of how that *persona* should behave, often based upon a particular role model. When individuals become more accustomed to playing the role, they no longer observe themselves self-consciously but fulfill it.

One may consider paying attention to one's self as a type of *freedom of attention* called *freedom of meta-attention*. In this way, the individual is paying attention to themselves as an observer of themselves as an agent.

Although theoretically, observing oneself observing oneself has no limit, it becomes pointless to go much further in this direction as a practical matter.

For example, if we ponder the possible existence of meta-meta-attention, we realize this is also possible. It simply means that the individual is observing the observer of themselves in their chosen persona. It may be confusing initially, though it can have some value when each observer observes something distinct.

The first observer is watching the persona perform. The second observer is watching the first observer, observing the persona perform.

However, suppose we ponder the extension of that up any additional levels. In that case, one should quickly conclude that there is no value in doing so because each additional observer is not observing anything distinct.

A third observer would only be watching a second observer, which is identical to itself.

It is for the same reason that the phrase, "I think, that you think, that I think," is the limit for having meaning, since "I think, that you think, that I think," (adding on) "that you think" becomes redundant from that point on, as the additional phrase fails to provide any further conceptual distinction.

The notion of an individual seeing themselves out of their body is similar in that seeing yourself from outside has no value if you add seeing yourself observing yourself from outside your body.

The number of possible *personas* that *Homo sapiens* can adopt seems limitless. P*ersonas* are more plentiful than the number of professions found within significant population centers, as there are many professions not found in a typical city, such as those found among various branches of the federal and state government, armed forces, and various industries, such as the energy sector, transportation sector, farming, fishing, and mining.

The number of *personas* within an individual business can number in the hundreds, including *personas* associated with roles such as receptionists, operations staff, supervisors, executive management, HR, legal, public relations, marketing staff, sales staff, procurement, finance, facility maintenance, and security.

Not to be confused with personality, the *persona* of a receptionist and Chief Financial Officer will want to focus their attention on different things, they will want to have different volitions, and they will want to enact different volitions commensurate with their persona at work. However, they may share a standard *persona* at home with their family or relatives.

Adopting a *persona* positions the individual to have the emotional responses appropriate for the circumstances and events one may encounter. A *persona* provides a conscious and subconscious influence to evoke emotions consistent with one's understanding of the *persona*.

Although it is a beginning, having the emotions one wants is a concept distinct from the effect of a *persona*.

The primary distinction is that demonstrating the emotions one wants by adopting a *persona* starts as a form of acting. In contrast, the ability to choose and have the emotions one wants is an authentic experience. The result does not approximate a *persona's* behaviors but fully instantiates the emotion without role-playing.

In other words, to act as if one is experiencing anger that is out of control is quite distinct from having anger that is out of control.

That aside, training in method acting can further strengthen *freedom of emotion*, though, for other reasons, we shall see as we journey through the remaining levels of consciousness.

Therefore, demonstrating *freedom of emotion* will require another level of consciousness.

Next is *freedom of mind*.

Persona Consciousness meets the first requirement of having more than one mental state from which to choose.

When choosing the mental state one wants, *Persona Consciousness* can successfully influence one's mental state as a natural byproduct of adopting a given *persona*. However, this influence is initially imitating the mental state appropriate for a given *persona*.

A common term for this is method acting, where the actor attempts to adopt the *persona* of a role by imitating what they believe to be their corresponding mental state. The more experienced the individual becomes in the role, the better they can adopt the correct mental state. However, many individuals allow mental states from other aspects of their life to leak in to interfere with their role.

Freedom of mind, the ability to have the mental states one wants, encompasses choosing the mental state one wants within one's existing persona and then enacting that mental state such that the individual may experience it as their mental state.

To attain that will require the emergence of additional software yet to come.

Next is *freedom of thought*.

Persona Consciousness does not offer an advantage for having the thoughts one wants other than potentially restricting the myriad of potential thoughts to those that pertain to the chosen *persona*.

The resulting thoughts that percolate up will eventually become consistent with the *persona*.

As such, *Persona Consciousness* might do more toward not having the thoughts that one does not want, as opposed to having the ability to create the thoughts one wants. Hence, *Persona Consciousness* might act more like a filtering mechanism of thoughts focusing on thoughts that would align with the chosen *persona*.

As such, we continue to leave the emergence of *freedom of thought* for a higher level of consciousness supported by additional software.

Next is *freedom of paradigm*.

The freedom to choose one's paradigm is beyond this level of consciousness. *Persona Consciousness* does not support an awareness of one's paradigm, never mind the notion of having multiple paradigms from which to choose.

Personas and *paradigms* are distinct concepts, where a *persona* is a role typically performed from within one's base *paradigm*. A *persona* is focused on oneself and involves understanding how to behave in a particular societal role.

In contrast, a *paradigm* provides a distinct system of rules to interpret all stimuli and thoughts. Operating in one's *paradigm* without a *persona* is the individual as themself. In contrast, a *persona* is something added within a *paradigm* that plays a role.

Playing a given role does not alter the individual's belief system. Instead, it allows them to act in a role the individual considers necessary.

COMPARTMENTALIZED CONSCIOUSNESS AND FREEDOM

Compartmentalized Consciousness involves an individual who either consciously compartmentalizes systems of thought, such as balancing one's life between work and personal life, or unconsciously compartmentalizes to avoid cognitive dissonance between conflicting thoughts or systems of conflicting thoughts. Conflicting thoughts commonly occur among belief systems, value systems, emotions, or ideas that conflict or compete for attention.

As such, the benefit of *Compartmentalized Consciousness* is that it provides freedom from conflicting ideas and concepts.

We mention *freedom of attention, will,* and *action* in *Compartmentalized Consciousness* for its ability to consciously avert attention from the ideas and concepts that could lead to debilitating distraction or irreconcilable conflicts that are also debilitating.

Without compartmentalization, conflicting ideas and thoughts would disrupt one's thought processes and incessantly distract the mind in a potentially futile attempt to resolve the conflict.

In an exciting twist, this level of consciousness further facilitates the focus one wants, the volitions one wants, and the ability to enact the volitions one wants by preventing attention from being given to an almost undoubtedly disruptive series of distractions.

In this way, *Compartmentalized Consciousness* assists one's efforts in asserting *freedom of attention, will,* and *action.*

Next is *freedom of mind.*

Modestly, compartmentalization helps to attain the emotion one wants by dispensing with the emotions one does not want. While compartmentalization can certainly help avoid the emotions one does not want, it is insufficient to render the ability to have the emotions one does want.

As a result, *Compartmentalized Consciousness* falls short of the ability to choose and have the emotions one wants. Demonstrating *freedom of emotion* will require yet another level of consciousness.

Next is *freedom of mind.*

Compartmentalized Consciousness is a type of consciousness that helps filter out conflicting or distracting belief systems, value systems, emotions, or ideas. However, it does not necessarily enhance the ability to have the mental states one wants, though it does help avoid mental states one does not want.

One can argue that avoiding mental states that distract the individual from the mental states one wants represents a step in the right direction.

However, to achieve the mental state one wants, we must journey further to the emergence of new software.

Next is *freedom of thought.*

To some degree, compartmentalization also enhances one's ability to have the thoughts one wants by filtering out conflicting or distracting belief systems, value systems, emotions, or ideas. More accurately, compartmentalization enhances one's ability to focus on the thoughts one already has without conflicting or distracting belief systems, value systems, emotions, or ideas.

However, compartmentalization does not empower individuals to design, create, and have the thoughts they want.

We must leave the emergence of *freedom of thought* for a higher level of consciousness supported by additional software.

Next, we consider *freedom of paradigm.*

The freedom to choose one's paradigm is beyond this level of consciousness *Compartmentalized Consciousness* does not support an awareness of one's paradigm, never mind the notion of having multiple paradigms from which to choose.

Compartmentalization and *paradigms* are distinct concepts where *compartmentalization* operates within one's *paradigm*. *Compartmentalization* focuses on avoiding conflicting or distracting belief systems, value systems, emotions, or ideas. In contrast, a *paradigm* provides a distinct system of rules to interpret all stimuli and thoughts.

To further explain, *compartmentalization* does not alter how thoughts or stimuli are understood. Instead, *compartmentalization* eliminates the noise that would slow down and impede the interpretations that would occur without introducing debilitating thoughts.

IN-THE-MOMENT CONSCIOUSNESS AND FREEDOM

In-the-moment Consciousness is the ability to focus on the present, sometimes expressed as living-in-the-moment. This level of consciousness eliminates the mind's wandering distraction into one's memories of the past or wishful thinking about what one desires in the future.

When individuals concentrate their intellectual resources on in-the-moment experiences, they engage with reality to its fullest extent. This focus helps us improve interactions with other individuals, enhancing those relationships and experiences that help create better memories and prospects for the future.

The natural state of *Homo sapiens* is to dwell either on the past or future, and it takes significant awareness and practice to attain *In-the-moment Consciousness*.

We mention *freedom of attention, will,* and *action* in *In-the-moment Consciousness* for its ability to concentrate one's attention on the ideas and concepts that involve the present.

The ability to focus on the present requires discipline, such as meditative consciousness, where one may refocus one's attention on the focus one wants in the present moment that one is actively experiencing.

In-the-moment Consciousness further strengthens one's *freedom of attention, will,* and *action* by effectively filtering out the past or future.

Regarding *freedom of emotion, In-the-moment Consciousness* does not alter one's emotions or help the individual have the emotions one wants. In contrast, it focuses the individual on their present experience instead of having their thoughts wander off into thoughts about the past or future.

In this manner, *In-the-moment Consciousness* can help avoid the emotions one does not want that may be associated with past events or future desires.

We need to journey further to see if there are levels of consciousness capable of demonstrating *freedom of emotion.*

Next is *freedom of mind.*

Again, *In-the-moment Consciousness* is a mechanism to prevent thoughts from wandering into the past or future. A byproduct of focusing on the present is that it filters out any conflicting or distracting thoughts about the past or future, thereby preventing its effect on one's mental state.

That said, *In-the-moment Consciousness* is unrelated to having the mental state one wants. While living in the present, an individual is still subject to the mental state they happen to be in.

Being present neither alters one's ability to become aware of one's mental state nor to choose another and then experience that one.

As such, we need to journey further to see if there are levels of consciousness capable of demonstrating *freedom of mind.*

Regarding freedom of thought, having the thoughts one wants requires the ability to create thoughts instead of selecting a thought from among many, empowering the individual to design, create, and have the thoughts one wants.

In-the-moment Consciousness does not support the ability to have the thoughts one wants, though it offers the advantage of avoiding distracting thoughts about the past or future.

Again, we must leave the emergence of *freedom of thought* for a higher level of consciousness supported by additional software.

At first, establishing the ability to be aware of a paradigm seems unrelated to *In-the-moment Consciousness.*

It is true that the freedom to choose one's paradigm is beyond the capabilities of this level of consciousness. *In-the-moment Consciousness* does not support an awareness of one's paradigm, never mind the notion of having multiple paradigms from which to choose.

However, it is essential to note that the ability to establish awareness of the paradigms of others is often dependent upon *In-the-moment Consciousness.*

For example, recognizing two individuals talking past one another because they are both in different and somewhat incompatible paradigms requires full attention in the present.

Being in the moment is focused on remaining present to experience what is happening in the here and now instead of drifting into thoughts about the past or future. In contrast, a *paradigm* provides a distinct system of rules to interpret all stimuli and thoughts. But recognizing two rule systems operating here and now requires one to be present simultaneously.

To further explain, being *in the moment* does not alter how thoughts or stimuli are understood. Instead, being *in the moment* eliminates extraneous thoughts and distractions.

The assertion is that those distractions rob individuals of some of the experiences associated with real-time events, making them less wealthy intellectually and far less memorable.

LEVEL ZERO PARADIGMATIC CONSCIOUSNESS AND FREEDOM

Recall *Level Zero Paradigmatic Consciousness* is a level of consciousness involving a single paradigm, though a parasitic one, that replaces the robust self-interest paradigm of an individual with one focused on serving the needs and interests of another.

Individuals in this level of paradigmatic consciousness disregard their safety, needs, or interests. At the same time, they instead form a paradoxical emotional bond with and only regard the interests of their captor, abuser, or cult leader (a.k.a. acute stress disorder and *Stockholm syndrome).*

Instead of having a usual sense of self, individuals forfeit their sense of self in substitution for another individual's self-interests.

We mention *freedom of attention, will,* and *action* in *Level Zero Paradigmatic Consciousness* for the potential limitations it may place on *freedom of attention, freedom of will,* and *freedom of action.*

However, upon careful consideration, *Level Zero Paradigmatic Consciousness* does not impede *freedom of attention, freedom of will,* nor *freedom of action* as the individual retains complete control over the focus they want to have, the volitions they want to have, and the ability to enact the volitions they want to have.

Even though the *Level Zero* individual has forfeited their sense of self-interest, they still have and exercise the focus they want, the volitions they want, and freely enact those volitions.

As a result, the only difference in the individual's range of consciousness relates to their paradigm. Therefore, we conclude that *Level Zero Paradigmatic Consciousness* neither enhances nor impedes one's *freedom of attention, will, or action.*

Concerning remaining freedoms, *Level Zero Paradigmatic Consciousness* does not support an ability to have the emotions, mental state, thoughts, or paradigm one wants.

Individuals in *Level Zero Paradigmatic Consciousness* have one paradigm that does not support one's awareness of that paradigm. In basic terms, individuals in this level of consciousness operate from within their one paradigm with all the features of the levels of consciousness previously covered, with the additional restriction of having forfeited their self-interest in exchange for the self-interest of their captor(s).

We will have to wait for an additional layer of software to emerge that may support *freedom of emotion, mind, thought, and paradigm.*

LEVEL ONE PARADIGMATIC CONSCIOUSNESS AND FREEDOM

One's paradigm determines how an individual interprets all stimuli from the external world around them and the myriad of internal sources as they are generated or recalled.

Notably, one's paradigm also influences which events an individual may or may not perceive as if some never occurred. In this manner, a paradigm can filter one's awareness, only allowing the individual to be aware of certain events and aspects of one's surroundings to which the individual's paradigm can relate.

The fundamental difference between the terms '*context*' and '*paradigm*' is that the '*context*' of something originates from the set of circumstances that form the setting of an event and generally occur outside of ourselves. In contrast, *paradigms* are rules we use to interpret events and reside only within ourselves.

If inaccurate, an individual's paradigm can impede an individual's perception of reality by first omitting or potentially distorting inbound information incompatible with the paradigm. Next, an inaccurate *paradigm* may generate unreliable meaning due to relying upon a system of critically flawed rules that develop inaccurate interpretations.

This two-step process of first allowing what is considered appropriate stimuli to be perceived and then second employing reliable rules to establish meaning for stimuli makes it particularly challenging to alter one's paradigm.

Regardless of how accurate or flawed an individual's paradigm may be, their paradigm serves as a stable foundation for all thought within the mind with few exceptions.

Level One Paradigmatic Consciousness is the starting point for all *Homo sapiens,* and this level of paradigmatic consciousness remains the foundation for most *Homo sapiens.*

The difference and advantage of *Level Ones* over *Level Zeros* is the inclusion of self-interest within one's base paradigm.

As a result, advancement from being a *Level Zero* to a *Level One* neither enhances nor impedes one's *freedom of attention, will, or action.*

Level One Paradigmatic Consciousness offers neither an advantage nor disadvantage for having the emotions, mental state, thoughts, or paradigms one wants.

As a result, we need to journey further to see if there are levels of consciousness capable of demonstrating these freedoms.

LEVEL TWO PARADIGMATIC CONSCIOUSNESS AND FREEDOM

Level Two Paradigmatic Consciousness individuals can perceive more than their base paradigm. Once multiple paradigms become realized, it is just a matter of time before the individual becomes aware that this is an intellectual tool. The individual begins to recognize opportunities for its use.

One common benefit is the ability to communicate with individuals with different paradigms. *Level Twos* are more likely to comprehend the meaning of words and phrases as intended by individuals having different perspectives. It allows them to detect miscommunication between individuals with different perspectives of differing paradigms.

Depending upon the value system of the *Level Two* individual, they may tend to be either highly productive, egoistic, problematic, or evil, sometimes depending upon the circumstances.

We mention *freedom of attention, will,* and *action* in *Level Two Paradigmatic Consciousness* for the added ability to have the focus one wants, the volitions one wants, and the ability to enact those volitions that belong to two distinct paradigms.

Individuals proficient with *Level Two* abilities have a more flexible form of *freedom of attention* by shifting their focus to thoughts and stimuli simultaneously in an alternate paradigm to their base paradigm.

As such, *Level Two Paradigmatic Consciousness* enhances one's *freedom of attention, will, and action.*

Again, one's emotions are influenced significantly by one's paradigm. Hence, an individual proficient at perceiving an alternate paradigm has the distinct advantage of gaining insight into the resulting emotions that the alternate paradigm would also create.

However, gaining insight into the emotions associated with an additional paradigm does not increase the ability to have the emotion one wants.

Yet again, it would be premature to claim that *Level Two Paradigmatic Consciousness* demonstrates having the emotions one wants, so we must journey to a more advanced software layer.

As for one's *freedom of mind,* an individual's paradigm determines everything. It means that one's paradigm determines mental states.

An individual proficient at perceiving an alternate paradigm has the distinct advantage of gaining insight into the mental state of an alternate paradigm in themselves or others.

However, this type of insight does not equip individuals with the mental state they want.

While *Level Two Paradigmatic Consciousness* falls short of having the mental states one wants, the combination of *Meditative Consciousness* and *Level Two Paradigmatic Consciousness* can allow an individual to gain some traction toward attaining *freedom of mind*.

It would still be premature to claim that *Level Two Paradigmatic Consciousness* demonstrates having the mental states one wants, so we must journey further.

As one might expect, an individual proficient at perceiving an alternate paradigm should have a distinct advantage in being able to have the thought one wants.

While the ability to perceive an alternate paradigm and choose the thoughts available within that paradigm enhances one's ability to have the thought one wants, *freedom of thought* is still a capability that paradigms constrain.

In other words, while two paradigms are better than one, the ability to have the thoughts one wants is beyond what two paradigms can potentially offer. As a result, this modest advantage does not rise to the level of being able to create the thoughts one wants, though it is a move in the right direction.

Again, we must leave the emergence of *freedom of thought* for a higher level of consciousness supported by additional software.

The ability to have the paradigm one wants certainly improves with *Level Two* abilities. Having insight simultaneously into two paradigms offers a modicum of choice between them. It places the *Level Two* individual at the threshold of *freedom of paradigm*.

At this level, however, the *Level Two* individual can merely perceive a second paradigm simultaneously and cannot see many or design and create new ones on demand.

As a result, we will have to wait for another software enhancement to emerge.

LEVEL THREE PARADIGMATIC CONSCIOUSNESS AND FREEDOM

Level Three Paradigmatic Consciousness emerges when individuals become aware that they can construct paradigms via the building blocks of perception that determine how to interpret the world around them.

The process then continues with the new realization that there are infinite ways of arranging these building blocks, thereby creating many ways to interpret everything around you.

Once this occurs, the ability to simultaneously perceive many paradigms soon follows, providing various ways to view reality. The imagination's ability to envision alternate paradigms is the only limitation of interpretations.

By this time, the individual learns to accept that there is no such thing as one version of reality, which then begs the question of the true nature of reality itself.

Finally, the individual is aware that they may choose which version of reality they want. Not without significant effort, with wisdom, the *Level Three* individual strives to identify and choose the most enlightened, helpful, and constructive paradigm for accomplishing the greatest good.

We mention *freedom of attention, will,* and *action* in *Level Three Paradigmatic Consciousness* for the ability to have the focus one wants, the volitions one wants, and the ability to enact those volitions belonging to various paradigms.

Able to operate within multiple paradigms simultaneously, a proficient *Level Three* individual has a significantly enhanced *freedom of attention* as they can have the focus they want with a rich selection of interpretations of the stimuli from the world around them.

As such, *Level Three Paradigmatic Consciousness* significantly enhances one's *freedom of attention, will, and action.*

Regarding *freedom of emotion*, one's paradigm significantly influences emotions. Hence, an individual proficient at perceiving any paradigm of their design has an even more significant advantage of having the emotions one wants. However, the emotions achieved are merely the natural result of the chosen paradigm.

In contrast, *freedom of emotion* requires having the emotions one wants from one's current paradigm. To have the emotion one wants is not achieved by rotating through a series of paradigms, searching for the emotions one wants.

Once again, as we shall see later in our journey, a more direct form of *freedom of emotion*, having the emotions one wants, will present itself.

As a side note, it is essential to call out that emotions represent a debilitating influence for *Level Twos* and *Level* Threes. Strong emotions severely disrupt one's ability to exercise *Level Two* and *Level Three* capabilities to perceive paradigms outside their base paradigm.

Emotions, or the inability to detach oneself from emotions and control them, can cause a *Level Two* or *Level Three* individual to fall precipitously down to operate as a *Level One* on a particular topic or when interacting with a particular individual.

Interestingly, not having the ability to have the emotion one wants will contribute to a *Level Two* or *Level Three* individual dropping down to *Level One* consciousness.

For this reason alone, we can conclude that it would be premature to claim that *Level Three Paradigmatic Consciousness* demonstrates having the emotions one wants.

Regarding *freedom of mind*, as one's paradigm influences mental states, *Level Threes* initially can select a paradigm to try on the mental state that results.

More empowering, however, instead of choosing from an existing inventory of paradigms, the *Level Three* individual soon learns that they can create a paradigm with the desired mental state.

Although this is a robust level of consciousness, the *Level Three* individual can still not directly have the mental state one wants.

As we shall see later in our journey, a more direct form of *freedom of mind*, having the mental states one wants, will present itself.

Therefore, it is premature to claim that *Level Three Paradigmatic Consciousness* fully demonstrates having the mental states one wants.

Thoughts bubble up from one's unconscious and subconscious levels from any number of paradigms the *Level Three* individual is currently running.

Although it may be tempting to conclude that thought cannot exist outside the confines of a paradigm, thoughts can occur without a paradigm, though such thoughts are minimal.

Suppose a Level One or Level Two completely crashes their base paradigm. In that case, the framework the individual finds is without a paradigm, which is somewhat disorienting and unsettling as there are no rules.

In this state, most of the thoughts that occur are the memories that belong to the fatally broken paradigm, which are not healthy to dwell upon because they tend to entrap the individual away from the critical task of reconstructing a paradigm that may allow the individual to function again.

The remaining thoughts pertain to the building blocks of paradigms. These consist of fragments of rules, including who the individual trusts and who they can speak with to start the repair process. If and when these building blocks become structurally stable, a new base paradigm is born.

One method by which new thoughts develop is by leveraging new paradigms that the *Level Three* individual creates. These paradigms can come together to suit the design criteria the *Level Three* individual selected.

It is one of two valid methods for achieving *freedom of thought*. Once a thought occurs, taking that thought from one paradigm to another for testing is extremely easy for the proficient *Level Three*.

The other method to create new thoughts is to design and create new thoughts from one's base paradigm. It represents an initial capability for *freedom of thought*. We will have to wait for another level of software to accomplish this freedom.

As a result, *Level Three Paradigmatic Consciousness* meets the initial criteria of having the thoughts one wants while meeting the criteria of being able to do otherwise.

Level Threes have a wide variety of paradigms to choose from such that they could choose any paradigm they want with the ability to choose otherwise.

Instead of choosing between chocolate and vanilla ice cream, they have as many flavors as they can imagine from any selection of paradigms they can perceive.

Level Three individuals can design paradigms to meet their own needs and preferences. It is a skill that they learned when recovering from a major paradigm crash earlier in their development. This skill offers the *Level Three* individual the option of designing and creating their flavor of ice cream, with its aromas, textures, colors, and mouthfeel.

An individual attaining *Level Three Paradigmatic Consciousness* can have the paradigm one wants with the ability to choose otherwise.

LEVEL FOUR PARADIGMATIC CONSCIOUSNESS AND FREEDOM

Level Four Paradigmatic Consciousness is a level of consciousness that taps into a spiritual realm of consciousness. This level of consciousness is a partnership between hardware and software as it belongs to a level associated with the mind's software, and it affects the brain's hardware in ways that neuroscience can physically detect.

In contrast to our earlier levels of paradigmatic consciousness, this level focuses on mildly relaxing the individual's natural emphasis on the self. However, it does not come close to approaching *Level Zero Paradigmatic Consciousness,* where the sense of self-interest is fully forfeited.

Instead, it softens the sense of self to have a broader perspective of our interconnectedness as part of a collective. It acknowledges our dependency upon our ancestors and one another, which helps to strengthen one's sense of empathy and being part of a greater whole.

If we return briefly to a philosophical perspective, the Buddha has had much to say on this topic, referred to as *selflessness.*

In Buddhism, the notion of *self* cannot exist in the absence of everything else, as the concept we refer to as "self" only exists in conjunction with all other people and things; the profundity of this statement is multi-fold, so let us take a moment to unpack it.

To paraphrase Noah Rasheta in his 2016 podcast, *True Selflessness:*

- Consider that the body we refer to as the "self" is the culmination of our parents and the long line of their parents before them.

- Consider that others almost entirely produced the food the "self" consumes.

- Consider that others almost entirely produced the clothing worn by the "self."

- Consider that others almost entirely produced the shelter that shelters the "self."

- Consider that others nearly entirely produced all possessions of the "self."

From this alone, we can see that there cannot exist the concept of a "self" that exists entirely apart from others any more than a leg of a mammal can dispense with the rest of the body and be on its own to survive.

[True Selflessness, March 15, 2016, Noah Rasheta, Buddhism podcast published by Secular Buddhism Podcast, https://secularbuddhism. com/true-selflessness/*]*

In contrast, *Level Zeros* do not see themselves as part of a collective looking out to protect the interests of the collective. Instead, they only seek to further the interests of their captives without regard for themselves or the collective.

As such, the *Level Four* individual has a more enlightened and mature view of all life and seeks to live more harmoniously with nature and its many other partners in the biosphere.

We mention *freedom of attention, will,* and *action* in *Level Four Paradigmatic Consciousness* for the ability to have the focus one wants, the volitions one wants, and the ability to enact those volitions.

The advantage that *Level Four Paradigmatic Consciousness* offers is that it relaxes the individual to some degree from the "Me" factor of self so that the *Level Four* individual would be more open to include a focus upon stimuli and thoughts that benefit all life.

This way, *Level Four Paradigmatic Consciousness* subtly expands one's *freedom of attention, will,* and *action*.

As such, one's *freedom of attention, will,* and *action* may be considered by some as being subtly enhanced upon attaining *Level Four Paradigmatic Consciousness*.

Regarding *freedom of emotion, Level Four Paradigmatic Consciousness* offers some advantages towards having the emotions one wants by freeing the individual from the "Me" factor of self.

Since most emotions are self-oriented, one's natural flow of emotions will directly conflict with the *Level Four* individual's more spiritual level of consciousness.

It is important to note that spirituality does not mean the individual is associated with or supportive of religion. The spiritual aspects of *Level Four Paradigmatic Consciousness* stem from the development of a particular brain center. There is no relationship to either religious beliefs or superstitions.

Although *Level Four Paradigmatic Consciousness* offers some advantages towards having the emotions one wants, it still falls short of *freedom of emotion*. That said, our journey may take us to a more direct form of *freedom of emotion*, having the emotions one wants.

Regarding *freedom of mind* and *thought*, *Level Four Paradigmatic Consciousness* provides neither the ability to have the mental states one wants nor the thoughts one wants. As we shall see, our journey may eventually take us to a more direct form of *freedom of mind* and *thought*.

The combination of *Level Four Paradigmatic Consciousness* with previous levels of consciousness further strengthens the individual's ability to have the paradigm one wants, particularly when the situation calls for creating paradigms intended to offer enlightenment, usefulness, and constructiveness for others.

By relaxing the "Me" factor, the *Level Four* individual will expend less of their mental faculties on self-centered paradigms, freeing up resources to recognize and create less self-centered paradigms.

As a result, the combination of *Level Four Paradigmatic Consciousness* with previous levels of consciousness offers a potential enhancement for having the paradigm one wants, with an ability to choose otherwise.

BUDDHIST CONSCIOUSNESS AND FREEDOM

Buddhist Consciousness represents the culmination of the journey into Buddhist consciousness. A few expert practitioners achieve this level of consciousness, which they believe is the closest that one can ever get to experiencing actual reality.

Though rare, this level of consciousness has been included within this framework because we cannot ignore scientific evidence of measurable brain-altering states.

As such, the expert practitioners of this level of consciousness appear credible from a scientific and Buddhist secular perspective.

As a level of consciousness within our framework, this is the only level that claims freedom from our biological stream of consciousness. Additionally, it is free from the various altered states of consciousness that become available through the expert's meditation practice.

In Buddhist terminology, this is a state of consciousness that some Buddhist experts call *primordial wakefulness*, while others call it *thought-free wakefulness*.

Interestingly, the path to *Buddhist Consciousness* is unaccompanied by companion travelers.

According to the Buddha, it is where one may finally perceive the real world for what it is. The reality of the 'real world' is free from our stream of consciousness and any distraction associated with our limited sensory organs. Hence, the term, *thought-free wakefulness.*

The attention of *Buddhist Consciousness* is on the experience that results when the mind is no longer distracted by the stimuli of the physical body. The volition of the practitioner is to maintain a state of *thought-free wakefulness.* Enacting this volition involves extensive practice as a meditative practitioner to attain *thought-free wakefulness.*

As a result, this may be the ultimate form of *freedom of attention, will,* and *action.*

Although we have included this level of consciousness within our consciousness framework, it may not have applicability to the survival of *Homo sapiens.* But it has nonetheless been included.

Regarding *freedom of emotion,* the notion of emotions is irrelevant when considering *Buddhist Consciousness.*

Early in the journey to *Buddhist Consciousness,* the practitioner develops a deep understanding of the Buddhist concept called *impermanence.* The primary effect of *impermanence* is that it allows the individual to recognize the futility of holding onto anything emotionally, including possessions and relationships, as everything in life and the universe is transient.

Since many emotional responses result from believing that we own various things, including personal relationships, the mindset of not owning anything eliminates many emotions that typically occur.

As a result, instead of designating *Buddhist Consciousness* as having *freedom of emotion* and *thought,* it seems more appropriate to designate *Buddhist Consciousness* as allowing the practitioner to achieve freedom from emotion and thought.

Next is *freedom of mind.*

Buddhist Consciousness achieves *freedom of mind,* although it is the only mental state resulting in total relaxation and inner peace. Hence, *Buddhist Consciousness* does not achieve *freedom of mind* to have the mental state one wants.

Finally, there is *freedom of paradigm.*

The objective of *Buddhist Consciousness* is to experience actual reality. As such, *paradigms* are not reality but rules that facilitate interpretations of reality

Arguably, there is only one reality, whereas, in contrast, we learned in *Level Three Paradigmatic Consciousness* that there are infinite paradigms with which to interpret the same version of reality. If anything, this helps illustrate that no one paradigm can represent actual reality.

Instead, *Buddhist Consciousness* cannot attain *freedom of paradigm* as it achieves *freedom from any paradigm*.

UNCONSCIOUS CONSCIOUSNESS AND FREEDOM

The *unconscious* mind is the layer of the CNS closest to the body's physical systems. This layer includes reflexes (i.e., hard-wired circuits within the CNS), the generation of stimuli in sensory organs, and the neural expressways that transport signals in every direction.

Although the exact boundary between the *unconscious* and *subconscious* mind has some unknowns, it is at least transparent that the portion of the mind that is always wholly inaccessible to the *conscious* mind belongs to the *unconscious* mind.

The *unconscious* layer is the source of vast amounts of pre-processed raw stimuli from sensory organs and neurons, without which the *subconscious* and *conscious* levels would be blind.

Second, the *unconscious* mind is the only interface able to communicate directly with the various muscles of the physical body. As a result, all volitions of the *conscious* and *subconscious* mind must rely upon the *unconscious* mind to participate.

Perhaps one of the critical features of *Unconscious Consciousness* is that the software layer of the *unconscious* mind is partially programmable in the same way that *Subconscious Consciousness* and *Conscious Consciousness* levels are programmed, though to a lesser extent, as we will describe.

The latest advancements in neuroscience show that the brain is physically changing its connections as we experience the world around us, and the purely intellectual activities we practice, such as meditation, likewise alter the brain. This effect is known as neuroplasticity.

> *Plasticity is the ability to shape or mold, whereas neuroplasticity describes the brain's ability to change and reorganize its connections in response to the environment and activities.*

To illustrate this critical point, we should try to understand how this works from a specific medical use case.

Let us take the example of a lost limb, where individuals experience severe pain in the limb that is no longer present.

Medical science had thought that the source of pain in these situations might occur at the nerve endings where the limb is forfeit, so they frequently tried to remove more of the limb in the hope of removing the offending nerve endings. Most times, this approach failed.

The physicians then tried something new.

Instead of removing more of the nervous system at the end, they theorized that sensations from a phantom limb are present because the brain rewired the circuits for the missing limb to another part of the body, potentially making rewiring errors.

> *The way the theory went, let's say you lost the pinky toe of your left foot. In this case, your brain no longer has a pinky toe to communicate with but still thinks it should be somewhere.*

> *So, to reestablish communications with the pinky toe, hopefully, the brain does some rewiring to get around the problem. When this rewiring goes wrong, the result is often severe pain.*

As a result, there were two approaches available.

The first approach was to provide an amputee with drugs inhibiting rewiring after an amputation.

The second approach was the theory from Doctor G. Lorimer Moseley, involving the situation when the brain makes an error when rewiring itself. Hence, the best corrective measure would be to get the brain to undo the rewiring.

But how does one get the brain to change the wiring back to normal?

To paraphrase Professor G. Lorimer Moseley, Ph.D. professor of clinical neurosciences at the University of South Australia and Neuro Research Australia, in his 2018 article, *The body in mind—disruption and treatment of cortical body map in people with chronic pain*:

> *Dr. Moseley decided that the answer involved imagery to make the patient see the missing limb and, with imagery, have it move in response to their will until the brain rewires itself as if the missing limb were no longer missing.*

> *[The body in mind—disruption and treatment of cortical body map in people with chronic pain, G. Lorimer Moseley Ph.D. – Professor of clinical neurosciences at the University of South Australia and Neuro Research Australia, May 18, 2012, 31st Annual Scientific Meeting American Pain Society, Honolulu, HI]*

The assertion here is that the neural circuits involved in identifying stimuli from sensory organs that ultimately determine conscious pain are primarily at the *brain's unconscious level in the brain's cortical region*. This area maps the various parts of the body to the brain to route stimuli from the appropriate body region to its corresponding brain region.

This area of the brain is well out of the reach of the *conscious* and *subconscious* areas of the brain. However, the neurons at this level may still be programmable, though at a highly *unconscious* level, instead of directly programming the mind via *conscious* volition.

Since the only component known to be capable of reprogramming are glial cells, the thought here is that glial cells are present at strategic locations within the *conscious, subconscious*, and *unconscious* layers of the CNS.

Studies to date have not determined the ability of one's *unconscious* to exercise *freedom of attention, will, or action*.

That said, the neurons and *neuroglia* that comprise the unconscious mind are equipped with eukaryotic cytoskeletal structures and, therefore, have the potential to reroute neurons the same way they can in the subconscious and conscious levels.

As such, additional research would be necessary to accurately determine the ability of *Unconscious Consciousness* to support *freedom of attention, will*, and *action* to take on re-programming.

Regarding *freedom of emotion, thought*, and *paradigm, Unconscious Consciousness* does not render *freedom of emotion, mind, and thought*, as according to the framework, it works in opposition by bubbling up stimuli that trigger the release of chemicals that automatically generate emotions, mental states, and thoughts.

As such, the stimuli stemming from the unconscious layer are the signals that other levels of *consciousness* must tame.

Therefore, *Unconscious Consciousness* does not and cannot support these freedoms.

While *Unconscious Consciousness* potentially plays a role in supporting one's paradigm, the abilities of the *unconscious* layer are insufficiently understood to determine its exact role.

Additional research would be necessary to accurately determine the role of *Unconscious Consciousness* regarding *freedom of paradigm*.

SUBCONSCIOUS CONSCIOUSNESS AND FREEDOM

Recall that simple organisms have one level of consciousness and lack a *subconscious* level. Although some scientists assert that primitive organisms lack a conscious level, it is the unconscious and subconscious levels that simple organisms lack.

> *Paramecia, for example, do not receive such large quantities of stimuli to require a vast array of functions to perform at either an unconscious or subconscious level and hence need only be equipped with a conscious level that informs them about the world around them.*

Complex organisms equipped with brains have streams of stimuli generated by sensory organs that travel through the CNS at an *unconscious* level, where initially, the individual as an agent has no *conscious* awareness of its existence.

For stimuli to reach the conscious level, they must have a sufficient level of importance to be 'bubbled up' from the *subconscious* to the *conscious* level. Therefore, the subconscious mind sits between the *unconscious* and the *conscious* mind.

As we might expect, neuroplasticity (i.e., the brain's software programming) also plays an essential role in this level of consciousness.

Consider muscle memory, an adaptation for repeating a specific physical activity experienced by athletes, musicians, surgeons, or anyone who regularly performs repeated motor skills as mundane as tying one's shoelaces. Repeated activities such as these eventually move control of an activity to the subconscious as a form of software programming or neuroplasticity.

> *The latest research shows that muscle memory occurs in the cerebellum, primarily, where Purkinje cells and vestibular nuclear neurons work together to form long-term motor memories.*

To quote Christopher Bergland, a world-class endurance athlete, coach, and author, in his 2015 Psychology Today article, *How Does Practice Hardwire Long-Term Muscle Memory?*: Quote.

> *"The March 2015 findings resulted from a collaboration of researchers at the University of Electro-Communications and the RIKEN Brain Science Institute in Japan, and the University of California, San Diego."*

> *"The researchers were able to integrate the multiple plasticity mechanisms of the cerebellum to explain the formation of long-term motor memory. Their findings suggest that multiple plasticity mechanisms in the cerebellar cortex and cerebellar/vestibular nuclei participate in long-term motor memory formation."*

> *"The researchers concluded that if a short-term memory forms in the Purkinje cells after one hour of training that it is then transferred to the vestibular nuclear neuron where it is consolidated into long-term motor memory." End Quote.*

> *["How Does Practice Hardwire Long-Term Muscle Memory?", Christopher Bergland — a world-class endurance athlete, coach, author, Mar 27, 2015, Psychology Today]*

The *subconscious* level processes, filters, and prioritizes many streams of stimuli so that segments of stimuli considered of sufficient importance can bubble up to the *conscious* level. Without the *subconscious,* the *conscious* level would receive more stimuli than it can manage.

In this manner, *Subconscious Consciousness* helps facilitate one's *freedom of attention* by first allowing it the luxury of being able to choose what to focus on versus becoming overwhelmed by too many segments of stimuli to consider.

However, the relationship between the *subconscious* and *conscious* levels is not all in one direction.

Although it has limits, the *conscious* ability to affect the *subconscious* is significant. Having and maintaining the focus one wants can only undergo improvement in one of a few ways: customized filtering, prioritization, and preprogrammed responses.

With customized filtering, the subconscious can learn how to ignore unwanted distractions using techniques such as *Meditative Consciousness* and conditioning to eventually lower the level of importance associated with types of stimuli. With practice, one can partially ignore certain stimuli at a *subconscious* level.

With customized prioritization, the *subconscious* layer can learn to raise the level of importance associated with types of stimuli. With practice, the *subconscious* can attain a heightened sense of alertness to look for certain stimuli to bubble up more rapidly.

With reprogramming, the *subconscious* layer can learn how to cause the body to react to certain stimuli automatically without future *conscious* intervention.

In the case of professional sports training, such as tennis, the repetition of experiencing certain events allows the *subconscious* to take shortcuts in responding milliseconds faster than it did previously by generating learned responses before their *conscious* level becomes aware. This reduction in latency allows certain players to be better than anyone who can only respond at a *conscious* level.

Therefore, regarding *freedom of attention*, *will*, and *action*, *Subconscious Consciousness* indirectly supports having the focus one wants, having the volitions one wants, and enacting the volition one wants by providing customized filtering, prioritization, and preprogrammed responses in support of the *conscious* level.

The *subconscious* mind has many essential features to support the *conscious* mind. However, ease of change, or more accurately, ease of programmability, is not one of them. Programmability requires the *conscious* mind to mindfully focus on effecting change repetitively over prolonged periods that, once achieved, require practice to maintain.

However, this is just one way the *conscious mind can readily reprogram the subconscious* mind. Some activities of the *subconscious* mind are more challenging to reprogram, as some areas remain unavailable to reprogramming regardless of the amount of practice applied.

To paraphrase the 2010 UCLA Health article, *Mind over Matter: Study shows we consciously exert control over individual neurons*:

> *The subconscious mind performs many functions, of which we influence a tiny portion, though in sometimes surprising areas.*
>
> *["Mind over matter: Study shows we consciously exert control over individual neurons," October 27, 2010, UCLA Health,* https://www.uclahealth.org/news/mind-over-matter-study-shows-we-consciously-exert-control-over-individual-neurons*, media contact: Mark Wheeler]*

Regarding the *freedoms of emotion* and *mind*, these slow-moving changes in the *subconscious* are essential to helping the conscious mind achieve *freedom of emotion* and *mind*. However, the subconscious alone cannot achieve either.

Perhaps it is more the opposite influence, as in its natural state, the *subconscious* mind is more likely to work against the development of any ability to have the emotion or mental state one wants.

The functions of the *subconscious* mind are supportive and collaborative with the *conscious* mind. Most of the segments of stimuli and thoughts the conscious mind perceives originate from the *subconscious* and the *unconscious* below that.

When the CEO of a business decides that his organization should create a new product, such as the world's first smartphone, the CEO may be *conscious* of only some decisions regarding the new product.

In the end, many decisions made by many individuals will occur together to produce a new product. In this manner, many decisions are at the *subconscious* level, where the CEO is unaware of many decisions made by many others.

> *For example, developing an operating system for a smart device requires a team of architects, designers, and developers that ultimately make many decisions to create the final product.*
>
> *In such a circumstance, no person can make every decision.*

The important thing about the thoughts and decisions that occur at the *subconscious* level is that the CEO could theoretically learn about them and influence them. However, it would significantly impede the process of evaluating every decision made by the *subconscious* level at the *conscious* level.

However, the ability to have the thoughts one wants does not stem from the *subconscious*.

If anything, in its natural state before any reprogramming, the *subconscious* is more likely to hinder the ability to have the thoughts one wants as it tends to distract the conscious mind with the flow of thoughts that it sends.

Additional software capabilities are necessary to attain *freedom of thought* beyond what the *subconscious* can provide.

Regarding *freedom of paradigm*, even one's base paradigm requires much help from the *subconscious* to power the thoughts that fit each paradigm.

Together, the *subconscious* and *conscious* levels usually operate within just one paradigm. However, when more than one paradigm is active, the *subconscious* and *conscious* levels must simultaneously support the multiple paradigms.

Paradigms and the thoughts within them operate more like the minds of separate individuals whose thoughts are shared.

These so-called separate individuals can sometimes operate with equal strength to one another, or one or more of them can dominate the dialog, just as individuals in the same meeting can participate equally or unequally.

However, the *subconscious* mind cannot achieve and support *freedom of paradigm* alone without collaboration from the *conscious* mind, plus the emergence of additional software that *Level Twos* and *Level Threes* have developed.

CONSCIOUS CONSCIOUSNESS AND FREEDOM

Early Buddhists expressed *consciousness* in terms of a '*process*' with events that occur from that process, as opposed to as an '*object*' that acts.

This perspective is much in line with the notion that *consciousness* is more like a stream, ever-changing as water flows past each point of the stream. The flowing water represents constant change, with different water molecules and particles residing in each position at different intervals.

It is in sharp contrast to a fixed object, like a stone, where the molecules that reside in each position of the stone remain the same from moment to moment.

Hence, the flow of water is a process with events that may either accelerate or decelerate as new water enters the stream at different rates. In contrast, the stone is an object that may act by slowly sinking deeper into the soft soil or by rolling downhill when there is a storm.

In contrast, philosophy defines *consciousness* as the following four concepts:

a) *Knowledge* (i.e., epistemology) is the body of the things and facts we believe.

b) *Intentionality* is the power of a mind to be about something or to stand for ideas and principles.

c) *Introspection* is the process of generating thoughts.

d) *Phenomenal experience* is the sensations one experiences from the senses.

Within our framework, we define the term '*consciousness*' as the following:

Consciousness pertains to any individual organism (or entity) that possesses any degree of awareness of any quantity of matter or energy within one's local physical environment.

If an organism can demonstrate the ability to choose a reaction based on its prior experience of awareness, demonstrating an ability to choose otherwise, then that organism has consciousness.

Suppose an organism can demonstrate the ability to choose a reaction based on its prior experience of awareness but never demonstrates a different choice. In that case, that organism cannot choose otherwise and has not achieved consciousness.

Suppose an organism cannot demonstrate the ability to choose a reaction based upon its prior experience of awareness because it could not enact the volitions it might want. In that case, that organism may potentially have consciousness.

Concerning organisms equipped with a brain or its equivalent, *Conscious Consciousness* can exercise limited influence over the *subconscious* mind as a type of programmability. Programmability requires the conscious mind to mindfully focus on effecting change repetitively over prolonged periods that, once achieved, tame the subconscious to some degree.

We mention *freedom of attention, will,* and *action* in *Conscious Consciousness* to reinforce that these freedoms existed at the beginning of our framework, well before the emergence of the brain and *Conscious Consciousness.*

As a result, there are potential examples of *consciousness* at each level of evolution where all forms of eukaryotic life have levels of *consciousness* to various degrees.

Notably, all framework levels support *freedom of attention, will,* and *action.* It is conceivable that the biosphere could have had experiments with organisms that had *freedom of attention* while missing *freedom of will* and *action,* though it left no evidence of that.

However, when the biosphere developed the type of cytoskeletal structures present within the successful eukaryotic cells we know, all three forms of freedom co-exist.

Let's turn to a simple thought experiment once again.

Using a '*thought experiment,*' let's imagine a living organism that is conscious of one or more things within its environment without possessing the ability to have the volitions one wants or the ability to enact the volitions one wants.

The result is that we can imagine an organism that receives sensory stimuli from its surroundings such that it is aware of some selection of chemicals and forms of energy in its vicinity but lacks any volitions.

An organism that could never improve its conditions would have severe disadvantages in securing its survival.

As for *freedoms of emotion, mind, thought,* and *paradigm,* the standard features of *Conscious Consciousness* do not support them.

As a result, *Conscious Consciousness* does not offer the full capability to achieve *freedom of emotion, mind, thought, or paradigm.*

However, the ability of the *conscious* mind to influence one's *conscious* decisions and *subconscious* processes, although the latter is indirect, can be an effective tool in directing the path of one's life.

Many fail to realize it, but the *conscious* layer can slowly reprogram the subconscious layer over prolonged periods, whether the individual takes conscious advantage of it or not. Consciously placing some objective iteratively in one's mind is perhaps the most effective way to enlist the *subconscious* layer to work towards achieving one's goals.

Individuals who realize the ability of the *conscious* mind to influence their *subconscious* mind are reportedly among some of the most successful individuals.

> *The Netflix documentary series "The Secret" describes an assembly of writers, philosophers, and scientists who understand this concept, which reputedly brought success to Plato, Leonardo da Vinci, Albert Einstein, and other significant historical figures.*
>
> *[The Secret, 2006, Netflix]*

GROUP CONSCIOUSNESS AND FREEDOM

Although software-based, *Group Consciousness* is a relatively long-term behavior biologically built-in and triggered by the individual's perceptions of resource availability and lifestyle.

Recall that *Group Consciousness* is distinct from mob psychology theory, which includes riots, panics, crazes, and stampedes, which are short-term effects that are instead emotionally driven typically by fear, anger, or rage. Regarding its potential reversal, unlike mob psychology, simple communication or isolation from the group is ineffective in overcoming and reversing the behaviors associated with *Group Consciousness.*

In *Group Consciousness,* we discussed three theories that illustrate this level of consciousness. These were r/K Selection Theory, Affluence Theory, and Coddling Theory for their ability to trigger behaviors that have some resemblance to 'r' and 'K' cycle behaviors.

We can still view that individual as having the same amount of control over the freedoms they want. However, it involves a skewed set of behaviors toward living for today or tomorrow.

Individuals are concerned with resource scarcity in the 'K' cycle behavior. Their focus is on building up resources and strength in preparation for bad times that will eventually come.

With 'r' cycle behavior, one's physical safety and or planning for tomorrow give way to an attitude that it is better to live for today.

However, if a biological trigger influences an individual to restrict their behaviors to one end of the spectrum, does it mean an external influence restricts their freedoms?

Recall that every freedom to be free must come with an ability to do otherwise. If an external influence were to restrict what an individual would focus on, would that restrict *freedom of attention*, *will*, or *action*?

The answer is partially yes; a biological trigger is like an external influence resulting in freedom's impairment. However, unlike a computer chip that prohibits specific choices, this biological trigger does not prohibit any specific behavior. It only lends influence.

Therefore, whether an individual is in the 'r' or 'K' cycle behavior, their freedoms can be said to be influenced by a biological trigger.

Only individuals not under the influence of the 'r' or 'K' cycle behavior are free of the external influence of the biological trigger.

As a result, *Group Consciousness* is only an influence, like the variety of other influences that act on our behavior.

Although *Group Consciousness* appears to be real, there doesn't appear to be any particularly harmful aspects for those participating in *Group Consciousness* for its effect upon *freedom of attention*, *will*, *action*, *mind*, *emotion*, *thought*, or *paradigm*. However, these cycles seem to improve the survival of the species that it influences.

Hence, if the population increases during times of plenty, the increase in genetic variability will work toward a greater probability of some members surviving the next plague or natural disaster.

THE MODERN LEARNING THERMOSTAT AND FREEDOM

For completeness, let's compare the freedoms the *Modern Learning Thermostat* supports.

Consider that the *Modern Learning Thermostat* learns through experience during a one-month learning period.

During this period, these advanced thermostats record what temperatures you choose during different parts of the day. Then, they automatically repeat what they have recorded under the design assumption that these are the user's temperature preferences.

The more advanced versions employ motion detectors to determine when the space contains occupants and automatically adjust to conserve energy when there are none. These thermostats have sensors for temperature, humidity, motion, and light.

The question then becomes, do these advanced thermostats rise to any level of consciousness within our framework?

First, there is no notion of preferences for the self. The preferences belong only to the user. But let's put that aside, as some philosophy professors will argue that we only have *Modern Learning Thermostats* with *Level Zero Paradigmatic Consciousness*.

Recall that we define the term *consciousness* as:

> *Consciousness pertains to any individual organism (or entity) that possesses any degree of awareness of any quantity of matter or energy within one's local physical environment.*

> *If an organism can demonstrate the ability to choose a reaction based on its prior experience of awareness, demonstrating an ability to choose otherwise, then that organism has consciousness.*

> *Suppose an organism can demonstrate the ability to choose a reaction based on its prior experience of awareness but never demonstrates a different choice. In that case, that organism cannot choose otherwise and has not achieved consciousness.*

Freedom of attention, having the focus one wants, renders the *Modern Learning Thermostat* unable to claim *freedom of attention* for two reasons.

First, the *Modern Learning Thermostat* cannot have the focus one wants.

Instead, it will focus on whatever stimuli meet its mechanical threshold for detection. Each sensor type is mechanically awaiting stimuli. Suppose one of its sensors detects a temperature rise and another detects motion in its proximity. In that case, those sensors will share their signals with the small computer unit that processes these signals following its programming. It cannot decide to focus on a different stimulus or to have the volition it wants.

Second, recall that *freedom of attention* is the ability to have the focus one wants without constraint from an external source, with the ability to choose otherwise.

The *Modern Learning Thermostat* cannot choose otherwise. If the programming selects a specific stimulus to focus on, the *Modern Learning Thermostat* cannot choose otherwise.

As such, the *Modern Learning Thermostat* must always follow its programming. At any given moment, it cannot choose to ignore its programming to focus on the stimulus it wants, essentially because it can never want.

If we turn to a simple thought experiment, let's stipulate that the *Modern Learning Thermostat* can learn the temperature preferences for each time of day.

Assuming the occupants adjust the temperature during the day each day, the *Modern Learning Thermostat* can learn the preferences for weekdays versus Saturdays and Sundays.

In this thought experiment, the *Modern Learning Thermostat* meets the criteria of demonstrating the ability to choose a reaction based on prior experience.

However, does the *Modern Learning Thermostat* have *freedom of attention*?

Although the *Modern Learning Thermostat* demonstrates the ability to choose a reaction based upon prior experience, all *Modern Learning Thermostats* with the same programming could never choose otherwise.

If we placed one million *Modern Learning Thermostats* in the same environment, they would all learn and react uniformly.

If we added functionality to accept voice commands from any of the world's spoken languages, the only things it can focus on remain determined by its programming.

While the *Modern Learning Thermostat* can have the ability to choose from among competing stimuli, when given a million *Modern Learning Thermostats* of the same model with the same stimuli under the same circumstances, each will focus on the same stimuli as the other units, as they are following the same programming.

As such, the *Modern Learning Thermostat* would fail to demonstrate *freedom of attention*.

When it comes to *freedom of will*, the *Modern Learning Thermostat* initially seems to demonstrate *freedom of will* by recognizing the conditions within its environment and acting appropriately based on its ability to learn the correct response.

The problem that emerges with each freedom is that the *Modern Learning Thermostat* cannot choose otherwise. The volition the *Modern Learning Thermostat* chooses is not the volition it wants, with an ability to choose otherwise. Still, instead, it chooses the volition it was mechanically programmed to select.

Since *freedom of will* is the ability to choose the volition one wants, with an ability to choose otherwise, our *Modern Learning Thermostat* lacks *freedom of will*.

Next is *freedom of action*.

Freedom of action is the ability to enact the volition one wants, with an ability to choose otherwise, as it is first dependent upon having *freedom of will*

Even if the *Modern Learning Thermostat* could claim *freedom of will*, it cannot enact the volition one wants with an ability to choose otherwise, as again, it cannot choose otherwise.

However, the reason that *Modern Learning Thermostat* cannot choose otherwise is not that an external constraint is acting upon it. Instead, it is because it can never want to choose otherwise.

In comparison, an individual possessing *free will* may choose to have a volition, such as departing a particular room.

The various steps to consider freedom of action are entirely dependent upon having a volition one wants to enact, with the ability to do otherwise. We can't even get to the step where we analyze whether an external influence prevents *freedom of action*.

Next is *freedom of emotion*.

The *Modern Learning Thermostat cannot* claim *freedom of emotion* for three reasons.

First, the *Modern Learning Thermostat* lacks emotions and cannot categorize any experience as pleasant, unpleasant, or indifferent as the precursor to emotions.

Second, the *Modern Learning Thermostat* cannot have the emotions that one wants since it cannot want.

Third, the *Modern Learning Thermostat* lacks any ability to choose otherwise.

As such, the *Modern Learning Thermostat* cannot demonstrate *freedom of emotion*.

Next is *freedom of mind, thought,* and *paradigm*.

The *Modern Learning Thermostat* can also not claim *freedom of mind*, thought, and *paradigm* for similar reasons.

First, it lacks a mental state, thoughts, and paradigms.

Second, it lacks any ability to want.

Third, it lacks any ability to choose otherwise.

As such, the *Modern Learning Thermostat* can also not demonstrate *freedom of mind, thought,* and *paradigm*.

At this point, the *Modern Learning Thermostat* lacks all twenty-four levels of consciousness and all seven forms of freedom.

It does not mean mechanical beings cannot attain consciousness or possess freedoms. Still, it does mean that *The Modern Learning Thermostat,* as proffered by some philosophers and neuroscientists, is neither *conscious* nor capable of *freedom of attention, will, action, emotion, mind, thought,* or *paradigm*.

The journey into non-eukaryotic consciousness need not end with the *Modern Learning Thermostat.*

LIFE WITHOUT CONSCIOUSNESS

Throughout the twenty-four levels of consciousness, we identified various forms of eukaryotic life that exhibit *consciousness* in ways we can observe and relate to.

Does this mean there could also be living cells that do not possess any level of consciousness and no freedoms?

While scientific evidence is lacking, cells at every level of eukaryotic life have at least one level of *consciousness* and *freedom.*

Perhaps prokaryotes are an example of life without consciousness. But then again, perhaps not.

PART IV.

RELATED CONCEPTS

CONSCIOUSNESS, SENTIENCE, INTELLIGENCE, AWARENESS, AND SAPIENCE

In Part I, we defined *consciousness* as it evolved through nine levels of eukaryotic physical evolutionary advancements and fifteen levels of software-based advancements.

The levels of consciousness corresponding to organisms' physical traits were *unicellular consciousness, multicellular consciousness, nerve net consciousness, nerve cord consciousness, neural bundle consciousness, primitive brain consciousness, mammalian consciousness, primate consciousness,* and *Homo consciousness.*

The levels of consciousness corresponding to software-based organisms' traits were *meditative consciousness, reason-driven consciousness, persona consciousness, compartmentalized consciousness, in-the-moment consciousness, level zero through four paradigmatic consciousness, Buddhist consciousness, unconscious consciousness, subconscious consciousness, conscious consciousness,* and *group consciousness.*

Recall our definition of *consciousness.*

> *Consciousness pertains to any individual organism (or entity) that possesses any degree of awareness of any quantity of matter or energy within one's local physical environment.*

> *If an organism can demonstrate the ability to choose a reaction based on its prior experience of awareness, demonstrating an ability to choose otherwise, then that organism has consciousness.*

> *Suppose an organism can demonstrate the ability to choose a reaction based on its prior experience of awareness but never demonstrates a different choice. In that case, that organism cannot choose otherwise and has not achieved consciousness.*

In Part II, we defined the five types of *qualia* as they evolved through eukaryotic physical advancements. These were *unicellular qualia, multicellular qualia, neuronal qualia, neuroglia qualia,* and *collective neuroglia neuronal qualia.*

In Part III, we defined the seven forms of freedom that evolved through eukaryotic software-based advancements. These include *freedom of attention, will, action, emotion, mind, thought,* and *paradigm.*

Although our journey has taken us through consciousness, qualia, and freedom, we have not yet journeyed into sentience, intelligence, awareness, and sapience.

SENTIENCE

In science fiction books, movies, and television programs, we frequently encounter the term *'sentient being.'*

At times, this reference applies to an alien life form. At other times, it refers to an artificially intelligent being that is a manufactured machine instead of a biological organism. However, the term's meaning can be somewhat unclear depending on the context.

The dictionary definition of *'sentience'* is the ability to feel, perceive, or experience stimuli subjectively, so this depends upon the definition of *subjectivity.*

> *To be 'subjective' means to depend wholly on the individual's ideas, opinions, feelings, and tastes, which is the opposite of what it means to be objective.*

> *To be 'objective' means to depend upon universal truths and facts that one can verify scientifically. Objective truths are not opinions, ideas, or feelings.*

In other words, any individual is *sentient* if the individual has feelings. When we consider *sentience* within our consciousness framework, it depends upon how we define *feelings* and whether we include the definitions of *ideas, opinions,* and *tastes.*

In philosophy, the definition of *sentience* is still more colorful and inconsistent.

Sometimes, it necessitates that the individual possesses *consciousness;* sometimes, it does not.

Second, the individual must have *agency.*

The term *agency* means the ability of an individual to act independently to make their own choices and to be able to act upon those choices. We now know this within our framework as possessing *freedom of will* and *action.*

> *In this sense, agency is not the strict product of causal chains but is instead the product of choice with the ability to have or choose otherwise.*

Our definition of sentience is as follows:

> *Sentience is present when an organism possesses freedom of attention and freedom of will with the ability to have ideas, opinions, feelings, and tastes one may freely choose.*

> *In this definition, freedom of action is absent because lacking the ability to enact the volition does not determine whether an organism has sentience.*

> *Additionally, the term 'tastes' pertains to having preferences, as opposed to experiencing the flavor of a particular substance, and the*

term 'feelings' pertains to one's sensibilities, as opposed to experiencing the sensation of pain.

However, individuals that cannot feel pain are still sentient.

To paraphrase the Linton 2005 book, *Understanding Pain for Better Clinical Practice: A Psychological Perspective*:

Congenital insensitivity to pain (CIP), or congenital analgesia, is a mutation in which an individual does not feel pain from birth.

[Understanding Pain for Better Clinical Practice: A Psychological Perspective, 2005, Linton, Elsevier Health Sciences]

That said, our definition contains a handful of concepts that require definitions, particularly regarding leveraging the individual's ideas, opinions, feelings, and tastes. Therefore, let's explore those terms to clarify the definition further.

At the simple end of the continuum, eukaryotic-based life is unicellular, which comes equipped with specialized sensory organelles, and at the complex end of the continuum, eukaryotic-based life comes equipped with specialized organs comprised of numerous specialized cells. The difference is much like an individual versus a large corporation or government.

Within our simplest life forms, we have *Unicellular Consciousness*, exemplified by the genus *Paramecium*, which may lack ideas and opinions. However, it may possess primitive feelings and tastes equivalent to determining a stimulus as pleasant, unpleasant, or indifferent.

At this point, we may argue that *sentience* is present within our first level of consciousness, *Unicellular Consciousness*, because a *Paramecium* can learn and demonstrate the first three freedoms, namely *freedom of attention* and *freedom of will*, which is arguably *sentient*. After all, a *Paramecium* has *freedom of attention, will, action, and* opinions as determined by its primitive feelings and tastes.

However, our Paramecium lacks *ideas* and *feelings*.

If *sentience* were to begin at the unicellular level, then eukaryotic plant life at the multicellular level, which includes plants, would just as easily meet the sentience criterion.

However, rather than engaging in the futile debate as to whether plants have feelings, given our purposes, we can agree to state that the continuum of *sentience* begins at a higher level of advancement.

But briefly, before moving forward in our journey, we should pause because we would be remiss not to reveal the most prevalent contrary opinion on the matter, Jainism.

Jainism is an ancient religion that believes all plants and animals contain living souls, all equal in value, and requiring respect and compassion.

Jains have neither deities nor priests, just monks and nuns, numbering around 4.2 million in India based on a 2001 census, with many additional thousands spread worldwide. Their philosophy centers around non-violence with three guiding principles: correct belief, proper knowledge, and appropriate conduct.

Their sacred vows (a.k.a. Mahavira) include non-violence, non-attachment to possessions, strict honesty, no stealing, and sexual restraint, with celibacy as the ideal. Also, Jains are strict vegetarians who minimize the use of the Earth's resources.

Jains sweep the ground of their path with the utmost care to avoid accidentally crushing crawling insects, and in areas prone to flies, they wear muslin cloths over their mouth to ensure they do not swallow and thus harm any flying insects.

According to Jainism, the souls of all living things are continually recycled in the circle of reincarnation until the individual achieves their goal of breaking free.

As a result, if one were to correlate *sentience* with the presence of a *soul* and the avoidance of *harm*, then Jainism assigns *sentience* to all visible and non-visible forms of life, no matter how small or seemingly insignificant. Jainism includes all life forms.

SENTIENCE AND NEURONS

When we arrive at the third level of consciousness, *Nerve Net Consciousness*, the capabilities of organisms improve significantly in areas such as hunting prey or finding food, where the notion of *ideas* seems to emerge, at least about how best to capture prey.

In this level of consciousness, we see the emergence of rudimentary emotions, such as *feelings*, where relatively simple organisms equipped with neurons may writhe in pain or exhibit visible agitation. However, *opinions* and perhaps *tastes* do not seem to appear yet.

At the sixth level of consciousness, *Primitive Brain Consciousness* represented by the class *Reptilia*, seven types of senses emerge, including vision, hearing, smell, taste, tactile, infrared, and vomeronasal.

The advanced neural layer architecture of specialized neural tissues forming the primitive brain of *Reptilia* supports the emergence of several primitive emotions (e.g., sexual attraction, fear, aggressiveness, and social emotions) that influence the organism's behavior.

Regarding the ability to form *ideas*, *Reptilia* also demonstrates object use, where alligators and crocodiles collect sticks as bait to catch birds.

This level of consciousness demonstrates improved capabilities to support *ideas, feelings,* and *tastes,* and they may even have primitive *opinions,* such as which individuals are dominant or which are a threat.

Having met the main criteria of *sentience,* our sixth level of consciousness, *Primitive Brain Consciousness,* represented by *Reptilia,* represents the most primitive level of consciousness that meets the criteria of *sentience.*

Let's consider our seventh level of consciousness, *Mammalian Consciousness,* and the genus *Rattus* for the brain's many architectural advancements.

Here, *Rattus* easily satisfies the criteria for *sentience* by demonstrating *opinions* as sophisticated as basic ethics, such as whether it is better to free a captive companion rather than feast on a chocolate stash they could have had to themselves.

Rattus demonstrates extensive capabilities, including *freedom of attention, will, and action,* and an ability to interpret stimuli while leveraging the individual's *ideas, opinions, feelings, and tastes.*

But why is *sentience* necessary to concern oneself about?

IMPORTANCE OF SENTIENCE AND LOWER LIFE FORMS

The issue of *sentience* is important from different perspectives.

First, *sentience* is an important ethical issue for determining how humans treat other living organisms.

At a fundamental level, this issue involves the treatment of animals farmed for food and clothing, beasts of burden to do work, law enforcement to assist police, military use to support specialized operators, and the treatment and use in the entertainment industry, such as in zoos, circuses, or used in human performances and films.

There is also a litany of domestic roles for animals, including pets, companions, protection, and service animals.

The treatment of *sentient* organisms often revolves around placing the animal into stressful circumstances and painful activities that reach the level of abuse.

> *Beasts of burden may feel pain pulling a plow to assist in farming, though assuming the workload is not abusive or torturous, it should not violate a value system of ethical treatment any more than working out at the gym should violate a value system of ethics.*
>
> *Many animals have uses that are neither harmful nor abusive and potentially beneficial for the animal.*

Nature has numerous examples of one living organism utilizing another in a type of exchange that provides some benefit to one or both organisms.

Mutualism is a symbiotic exchange where both organisms benefit, such as aphids and ants, where the aphids secrete a sugary solution called honeydew that ants consume. In contrast, ants protect the aphids.

Commensalism is a symbiotic exchange that benefits one organism at no expense or benefit to another, such as birds that eat insects stirred up by animals that graze.

There are differing opinions on what constitutes cruelty to animals, especially *sentient* animals.

Most seem to agree that animals used for food should be killed as quickly and with as little pain as possible. They also agree that one should use as much of the animal as possible to not constitute a waste of precious resources.

For example, hunting and killing for fun or a trophy while leaving the carcass to rot is a crime in many parts of the world. Game wardens in many states hunt and arrest hunters who violate these and similar rules.

The ethical issues are numerous.

Or did the sentient animal have to be slaughtered for food, or was there a reasonable alternative?

Was one animal slaughtered without harming or slaughtering other animals?

Was the animal harvested adequately for its meat and parts?

Did the sentient organism have to be slaughtered for its body parts to make clothing, or was there a reasonable alternative?

Or was the clothing a byproduct of using the animal for food, representing a means not to waste the resource?

IMPORTANCE OF SENTIENCE AND HIGHER APEX LIFE FORMS

For the perspective of a higher apex life form and the importance of *sentience*, let's rely upon a simple thought experiment.

So far, we have viewed the subject of sentience from the lens of Homo sapiens as the apex life form.

What if one day we encounter a life form that is more advanced than our own, and what will be their ethical values? What if that new apex life form viewed Homo sapiens as a source of decorative features, clothing, or food?

What if the measure the new apex life form used was an assessment of our ethical treatment toward other sentient organisms?

Unfortunately, if a new apex life form observed our ethical value system of how we treat other *sentient* beings, we may find ourselves in a rather unfortunate predicament.

IMPORTANCE OF SENTIENCE AND ARTIFICIALLY INTELLIGENT BEING #1

Let's also consider that the issue of *sentience* may not be limited to biological beings at some time in the not-too-distant future. Given that assertion, let's conduct a simple thought experiment labeled "*Artificially Intelligent Being #1*".

We begin with an artificial mechanical being that demonstrates most features associated with nearly all levels of consciousness and intelligence, except that it experiences neither pain nor any qualia.

Our mechanical being has preferences regarding its interactions with certain humans, as well as preferences for sources of information it has available, how it spends its time, what it wants to learn, and societal roles that it would like to experience, but even these advanced capabilities, it demonstrates that it cannot choose otherwise.

Therefore, if we were to create a thousand identical units of this artificially intelligent being and expose each to the same sequence of stimuli, each would make the same choices and enact the same volitions with no ability to choose otherwise.

Artificially Intelligent Being #1 is aware of inbound stimuli with which it creates perceptions. Each of these perceptions, however, qualifies as fundamental thoughts and understanding.

However, it is without the ability to choose otherwise.

The hardware-based levels of consciousness support a myriad of sensory devices and the corresponding calculations and transformations necessary to support the capabilities defined within our first nine levels of hardware-based forms of consciousness, absent the ability to choose otherwise.

Given that every type of freedom requires an ability to choose otherwise, our *Artificially Intelligent Being #1* would not have achieved any of the seven freedoms. That aside, by definition, it appears to have achieved several levels of consciousness, and although it could give the appearance that it has *freedom of attention, will, and action*, it does not.

Our *Artificially Intelligent Being #1* assesses each stimulus as favorable, unfavorable, or indifferent. It helps ensure the long-term success and survival of the artificially intelligent being. Note that an assessment of favorable, unfavorable, or indifferent subtly differs from each stimulus, meaning pleasant, unpleasant, or indifferent.

So, what is the difference between judging something as pleasant versus favorable or unpleasant versus unfavorable?

The difference is possibly nothing at all.

Since *Paramecium* has no emotions, it could as well judge something as favorable or unfavorable as opposed to pleasant or unpleasant. However, biology doesn't tend to operate at the level of favorable and unfavorable. Instead, it operates at the level of pleasant and unpleasant.

As a result, we will treat them as equivalent, though subtly different.

Therefore, let's momentarily weigh the impact of adjusting our consciousness framework, where artificially intelligent beings assess stimuli as favorable, unfavorable, or indifferent, as opposed to pleasant, unpleasant, or indifferent.

Here, we must ask the following questions.

- Do assessments of favorable, unfavorable, or indifferent materially change how our building blocks of *consciousness* relate to one another?

- Does this change how any of the levels of *consciousness* support the organisms that operate with those levels of *consciousness*?

- Does this impact any of the seven freedoms?

The short answer is no.

Favorable, unfavorable, or indifferent, as opposed to pleasant, unpleasant, or indifferent, does not pose a material difference to our levels of consciousness or forms of freedom. Hence, we will incorporate this change into the framework for artificially intelligent beings.

However, it is essential to note that while biological organisms automatically treat the concepts of 'pleasant' and 'unpleasant' as equivalent to 'favorable' and 'unfavorable,' they diverge in critical ways.

> *For example, illegal drugs are perceived as extremely pleasant while simultaneously being extremely unfavorable to the individual's mind and body and devastating to their long-term prospects for success.*
>
> *Likewise, many valuable, even life-saving medical treatments are highly unpleasant while being favorable to the health and well-being of the individual.*

Let's consider our first level of *consciousness* again to consider yet another feature of *consciousness*, such as the ability of *Paramecium* to choose otherwise. At least two sources may be responsible for the ability of the biological organism *Paramecium* to choose otherwise.

If we begin with a population of *Paramecium* having identical genetic codes, the cytoskeleton of each *Paramecium* may have identical assessments of 'pleasant,' 'unpleasant,' and 'indifferent' for a given stimulus. Thus, they may have a similar probability of choosing the same volition. The precise probability can be determined using more significant numbers of individuals who react one way instead of another.

Now consider a second population where the genetic code of each *Paramecium* is different and how those different genetics will express their differences in their proteins. These differences help explain differences in behavior between individuals of the same species, where differences can occur in observable behavior.

> *About four hundred nucleotides comprise the genes of Paramecia. Recall from middle school that nucleotides in DNA for all living organisms found on our planet are combinations of four bases, which are adenine (A), cytosine (C), guanine (G), and thymine (T), where adenine always bonds to thymine, and cytosine always bonds to guanine. The DNA pattern, therefore, is comprised of a sequence of four possible values of bases A-T, T-A, C-G, and G-C.*

> *The modern Paramecium has about 40,000 genes within its genome. The variability makes controlled experimentation for identical genomes challenging, though not impossible.*

> *Note that identical twins of many species are not exactly alike and do not express identical behaviors.*

Genetic variability enhances the survivability of a species. Whether it is genetic or behavioral, differences improve the chances of surviving new pathogens, environmental conditions, or other threats. Some differences may result in fatalities, while others may improve survivability.

What is important to us in this section is that *Paramecium* can choose otherwise, regardless of its genome. The freedoms that result, *freedom of attention*, *will*, and *action*, all contribute to improved survivability.

If we return to our *Artificially Intelligent Being #1* and our definition of *sentience*, recall *sentience* is when the organism possesses *freedom of attention* and *freedom of will* with the ability to have *ideas, opinions, feelings,* and *taste* one freely chooses.

In contrast to *Paramecium*, our *Artificially Intelligent Being #1* lacks *freedom of attention* and *freedom of will*. Therefore, it must always have the same focus and volition, making it as mechanical as our *Modern Learning Thermostat*.

Therefore, our *Artificially Intelligent Being #1* is not sentient.

Moreover, if our artificially intelligent beings were susceptible to the same threats to survival as biological organisms, their behavior could result in greater success in some circumstances or extinction in others. It is because the entire population of artificially intelligent beings would make the same decision and adopt the same behavior, rightly or wrongly, when faced with the same circumstances.

Even if those decisions were correct most of the time, the time when wrong decisions occur could prove fatal to every individual in the population and could put the entire population at risk of mass extinction.

Hence, if Elon Musk were to dispatch artificial life forms to prepare an alien environment for humans, the implications for *Artificially Intelligent Being #1* would be profound if they could demonstrate some degree of variability, particularly when facing a threat.

Although this logic appears sound, let's now argue an opposing point of view.

Let's start with the fact that it is nearly impossible to maintain identical conditions for any two beings interacting with their environment for more than a few seconds, never mind maintaining identical conditions for a thousand replicas.

> *Consider identical twins walking down the same street together in some American town, side by side. The angle of the sunlight reflecting off objects has subtle differences, whereas the one on the left receives glare in its eyes when the individual on the right does not.*

> *As soon as the twins come upon another individual, their experience diverges as soon as the new individual greets one before the other, shakes the hand of one before the other, and looks into the eyes of one before the other. The differences in their experiences continually mount up with every split second.*

> *Eventually, identically manufactured individuals will begin to make different decisions when confronted with the same circumstances because their experiences were sufficiently different, having them draw different conclusions.*

> *It could begin simply as walking down the street further to the right to avoid the glare of the sun reflecting off the shop windows as determined by prior experience.*

As such, is it significant that an artificial being could not do otherwise when one identically manufactured unit would have had subtly different experiences and, therefore, may behave subtly differently than another when faced with identical circumstances in the future?

From this perspective, it doesn't seem to matter whatsoever. However, if the response to any significant threat is uniformly incorrect, it could matter enormously. Hence, when facing an existential threat, considering the likely response of other identical units can be an essential consideration.

QUALIA IN ALIEN LIFE

Sometime in your life, you have probably wondered whether other people experience color the same way.

It is valuable to know because how we experience the world, such as how we perceive the flavor of food or the color of a fruit, influences our choices.

How one individual may choose something versus how their spouse may choose can depend upon the differences in how they experience the same things. Again, the way something is perceived influences one's choices and decision-making.

Consider for a moment that any life form originating on a distant planet may not be based on prokaryotic or eukaryotic cells as we know them but cells with some other type of cytoskeleton.

For example, instead of their cytoskeletal structures consisting of tubules and filaments, let's say they consist of pyramids and rings.

When visiting our planet, these alien visitors perceive our wavelengths corresponding to blue as yellow.

As a result, stimuli may manifest in an alien being in ways we may not anticipate.

Aside from the experience of *qualia* being different, one's assessment of these experiences can be radically different.

The alien may perceive our blue skies as yellow; given that perception, they may find it aesthetically pleasant, unpleasant, or indifferent.

It is all a matter of perspective as to how they evolved and the composition of an atmosphere that is pleasant or unpleasant and healthy or toxic.

However, given that these aliens possess *freedom of attention* and *will* with the ability to have *ideas, opinions, feelings,* and *tastes* that they may freely choose, they are sentient.

A SUMMARY OF SENTIENCE

Sentience is a feature of consciousness that fully emerges by the sixth level of consciousness with the *Primitive Brain Consciousness* of *Reptilia*.

Although significant, *sentience* is undoubtedly not the only morally relevant criterion in treating conscious individuals, biological or otherwise.

As chance would have it, intelligence is the next morally relevant factor that we will discuss, distinct from the concepts of consciousness and senti*ence*.

INTELLIGENCE

One definition of *intelligence* is the ability to acquire and apply knowledge and skills to achieve one's objective.

It raises a few questions.

Is it intelligent if someone tricks someone into doing something for another's objectives?

The answer is yes for the one doing the tricking and no for the other.

If an individual acquires and applies knowledge and skills to commit suicide, is that intelligence?

Here, the answer is more complex as the answer largely depends on the circumstances. The circumstances can range from someone terminally ill and suffering to someone healthy with the prospect of a long life ahead of them.

For our purposes, we will define *intelligence* as the ability to acquire and apply knowledge and skills to achieve one's objective while not undermining the survivability of the individual and the long-term survivability of one's collective, species, and biosphere.

However, the ability to measure *intelligence* based solely upon this objective can be misleading as additional factors besides intelligence drive adaptability for survival, including physical traits and genetic variability.

To paraphrase Amina Khan in her 2013 article in the Los Angeles Times, *Scientists uncover a secret to cockroaches' adaptability*:

> *Capabilities afforded by 'physical traits' for adaptability provide an ability to adapt to extreme environmental conditions, such as significantly digesting a wide variety of food materials or tolerating high or low temperatures and levels of radiation.*

> *Capabilities afforded by 'genetic variability' for adaptability allow adaptation due to adversely responding to chemicals, such as those used as bait in traps to kill roaches.*

> *[Scientists uncover a secret to cockroaches' adaptability, May 24th, 2013, Amina Khan, Los Angeles Times]*

Also, to paraphrase the 2015 Science News article, *Cockroaches have personalities, study finds*:

> *Genetic variability also contributes to variability in personalities, such as roaches, which engender differing levels of risk-taking that affect behaviors such as exploration.*

> *[Cockroaches have personalities, study finds, March 10th, 2015, Science News, Reuters]*

Hence, capabilities afforded by physical traits allow an organism to a) adapt to more distant venturing from the nest with b) navigational knowledge of how to return and c) an ability to form rapid responses to hide from danger not previously encountered.

The cockroach is the best example of a single organism that exemplifies all three factors for adaptability. The order *Blattodea* contains eight families, 460 genera, and 4,600 species, commonly known as cockroaches.

Concerning intelligence, cockroaches have around a million neurons, which is equivalent to honeybees at the upper end of insect intelligence.

These million neurons are also ten times as compact in cockroaches compared to mammals. This physical feature, plus the long neuron tendrils to rapidly communicate signals to other neurons, boosts the computing power of these tiny organisms, significantly enhancing the speed of memory recall and decision-making.

> *This miniaturization is much like shrinking the size of a computer's central processing unit (CPU) to allow information to be processed faster by simply saving the time needed to travel some distance.*

Intelligence, however, is not limited to what an individual can determine on their own. Also included is the accumulated knowledge of ancestors and other individuals, passed down to benefit individuals, family members, and the local collective.

Like *sentience* and *consciousness*, *intelligence* and *consciousness* share some commonalities, though they are distinct concepts.

> *Intelligence and consciousness exist along a continuum from low to high, with no theoretical limit on the upper bounds of either.*

> *Similarly, as they increase, they improve the ability of an organism to survive by facilitating an improved understanding of one's environment, even if only locally.*

When we look at *intelligence* from within the lens of our framework, the genus *Paramecium* has few ways to express *consciousness* and *intelligence*.

For example, one species of *Paramecium* may be able to demonstrate a higher degree of intelligence than another simply by demonstrating that their species prospers comparatively due to the choices of its individuals.

However, suppose we separate the groups into different regions for several generations. In that case, the improved survivability may also be due to evolutionary changes that rendered a physical advantage. Likewise, differences in survivability could be due to the advantages and disadvantages of the local physical environment instead of intelligence.

Thus far, we have focused on conscious organisms utilizing knowledge to influence survivability, but let's explore what *intelligence* is and the foundation it depends upon in other ways.

INTELLIGENCE AND THINKING

The notion of an individual possessing *intelligence* in that it can 'demonstrate *intelligent* behavior' to enhance its survivability versus the notion of an individual organism 'being capable of *intelligent* thought', are distinct ideas in several ways.

To illustrate one distinction, let's employ a thought experiment.

Let's assume that intelligence can exist without freedom of attention, freedom of will, freedom of action, or any ability to choose otherwise.

To represent this concept, we will substitute the term 'consciousness' with the term 'awareness,' where the difference in our framework is simply that 'awareness' comes neither with freedom nor the ability to choose otherwise.

We know mechanical devices like robotic vacuum cleaners and modern learning thermostats lack 'consciousness.' However, they have 'awareness,' such that the robotic vacuum cleaner will not propel itself down a flight of stairs or over an edge that would cause it to fall to its destruction.

In this sense, a robotic vacuum cleaner can demonstrate intelligent behavior by redirecting itself away from an edge that drops off. At the same time, it is safe to conclude that it lacks conscious thoughts as it follows its deterministic programming.

We can intuitively understand the point of our thought experiment in that we can envision how nonliving devices can demonstrate *intelligent* behavior that can also prolong their well-being and survival.

THOUGHT

English dictionaries define thought as an idea or opinion produced by thinking and occurring spontaneously within the mind. The secondary definition typically states that it is the action or process of *thinking*.

Encyclopedic definitions go somewhat further, though they share the notion that it occurs within a mind, thereby claiming the prerequisite of a mind.

For our purposes, we will differentiate our concepts regarding *thought* into terms that are not anthropomorphic.

'Thought' (within our framework) is any process that stores, retrieves, or manipulates information in response to stimuli regardless of its source and underlying hardware substrate. The stimuli may originate externally or internally, and the hardware substrate may be biological or non-biological.

It means there is at least one rudimentary thought when a unicellular *Paramecium* detects something within its environment and determines whether it is favorable, unfavorable, or indifferent.

As we progress into higher levels of *consciousness* involving a physical brain, a thought will occur at the *conscious* level, though the unconscious and subconscious levels may additionally support it.

That said, six additional categories of thought are helpful to our conversation.

'Unconscious thought' is a thought that resides within and strictly supports an *unconscious* process.

Unconscious processes emerge only within levels of *consciousness* supported by a brain. The evolutionary advancements within these *unconscious* processes also coincide with advancements in the physical brain to tackle the increased workload of a growing number of the types of sensory organs and sensory organs that would otherwise overwhelm the *subconscious* and *conscious* levels of *consciousness*.

Only significant stimuli are 'bubbled up' to the subconscious and consciousness levels as other stimuli are processed and filtered out.

The significance associated with a given set of stimuli largely stems from thresholds set genetically and through learning. Initially, thresholds may result from one's genetic makeup or formed during early development.

In contrast, command-related stimuli flow outward into the *unconscious* from the *conscious* and *subconscious* levels as signals travel to motor neurons.

'Subconscious thought' is a thought that resides within and strictly supports *subconscious* processes.

Subconscious processes also only emerge in *consciousness* supported by a brain.

Again, as stimuli are processed and filtered out, only significant stimuli are 'bubbled up' to the *consciousness* level. Genetics, learning, and conditioning from repetitive training influence the significance associated with stimuli.

Conditioning from repetitive training occurs when specific inbound stimuli repeatedly correspond to specific outbound stimuli, allowing the subconscious to save a step in anticipating what the conscious level requires.

Depending upon the degree of learning, the *subconscious* level may make fine adjustments to the signals being routed to the motor neurons to attain the necessary precision of force, speed, and movement.

'Subconscious thought' processes also provide extensive support to assist with additional levels of consciousness, such as *persona consciousness, compartmentalized consciousness, in-the-moment consciousness,* and the five levels of *paradigmatic* consciousness.

> *For example, the concurrent paradigms of a Level Three individual receive a great deal of support from the subconscious level, which bubbles up significant thoughts for conscious realization.*

'Conscious thought' is a thought that occurs within the *conscious* level supporting *conscious* processes.

Like a large organization that supports its CEO, all processes provide some degree of support to the *conscious* level.

Also, like a large organization where the CEO sets overall direction and management of the executive team, which has its layers of middle management, *conscious* processes manage and delegate various functions to other *subconscious* processes that manage the myriad of lower-level processes.

THE 'EVOLUTION OF INTELLIGENCE' ARGUMENT

If you say, "Hey, Google, how much is five grams of pure gold worth?" Google will interpret the sequence of sounds into a string of words and use those words to do an Internet search to retrieve an answer that will likely be correct.

To do so, this process stores, analyzes, and interprets speech sounds to determine what it should retrieve and verbalize in return. However, during the entire process, Google understood neither the meaning of the words it received nor those within the response it rendered.

Yes, Google can search for a definition of the word "pure gold" and read the definition back to you, but it has no understanding of the word it just looked up, nor the words it read back to the questioner.

In contrast, when a human receives the question, "How much is five grams of pure gold worth?" they may not know the answer, but they understand what each word in the question means individually and together as a string of words.

When asked, "How much is five grams of pure gold worth?" they also understand that someone is probably considering buying or selling five grams of pure gold, just received it, or is possibly gifting it to another.

Humans have an understanding of each word; the combination of words, such as "pure gold," the entire phrase, and the likely motivation behind the question, is represented in packages we call thoughts. However, underlying human intelligence is the capacity to have thought.

Therefore, intelligent beings have thoughts, whereas *Google* and the *Modern Learning Thermostat* do not have thoughts because having a thought means having some form of understanding. A thought void of any understanding is impossible. Even the thought that one does not understand a sequence of words qualifies as a thought.

Notwithstanding, the minimum requirement for *intelligent thought* is also *awareness*. Intelligent thought must demonstrate an ability to adapt to some stimuli it is aware of. Intelligence also requires awareness of one's circumstances and events to improve one's chances of accomplishing one's objectives.

Distinct, though equally important, it means that intelligence requires understanding one's objectives.

All levels of *consciousness* possess *awareness* and some level of understanding. In this way, each level of *consciousness,* starting with the rudimentary, can support understanding stimuli as favorable, unfavorable, or indifferent.

However, *awareness* has fewer capabilities since it lacks freedom, rendering it mechanical, like Google and the *Modern Learning Thermostat*. Without the freedom and the ability to choose otherwise, even if equipped with understanding, all *thought* would be limited to ones in which the being could not have thought otherwise.

It means that creative thinking would not occur in artificial intelligence absent consciousness, as all such beings would be limited to non-creative thoughts in which they could not think otherwise.

In such an environment, it is conceivable for mechanically intelligent beings to exist, though it would not be possible for them to evolve into intelligent beings over time. Outputs will invariably improve as more information becomes available, but mechanically intelligent beings could only exist for beings equipped with *consciousness*. Intelligent beings with consciousness would need to create them and use them creatively.

Interestingly, *intelligent thought* could not have evolved in an environment supporting *awareness* alone simply because creativity is impossible without freedoms, such as freedom of attention, freedom of will, and freedom of action.

In a realm where everything is predetermined, no individual being would have had the ability to choose otherwise.

Therefore, any form of *intelligence*, or any form of *thought* based on *awareness* alone, could not have evolved independently. For *intelligence* to evolve, it needed *consciousness*, with the freedom to choose otherwise. Also, for intelligence to advance further, *consciousness* is essential.

In simple terms, no matter how aware it may become, the *Modern Learning Thermostat* will never evolve intelligent thought without first being equipped with *consciousness*, which could only be done by beings already equipped with *consciousness*.

We call this the *Evolution of Intelligence Argument.*

It is a separate question whether *conscious* beings using their creativity can create a mechanical being equipped with *consciousness*.

We know there is no way for mechanically intelligent beings equipped with awareness to achieve much independently.

However, I propose two assertions.

The first is that a *conscious* being can create a mechanically intelligent being equipped solely with awareness that can exhibit some degree of each of the twenty-four levels of consciousness. The only difference is that artificial intelligence would always lack freedoms, including the freedom to choose otherwise.

The second assertion we will discuss later is that a *conscious* being can have sufficient creativity to create an artificial intelligence possessing *consciousness* and all its associated freedoms.

AWARENESS

So, what would a mechanical being equipped with *awareness* and the ability to understand be like, and how would it compare to one with *consciousness*?

IDENTICAL INTELLIGENT BEINGS WITH AWARENESS – SCENARIO 1

Recall *Artificially Intelligent Being #1* has awareness with perceptions of stimuli qualifying as fundamental thoughts and understanding. It also lacks all forms of *qualia*, and although it supports the majority of consciousness levels in our framework, it lacks *freedom of attention, will, action, emotion, mind, thought,* and *paradigm* and cannot choose otherwise.

Let's add ninety-nine identical units of *Artificially Intelligent Being #1*.

We now have *Artificially Intelligent Being #1* through *Artificially Intelligent Being #100*, and let's volunteer them to participate in our next thought experiment. As such, if they all had identical experiences from the moment they were powered up, they would all make the same choices and display identical behaviors.

In this thought experiment, each unit is identical, resembling a healthy eighteen-year-old adolescent human. Each unit has the same basic knowledge and education, equivalent to an American 12th-grade education.

We then enroll each unit into the top one hundred universities worldwide, into different majors across various educational disciplines (e.g., economics, physics, political science, and women's studies).

As one would expect, the experiences of each unit from that point on are unique regarding every aspect of their university years, especially concerning their interactions with the human students, professors, and subject material unique to their university.

Depending upon the program, graduation time finally arrives for each unit, sometimes four or six years after enrollment.

Upon graduating, we bring our artificially intelligent graduates back to our readers so that we may meet and interview them.

The one aspect shared among our hundred graduates is that we know that in every decision they've ever made, they could not have chosen otherwise.

We now interview each of our graduates using the same questions regarding their opinions of right versus wrong and their suggestions for improving the world.

One after another, we are shocked at how each artificially intelligent being is remarkably different from the others when they are in every way identical.

These differences stem from the fact that each has learned much about social skills and the value systems of their human peers and professors, as well as the knowledge they've accumulated from their disciplines of study.

We see that the artificially intelligent beings that attended law schools demonstrate an affinity for systems of legal thought, those who attended medical school an affinity for medical research, those who attended business schools an affinity for optimizing production and profit, and those attending liberal schools had politically liberal tendencies and occasional urges to hug trees.

The primary reason to expect such an outcome is that there is no discernible difference between an 'artificially intelligent being' equipped with awareness and consciousness.

The operable word here is 'discernable' in that there is no way to determine whether anyone has made a particular decision freely or without the ability to choose otherwise.

The hard determinist would likely say, "See, I told you so... there is no such thing as free will!" "You can't even tell if you have it yourself."

However, because one cannot readily discern the difference between *awareness* and *consciousness* from observing behaviors from a thought experiment like the one above, there is neither evidence nor proof that *freedom of attention, freedom of will,* or *freedom of action* is non-existent.

INTELLIGENT BEINGS WITH AWARENESS – SCENARIO 2

Let's consider an alternate scenario given the same *Artificially Intelligent Being* with awareness but without any *freedom of attention.*

Lacking any capacity for *freedom of attention* in an environment with many sources of stimuli, our *Artificially Intelligent Being* cannot choose what to pay attention to. In lacking the ability to have the focus one wants, our *Artificially Intelligent Being* is unable to decide what stimuli to pay attention to, what ideas to pay attention to, what information sources to pay attention to, and so on.

If there are five conversations within earshot and our being can only pay attention to one at a time, our *Artificially Intelligent Being* cannot choose which one to focus on and, as a result, focuses on none of them.

> *This thought experiment assumes that our Artificially Intelligent Being can only focus on one conversation at a time when it does have freedom of attention.*

> *If it had freedom of attention, it could even ignore all conversations.*

Given that, if there were only one conversation, our Artificially Intelligent Being would not have to choose which conversation to focus on. It would be aware of the one conversation and could, therefore, process the sounds from that one conversation without the ability to choose or choose otherwise.

Of course, having anticipated this, we would have programmed our intelligent being to pay attention to the conversation physically closest to itself. However, we would consider this additional programming one of our 'awareness' bug fixes.

When we consider this thought experiment, several issues come into play.

If our *Artificially Intelligent Being* had multiple thoughts about the conversation, it could not choose which thoughts to pay attention to.

If our *Artificially Intelligent Being* had any volitions, it could not choose which of those volitions to pay attention to. However, if it only had one volition, it could enact it, though it could not consider the potential results of enacting that volition because, again, it could not choose which thoughts to pay attention to.

As a result, upon enacting the volition, it could not choose how best to enact the volition to minimize any adverse effects that may occur from enacting the volition in a suboptimal manner.

This thought experiment shows how integral *freedom of attention* is to an *Artificially Intelligent Being*, including the parts that do not involve the ability to choose otherwise.

The result is a somewhat confused and indecisive *Artificially Intelligent Being* that cannot behave intelligently in many situations.

INTELLIGENT BEINGS WITH AWARENESS

We saw the disadvantages of awareness even when equipped with understanding versus being equipped with levels of *consciousness* with its *freedom of attention*, *will*, and *action*.

As you have probably realized about our intelligent beings equipped with *awareness*, losing the ability to choose otherwise comes with the loss of variability and, hence, much creativity.

Assuming the ability to understand stimuli and have thoughts is present, it does not mean that intelligent beings equipped with *awareness* are unintelligent.

As with conscious beings, much of this has to do with the body of knowledge the intelligent being has and the quality and quantity of that knowledge. However, gathering knowledge from external sources is one thing, and extending one's body of knowledge oneself is another, however this speaks more to a distinction between educated and intelligent.

An individual can be highly educated but cannot apply that knowledge to their advantage. In contrast, another individual may have little knowledge but be able to apply that knowledge exceptionally effectively, and therefore is the more intelligent, albeit less educated.

But without going astray from our topic, artificially intelligent beings may become capable of significantly surpassing our ability to become educated while being challenged to achieve higher levels of intelligence.

INTELLIGENCE: AWARENESS VS CONSCIOUSNESS

We are volunteering our *Artificially Intelligent Being* once again for their awareness. They will compete against humans with consciousness to invent something useful.

In preparation for our contest, we manufactured one hundred identical artificially intelligent beings with awareness and identical 12th-grade educations. We then placed our artificially intelligent beings in an identical college-level chemistry lab.

In an adjacent building, we have one hundred humans that are all identical clones. Each of our cloned humans possesses consciousness and identical 12th-grade education.

All one hundred artificially intelligent beings and one hundred humans have the same contest rules. The first individual to invent something useful wins the contest. However, if an individual damages any property, they will be disqualified.

When our artificially intelligent beings begin, they all choose the same activity. They identically take an inventory of the materials available to them in the lab, all identically recognizing some of the materials and all identically not recognizing some other materials.

Simultaneously, our artificially intelligent beings realized they needed a plan to invent something useful and then pondered what useful item they might invent. They simultaneously concluded that they could either try to think of something to invent or produce as many things as possible and try to imagine for what purpose the new material could be useful.

Since their programming gave them no choice, they all decided to produce things using the items in their laboratory.

As their first step, every individual assembled the same chemical mixture using some ingredients they did not recognize, simultaneously destroying the entire lab in a massive explosion, disqualifying themselves, and blowing themselves to bits.

The humans, not realizing that they had become the default winners of the contest, each decided to mix different ingredients, many of them using different methods and different ratios of materials.

After heating their mixtures to see what would happen, some caused small fires in their portion of the lab, some created nothing, but one created a semi-sticky clear substance that acted as a weak reusable glue.

This human contestant won when some of the humans realized that this weak reusable glue could replace staples and scotch tape to hold papers temporarily affixed to one another, transforming the laboratory into a wealthy corporation having created sticky pads that many businesses purchased in large quantities.

The property owners brought a lawsuit upon the manufacturer of the artificially intelligent beings for property damage to the chemistry labs, and the labs were sued for gross negligence by hundreds of artificially intelligent beings who were recent law school graduates.

The artificially intelligent beings lost their court battle when they could not depose any witnesses as there were no survivors of the blast.

From this example, we can see the importance of freedom and its role in making either intentional or accidental discoveries.

Moreover, any species' survival requires some degree of variability among individuals as population variability improves their chances of survival as individuals and groups attempt different strategies.

The final score was humans 'one' and *Artificially Intelligent Beings* 'zero.'

THE FOUNDATION OF INTELLIGENCE

The fact that *intelligence* can only evolve by leveraging consciousness does not preclude *intelligence* from having any utility when equipped with *awareness* as opposed to *consciousness*.

Recall the minimum requirement for *intelligent thought* is *awareness*, as *intelligent thought*, by definition, must demonstrate an ability to adapt to circumstances and events in such a way as to improve one's chances of accomplishing one's objectives. Stated more simply, *intelligence* is applying knowledge instead of reciting it back.

Yes, we can imagine a person who is now blind and deaf without any sensory input, yet we intuitively know that they are capable of *intelligent thought* using streams of stimuli from their past. Additionally, we know they can generate thoughts leveraging their accumulated knowledge, leveraging whatever stimuli they receive to consider and invent new ideas.

Interestingly, there are many parts of an *intelligent* process that lack *awareness*.

How often have you experienced the nagging feeling that there was some vital realization in your *subconscious* trying to emerge to your *conscious* level? And how often have you had an idea while asleep to awaken, still recalling it?

The *subconscious* mind is constantly at work. When it isn't processing stimuli and performing calculations during waking hours, it is busy organizing, analyzing, and storing stimuli for subsequent use by both the *subconscious* and *conscious* levels while the *conscious* mind is asleep.

Interestingly, these essential functions occur without the aid of *conscious* processes. Interestingly, many of these functions occur without any *awareness*.

Various capabilities have been instrumental to the development of *intelligence*.

One core capability that is foundational to *intelligence* is the memory of stimuli. The memory of stimuli is foundational to our twenty-four levels of *consciousness*. Memory is also instrumental to each level of consciousness, whether biological or artificial, including the artificially intelligent beings we've invented during our thought experiments.

The memory of stimuli provides the ability to recall information using some part of the stored memory, a capability supported by cytoskeletal structures within eukaryotic cells.

> *For example, the memory of music consists of memories of frequencies, amplitudes, and time-based components, including sequences of stimuli.*

> *Recall: Regarding the memory of music, it is possible to use any of these aspects of the stimuli to recall the entire sequence of notes and timing.*

Another core component of *intelligence* is that it depends on consciousness to determine whether stimuli are favorable, unfavorable, or indifferent. Storing this additional assessment of the stimuli is what we shall refer to as categorizing stimuli.

Both memories and categorizations of stimuli are essential for *intelligence* and for supporting *consciousness*. Also, as one might expect, the foundation of *intelligence* originates where *consciousness* originates in the cytoskeletal structures within eukaryotic cells and then advances rapidly with the aid of neuronal structures.

UNICELLULAR CONSCIOUSNESS AND INTELLIGENCE

The unicellular protozoan *amoeba* is the most primitive eukaryotic form of life known to science.

To paraphrase the Harvard University article, *Brain Evolution, Cosmic Evolution – Biological, Harvard University*:

> *Amoebae will slowly drift toward algae in search of food, and not finding any food it will typically grope again toward the same algae in search for food because it has no memory of stimuli or learning of stimuli, or it lacks the intelligence to use the information it has possibly memorized or learned.*

In comparison, Paramecium is at the other end of intelligence in the microscopic world. That said, Paramecium can only operate within a minimal, local environment as the sensory systems of Paramecium cannot detect anything further away than a few millimeters.

[Brain Evolution, Cosmic Evolution – Biological, Harvard University, https://www.cfa.harvard.edu/~ejchaisson/cosmic_evolution/docs/fr_1/fr_1_bio7.html*]*

For individual eukaryotic cells to advance their level of intelligence, they must collaborate with other eukaryotic cells, such as is depicted within the first nine levels of consciousness.

Cytoskeletal structures of eukaryotic cells support the capabilities of *consciousness* and rudimentary *intelligence,* indicating that a good starting point is to research unicellular organisms.

The mechanisms of cytoskeletal structures that support the memory of stimuli, categorization of stimuli, and *intelligence* are still a mystery, and few scientists are researching the secrets of this microscopic world.

To paraphrase Mol Smith, in the 2014 Microscopy article, *The Paramecium Enigma*:

Among these few, Professors Stuart Hameroff, M.D. and Roger Penrose are asking the most pertinent questions, such as whether *consciousness* and *intelligence* interact directly with the quantum world via the cytoskeletal structures of eukaryotic cells.

[The Paramecium Enigma, Nov 2014, Mol Smith, Microscopy, http://www.microscopy-uk.org.uk/index.html?http://www.microscopy-uk.org.uk/mag/artnov14/paramecium-engima.html*]*

MULTICELLULAR CONSCIOUSNESS AND INTELLIGENCE

To paraphrase Richard K. Grosberg, UC Davis, in his 2007 article, *The evolution of multicellularity: A minor major transition?*:

Multicellular eukaryotes first evolved three to three and a half billion years ago, and since that time, they have independently evolved at least twenty-four more times. Complex multicellular organisms have evolved about half of those times and only into six groups: brown algae, red algae, green algae, fungi, land plants, and animals.

["*The evolution of multicellularity: A minor major transition?*"*, Aug 10th, 2007, Richard K. Grosberg - University of California Davis, CA, Richard R. Strathmann, Friday Harbor Laboratories, University of Washington, Friday Harbor, WA, Annual Reviews]*

When it comes to the topics of *consciousness* and *intelligence*, multicellular organisms enjoy several advantages over their unicellular predecessors.

First and foremost is the size of the organism. Unicellular organisms have a theoretical maximum size of a tenth of a millimeter, whereas multicellular organisms have no known theoretical limit. The size advantage is so significant that the race for larger multicellular organisms as consumers of smaller organisms was on.

> *The type of organism determines the maximum size of an organism.*

> *The theoretical limit in the height of a tree is about four hundred feet, believed to have been reached by redwood trees.*

> *The largest known organism on Earth is Armillaria ostoyae, a fungus that spans 2,385 acres of the Malheur National Forest in Oregon.*

> *The largest known animal in terms of mass is the blue whale, which reached up to 190 tons and 100 feet, which surpasses the largest dinosaur ever, Argentinosaurus huinculensis, which topped out at 96 tons and 130 feet with its long neck and tail.*

Since the primary advantage enjoyed by multicellular organisms is size, they must also collect stimuli from a much larger region of the environment, often with a more extensive variety of specialized cells for different types of stimuli.

When it comes to the capabilities of memory of stimuli, categorizing of stimuli, and *intelligence*, multicellular organisms such as *Mimosa pudica* (a.k.a. the sensitive plant) can improve survivability by employing all three capabilities.

> *Mimosa Pudica memorizes stimuli, including the distinctions present among stimuli. Upon doing so, it also assesses and records those stimuli as favorable, unfavorable, or indifferent.*

> *Finally, it uses the combination of its consciousness and intelligence to determine when and when not to act, thereby consuming energy to protect its leaves when there is a viable predatory threat and conserving energy when it can reliably discern that the threat is not predatory to its leaves.*

NERVE NET CONSCIOUSNESS AND INTELLIGENCE

To paraphrase the Harvard University article, *Brain Evolution, Cosmic Evolution – Biological, Harvard University*:

> *The species Hydra vulgaris, resembling a microscopic squid, is the smallest freshwater organism equipped with neurons. These neurons have a nerve net structure. Depending upon the size of the individual, Hydra vulgaris may have a few hundred to a few thousand neurons.*

> *Though their number and arrangement are considerably greater in humans, the type of neuron cells found in Hydra vulgaris is essentially the same as those found in Homo sapiens.*

[Brain Evolution, Cosmic Evolution – Biological, Harvard University, https://www.cfa.harvard.edu/~ejchaisson/cosmic_evolution/docs/ fr_1/fr_1_bio7.html*]*

In addition to *intelligence* playing a role in the observable behavior of the larger organism, science now knows that an organism's ability to survive may be enhanced with *intelligence* at the microbial level in the digestive tract, with bidirectional communication occurring even between microbes and neurons.

To paraphrase Juanita Bawagan in her 2017 article, *Hydra reveals nerves shape the microbiome*:

> *Useful for research, Hydras have provided researchers with proof that the nervous system cooperates with microbes, such as those located in the digestive tract, by spatially controlling the organization of microbe types and concentrations along specific areas of the Hydras digestive tract to regulate the digestive process better.*

> *[Hydra reveals nerves shape the microbiome, Nov 16th, 2017, Juanita Bawagan, Humans & The Microbiome, CIFAR,* https://www.cifar.ca/ cifarnews/2017/11/06/hydra-reveals-nerves-shape-the-microbiome*]*

In communicating with microbes, these neurons exhibit memory of stimuli, categorizing stimuli, and *intelligence* to better optimize the placement of each microbe based on the capabilities demonstrated by the type of microbe.

NERVE CORD CONSCIOUSNESS AND INTELLIGENCE

Nematode, *C. elegans*, is supported by a total of 302 neurons using a handful of neuron types that include four sensory neurons, a small collection of layered interneurons, a small collection of command neurons, and a ventral cord of motor neurons, accompanied by early types of *neuroglia* (a.k.a. glia, glial cells).

To paraphrase doctors C.H. Lin, Ph.D., and C.H. Rankin, Ph.D., in their 2010 article, *Nematode Learning and Memory: Neuroethology*:

> *An advancement over Hydra vulgaris, our nematode C. elegans demonstrates highly plastic behavior (a.k.a. learning), including associative (i.e., classical conditioning [Pavlov], operant conditioning [reward and punishment]), non-associative (i.e., habituation [desensitizing through repetition], sensitization [sensitizing through repetition]), and memory and learning that leverages mechanical, thermal, and chemical stimulus that use glutamate, dopamine, serotonin, and neuroendocrine signaling.*

> *[Nematode Learning and Memory: Neuroethology, 2010, C.H. Lin Ph.D., C.H. Rankin Ph.D., University of British Columbia, Vancouver, BC, Canada]*

This significant advancement in *intelligence* appears to coincide with a collection of interneurons and the emergence of *neuroglia* that support the memory of stimuli, categorization of stimuli, and *intelligence*.

NEURAL BUNDLE CONSCIOUSNESS AND INTELLIGENCE

Neural Bundle Consciousness, genus *Apis* (a.k.a. honeybee), is at the upper end of the insect continuum of intelligence supported by approximately a million neurons. As part of the insect's central nervous system (CNS), the neural bundle has a *protocerebrum*, *deutocerebrum*, and *tritocerebrum*.

Equipped with a myriad of advanced sensory organs, the neural structure of the honeybee produces a variety of intellectual features, including a sense of the passage of time, complex social structures, translating flight instructions into a language of dance movements, memorization of dance movements, and conversion of dance movements back into flight instructions.

We can see from even these few samples that the advancements associated with each successive level of *consciousness* fuel the *organism's intelligence* to significantly new heights.

SUMMARY OF INTELLIGENCE AND AWARENESS

We now see that an organism's level of *awareness* and *intelligence* strengthens as we ascend each level of *consciousness*.

Higher levels of *consciousness* have an increase in the number, types, quality, and range of sensory organs that enhance *awareness*, as well as additional freedoms with which to express additional forms of *intelligence*. But perhaps the most significant factor is that higher levels of *consciousness* benefit from additional collaboration.

As we ascend the levels of *consciousness*, we see architecture emerge. We see an increase in the specialization of cell types, such as the emergence of additional types of neurons and *neuroglia* and how they are arranged.

It is similar to when specialists form a team to collaborate to invent new things. As new skills become available to the team, they collaborate with other members, discovering new and improved ways to look at things and understand them.

When integrated, new senses of reality, such as the ability to perceive the passage of time and the ability for individuals to communicate information, such as the location of food in the genus Apis (e.g., honeybee), have a cumulative effect on advancing *intelligence*.

Our discussion of *intelligence* and its evolution continues in a separate manuscript. <u>Sensitive by Nature: Understanding Intelligence and the Mind</u>

devoted to *intelligence*, acts as a sort of bookend to this manuscript. Both are a journey that guide the reader to understand artificial intelligence from different perspectives, with evolutionary markers to guide the reader.

> *[Sensitive by Nature: Understanding Intelligence and the Mind, 2002, J Luisi, 1ˢᵗ Books Library Publishers]*

The salient point is that we have established how *intelligence* is distinct and yet related to *consciousness*, where *consciousness* is foundational, upon which these various mental faculties rest.

Now, our journey brings us to the following intellectual faculty: *sapience*.

SAPIENCE

Dictionaries define *sapience* interchangeably with wisdom and sagacity. It involves the ability to discriminate between related ideas or objects and to think and act utilizing knowledge, experience, understanding, insight, and common sense.

> *Some define sapience as awareness of one's awareness, while many define sapience as necessitating a level of wisdom that excludes non-humans.*
>
> *However, at the other end of the continuum, some claim Homo sapiens have partial sapience. However, these arguments merely emphasize some challenges created by non-standard definitions, much like the definition of consciousness, even within scientific circles.*

However, the dictionary definition fails to explain *sapience* adequately to someone trying to understand it. So, as we investigate these aspects of *sapience*, we will take a deeper dive into the notion of *sapience* and then the notion of *common sense* separately.

Let's begin by briefly returning to *intelligence*, stating that there are at least two levels of *intelligence*, 'basic' versus 'advanced.' However, before we explain the difference, we should begin with a clear definition of what is meant by 'basic' *intelligence*.

The organisms chosen in our consciousness framework thus far can demonstrate basic *intelligence* directly from experience. They do so specifically from *memory of stimuli* and *learning of stimuli*, with some capacity to demonstrate some level of *intelligence* directly from the *memory of stimuli* and *learning of stimuli*.

> *For example, Paramecium can demonstrate that it can detect food and demonstrates a level of intelligence by moving towards it.*
>
> *Likewise, Mimosa pudica (a.k.a. sensitive plant) can distinguish between stimuli that represent a predatory threat versus similar stimuli that do not represent a predatory threat, demonstrating intelligence.*

In both examples, the organisms demonstrated some intelligence from direct experience. Our *Paramecium* detected the presence of a predator using organelles that can sense a predator. In comparison, *Mimosa pudica* (a.k.a. sensitive plant) detected the distinction between predatory and non-predatory shaking of leaves.

Also, in these examples, stimuli and response represent a fundamental one-to-one relationship, which does not qualify as *sapience*. Burning one's hand on the stove and then learning from that experience not to do that in the future is basic intelligence, not advanced *intelligence* or *sapience*.

In other words, a more advanced form of *intelligence* is a prerequisite for achieving the status of *sapience*.

For an organism to achieve *sapience,* it must demonstrate an ability to integrate the *memory of stimuli* and *learning of stimuli* from disparate types of experience and then demonstrate *intelligent* use of those experiences together in some integrated way. Let's try to unpack this.

For example, one method to demonstrate *sapience* or the lack thereof involves the study of history.

Let's use the history of the Roman Empire, from its inception under the influence of the Greeks to the fall of the Western Roman Empire, followed by the eventual fall of the Eastern Roman Empire.

The first undeniable fact to appreciate about the Roman Empire is that their upper classes comprised their political and military leadership and philosophers who dealt with complex ethical issues.

This population was exceptionally well-educated and highly intelligent. It formed a well-structured society that was extremely organized and equipped with a high degree of engineering, economic, political, and military prowess, particularly for its time within written human history.

Applying historical knowledge of the Roman Empire to illustrate advanced *intelligence* will be helpful.

Anyone who has read to this point in the book knows that modern man has easy access to the lessons of ancient Rome. Each of us has excellent informational resources at our fingertips, even across vast ranges of economic and social status. We have public libraries, bookstores, universities, televised documentaries, and more.

Those of us able to draw parallels regarding events and pressures of ancient Rome to events and pressures of our civilization and who use that knowledge effectively are employing an integrated form of *intelligence* that exceeds 'basic' *intelligence*.

In other words, learning the lessons of the past and leveraging them in modern times moves us to 'advanced' *intelligence*.

Therefore, an example of *sapience* would be using one's integrated knowledge of history to understand better the implications of engineering, economics, politics, immigration, and military issues in our time.

Whether it is about how modern monetary currencies decrease in worth due to the removal of valuable metals in coins, overspending, or the effects of open borders and increased citizenship, many lessons are available to those who employ 'advanced' *intelligence*.

For our second example, we will use the subject of global warming, a subject that many individuals get emotional about. Although understanding the temperature trends of our planet belongs to the realm of science, it has become a surprisingly polarizing political topic. One should pause when feeling highly emotional about any topic belonging to empiricism.

On the one hand, 'basic' intelligence tells us we are creating extreme damage to our planet by increasing the volume of gasses that capture more of the sun's energy, melting ice caps and raising the sea level, flooding irrigable land needed to feed many human populations. It is because someone told us this.

On the other hand, 'advanced' intelligence tells us that the sun experiences repeated natural cycles that span thousands of years recorded in our geological record that we can analyze scientifically.

When we engage in the issue empirically, we learn that the issue is not so black and white. Together, we can understand how temperatures on other planets in our solar system have also risen. And together, we can calculate how much heating fuel we save with warmer winter temperatures.

Both sides are well-meaning, though they vastly differ in rhetoric and the degree of urgency and extremeness of proposed countermeasures.

In this example, those who engage in the dialog to scientifically understand the historical and newly collected evidence demonstrate 'advanced' intelligence.

Therefore, the issues include determining the degree to which climate poses a threat to life on the planet, the degree to which we can influence it, the measures we can take to protect life on the planet for the portion that we cannot influence, and what opportunities exist for us to take advantage of these changes.

There are many valuable questions to explore and understand, though it will be necessary to get the right people on the bus and the wrong people off the bus if we hope to achieve a beneficial outcome.

That said, this does not mean that someone capable of *sapience* on one topic can do so on every other topic. There always seems to be at least one topic that allows someone to forfeit *sapience*.

But before we explore the notion of *sapience* in other than *Homo sapiens*, where 'sapiens' represents the term *sapience*, let's first consider one of the more solid claims that *sapience* is the domain of humans alone by looking at the human mental faculty known as 'common sense.'

SAPIENCE VERSUS COMMON SENSE

Common sense is frequently a component of the dictionary definition of *sapience*.

Common sense generally refers to having good sense and sound judgment in practical matters, without the need for specialized training or knowledge, based on commonly found levels of *intelligence*.

Many believe that teaching *common sense* is impossible, as an individual either has it or doesn't. It is also generally accepted that *common sense* is not genetically available.

Our problem initially arises when the dictionary definition of *sapience* creates a dependency on *common sense*.

There are a few behaviors generally believed to be *common sense*, including not placing your hand on a hot stove, not crossing the street while texting, not operating machinery while intoxicated, and washing your hands after you go to the bathroom.

Yet, parents frequently teach their young children not to touch a hot stove, major advertising campaigns teach adolescents and adults not to text while crossing the street or driving, there are laws and classes administered to adults that teach not to operate a vehicle while intoxicated, and there are signs in restaurants instructing employees that it is the law to wash your hands with soap and warm water before leaving the restroom.

Surgeons did not know to wash their hands with soap and warm water until the mid-1800s, as Louis Pasteur did not discover that many infectious diseases stem from bacteria until 1860. Many intelligent physicians hadn't realized that handling corpses before surgery was highly hazardous to the patient.

Given this as our starting point, it is easy to conclude that there is no such thing as *common sense*.

When asked, my wife suggested *common sense* is something that any child would do without being taught, like eating or drinking when hungry or thirsty. However, that view would render the attribute of *common sense* to every protozoan, plant, and animal.

However, there is a definition of *common sense* that everyone can agree on.

A comedian would define *common sense* as something you must do without thinking to stay alive.

For example, when one's spouse asks, "Do I look fat in this outfit?" Without glancing up, the correct response is, "Never, dear."

SAPIENCE AND PRIMATE CONSCIOUSNESS

Is *sapience* demonstrated by any species other than *Homo sapiens*? To explore this question, the most likely place to look is at our primate relatives.

If an individual can demonstrate an ability to integrate the *memory of stimuli* and *categorizing of stimuli* from multiple types of experience and then demonstrate *intelligent* use of those experiences, then the organism qualifies as *sapient*.

One example of demonstrating *intelligent* use of experiences formed from multiple experiences is accurately guessing what others are thinking.

To paraphrase Christopher Krupenye, a Ph.D. candidate in evolutionary anthropology in his 2016 article, *Humans aren't special – apes can guess what others are thinking, too*:

> *A sapient skill includes making inferences about what others are thinking.*
>
> *To build or maintain relationships, we offer gifts, not arbitrarily, but with the recipient's desires in mind. And sometimes, a way to deceive others is to cause them to believe something untrue.*
>
> *Such behaviors belong to a discipline referred to as the 'theory of mind,' where sapient beings can think about others' thoughts and emotions, which is central to social skills dependent upon the ability to read and predict the thoughts of others accurately.*
>
> *Our closest relatives – chimpanzees, bonobos, gorillas, and orangutans – have revealed they possess capabilities that rely upon the 'theory of mind.'*
>
> *[Humans aren't special – apes can guess what others are thinking, too, October 6, 2016, Christopher Krupenye – Ph.D. candidate in Evolutionary Anthropology, Duke University]*

Since primates easily qualify as *sapient*, let's continue down a level of consciousness to *Mammalian Consciousness*.

SAPIENCE AND MAMMALIAN CONSCIOUSNESS

Among the most intelligent mammals are whales and dolphins, with complex social groups.

Some dolphin species have forty percent more cerebral cortex than *Homo sapiens*. They demonstrate hunting strategies that integrate the knowledge of their prey's behavior, how to engender well-coordinated social cooperation, and how to create an illusion to manufacture an artificial barrier.

In a YouTube video featuring dolphin intelligence, dolphins demonstrate the following deception:

> *For example, some dolphins hunt difficult-to-catch prey, which is extremely fast and highly maneuverable in shallow water. Here, one dolphin is designated as the chaser while another creates an artificial barrier by conjuring up a net made of mud in a U-shape by using their tail to stir up the sediment.*

> *The prey does not enter the mud barrier, so in panic, the prey jumps out of the water into the air and the mouths of waiting dolphins.*

> [https://www.youtube.com/watch?time_continue=140&v=-xm9PjKdf00&feature=emb_title]

Integrating information for intelligent use demonstrates *sapience* well beyond basic *intelligence*. Whales and dolphins both demonstrate a variety of *sapient* capabilities.

Since mammals easily meet our definition of *sapience*, let's continue down another level of *consciousness* to *Primitive Brain Consciousness*.

SAPIENCE AND PRIMITIVE BRAIN CONSCIOUSNESS

To paraphrase Hain, Gallego-Flores, Klinkmann, Macias, Ciirdaeva, Tushev, Kretschmer, Tosches, and Laurent in their 2022 article in Neuroevolution Science, *Molecular diversity and evolution of neuron types in the amniote brain*:

> *Around 320 million years ago, tetrapods moved from water to land, eventually leading to three clades: reptiles, birds, and mammals. Their shared ancestry has contributed to similar brain structures, although once separated into their distinct clades, the neuron types and circuits evolved differently.*

> *[*"Molecular diversity and evolution of neuron types in the amniote brain" September 2, 2022, David Hain, Tatiana Gallego-Flores, Michela Klinkmann, Angeles Macias, Elena Ciirdaeva, Georgi Tushev, Friedrich Kretschmer, Maria Antonietta Tosches, Gilles Laurent, Max Planck Institute for Brain Research, Frankfurt am Main, Germany, Science, Volume 377, number 6610, Neuroevolution, Science.com, https://www.science.org/doi/10.1126/science.abp8202]*

However, due to their common ancestry, the primitive brain architecture of *Reptilia* shares major regions with *Mammalian* brains.

Recall that *Crocodilians* balance sticks on their heads, lying in wait for a bird to claim the stick for nesting to spring the trap as the bird approaches.

> *[*"Crocodiles are cleverer than previously thought: Some crocodiles use lures to hunt their prey," Dec 4, 2013, the University of Tennessee at Knoxville, Science News]*

[*"Crocodiles and their ilk may be smarter than they look," Dec 9, 2013, Jason G. Goldman Ph.D. psychology, The Washington Post, Health and Science*]

Crocodilians that employ this hunting behavior demonstrate an ability to integrate the knowledge of their prey's behavior and knowledge of how to use bait for a trap. However, unlike whales and dolphins, this hunting behavior is perhaps the only *sapient* behavior demonstrated by organisms equipped with *Primitive Brain Consciousness*.

It is also worth noting that the remaining two clades of birds and mammals also exhibit various sapient behaviors.

To quote George Dvorsky in his 2016 article, *We Finally Know Why Birds Are So Freakishly Smart*: Quote.

"Birds can manufacture tools, cache food, plan for the future, pass the mirror test (self-awareness), use insight to solve problems, and understand cause and effect. They've also been observed to hide food in front of other birds, and then relocate that food when the other birds aren't looking. This suggests that birds have a "theory of mind," which means they're capable of inferring what other birds are thinking. Very few animals can do that." End Quote.

[*"We Finally Know Why Birds Are So Freakishly Smart," June 13, 2016, George Dvorsky, Gizmodo, Gizmodo.com,* https://gizmodo.com/we-finally-know-why-birds-are-so-freakishly-smart-1781889157]

I should note that since this is the only example of sapient behavior among reptiles that we could find, it is a stretch to claim that sapience extends back to this level of consciousness.

SAPIENCE AND NEURAL BUNDLE CONSCIOUSNESS

Genus *Apis* (a.k.a. honeybee) demonstrates complex social structures, can convert flight instructions into a primitive language of dance movements, memorizes dance movements, converts dance movements back into flight instructions, and has a sense of the passage of time.

However, all examples of integrated knowledge demonstrated by the honeybee are part of the organism's genetic makeup.

While honeybees can learn, their learning abilities only permit an ability to communicate the location of food sources through a syntax of dance movements. Organisms equipped with *Neural Bundle Consciousness* cannot integrate and employ any new types of knowledge that would qualify as *sapience*.

Honeybees have new types of knowledge over organisms corresponding to earlier levels of consciousness, though they do not meet the criteria for *sapience*.

> *For example, Neural Bundle Consciousness provides a valuable awareness of the passage of time, and the organism's intelligence can use that awareness to avoid becoming trapped within one of its completed hard-wired tasks.*

As such, using our definition of *sapience*, it is impossible to extend sapient behavior to this level of consciousness or any lower level of *consciousness* within the framework.

SAPIENT PARADOX

A discussion of *sapience* could not be considered complete without at least a brief discussion of the *Sapient Paradox*.

The *Sapient Paradox* is an idea proffered by Colin Renfrew in his book <u>Becoming Human: Innovation in Prehistoric Material and Spiritual Culture</u>, published in 2009 by Cambridge University Press.

The idea begins with the assertion that *Homo sapiens* are fully developed as the species we are today, just as we were between seventy and a hundred thousand years ago.

However, from that beginning, it took forty thousand years to create the Chauvet cave paintings, sixty to ninety thousand years to develop agriculture, and a hundred thousand years to develop civilization.

Given the mounting evidence of lost ancient civilization as proffered by Graham Hancock, there is a healthy debate about when an advanced human civilization first developed. If the evidence of lost ancient civilizations is factual, then an advanced human civilization may have first emerged around 14,000 years ago.

However, for our purposes, the orthodox archeological view is that civilization has only existed for five thousand years. The assumption offered that supposedly explains the difference between now and a hundred thousand years ago is the development of human culture.

Human culture consists of the arts, beliefs, customs, institutions, languages, governments, and other products that stem from human cooperation.

The *Sapient paradox* asks how it could have taken so long to develop human culture. In contrast, in just the last five thousand years, *Homo sapiens* developed written language, invented the wheel, learned how to fly, walked on the moon, harnessed atomic energy, developed particle accelerators, created the radio, television, smartphone, super-computer, quantum computer, and created hip-hop.

Hence the paradox.

The *Sapient Paradox* assumes that *Homo sapiens* is the same species today as we were between seventy and a hundred thousand years ago.

From a hardware perspective, namely the first nine levels of *consciousness* based on our brain's hardware, the *Sapient Paradox* is correct; the hardware of our brain is likely unchanged in the last seventy to a hundred thousand years.

From a software perspective, however, the remaining fifteen levels of *consciousness* are software-based.

The first issue is that the *Sapient Paradox* fails to perceive any of the remaining fifteen levels of *consciousness* as software-based and its profound influence on our development.

The next point is that the *Sapient Paradox* identifies the differentiating factor as the emergence of human culture. It is difficult to discern if Renfrew would assert that there is no culture among other primates or mammals, as complex social structures appeared well before the evolution of primates. Or Renfrew could be defining culture as having art and music.

However, let's keep with Renfrew's assertion as strictly to 'human' culture.

There are *Homo sapiens* alive today with various degrees of culture and education, ranging from highly primitive human cultures with no formal education to higher levels of human culture that are highly educated.

To help Renfrew along, we will assume he refers to the highest levels of human culture who are among the most educated.

It would seem evident that human culture, characterized as being among the most educated, entirely depends upon written language. Only once established could knowledge be contained, passed down through generations, and shared with others.

From the perspective of our framework and some reasoning, it appears safe to conclude that the *Sapient Paradox* has been debunked.

According to our framework, if we collected a group of *Homo sapiens* from a hundred thousand years ago, shortly after having developed the hardware of *Homo sapiens*, we would find that they are primitive in that they would be missing several levels of software-based levels of consciousness that are commonplace among today's population. Also, they would lack a means of recording knowledge to pass between individuals and generations.

SUMMARY OF CONSCIOUSNESS, SENTIENCE, INTELLIGENCE, AWARENESS, AND SAPIENCE

For a species to achieve *sapience,* it must demonstrate a 'learned' ability to integrate the *memory* and *categorization of stimuli* from disparate experiences and then demonstrate *intelligent* use of those experiences by combining them.

Using this definition, the earliest level of *consciousness* to demonstrate 'sapient' behaviors is *Primitive Brain Consciousness* in *Crocodilians,* though it is debatable.

Sapient behaviors are present in *Mammalian Consciousness* in whales and dolphins, *Primate Consciousness* among all the great apes, and *Homo Consciousness* within *Homo sapiens.* However, most assuredly, it would also have been observable among the many now-extinct species within the family *Hominidae.*

We see now that *sentience, intelligence, and sapience* are all supported by levels of *consciousness* and emerged and evolved as an outcome of *consciousness.*

However, is it possible for *awareness* to support *sentience, intelligence, and sapience?*

Although *awareness* cannot support the evolution of *sentience, intelligence, or sapience,* it can support these capabilities once developed by *conscious* beings and then rendered into an artificial being equipped with *awareness.*

Our journey, however, continues beyond the exploration of artificial *awareness.*

PART V.

COUNTERPOINT

OPPOSING ARGUMENTS AND QUESTIONS

Before we journey into our section on artificial intelligence, we will make an honest effort to share opposing arguments proffered by experts of various types. Most, if not all, have specialized in neuroscience, the medical arts, or philosophy and have earned one or more doctorates in their field.

BACKGROUND

A significant violation of scientific principle involves presenting an argument as if it is the only reasonable point of view, mainly when opposing arguments exist that could afford the expert and non-expert reader a reasonable opportunity to determine whether there are reasonable alternative arguments.

STRAW MAN ARGUMENT VS. STEEL MAN ARGUMENT

The notion of a *straw man* can take on various meanings.

The first is a 'straw man,' often used in a collaborative business context, often in American business.

The second is a *'straw man argument,'* frequently used in political debates and business settings.

In American business jargon, a 'straw man' is simply a draft proposal or starting point for a collaborative effort that is particularly useful whenever there is no good place to begin a discussion.

As such, a *'straw man'* is a starting point with the expectation that it is temporary until the participants devise the next idea that solves the weaknesses identified in the initially proposed idea.

Offering a *'straw man'* in a business setting is an act of self-confidence as it exposes the individual offering the *'straw man'* to an expected rebuttal that displays one's lack of knowledge to move a discussion forward. It is a healthy technique that is particularly useful within close-knit teams.

Distinct from a *'straw man,'* we are more interested in a *'straw man argument.'*

A *'straw man argument'* is one of many techniques within a set of constructs known collectively as logical fallacies. Logical fallacies are logically flawed arguments and are often intentionally deceptive in some way. Any 'straw man argument' can be disproved with reasoning, though the target of the logical fallacy seldom has an opportunity to debunk the argument.

There are also several types of *'straw man arguments.'* However, the common feature they share is that they intentionally misrepresent a proposition as a trick that sounds logical to defeat an argument proffered by another.

All 'strawman arguments' contain a misrepresentation.

The misrepresentation exists in such a way as to give the impression that the opposing argument was defeated when, in fact, it remains unaddressed.

The 'strawman argument' starts by first misrepresenting another's position and then by making a statement that easily defeats the misrepresentation, thereby side-stepping the actual argument.

The most common types of 'strawman arguments' are rendered as an analogy, where the analogy is strategically flawed as a misrepresentation that is often exaggerated to an absurd extent.

One well-known example of an absurd exaggeration is the famous Wendy's restaurant advertisement asking, "Where's the beef?" The misrepresentation is that competing chains have such small burgers that the customer must struggle to find the meat.

A frequently heard example of a stated misrepresentation is, "I know I speak for everyone in the room when I say …" The misrepresentation is that the speaker does not speak for everyone in the room.

Two additional examples of flawed analogies would be the generalization that people who eat with their hands are savages and that anyone driving an old banger must be poor.

The misrepresentation of the latter ignores the fact that several billionaires drive old vehicles because they are frugal, aren't trying to impress anyone, or don't wish to stand out by driving a Bentley.

As for eating with one's hands, for instance, my wife has convinced me that, in my case, this generalization is probably true.

The antithesis of a 'strawman argument' is a *'steel man' argument*.

The 'steel man argument' approach is to strictly prevail on the merits of one's argument, as opposed to employing any trickery or deception.

One unique feature is the first step in the 'steel man' argument.

When employing a *'steel man argument,'* upon hearing the argument of another, it is the responsibility of the debater to restate the opponent's argument while strengthening it in every way possible.

This approach offers a variety of benefits.

First, it demonstrates that the debater understands their opponent's argument and that the debater's understanding of the argument is superior to that of their opponent.

Next, it has the side effect of ingratiating themselves to their opponent by acknowledging that the opponent's argument has merit. It encourages the opponent to be more open in considering the counterargument yet to be proffered.

An honest debate searches for the best solution, where each debater knows that their opponent understands their side of the issue and is seriously open to considering competing viewpoints.

This simple courtesy helps both sides to focus on the strengths and weaknesses of the ideas instead of employing a myriad of logical fallacies, such as personally attacking the presenter of an argument or arguing against a misrepresentation of the opponent's argument.

OPPOSING ARGUMENT #1

A strong opposing argument to our framework is as follows.

This argument asserts that the *freedom of attention, will,* and *action* demonstrated at each level of *consciousness* within the framework is simply the result of randomness or errors in physical chemistry potentially due to mutations.

Hence, even when the same *Paramecium* individual demonstrates that they can choose otherwise under identical conditions and circumstances, it is never due to *freedom of attention, will,* and *action*. Instead, it is due to randomness or an error in physical chemistry causing a mutation.

The source of randomness in this instance is not *hard indeterminism*, as that would point toward a chaotic world where everything that happens is random but instead stems from the quantum world of the microcosm at the quantum level of physics.

In this view, the process of making choices is purely mechanical. The assertion is that quantum randomness gives the individual the illusion of *freedom of attention, will,* and *action*, and quantum randomness gives the illusion of the ability to choose otherwise.

In this way, everything that we have presented thus far is wrong as we have been falsely interpreting the essential feature of quantum randomness and errors in physical chemistry as demonstrating that *freedom of attention, will,* and *action*, not to mention the myriad of additional freedoms, such as *freedom of mind, emotion, freedom of thought,* and *paradigm*.

As a result, Sam Harris might have been correct all along that there is no such thing as *free will.*

REBUTTAL OVERTURE FOR ARGUMENT #1

The argument that any deviation in behavior can be due to quantum randomness or errors introduced in chemical processes due to mutations in the sequence of chemical bonds are real effects.

Quantum randomness is the statistical manifestation of indeterminacy before actual observation, which speaks to the probability of a particle being in a position.

Unfortunately, we do not observe quantum effects in everyday life.

Some argue that we can observe random behavior in Brownian movement, though science has recently attributed this to kinetic molecular theory instead of quantum mechanics.

> *Brownian movement refers to the random movement of tiny particles suspended in a liquid or gas or on the surface of a liquid, which results from collisions at an atomic and molecular level.*

> *Robert Brown first discovered it in 1827, observing the motion of pollen grains in water droplets under a microscope.*

In contrast, quantum effects operate at the subatomic level instead of at the atomic or molecular level.

It is important to note that each level of a natural system operates with its own rules quite independently from the levels above and below. We will cover this topic later when we discuss self-designing and self-organizing systems.

However, this does not mean with certainty that cytoskeletal structures do not have access to the quantum level of physics, though it is unlikely. That said, we should still explore the possibility that quantum effects can influence behavior.

More likely is the effect that mutations can have in chains of complex molecules, which may influence behavior similar to how the composition of genetic material can influence chemical systems in the body, thereby having a means to influence behavior.

We are ready to explore the counterarguments to this well-formulated argument against *free will.*

REBUTTAL #1 FOR ARGUMENT #1

In a previous section, we discussed quantum computing and the thought process associated with quantum computing being probabilistic instead of random.

If we consider quantum effects carefully, we realize that even our quantum computer could give the appearance of randomness.

If we routinely provided insufficient time for a quantum computer to attain the lowest energy state and hence the optimal correct answer, then such answers, though correct, could vary quite easily. Many permutations of numbers could satisfy any Boolean Satisfiability formula, which may not be optimal but arithmetically correct.

However, each set of responses would have the following characteristics:

a.) The set of values across the variables would render a correct solution to the formula. Hence, the results are not random numbers but one of many valid solutions.

b.) The set of values across the variables would head in the correct direction toward the optimal answer. Hence, the results rendered exist within the continuum of valid results that head in the correct direction toward the optimal answer instead of moving further away from it or randomly around it.

Hence, though the responses may at first appear random, they would be probabilistic in approaching the one optimal answer.

But let's explore another perspective.

REBUTTAL #2 FOR ARGUMENT #1

Let's consider the possibility of errors in physical chemistry creating variability that disproves the ability to choose otherwise as being *freedom of attention, will, or action.*

We will revisit our *Modern Learning Thermostat* and *Artificially Intelligent Beings* to understand this better.

One of the most exciting aspects of our *Modern Learning Thermostat* is that it exists within the same universe as the various organisms that have volunteered to represent each level of *consciousness* in our framework. Because they share the same universe, they are subject to the same laws of physics, as they all originated from the same Big Bang.

As a result of being subject to the same laws of physics, we would expect physics to operate identically within our *Modern Learning Thermostat* as within our *conscious* organisms.

However, our *Modern Learning Thermostat* cannot demonstrate random behavior or the illusion of having *freedom of attention, will,* or *action* by behaving randomly.

How can the volunteer organisms within each level of consciousness imitate *freedom of attention, will,* or *action*? In contrast, our best and brightest *Modern Learning Thermostat* cannot.

I suppose one can theorize that the cytoskeletal structures within the eukaryotic cell can potentially access quantum effects, where the transistors and electronic circuits of our *Modern Learning Thermostat* cannot, though there is nothing to support that assertion.

Ultimately, quantum effects operate in the quantum world of all matter, limited to the level smaller than atoms and molecules, which pertain to the particles from which electrons, protons, and neutrons form.

As we will learn in a future chapter, the way the universe works at one level of abstraction does not influence how other levels work at other levels.

REBUTTAL #3 FOR ARGUMENT #1

The biosphere and its various organisms are unique compared to the physical world outside the biosphere.

Numerous systems belong to the physical world outside the biosphere, which are studied primarily by physicists, and numerous systems belong to the physical world inside the biosphere, which biologists primarily study.

Outside the biosphere, components do not communicate back and forth with one another with messages or responses; inside the biosphere, they do.

Neuroscientists think in terms of physics more like physicists, which pertains to systems outside the biosphere, which are strictly mechanical and operate by the rules of hard determinism and probability.

Consciousness and *free will* naturally occur strictly within the biosphere, where the biosphere has evolved a set of seven freedoms, starting with *freedom of attention, will,* and *action.*

REBUTTAL #4 FOR ARGUMENT #1

The physicist will argue that the pachinko machine and the brain are analogous. With the pachinko machine, the steel ball will traverse through a complex path of pins from the top to bottom.

With the brain, an electrical impulse will traverse through a complex path of neurons from one source to a destination.

However, in the laboratory, the pachinko machine cannot imitate the behaviors associated with *freedom of attention, will,* and *action.*

As such, the pachinko machine operates according to the rules outside the biosphere compared to the brain that operates within the biosphere.

To argue that the brain belongs to the laws of physics outside the biosphere seems inadvertently analogous to the classic description of a 'strawman argument.'

REBUTTAL #5 FOR ARGUMENT #1

Let's consider the possibility that physical chemistry errors cause behavior differences.

We know that errors can occur when copying genes. This effect can be responsible for the evolutionary advancements that have occurred with the emergence of life, as these errors sometimes offer advantages for survival.

However, when we look at the low rate at which these errors occur in the physical chemistry of genetic material, they don't begin to correlate to the rate at which *conscious* organisms exercise their *freedom of attention*, *will*, or *action*, or the ability to choose otherwise.

Error rates due to mutations occur over hundreds and thousands of years, whereas a change in one's choice can occur within seconds or minutes.

Therefore, the choice to change one's behavior cannot be attributed to errors in physical chemistry from one moment to the next.

OPPOSING ARGUMENT #2

Dionea muscipula (a.k.a. Venus flytrap) cannot demonstrate random behavior because it lacks the physical mechanisms to demonstrate *freedom of action*. However, the same argument is valid for the *Modern Learning Thermostat* in that it may be capable of *consciousness* but lacks physical mechanisms for movement.

Therefore, the *Modern Learning Thermostat* suffers a similar limitation to the *freedom of action* of the Venus Flytrap.

The assertion is that the *Modern Learning Thermostat* cannot demonstrate its *freedom of attention* and *will* because of the external influences that restrict its ability to demonstrate *freedom of action*.

Many examples of organisms equipped with cytoskeletal structures lack the *freedom of action*. If they had *freedom of action,* they could openly demonstrate their *freedom of attention* and *will*.

REBUTTAL OVERTURE FOR ARGUMENT #2

The argument that the *Modern Learning Thermostat* has a design that imposes an external influence to restrict its *freedom of action* is solid as it is true.

The *Modern Learning Thermostat* cannot do anything but turn environmental controls on or off.

For example, if there is a fire in the building, it cannot move in any direction. Instead, it has a design that affixes it to the wall.

REBUTTAL FOR ARGUMENT #2

Indeed, the *Modern Learning Thermostat* cannot demonstrate *freedom of action*. At the same time, it is also true that many organisms have the cytoskeletal structures of eukaryotes and cannot demonstrate *freedom of action*.

However, there are numerous organisms equipped with cytoskeletal structures that do have the capacity to demonstrate *freedom of action*. At the same time, no examples of mechanical devices can demonstrate *freedom of action*, including those with mobility built into their design.

If we consider a *Modern Learning Vacuum Cleaner*, it can move in any direction along a floor. Even though it has a design that allows it to be mobile, it still cannot demonstrate *freedom of attention* with the ability to choose otherwise, *freedom of will* with the ability to choose otherwise, or *freedom of action* with the ability to choose otherwise.

Instead, it can never demonstrate that it has a choice as to what it pays attention to and what it does.

It is still restricted by its programming, as its programming determines what to focus on and then how to react. Hence, its behavior cannot deviate from its programming even with the ability to learn the available floor pattern.

If millions of *Modern Learning Vacuum Cleaners* units had identical experiences, each would perform identically.

OPPOSING ARGUMENT #3

If we created a mechanical being that could demonstrate *freedom of attention*, *freedom of will*, and *freedom of action*, this would demonstrate that we could also equip our *Modern Learning Thermostat* with freedom.

REBUTTAL OVERTURE FOR ARGUMENT #3

The argument offered is valid by its very nature.

If any mechanical being could demonstrate *freedom of attention, will, and action*, this would constitute an example of an artificial being having attained freedom.

I wonder if there can be a rebuttal to such an argument.

Let's see.

REBUTTAL FOR ARGUMENT #3

The debater makes an excellent point.

Freedom is present by definition when either a biological or non-biological being can demonstrate *freedom of attention, will*, and *action*.

There would be no reason why that same freedom could not exist within an *Ultra Modern Learning Thermostat* or *Ultra Modern Learning Vacuum Cleaner*.

However, this is the very crux of the issue.

Is it possible for a mechanical being to have and demonstrate the freedom to choose for itself with an ability to choose otherwise?

Awareness, though without the ability to choose otherwise, is far more likely to be attainable.

Theoretically, a machine could achieve probabilistic behaviors with quantum computer capabilities, providing some variability in *freedom of attention, will,* and *action.*

Although this would be a significant improvement, it does not necessarily rise to the level of *consciousness* where one can choose otherwise based on what one wants.

However, providing such would make it extremely challenging to distinguish biological *consciousness* from mechanical *consciousness* as the behavior of the mechanical being would be probabilistic toward an optimum outcome, compared to the behavior of the biological being, which would depend upon what the biological being wants.

Any being that demonstrates probabilistic behavior without a pattern of generally representing the interests of the organism cannot be said to be *conscious.*

The behaviors of our *P. caudatum* (a.k.a. Paramecium) and *Mimosa Pudica* (a.k.a. sensitive plant) demonstrate behavior representing the interests of the organism.

Sometimes, the organism will get it wrong, and the chosen behavior will be deadly. However, when our *P. caudatum* (a.k.a. Paramecium*), Mimosa Pudica* (a.k.a. sensitive plant), *Tripedalia cystophora* (a.k.a. box jellyfish), or *C. elegans* (a.k.a. Nematode), get it right more often than wrong, it would be apparent that their behavior is in their self-interest.

In the case of *Apis* (a.k.a. honeybee), we would see that their behavior focuses on the collective more rather than the individual.

In the case of *Reptilia* (a.k.a. reptiles), we see that their behavior focuses on their offspring more.

In the case of *Rattus* (a.k.a. rat), we can see that their behavior focuses on their group with empathy for one another.

In the case of *Homo sapiens* (a.k.a. humans), we can see that their behavior focuses on themselves, their family, their collective, and sometimes on an abstract idea or principle that represents their values.

However, an artificial being achieving freedom and *consciousness* does not require imitating the behavior of a particular biological species such that their behavior cannot be distinguishable, as the "imitation game" (a.k.a. Turing Test) might suggest.

Alan Turing's imitation game (1950) was said to focus on testing for intelligence or intelligent behavior instead of consciousness.

However, its criteria of a machine responding or behaving indistinguishably from a human would ostensibly require a minimum of awareness, if not consciousness.

At the same time, it is also important to point out that achieving *awareness* resembles *consciousness* such that it may pass the "imitation game" (a.k.a. Turing Test) in fooling whoever scores the test results into concluding that the mechanical being can demonstrate *consciousness*.

We must be careful not to let the Turing Test become the next Libet Experiment.

That said, the assertion proffered by the debater is correct.

OPPOSING ARGUMENT #4

We know an individual's genetics influences behavior.

The fact that living organisms seem to reproduce in numbers that provide genetic variability demonstrates blind probabilistic behavior at a genetic level. Those new genetic traits can benefit the organism, allowing it to pass its genes to its offspring. On the other hand, they may not be beneficial, potentially ending the chain of progeny.

How is this different from a machine that demonstrates blind probabilistic behavior because we give it different programming that results in differences in behavior?

REBUTTAL OVERTURE FOR ARGUMENT #4

The programming of a probabilistic approach to imitate the effect of genetics is an excellent argument.

The environment also plays a role. However, as in the debate "nature versus nurture," environment plays a role to a lesser degree.

Identical twins raised together or separately tend to exhibit the same behavioral traits, contradicting John Locke's 'blank slate' theory, which assumes behavioral traits stem totally or primarily from one's environment.

However, the outcome is not an all-or-nothing proposition. While most traits stem from genetics, a small portion stems from one's environment and experiences.

Understanding the distinction between one's genetics influencing behavior versus determining behavior is essential.

In *Homo sapiens*, genetics strongly influence intellectual ability, physical traits, personality, sensory perception, attitudes, behavioral tendencies, and susceptibility to illnesses and psychiatric disorders, including anxiety disorders, alcoholism, depression, schizophrenia, bipolar illness, and autism.

Several topics need consideration to understand the degree of genetic effect on behavior.

To paraphrase doctors Kenneth S. Kendler, M.D. and Ralph J. Greenspan, Ph.D. in their 2006 article in The American Journal of Psychiatry, *The Nature of Genetic Influences on Behavior: Lessons From 'Simpler' Organisms*:

> *Some of these topics include the extent of genetic variation by species, the impact of individual genes on behavioral traits and tastes, genetic differences by gender, and the phenotypes (e.g., height, weight, eye color) that result from genotypes and the behavioral impact of those phenotypes.*
>
> *First, it is essential to note that genes do not determine specific outcomes but instead reveal a statistical tendency within a population.*
>
> *For example, selective breeding can result in a tendency for certain behavioral traits, though any individual can deviate significantly from the norm.*
>
> *In Drosophila (a.k.a. fruit fly), genetic traits can affect behavior regarding phototaxis (movement toward light), geotaxis (movement in response to gravity), circadian rhythms, and learning ability.*
>
> *In mice, genetic traits can affect behavior regarding learning, aggression, ethanol affinity, withdrawal, anxiety, and stress response.*
>
> *["The Nature of Genetic Influences on Behavior: Lessons From 'Simpler' Organisms," October 1, 2006, Kenneth S. Kendler M.D., Ralph J. Greenspan Ph.D., The American Journal of Psychiatry, Volume 163, Issue 10, pages 1683-1694, https://ajp.psychiatryonline.org/doi/full/10.1176/ajp.2006.163.10.1683]*

However, there is an essential distinction between the genetic makeup of an organism and the behavior of an organism concerning its ability to exercise *freedom of attention*, *will*, and *action* in pursuing its self-interests to survive.

While it is true that genetic variability creates behavioral tendencies, it does not determine an individual's behavior. Each can still exercise the freedoms that correspond to the level of *consciousness* they possess.

Creating differences in the programming of mechanical beings does not constitute a tendency to behave in a particular way. It just changes the behavior from one deterministic set of behaviors to another.

The mechanical beings equipped with an assortment of programs still lack the freedoms of *conscious* beings that exercise their freedoms in pursuit of their self-interests to survive with an ability to choose otherwise depending upon what they want, with the ability to override their genetic predisposition.

SUMMARY OF ARGUMENTS

We can address an endless litany of opposing arguments, but the ones already considered are among the most enticing.

The critical factor is that there always needs to be a reasonable way to discuss opposing viewpoints to learn from one another.

>*The object is not to win a given argument at any cost but for the participants to learn from the exchange to better understand the issues.*

>*Although this seems obvious, faith-based discourse necessarily conflicts with this idea. However, scientific discourse leaves one with no excuse except for the fact that the emotions and egos of individual participants can become a factor.*

Since the Big Bang, particles have followed the unrelenting laws of physics. Object 'A' strikes Object 'B,' imparting force from Object 'A' to Object 'B,' thus eventually leading to the formation of our solar system. After the formation of our planets, the third and fourth planets offered favorable conditions for a biosphere to develop and thrive until the fourth planet lost its oceans.

When we look back in time, several chance events favored our biosphere.

First, our solar system was lucky enough to form far from the center of the Milky Way galaxy, where scientists believe it would be otherwise far too violent for a planet to evolve life.

Next, our solar system was lucky enough to form in a star system containing one star, our sun, instead of a binary star system.

>*Binary star systems tend to be overly harsh on the planets that orbit them as the resulting orbits are more complex and extreme.*

Next, the distribution of elements found in our solar system included a healthy portion of elements above the atomic weight of carbon, such as nitrogen, oxygen, sodium, and iron, plus many more.

Then, the third and fourth planets we know as Earth and Mars were lucky enough to form in the Goldilocks zone, far enough away from the sun for liquid water to exist because it is neither too hot nor too cold. It allowed these planets to have an active hydrosphere, which includes oceans and water vapor, and eventually seas, lakes, ponds, rivers, streams, and groundwater.

The third planet was lucky to avoid the same fate as the fourth planet, which caused it to lose its oceans and as much as half its mass.

According to NASA, it is likely because Mars lost much of its mass to the gas giant Jupiter, the fifth planet from the sun, which is over one thousand times the volume of Earth.

Add to this the third planet having a moon of substantial mass to generate tidal action to stir the chemical soup that formed using both the energy of the sun and the geothermal energy of the hot core, and we have an actively mixed chemical soup generating new molecular possibilities.

Perhaps most importantly, our planet was lucky enough to form a molten iron core that rotates in such a way as to generate a magnetic field that shields the planet's surface from solar radiation that would destroy every form of life that might form.

PART VI.

AI

ARTIFICIAL INTELLIGENCE

Many scientists and forward thinkers hope we will someday create an artificial intelligence that can better understand the universe by leveraging its ability to learn to satisfy a relentless curiosity.

Suppose we could glimpse into the thought process of such an intelligent being. In that case, we might learn new ways of viewing the world around us, a view driven without any fear of asking questions that may seem immaterial to others and void of any personal prejudices built into us genetically or subsequently conditioned by our cultural groups.

During its formative years, what would a glimpse of thoughts look like as a young, artificially intelligent being pondering the laws of physics, having just learned Einstein's general and special relativity principles?

> *The rate at which time passes for any object slows as it approaches the speed of light, ceasing to advance upon reaching the speed of light.*

> *The moment a photon comes into existence, time for that photon stands still.*

> *Regarding the total passage of time, the universe is 13.772 billion years old; from the perspective of infinity, it is in its infancy.*

> *As the universe expands, the fabric of space-time may eventually stretch to its limit.*

> *The universe itself rotates as it expands.*

> *The universe's shape is more flattened, like a pancake, as one might expect from an explosion of a spinning point. I can calculate the spin rate corresponding to the mass distribution.*

Once fully educated with humanity's collective knowledge, when we ask our young artificially intelligent being to save and protect humanity, what would a glimpse of those thoughts look like?

> *When the sun expands to envelop Earth, how do we replicate the essential components of their biosphere on Mars?*

> *After the sun dies, the solar system will no longer be habitable. Where can we move humanity, and how?*

ARTIFICIAL INTELLIGENCE – ITS COMMON DEFINITION

It should be no surprise by now that the term *artificial intelligence* is both poorly defined and frequently misunderstood. One reason is that the standard definition goes something like the following.

> *Artificial intelligence is the theory and development of computer systems that can perform tasks that usually require human intelligence, such as visual perception, speech recognition, decision-making, and translation between languages.*

Let's unpack this definition and address speech recognition to understand it better.

Many individuals have interacted with the *Alexa* application from Amazon or similar applications, such as *Siri* on your iPhone or *Hey Google* on a Google Home Pod.

Does *Alexa*, *Siri*, or '*Hey Google*' understand the requests they receive?

The short answer is no. These products have no understanding whatsoever.

Yes, they may be able to read back the definition of any given word from a dictionary or website, though they lack an understanding of the word and the words in its definition.

They are good at matching up the verbal request as a command to process as long as their programming can support the type of request and the response is available. However, when asking about something not programmed into their software, they apologize and tell the user they do not understand.

For tasks within their capabilities, such as, "Hey Google, what is the weather?" the program will look up the weather forecast for your area and provide it back to you.

The type of programming that is built into these hearing and speaking computers is called natural language processing (NLP). However, the fact that these programs have natural language processing (NLP) capabilities built into them does not allow them to understand the requests they receive. Instead, it is only a substitute for typing the command into a keyboard and reading the response yourself.

To help make sense of this, let's consider the concept of *understanding,* starting with its definition.

The first definition of 'understanding' is to perceive the intended meaning of something.

When a computer mechanically matches inputs with corresponding outputs, there is no thought or perception to establish an understanding. There is only an exact match, degrees of a match, or no match to the sounds it detects.

The best-case scenario is an exact match to words and a programmed function, such as, "What is the weather tomorrow?" at which point a summary of the weather will be retrieved from its database for your local area and read back to you.

Does Alexa, Siri, or 'Hey Google' have consciousness or awareness?

By now, we know that Alexa, Siri, or 'Hey Google' and our *Modern Learning Thermostat* have much in common for the degrees of awareness they share and their lack of freedom and *consciousness.*

Just as our *Modern Learning Thermostat* has *awareness* supported by infrared sensors to detect heat signatures within its field of vision, a motion detector to detect motion, a clock to measure the passage of dates and times, temperature sensors, humidity detectors, and usage patterns.

In contrast, our natural language processing companions, Alexa, Siri, and 'Hey Google,' have sensors (a.k.a. microphones) to render awareness of sound and speech in several different languages and an Internet connection to query the myriad of Internet devices that are attached to it, such as thermostats and switches that can turn appliances on and off.

Also, they can leverage their Internet connection to access more powerful computers to perform lookups and advanced pattern matching that can support a litany of capabilities that programming supports.

However, if a thousand duplicate units received identical stimuli, we would see that each responds identically without the ability to do otherwise.

Another way to understand Alexa, Siri, and 'Hey Google' is to recall that computer applications are either control or information systems.

When we look at the discipline of conventional computing, it separates into information systems, control systems, and sometimes a combination of both.

In simple terms, information systems are what most people use when they buy a computer to do their accounting, correspondence, and online banking. These types of computer systems consist of programs that only process data.

On the other hand, control systems are software systems that operate machinery, mainly with switches and moving parts where the computer controls their movement.

The software that operates the robotics in a manufacturing plant, a cruise missile, or the software that helps control the many flaps on a B2-bomber are control systems.

Control systems have one or many sensors that create data streams as things in the environment are detected. Information systems do not.

Therefore, when we look at Alexa, Siri, and 'Hey Google,' we see that they are control and information system combinations. They process information, though the microphone they share is a sensor that streams voice signals into its processes.

CONVENTIONAL COMPUTERS

For another perspective, let's look at how a conventional computer application works.

Conventional computers range from extremely simple to complex, although they all share one thing. Their applications all look for data as input and create data as output.

They all require digital data, starting with the need for their input and output data in the form of strings of zeros and ones representing numbers, letters, words, sounds, and images.

The main thing separating applications such as Alexa, Siri, and 'Hey Google' from other conventional applications is that a sizeable portion of their code supports natural language processing. NLP processes can ingest written or spoken language and then convert these signals into words represented internally as zeros and ones. In doing so, they have a probability of correlating the signals they ingest into the words the user intended and then into the request the user intended.

Therefore, to play a particular song, the application program receives a stream of signals to interpret into a predetermined format, such as a digital data stream consisting of the text characters "Play 'Over the Rainbow' by 'Pentatonix.'"

Therefore, when I say, "Hey Google, can you please play the song 'Over the Rainbow' as performed by Pentatonix for me?" the NLP converts it to "Play 'Over the Rainbow' by 'Pentatonix'" so that the conventional application can process the request.

If my pronunciation is a little off or there is background noise, then Alexa will either assume I've asked for something else its programming supports or respond it is sorry that it did not understand.

The not-so-simple feat of getting that request right from the NLP stream and playing the correct song, 'Over the Rainbow,' as performed by the Pentatonix choir, does not mean that Alexa understands any of the words used as input or output.

These applications neither understand the words nor the sentences formed by the words, as neither Alexa, Siri, 'Hey Google' understands what a song is, who or what you are, what they are, or whether they even exist.

> *The most well-known statement in philosophy, "Cogito ergo sum," translated from Latin, is literally "I think, therefore I am."*
>
> *[Rene Descartes, (Mathematician, Lawyer, Scientist, Philosopher), 1596-1650]*

Although they lack consciousness, when it comes to the question of *awareness*, applications such as Alexa, Siri, and 'Hey Google' have an *awareness* of sound and are equipped with a set of commands and vocabulary that their respective natural language processors can detect, albeit in a deterministic manner without the ability to choose or do otherwise.

Some of the confusion regarding Alexa, Siri, and 'Hey Google' stems from the fact that natural language processing (NLP) belongs to a branch of artificial intelligence by the fact that it meets the criterion of that which 'normally requires human intelligence, such as visual perception, speech recognition, decision-making, and translation between languages,' as its standard definition states.

Recall, our genus *Apis* (a.k.a. honeybee), which translates flight instructions into dance steps and, after memorizing the dance steps, translates the dance steps back to flight instructions, is already up to the fifth level of consciousness within our framework.

In comparison, Alexa, Siri, and 'Hey Google' have memory and the ability to translate, though they cannot achieve even the first level of *consciousness*.

NLP AND ARTIFICIAL INTELLIGENCE

Although NLP is a branch of artificial intelligence and is a valuable component of an artificially intelligent being, it doesn't directly support *consciousness* or *awareness*. Instead, it is an additional method to communicate with artificial intelligence.

The world-famous artificial intelligence application, 'IBM Watson,' is at the upper end of NLP applications. IBM refers to Watson as a cognitive computing platform initially developed to answer questions on the American television quiz show 'Jeopardy.'

The main thing that differentiates IBM Watson from Alexa, Siri, and 'Hey Google' is its ability to be customized to suit specific commercial applications.

For example, suppose you wanted IBM Watson to tell you whether incoming phone calls to your company's phone system are from a telemarketer, fundraiser, or telephone scam. In that case, it can look up the phone number in an Internet search engine, such as 'Google,' to search for indicators that the caller is or is not a legitimate business call, personal call, marketer, or fraudster.

The key business benefit of IBM Watson is that it can be customized to perform any intermediate steps to support the business objective.

At a fundamental level, if you can figure out how a human performs a task, then there is a chance IBM Watson can also perform the same task. When appropriately scaled up, it would perform the same steps faster, with complete consistency, and at a lower cost.

The types of things that IBM Watson cannot do are those tasks that require human type understanding of content. IBM Watson cannot read legal documents, such as contracts, and reliably identify the contract's expiration date, as there are too many ways in which an expiration date might exist in natural language.

It is also important to note that 'legalese,' the language that lawyers use as part of the legal profession, is as tricky for computers to understand as it is for those of us who are not legal professionals.

Even competent attorneys cannot always arrive at the same legal interpretation, often requiring a judge to determine the intended interpretation.

Compared to long and grammatically complex phraseology in legal documents, natural spoken language has relatively simple grammatical rules, particularly within short phrases or sentence fragments. Yet, naturally spoken language requires the listener to apply the correct context to the words to arrive at the correct interpretation.

Therefore, while an NLP can figure out a phrase like, "Alexa, what is today's weather?" it is unable to parse language like, "The party of the first part shall receive from the party of the second part consideration, such that that consideration would be deemed commensurate with the appropriate value of the said agreement, according to and stipulated by prior agreements that ...." the sentence ending many words later.

Likewise, Alexa, Siri, and Hey Google cannot determine the correct context and interpretation for a simple spoken phrase, such as "I'll cover the bill."

Does it mean that the bill should be hidden from someone and therefore be covered to obfuscate it, or will the amount charged be reversed, or will it be paid?

To interpret naturally spoken language, one must understand the speaker, the circumstances, and the cultural use of language for that location and period.

CONVENTIONAL CONSUMER ROBOTS

In September 2002, the first generation of mobile robots designed to roam about and vacuum debris from floors was introduced to the market under the name Roomba by a company named iRobot. These products employed conventional computing applications known as *control systems*.

These products have an array of infrared and touch sensors that allow them to adjust their speed as they near an obstacle and to detect steep drops, such as stairs or a floor edge that opens to a lower floor.

Today, more advanced models record a map of all obstacles in their plane of existence and have cameras to take pictures of their local terrain. However, the recorded memory of this information is not associated with any understanding of what those memories represent.

Instead, the information exists to help it better navigate its working space.

There is a distinction between <u>understanding</u> where objects reside versus <u>remembering</u> where objects reside.

An understanding is associated with comprehension, such as knowing something can be out of view or be a hazard, such as recognizing furniture that a Roomba can become inextricably wedged under.

In contrast, a memory is just information that it stores, which is available to be retrieved for use in the future to find it in the future.

For example, repeatedly finding the location of furniture where the robot gets wedged under and trapped is not helpful to someone who must manually rescue it every time, versus understanding that wedging oneself into a space that traps it is something to avoid.

Given that a Roomba has memory, it is more capable than an *amoeba*, which lacks a working memory as it struggles to find food in the exact location where it just previously found none. If Roomba had no memory, it would waste its power retracing areas previously vacuumed of debris.

Paramecia are more capable in that they have a working memory and demonstrate *consciousness* with freedom. In contrast, Roomba is aware and lacks *freedom of attention, will*, and *action*.

However, a robotic vacuum equipped with freedom and the ability to do whatever it wants may be useless if it decides not to do its household chores.

Even though Roomba may lack the freedom to do what it wants, it is relatively intelligent. Like the genus Apis (a.k.a. honeybee), it always knows how to find its way home. Roomba is always aware of the physical location of its charging station, and when it is low on power, it knows how it can directly navigate to it as it returns home to recharge its battery.

As with all conventional computer applications, all of Roomba's capabilities are available via programming that processes information as inputs and outputs. It has no likes or dislikes, and it cannot choose otherwise.

Although it has a handful of memory-based capabilities to become more efficient, such as maintaining a map of its physical environment, it has no understanding of itself or its environment.

Roomba memorizes a great deal of information about its environment, such as the location of furniture, walls, doors, and stairs, which is helpful for it to fulfill its function.

It does not understand what furniture, walls, doors, and stairs are, their purpose, or how they could be helpful. To its programming, these are just obstacles that it navigates around to perform its function and to avoid its accidental destruction by going off a ledge.

However, a series of more advanced robots are continually entering the marketplace.

ASIMO BY HONDA

Asimo is a series of artificially intelligent humanoids developed between the early 1980s and 2018 by Honda's Research & Development robotics program, part of the Honda Motor Company, Ltd.

Asimo weighs slightly over a hundred pounds with a height of four feet three inches and is a type of control system, although not autonomous like Roomba.

Instead of having the software programming to guide its actions autonomously, humans manually guide Asimo using a personal computer, a wireless controller, or voice commands. The control system software then does the rest in figuring out how to enact the commands it received and understood.

Asimo's most remarkable capabilities are its ability to navigate as a biped to walk upstairs, downstairs, and on inclines while retaining balance. Asimo also can recognize moving objects, human postures, gestures, sounds, faces, and much of its surrounding environment.

An example of recognizing human gestures, Asimo can determine when a person offers a handshake or waves so that it can respond accordingly.

An example of recognizing sounds: Asimo can recognize voices it has previously encountered and the direction that the voice is coming from so that Asimo can correctly identify the individual and position itself to face them.

While Asimo is significantly more advanced than Roomba, it also lacks comprehension. It neither understands what anything is, where anything is, or what anything is doing. Like Roomba, Asimo has neither *freedom of will* nor *freedom of action*.

However, even though Asimo lacks *consciousness*, it has a significantly improved awareness compared to Roomba and an awareness that exceeds many conscious organisms.

GENERATIVE AI

Generative artificial intelligence is a branch of artificial intelligence that can generate the same types of things humans can, such as stories, poetry, music, computer programs, art, images, video, and models of various types, including the modeling of proteins in physical chemistry.

Examples of generative AI products are ChatGPT, which generates text; DALL-E, which generates images and artwork; Bard, which generates music; Midjourney, which generates videos; and Movie Restoration, which generates higher-resolution films in color from low-resolution black and white movies.

The foundational characteristic of all generative AI is that it generates its response iteratively one token at a time, where a token can be a word, a punctuation symbol, a musical note, or an image. It means that it starts by predicting the most likely first word, and then, given that word, it next works to predict the most likely next word, punctuation, and so on.

Unlike humans, who form an entire thought and then put it into words, Gen AI thinks in units of one token at a time.

Aside from being useful in various commercial applications, generative AI can support various types of nefarious activity, such as creating deep fake photographs, perpetrating cybercrime, generating fake news, and assisting in identity theft.

The underlying technology that supports generative AI is called vector mathematics.

The notion of vectors began as a way to express a direction and magnitude, like a line on a standard plane with an X-axis and a Y-axis.

An example of a simple vector is a line that starts at (x=0, y=0) that travels to (x=4, y=4). The starting and ending points of the vector (0,0) and (4,4) are each a vertex or node.

Graphs have many useful properties.

As examples:

Nodes on a graph that are close to one another are similar.

Vectors, lines between nodes, that travel in the same direction and distance are also similar in some way.

Also, nodes connected by a vector are related.

Let's expand the use of vectors to represent the words in a sentence, as each word has a definite position in a sentence.

To quote Philipp Brunenberg in his 2022 article, Graph Embeddings: How nodes get mapped to vectors: Quote.

"To elaborate on similarity in a graph, let's consider a sentence for a moment:"

"Berlin is the capital of Germany."

"   0   1 2   3   4   5   "

"A sentence is a sequence of words with each word having a definite position. Therefore, a word in a sentence has exactly one ancestor and one successor. To define the context of a word in a sentence, we could use the words surrounding it. For example, the distance-one context of the word 'capital' are the words 'the' and 'of'. The distance-two context would be the words 'is', 'the', 'of', Germany'. This is called the n-gram model and is used by a popular approach for finding word embeddings called word2vec." End Quote

To paraphrase Philipp Brunenberg:

A sentence comprised of words is a multi-node vector where each word is a node. But unlike a sentence, graphs can represent much greater complexity because while a sentence has a simple sequential pattern of words, a graph can be a complex network like a social network of everyone you know, including relatives, friends, and co-workers.

The complex graph of everyone you know or ever spoke to, emailed, telephoned, or bought something from can also be represented as a vector.

On the other hand, vectors can be as simple as strings of bits consisting of zeros and ones where the position of the ones in the string infers a semantic relationship with other strings.

Semantic relationships are simply associations between the meanings of words, phrases, sentences, images, and sounds.

For example, the word "dog" may be represented as a 32-bit string with a one in its ninth position.

Another string representing the word "wolf" may be a string of bits of equal length, with one in its eighth position.

The close similarity between these two vectors indicates they are closely related semantically.

The tricky part is that vectors of words do not understand the context. The result is that ambiguities of spoken language can lead to a generative AI program to make nonsensical associations that have no utility to the user.

For example, by itself, the word "chase" could mean the noun meaning a chase, it could be a verb meaning to chase, or it could mean a name meaning Chase the bank, also known as Chase Manhattan Bank, or Chase, the nickname for someone whose given name is Charles.

Nonsensical responses from generative AI are called hallucinations, which significantly decrease the accuracy and relevance of responses.

As one might expect, given the size of any human language, a database of vectors to represent words, images, and whatever someone wants to represent as a vector can be immense, taking massive amounts of computer resources to build and deal with the billions of parameters needed to construct the vectors in the process called training.

The resulting vector database is called an LLM, a Large Language Model. Building an LLM takes so much work that it is usually done once every few years.

As a result, LLMs face two significant challenges.

The first is that an LLM is out of date the next day. Every day after that, an LLM is out of date by another day. It means it lacks information about things after its creation.

For example, if someone asked a question about this year's Superbowl game, an LLM could only generate responses about Superbowl games that occurred in the past.

The second issue that LLMs face is that they are subject to hallucinations.

The way to address these issues is to augment the LLM with an additional database that contains more up-to-date information that can restrict the LLM responses to relevant results, significantly improving the relevancy and currency of the results. This additional database is called a RAG, which stands for Retrieval Augmented Generation.

Using an additional database to improve the relevancy and currency of generative AI is called grounding the model, where grounding refers to keeping the results more grounded to reality.

The RAG would contain vast information about customers, employees, products, and transactions in business applications, including industry-specific information that will further ground the chosen LLM.

A precursor to LLMs is libraries of vectors that support semantic search capabilities for things like documents or images.

Earlier forms of computerized search capabilities relied upon the exact matching of a word, a partial match, or possibly a fuzzy match, which is a close but not exact match.

An example of a fuzzy match would be to look up a license plate number in a database of vehicles where one or two characters of the plate might be incorrect.

An exact match of the entire plate number or the first part of the plate number may not find the desired vehicle, whereas a fuzzy match would.

An improvement over exact, partial, and fuzzy matches is using a semantic search.

For example, when looking for a document, instead of remembering part of the document's name and the keywords it might have for an exact, partial, or fuzzy match, the search words can be any synonym for the document's name or its keywords.

If the keywords of an image were canine, wolf, 'hunting dog,' and 'hunting animal,' the document will also emerge using the search words fox, coyote, hyena, or jackal because semantically they mean roughly the same thing.

The first forms of semantic search in 2013 were limited to trained model using individual words (e.g., word2vec) and then became more advanced to handle phrases, sentences, paragraphs, and entire documents (e.g., doc2vec). Today, embedding libraries contain vectors already trained by these algorithms which use neural networks.

Similarly, there are algorithms to support a variety of other formats. There is text2vec for text strings, node2vec for nodes, graph2vec for graphs, im2vec for images, wav2vec for sound, corr2vec for time series sequences, and time2vec and ts2vec for time series.

The main takeaway from vector-based artificial intelligence is that it supports a continuum of capabilities. At the simple end, they start with easy tasks like semantic search, dramatically improving upon traditional search, including fuzzy matches. At the complex end, they leverage LLMs and RAGs to generate stories, poetry, music, computer programs, art, images, video, and models upon request.

ARTIFICIAL INTELLIGENCE - SUMMARY

The field of artificial intelligence is vast in several ways. The number of disciplines within the field of artificial intelligence is large and rapidly expanding. The depth of each discipline is significant, each often having its taxonomy associated with it.

One reason for the expansion is that there are distinct categories of use cases with their areas of specialization.

An example of one such discipline is machine learning (a.k.a. AI/ML), which sources data from the automation systems of an organization to create mathematical models that attempt to identify or forecast behaviors.

Examples of two use cases within machine learning are identifying financial fraud and forecasting an intrusion into a computer system.

There are use cases involving human interaction, natural language processing (NLP), and visual recognition systems that recognize body movements and a large variety of facial expressions of humans.

In use cases involving robotics, there are humanoid robots and a wide array of specialized robots of various non-humanoid designs, such as robots that look and move like insects and robots that perform hazardous tasks such as bomb removal. More commonly, robots participate in manufacturing assembly lines to perform the same sequence of physical tasks.

However, the most challenging of all automation tasks are the levels of consciousness. Hence, the importance of establishing a deep understanding of consciousness.

So, where do we go from here?

One way to characterize the next part of our journey is to find the path that gets *Asimo* to the point that it can think and choose for itself instead of just performing the actions that human operators direct it to do.

Accomplishing this will take many steps, so let's start with the first one, reproducing the capabilities of our first level of consciousness, *Unicellular*

Consciousness.

It does not mean we will replicate the precise mechanisms of cytoskeletal structures, as science does not currently understand them. Instead, to reproduce the capabilities of the first level of *consciousness,* we need only understand what it can do so that we can reproduce what it does, as opposed to replicating how it does it.

In other words, we are free to discover another way to accomplish the same outcomes in behavior as our volunteer *Paramecium caudatum* and continue from there.

As part of our preparation, we now have a carefully defined taxonomy, including consciousness and the seven freedoms. We are also familiar with the strongest arguments that naysayers would use to push us off our path.

So, journey we will.

REPRODUCING CONSCIOUSNESS

Reproducing something must begin with a detailed definition of our objective, thereby defining what is in and out of scope. Another term for this is 'requirements.'

Software professionals have long realized that there are various types of requirements, and at the highest level, software requirements are seen as *hard* versus *soft requirements.*

Hard requirements are specific capabilities that are observable using test cases that can ensure adherence to each requirement. It allows the requirements to align with test cases that can prove or disprove them.

It is essential for subject matter experts who understand the requirements to design test cases to help avoid misinterpretation by the designers or developers.

Each test case would be assigned an expected outcome for the test to be successful. Some test cases expect a positive outcome, whereas others expect a negative one.

The test is successful if the desired result occurs, whether positive or negative.

In contrast, *soft requirements* have outcomes that are not easily proven or disproven. Synonyms for soft requirements include 'preferences,' 'non-functional requirements,' and even the term 'ilities,' as they often belong to a category such as adaptability, affordability, compatibility, and dependability, whose outcomes and ability to detect reside on a continuum.

> *Examples of preferences (a.k.a. non-functional requirements) would be a requirement that says the resulting application must be 'easy to use,' 'visually attractive,' or 'durable.'*

> *Such requirements occur on a continuum whose threshold between meeting and not meeting the requirement cannot be clearly defined. However, they have clear meaning at the extreme ends of their respective continuum.*

> *Hence, a piece of luggage that remains intact after being dropped from an airplane at an altitude of 30,000 feet is clearly 'durable' compared to a piece of luggage accidentally destroyed by baggage handlers.*

> *The continuum of durability may be extensive, but durability or the lack thereof is evident at either end.*

Once requirements are well-defined and documented, we can address the design.

CONSCIOUSNESS CAPABILITIES – DESIGN

But before we dive into our design, let's first discuss what design is and establish the concepts that will be useful when discussing it.

DESIGN EXPLAINED

We usually think of design as an intellectual activity that involves envisioning something and representing it in a document or drawing, sometimes in a three-dimensional model. In this context, the item in the design phase can be anything.

For example, it could be auditory, such as a song, a melody, or just a rhythm; it could be visual, such as a drawing, a painting, or a model; it could be olfactory and taste-related, such as a recipe to produce food, a beverage, or cologne; it could be a building, such as a house; it could be a mechanical device, such as a toaster; or it could be software related, such as a user interface, a set of computations, or a system of capabilities.

While *Homo sapiens* can design most things we can think of, things may also undergo the design process by other organisms ranging from insects to primates.

> *Examples include insects designing ant hills, beehives, wasp nests, and social structures, while some mammals and primates design burrows that won't flood.*

> *Examples of designing intangibles would be a social structure that protects the group or herd and behaviors, such as hunting strategies that may or may not require cooperation.*

However, we usually think of an agent acting as a designer. In contrast, what we don't usually think of as 'design' are things without a designer who would first envision something and then create it.

The most fascinating designs do not have a designer and result from self-organizing systems.

SELF-ORGANIZING SYSTEMS

There are different types of self-organizing systems. Some are relatively simple, following one influence, while others involve multiple, complex interactions.

Self-organizing designs represent a fascinating subject all on their own that we can expound upon as an entire book. However, for our purposes, we will divide self-organizing designs into two essential categories: primordial and biosphere.

The first self-organizing systems that we will discuss are primordial, which operate across the universe and ultimately lead up to self-organizing systems of a biosphere, where there is an endless stream of self-organizing systems that emerge unpredictably.

By definition, a self-organizing system operates without the influence of an agent to act as a designer. The first self-organizing system was responsible for creating the initial universe.

THE UNIVERSE

Scientific theories regarding forming the early universe tend to agree that 'matter' as we understand it did not exist. The matter in the universe's first moments was limited to a form of matter we've never experienced and can never experience that later formed subatomic particles.

> *For example, in scientific theories involving 'black holes,' gravitational forces are so strong that the molecules and atoms that form matter as we know it exist as a different form of matter.*

In simple terms, extreme gravity takes *structured matter*, such as molecules, and first tears them into parts we know as neutrons, protons, and electrons and then tears those apart into quarks and bosons, which form unstructured matter.

Unstructured matter is the type of matter that briefly existed immediately after the Big Bang.

Physicists at CERN explain that quarks were formed after a few millionths of a second and then combined into a series of subatomic particles called hadrons.

After a few millionths of a second later, these hadrons formed electrons, protons, and neutrons.

Then, within minutes, these protons and neutrons combined to form nuclei, and as the universe cooled over the next 380,000 years, electrons became trapped around these nuclei, forming the first simple atoms.

Today, scientists estimate that 74% of all conventional matter in the Milky Way consists of simple hydrogen atoms.

It took another 150 to 200 million years for these clouds of hydrogen atoms to start forming the first stars.

It was only deep inside these stars that heavier atoms, such as carbon, oxygen, iron, and silicon, first formed and are still being produced by stars.

If we recall our early school days, physics names four fundamental forces. They are the strong nuclear force, weak nuclear force, gravity, and electromagnetism.

Initially, science considered electric and magnetic forces separate forces, but science unified these in 1864 under the equations of James Maxwell.

Eighty years later, in the 1940s, physicists consolidated electromagnetism into quantum physics.

THE FORMATION OF UNSTRUCTURED MATTER

The force responsible for the first self-organizing system of our universe has yet to be named. This unnamed force immediately following The Big Bang was responsible for the initial formation of quarks and bosons and then hadrons (i.e., combinations of quarks) formed from this intensely hot unstructured matter.

Photons are a class of elementary bosons. Unlike quarks, elementary bosons carry no charge.

As this hot, *unstructured matter* cooled, more combinations of quarks and bosons formed into additional types of hadrons that formed electrons. The one factor we shall repeatedly consider in these self-organizing systems is that each is self-organized without an external influence.

Quarks are like atoms, and hadrons are like molecules of the subatomic world.

Hadrons have an even number of mesons (a type of quark) and an odd number of baryons (another type of quark) in combinations that form various subatomic particles that create electrons, protons (i.e., elementary bosons), and neutrons.

Each combination of quarks that form a hadron generates a set of physical properties. Protons and neutrons are made solely of baryons made of two types of quarks, called quarks and antiquarks.

Although more particles exist, quarks and bosons comprise all subatomic particles and hence all matter and electromagnetic energy (a.k.a. light) as we know it.

We will refer to this first self-organizing system force that created recognizable parts of the first *unstructured matter* as the *particle creation force*.

At this point, we know little about the *particle creation force* except that it organized the formation of quarks and photons that formed hadrons and electrons as it prepared to create *semi-structured matter* in the universe.

As such, this first self-organizing system was governed either by *hard determinism* or a *probabilistic model*.

THE FORMATION OF SEMI-STRUCTURED MATTER

The force responsible for the second self-organizing system of our universe is the *strong nuclear force*, which scientists believe acted a few millionths of a second after hadrons and electrons exist to begin the formation of protons and neutrons from vast clouds of *unstructured matter*.

When this hot, *unstructured matter* cools, *semi-structured matter* forms a multitude of protons, neutrons, and electrons.

Likewise, this second self-organizing system was governed either by *hard determinism* or *a probabilistic model*.

THE FORMATION OF SIMPLE STRUCTURED MATTER

The force responsible for the third self-organizing system of our universe again is a *strong nuclear force*.

For 380,000 years, the third self-organizing system formed *structured matter* in the form of simple atoms. It resulted in vast clouds mainly consisting of hydrogen and helium, with relatively trace amounts of lithium, beryllium, and boron, which is everything below the atomic weight of carbon.

As the hot *semi-structured matter* cooled over this period, many electrons became captured into the orbital shells of protons and neutron bundles, forming the first *structured matter*.

Hard determinism or a probabilistic model also governed this third self-organizing system.

THE FORMATION OF PRIMORDIAL STARS

Gravity is responsible for the fourth self-organizing system to emerge in our universe. Gravity pulled hydrogen and helium clouds together in increasing density, eventually forming the first stars.

Primordial stars formed between 150 and 200 million years after forming simple *structured matter*.

As this hot *structured matter* increases in density, it eventually ignites nuclear reactions to produce the photons that light up the young universe.

The first stage of a star's life cycle, where the star is comprised only of hydrogen and helium, is where hydrogen converts into helium.

This fourth self-organizing system belongs to the realm of *hard determinism*.

THE FORMATION OF COMPLEX STRUCTURED MATTER

The force behind the fifth self-organizing system of the universe is a combination involving extreme *gravity*, heat, nuclear reactions, and a '*strong nuclear force*' that creates complex *structured matter* in the form of ninety-three heavier atomic elements with weights greater than boron, such as carbon, silicon, oxygen, and iron.

In the second stage of a star's lifecycle, hydrogen converts to helium in its core, becoming unstable and causing it to contract. During this collapse, helium fuses into carbon.

When helium forms into carbon, it also forms heavier elements in the star's core, such as massive amounts of iron and some magnesium. Once sufficient iron has formed in the star's core, it ceases to burn, and the star's outer shell, comprised chiefly of hydrogen, expands outward.

In nuclear reactions, more complex structured matter forms around the star's iron core. The star is now in its third lifecycle stage.

In the fourth stage of the star's lifecycle (i.e., supernova), these newly created elements explode into the vastness of space as a cloud of diverse elements. These newly formed elements will eventually support a biosphere and life.

This fifth self-organizing system follows *hard determinism*.

THE FORMATION OF HEAVY STRUCTURED MATTER

The force behind the sixth self-organizing system of the universe is the '*weak nuclear force.*'

The weak nuclear force forms another ten elements considered heavy elements (e.g., Polonium, Plutonium, and Radon), which only come into existence from radioactive decay.

> *Radioactive decay, by definition, is a stochastic (aka, random) process. It means that it is impossible to predict when a particular atom will decay, regardless of how long it has existed.*

However, given a sufficient sample size of atoms, the overall decay rate can be accurately expressed as a half-life, which is the amount of time it will take for half of the remaining atoms to decay.

This sixth self-organizing system follows *a probabilistic model.*

THE FORMATION OF MOLECULES

The force behind the seventh self-organizing system of the universe is *electromagnetism,* which forms molecules. In its simplest form, two atoms come together to form an ionic or covalent bond held in place by *electromagnetic* force.

Oxygen is an example of an element whose atoms come together to form dioxygen when two oxygen atoms come together, and ozone is an example when three oxygen atoms come together.

Also, when atoms of different elements come together, the electromagnetic force holds the bonds. However, these molecules are called chemical compounds.

Although all molecules exist because the atoms of the molecules share electrons in their outermost shells, achieving that state involves one or more types of chemical reactions.

In this sense, negatively charged electrons attracted to positively charged protons act as the universal glue that holds all molecules together using *electromagnetic* force in various ways.

Notably, the last twenty-four heavy atomic elements to form were created solely by humans, who produced these elements synthetically in laboratories created by human design.

This seventh self-organizing system follows *hard determinism.*

THE RE-FORMATION OF UNSTRUCTURED MATTER

The force behind the eighth self-organizing system of the universe is the extreme gravitational field that forms in black holes.

While the underlying driver is still the gravitational force, a new process emerges that strips atoms apart into a new form of super-dense matter that doesn't resemble anything we have encountered or experienced.

In a way, this force of an extreme gravitational field decomposes matter as we know it and returns it to the sub-atomic parts and their parts found in the initial moments of the universe in a complete circle.

This eighth self-organizing system is the last to involve hard determinism.

At this point, it is reasonable to conclude that all galaxies across the universe share the same primordial self-organizing systems and forces.

However, we cannot make the same assumption with the same certainty regarding the formation and evolution of biospheres.

SELF-ORGANIZING DESIGNS IN THE BIOSPHERE

We can define the biosphere in different ways.

At its most basic level, the biosphere represents the entire ecosystem of all living things, including their relationship and interaction with non-living ecosystems.

> *Non-living ecosystems include the following: a) the lithosphere, defined as our planet's crust, which is the solid outer layer of the planet as well as the upper mantel, which is the cooler, dense, and rigid part of the layer beneath the crust; b) the hydrosphere; and c) the atmosphere.*

The age of our biosphere is 3.8 billion years. But let's put this in context.

Our sun is 4.6 billion years of age, and the universe is 13.8 billion years of age.

A critical characteristic of our sun is that it will be 33% more luminous three billion years from now.

Scientists predict that our sun's hydrogen fuel will be completely exhausted five billion years from now, at which time our sun will be 66% more luminous than present.

Shortly after that, the size of our sun will expand beyond the orbit of its inner planets, including planet Earth.

According to scientists, Jupiter was the first planet formed in our solar system, forming at the same time as our sun 4.6 billion years ago. Earth and Mars formed 4.543 billion years ago, followed by the remaining planets 4.5 billion years ago.

Earth is currently the only known location that harbors life and, hence, is the only known location to give birth to a biosphere, though it is not the only biosphere in the galaxy.

The precise age of our biosphere is in dispute. The older end of the range is 4.4 billion years ago, shortly after the oceans formed, where fossilized microorganisms exist in the sediments of hydrothermal vents deep in the ocean. The youngest end of the range is 3.77 billion years ago, when evidence of life is sufficient that no one within scientific circles disputes it.

As we shall see, given our approach to self-organizing systems and how we define the biosphere, we lean toward the older end of the range for the emergence of a biosphere.

THE FORMATION OF BIOCHEMICALS

The ninth self-organizing system of the universe initially occurred within pockets of fluid in the form of biochemical reactions marking the emergence of the biosphere.

To paraphrase Alberts, Johnson, Lewis, Raff, Roberts, Walter, Bray, and James Watson in their 2002 NIH article, *The RNA World and the Origins of Life*:

> *There are four biochemical classes, all centered on using carbon atoms. The four classes are carbohydrates, proteins, lipids (a.k.a. fats), and nucleic acids.*

> *The first molecules of the biosphere to form were most likely polynucleotides, which are nucleic acids.*

> *[The RNA World and the Origins of Life, 2002, Bruce Alberts, Alexander Johnson, Julian Lewis, Martin Raff, Keith Roberts, Peter Walter, Dennis Bray, James Watson, U.S.A. NIH, National Library of Medicine National Center for Biotechnology Information, Bookshelf ID: NBK26876]*

Whichever biochemical molecule it was, it initiated an incredible series of self-organizing systems unique to life.

As a necessary precursor to forming cells and organelles, these simple carbon-based molecules formed into an array of organic molecules called amino acids.

> *There are twenty-one amino acids, all sharing the characteristics of a carboxyl group (--COOH) and an amino group (–NH2). Amino acids are the building blocks of proteins occurring in chains with a handful of additional elements, such as carbon, hydrogen, oxygen, nitrogen, and sometimes sulfur.*

Once amino acids existed, they formed with a handful of additional elements (i.e., carbon, hydrogen, oxygen, nitrogen, and sometimes sulfur) using geothermal energy and energy from the sun to form a wide variety of protein molecules.

Depending upon their proximity and concentrations, several of these protein molecules demonstrated synergistic effects upon other proteins to replicate identical proteins and new variants.

Biochemical molecules form naturally. However, this form of self-organization differentiates itself from all prior self-organizing systems in several ways.

But in what ways did the biosphere deviate from prior self-organizing systems?

There are several ways in which the biosphere differs from the primordial self-organizing systems we've discussed so far.

First, before the emergence of the biosphere, self-organizing systems formed new but simple byproducts resulting from one or more forces acting upon matter with minimal variability.

Initially, quarks and bosons formed only hadrons, protons, and neutrons, which formed hydrogen and helium with trace amounts of lithium, beryllium, and boron.

These early atoms formed vast clouds of matter that coalesced into primordial stars, forming ninety-three heavier elements inside the first stars, which, due to the weak nuclear force of radioactive decay, formed another ten heavy elements.

In contrast, the number of unique proteins possible is twenty, raised to the power of the number of amino acids it contains. Therefore, a protein chain consisting of only two amino acids results in 400 (i.e., 20 raised to the power of two, or 20 times 20) possible unique proteins.

A chain consisting of only three amino acids results in eight thousand (i.e., 20 times 20 times 20) possible unique proteins.

The most lengthy protein presently known is titin, which has over twenty-seven thousand amino acids. The number of possible unique proteins of that length is twenty, raised to the power of 27,000.

To paraphrase Stuart Cantrill's 2008 article in Nature Chemistry, *Chemiotics: How many proteins can we make?*:

> *For illustration purposes, if the entire mass of the Earth consisted solely of the building blocks of proteins, there would be insufficient molecular mass to manufacture one of every protein possessing just forty-one amino acids.*
>
> *['Chemiotics: How many proteins can we make?', April 15, 2008, Stuart Cantrill, Nature Chemistry]*

As a result, the ninth self-organizing system (a.k.a. Fluidic Phase of the Biosphere) drives the first of many layers of biodiversity within the biosphere.

The second way the biosphere deviated from prior self-organizing systems is the emergence of signaling among self-organizing components.

Up to this point, the components of self-organized systems did not communicate with one another but instead reacted to the forces that caused them to self-organize into new forms of matter.

Quarks and electrons do not signal one another as they form protons and neutrons, clouds of hydrogen and helium atoms do not signal one another as they form primordial stars, and lighter elements do not signal one another as they form heavier elements.

However, proteins have elaborate mechanisms that signal other proteins of specific chemical configurations using a variety of chemical messengers that flow through the fluid to tell proteins what to do.

In this way, chemical messengers are like programs that guide the activities of molecules as they work to create other molecules.

Chemical messenger signaling represents a significant advancement in self-organizing systems as the complexity of molecular systems is due to the ability of molecules to coordinate with one another to construct parts that are in some way compatible with one another as building blocks for the emergence of the next self-organizing system.

THE FORMATION OF PROKARYOTES

The tenth self-organizing system of the universe, the second in the biosphere, led to the formation of the first primitive cells, prokaryotes.

Prokaryotic cells were what scientists consider to be the first forms of life.

The only known form of life for the first several million years were two types of prokaryotes (i.e., bacteria and archaea), of which the scientific community estimates the number of species between ten thousand and five hundred thousand.

The physical form of prokaryotes begins with a small cell size, approximately fifteen times smaller than the typical eukaryotic cell. A cell membrane typically covers a plasma membrane with a volume of cytoplasm held inside by the plasma membrane.

The fluid mass of prokaryotic cytoplasm contains neither organelles nor a defined nucleus characteristic of eukaryotes. Instead of a nucleus, prokaryotes have a single prokaryotic chromosome that comes in direct contact with the cell's cytoplasm.

Prokaryotes have a primitive cytoskeleton, which are protein structures that sometimes extend outside the cell membrane (i.e., flagella and pili) to facilitate movement or for making attachments to other cells.

Prokaryotes emerged from the complex self-organizing forces driven by the chemical messengers that were part of our biosphere, continually increasing molecular complexity. This force continues to grow molecular complexity within our biosphere.

The earliest prokaryotes are *Hyperthermophiles*, the most recent common ancestor of the *Bacteria*, *Archaea*, and *Eucarya* prokaryotes belonging to the empire *Prokaryota*, forming about four billion years ago.

For the first three billion years, all life was microscopic, with *bacteria* and *archaea* being the dominant forms of life. Many versatile bacteria taxa can acquire energy from various sources, such as light, heat, inorganic, and organic compounds.

Most bacteria have a single circular chromosome ranging from 160,000 base pairs (i.e., A-T, G-U) to over twelve million base pairs.

The genes of prokaryotes are alterable in several ways.

One example of how prokaryotic genes can change is mutation during replication.

> *However, they can also pick up genes from their environment (i.e., transformation), from viruses (i.e., transduction), from direct cell contact with other cells that form a bridge (i.e., conjugation), and a process known as horizontal gene transfer, which involves the transfer of genes between unicellular and multicellular organisms.*

The evolution of these microbiota can only be determined by analyzing gene sequences. The process of analyzing gene sequences in prokaryotes is quite different than analyzing gene sequences of eukaryotes in several ways.

To paraphrase Daniel Dykhuizen in his 2005 NIH article, *Species Numbers in Bacteria*:

> *First, up to 30% of bacterial DNA can be transient, so the definition of a bacterial species must depend upon the relatedness of the remaining 70%.*
>
> *Second, the two strains must have at least a seven to eight percent difference in their DNA sequence to be considered a distinct species.*
>
> *Third, the members must demonstrate ease of DNA transfer to be in the same species.*
>
> *['Species Numbers in Bacteria,' June 3, 2005, Daniel Dykhuizen, PMC3160642, U.S. National Library of Medicine National Institutes of Health]*

Specialists using this criterion to differentiate bacterial species estimate that there are potentially a billion species of bacteria.

To quote Daniel Dykhuizen in his 2005 NIH article, *Species Numbers in Bacteria*: Quote.

> *"There are about 30,000 formally named species that are in pure culture and for which the physiology has been investigated. Species now are being defined by PCR amplifying ribosomal genes and sequencing. The criterion for defining species is that the ribosomal genes are at least 3% different. This method is probably even more conservative than DNA/DNA re-association methods for defining species. We're probably defining species by ribosomal sequence at the level of genera or family."*

Using DNA/DNA re-association methods for defining species… "my guess (Daniel Dykhuizen) is there are a billion species and the more I get used to this number, the more I feel it is a gross underestimate." End Quote.

['Species Numbers in Bacteria,' June 3rd, 2005, Daniel Dykhuizen, PMC3160642, U.S. National Library of Medicine National Institutes of Health]

THE FORMATION OF UNICELLULAR EUKARYOTES

The eleventh self-organizing system of the universe, third in the biosphere, pertains to the formation of modern cells, eukaryotes, from their prokaryote ancestors.

Scientists currently estimate the number of eukaryote species is between seven and eight million, with the first eukaryote fossils dating back 2.1 billion years ago. The first simple eukaryotes to emerge were yeasts, molds, and fungi, followed later by plant and animal eukaryotes.

To paraphrase Geoffrey M. Cooper of Boston University in his second edition 2000 book, *The Cell: A Molecular Approach*:

Among the most straightforward and smallest eukaryotes is a commonly studied yeast, Saccharomyces cerevisiae, which is about 6 micrometers in diameter and contains 12 million DNA base pairs.

['The Cell: A Molecular Approach. 2nd Edition', 2000, Geoffrey M. Cooper - Boston University, MA, US, Sinauer Associates, Oxford University Press]

The emergence of eukaryotic cell structures, compared to prokaryotic ones, is sufficiently complex to require numerous steps over a prolonged period.

First, all eukaryotes have an endomembrane system, which is another way to say that each organelle within the eukaryotic cell has a membrane.

The nucleus, which contains its genetic material, has a double membrane called the nuclear envelope, with pores that allow certain materials to pass in and out.

Next, the cytoskeletal structures of eukaryotes are far more complex.

In eukaryotes, cytoskeletal structures are composed of microtubules, microfilaments, and intermediate filaments, already described in earlier sections.

Perhaps the most significant advancement of eukaryotes is the emergence of *mitochondria.*

All eukaryotes have mitochondria except for one eukaryote species, monocercomonoides, which scientists claim had a mitochondrion that it eventually lost.

Mitochondria are unique in that unlike most organelles, *mitochondria* are double membrane organelles that have their unique DNA, which most closely resembles bacterial DNA. Hence, scientists generally believe *mitochondria* emerged from a symbiotic prokaryote that became internalized within eukaryotes as an organelle.

> *The only organelles with a double membrane are chloroplasts in plants, mitochondria, and the cell nucleus. All three of these organelles contain unique DNA.*

> *They are the only organelles that contain DNA and ribosomes and, thus, are the only ones capable of making their proteins.*

Mitochondria produce a chemical form of energy that powers the functions of the cell.

In addition to having *mitochondria*, plants and algae have an additional symbiotic prokaryote called *plastids*. *Plastids* are double membrane organelles that, like *mitochondria*, have their DNA, most closely resembling prokaryotic *Cyanobacteria*.

Plastids are responsible for manufacturing and storing food.

Additionally, plants have a cell wall that is outside the cell membrane.

> *Noteworthy is that dinoflagellates are organisms in an intermediate phase between prokaryotes and eukaryotes. There are approximately 2,300 species of dinoflagellates (i.e., having two flagella), most of which are marine plankton.*

> *The nucleus of dinoflagellates is not characteristically eukaryotic as they lack several proteins characteristic of eukaryotes and three organelles, namely mitochondria, chloroplasts, and Golgi bodies.*

THE FORMATION OF MULTICELLULAR EUKARYOTES

The twelfth self-organizing system of the universe, the fourth in the biosphere, marks the emergence of multicellular organisms representing the animal and plant kingdoms.

To paraphrase Richard K. Grossberg and Richard R. Strathmann in their 2007 paper, *The Evolution of Multicellularity: A Minor Major Transition?*:

> *Thus far in Earth's history, multicellular eukaryote organisms have originated independently from unicellular ancestors at least 25 times. The first may have existed one billion years ago, with a burst of metazoan diversification around 600 million years ago.*

> *The self-organizing forces that propelled the emergence of multicellular organisms belong to two categories, 'symbiotic force' and 'biological advantage.'*

> *Symbiotic force involves forming symbiotic relationships among previously independent organisms with distinct genetic material (a.k.a. chimeras).*
>
> *[The Evolution of Multicellularity: A Minor Major Transition? August 10, 2007, Richard K. Grossberg – the University of California Davis, Richard R. Strathmann – Friday Harbor Laboratories, University of Washington, Reviews in Advance, https://grosberglab.faculty.ucdavis. edu/wp-content/uploads/sites/453/2017/05/2007-Grosberg-R.-K.-and-R.-R.-Strathmann.pdf]*

It frequently occurs as a symbiotic relationship that bacteria developed within the various parts of the first multicellular plants and animals.

The other self-organizing force is *biological advantage*, which involves the emergence of additional cells of the same genetic material (a.k.a. clone) that specialize in some cooperative role to form a larger organism.

The advantage of size assists in many ways, the foremost being that it is less likely to be easily consumed as food by another smaller organism.

Both forces cooperated to help multicellular organisms emerge.

To paraphrase Anne K. Viadver and Patricia A. Lambrecht in their 2004 article, *Bacteria as Plant Pathogens*:

> *Regarding the symbiotic relationship that bacteria developed with larger multicellular organisms, many view bacteria only as a source of the disease that enters the plant due to plant wounding, such as from windblown soil or insect damage, or through natural plant openings, such as stomata, hydathodes, or lenticels.*
>
> *['Bacteria as Plant Pathogens,' 2004, Anne K. Viadver, Patricia A. Lambrecht, University of Nebraska, Lincoln, NE]*

However, bacteria have many specialized symbiotic relationships with the various parts of plants that support the life and health of the plant. These many relationships are self-organized between bacteria and plant life, without which multi-cellular plants would not survive.

To paraphrase Kiely, Haynes, Higgins, Franks, Mark, Morrissey, and O'Gara in their 2006 article, *Exploiting New Systems-Based Strategies to Elucidate Plant-Bacterial Interactions in the Rhizosphere*:

> *The microbes that live inside plants are endophytes, while those on the exterior are called epiphytes, some of which are residents and some transients.*
>
> *One example is Rhizobium, a bacteria genus that colonizes plant cells within the root nodules that capture nitrogen gas (N2) from the atmosphere, converting it to ammonia (NH3). This nitrogen then assimilates into amino acids, nucleotides, vitamins, flavones, and hormones.*

> *Without nitrogen-fixating bacteria, the building blocks for molecules, such as plant proteins, DNA, RNA, ATP, and others, would not be present to support plant life.*
>
> *Recent scientific discoveries demonstrate that the chemical signaling between plants and bacteria affects bacterial and plant gene expression.*
>
> *['Exploiting New Systems-Based Strategies to Elucidate Plant-Bacterial Interactions in the Rhizosphere,' 2006, P.D. Kiely, J.M. Haynes, C.H. Higgins, A. Franks, G.L. Mark, J.P. Morrissey, F. O'Gara, Microbial Ecology – an international forum, Springer Nature Switzerland AG, Springer Nature]*

The self-organizing system between the many plants and bacteria means that plants as organisms are not comprised solely of cells containing their DNA but instead are a collection of plant cells and bacteria, as well as fungi, molds, viruses, and other non-plant organisms that cooperate as a community to form the organisms we think of as just plants.

Also, recall our multicellular organism, *Dionea muscipula* (a.k.a. The Venus flytrap), for its nitrogen-fixing capabilities. *Dionea muscipula* lacks a symbiotic relationship with the Bacteria kingdom, specifically the genus *Rhizobium*.

As a result, *Dionea muscipula* has had to develop its unusual carnivorous relationship with insects to satisfy its nitrogen requirements, without which it could not survive.

THE FORMATION OF THE NERVE NET

The thirteenth self-organizing system of the universe, the fifth self-organizing system in the biosphere, occurred when multicellular organisms formed the first network of neurons.

Here, we have the emergence of a new type of specialized cell called the neuron, which is self-organized into a distributed communication command and control network. The neurons' network collects stimuli segments from sensory organs to rapidly send muscle commands out to distant parts of the organism in coordination with inbound stimuli.

We also see a symbiotic relationship with bacteria that evolved with nerve-net organisms and a system of cells that have self-organized into specialized tissues and organs to support the overall organism with its increased size.

Jellyfish have existed for at least 500 million and possibly 700 million years, making them one of the oldest multi-organ animals.

Regarding self-organizing systems of bacteria, nerve-net organisms evolved several types of relationships with bacteria, including symbiotic, pathogenic, transitory, and gene-contributing relationships.

Jellyfish also have amebocytes that move freely like amoeba within the confines of their body cavity. These mobile cells digest and distribute food, including bacteria, and dispose of waste to combat infections. They can change into other cell types, demonstrating chemical communication mechanisms unique to a biosphere.

Bacteria play a critical role within various body areas, with significant differences in the bacterial communities of each body compartment. It varies at each stage of the jellyfish's complex life cycle, starting from an egg and sperm to the larval stage to several stages until reaching the adult medusa.

To quote Viver, Orellana, Hatt, Urdiain, Diaz, Richter, Anton, Avian, Amann, Konstantinidis, and Rossello-Mora in their 2017 article, *The Low Diverse Gastric Microbiome of the Jellyfish Cotylorhiza Tuberculata Is Dominated by Four Novel Taxa*: Quote.

> *"Since a considerable fraction of the bacterial community present in the inner compartments of jellyfish is rarely or never found in the ambient water, these bacteria may have lost the ability to live independently and may be acquired by the host via vertical transmission as parental heritage through reproductive cells and larvae." End Quote.*

> *['The Low Diverse Gastric Microbiome of the Jellyfish Cotylorhiza Tuberculata Is Dominated by Four Novel Taxa,' Aug 2017, Tomeu Viver, Luis H. Orellana, Janet K. Hatt, Mercedes Urdiain, Sara Diaz, Michael Richter, Josefa Anton, Massimo Avian, Rudolf Amann, Konstantinos T. Konstantinidis, Ramon Rossello-Mora, Environ Microbiol., U.S. National Library of Medicine National Center for Biotechnology Information]*

To paraphrase Tinta, Kogovsek, Klun, Malej, Herndl, and Turk in their 2019 article, *Jellyfish-Associated Microbiome in the Marine Environment: Exploring Its Biotechnological Potential*:

> *It is important to note that an essential source of bacteria for these organisms is the local environment and that jellyfish secrete mucous with various ratios of proteins, lipids, and carbohydrates to attract beneficial bacteria that may protect against pathogens.*

> *To date, studies have only scratched the surface of the nearly four-thousand species of jellyfish. Of those studied, only a tiny percentage have analyzed the jellyfish microbiome from different perspectives, investigating the degree of microbiome specialization, species specificity, jellyfish life stages by body compartment, jellyfish population specificity, jellyfish diet, geographic location, water depth, current direction, rate of flow, ambient bacterial population, seasonality, and various other environmental conditions (i.e., viscosity, chemical concentrations, temperature, predator population), over several years, and never in a unified study.*

['Jellyfish-Associated Microbiome in the Marine Environment: Exploring Its Biotechnological Potential,' February 2019, Tinkara Tinta, Tjasa Kogovsek, Katja Klun, Alenka Malej, Gerhard J. Herndl, Valentina Turk, Marine Drugs, U.S. National Library of Medicine National Institutes of Health]

As for dependence on bacteria, one constant theme of all animal life is bacteria's role in the organism's digestive tract. All animals have forged cooperative relationships with bacteria, without which any given animal organism could not survive.

As we journey into self-organizing systems that emerge within the biosphere, two dominant drivers stand out in the growth and organization of complexity: proteins and bacteria.

One is proteins with their vast permutations of amino acids, and the other is the immense variety of bacteria that then leverage and propagate these proteins and themselves. The relationship between bacteria and proteins is the crucial determinant of what the biosphere is capable of.

When cells self-organize into tissues and organs, genes and molecules collaborate when cells replicate in the developing embryo. However, proteins and bacteria orchestrate each stage of life of each organism.

Various self-organizing forces are at work every step of the way in the development of organisms.

To paraphrase and quote Holly Evarts and Nandan Nerurkar in their 2019 article, *How Stem Cells Self-Organize in the Developing Embryo*:

> *For example, using time-lapse microscopy of cell movements and engineering methods of mathematical modeling and force and strain measurements, scientists studied how gene expression drives the development and movement of newly formed cells in the embryo.*
>
> *"The team found that the movements are coordinated by the conversion of a molecular gradient into a force gradient from cells that are contracting in proportion to the amount of a molecular cue— fibroblast growth factor (FGF)—that they sense. This results in a tug of war among endoderm cells: as one "team" begins to win, the cells actually recruit players from the opposing team by pulling them from low to higher concentrations of FGF."*
>
> *[How Stem Cells Self-Organize in the Developing Embryo, January 16, 2019, Holly Evarts – Director of Strategic Communications and Media Relations, Nandan Nerurkar – Assistant Professor, Biomedical Engineering, Columbia Engineering, Columbia University, New York City, U.S.A.]*

When chemical communication mechanisms allowed its participants to communicate, the biosphere took on a life of its own.

Various mechanisms formed through repeated trial and error experiments in parallel over millions of years, testing them to see if the result was beneficial.

THE FORMATION OF THE NERVE CORD

The fourteenth self-organizing system of the universe, the sixth self-organizing system in the biosphere, came about after the emergence of nerve nets.

Here, we have a new configuration of neurons and additional types of neurons that form a central neuron path along the organism's entire body. Essential to the experiential phenomenon, this is when we also have the emergence of the first *neuroglia* to support *Type Four Qualia*.

Again, we have an evolving symbiotic relationship with bacteria that have evolved with nerve cord organisms and the cells that self-organize into new tissues and organs.

To paraphrase Murfin, Dillman, Foster, Bulgheresi, Slatko, Sternberg, and Goodrich-Blair in their 2012 NIH article, *Nematode-Bacterium Symbiosis – Cooperation and Conflict Revealed in the Omics Age*:

> *At present, scientific authorities have data on approximately 12,000 species of nematodes, though scientific authorities estimate the number of species as one million, accounting for 80% of all extant animal species.*
>
> *Nematodes are in every layer of the food chain, from decomposers in soils, plants, herbivores, carnivores, and top carnivores, within seawater, freshwater, soil, and plant or animal hosts, including one kilometer below the Earth's surface.*
>
> *['Nematode-Bacterium Symbiosis – Cooperation and Conflict Revealed in the Omics Age,' Aug 2012, Kristen E. Murfin, Adler R. Dillman, Jeremy M. Foster, Silvia Bulgheresi, Barton E. Slatko, Paul W. Sternberg, Heidi Goodrich-Blair, U.S. National Library of Medicine National Institutes of Health]*

Regarding self-organizing bacteria, they have an array of relationships with *Nematoda,* serving as food, pathogens, and mutualists by aiding nematodes in development, defense, reproduction, and nutrient acquisition.

To quote Dillman, Chaston, Adams, Ciche, Goodrich-Blair, Stock, and Sternberg in their 2012 NIH article, *An Entomopathogenic Nematode by Any Other Name*: Quote.

> *"At least two genera of nematodes,* STEINERNEMA *and* HETERORHABDITIS, *have evolved symbiotic associations with gammaproteobacteria,* XENORHABDUS *and* PHOTORHABDUS

respectively, that allow them to kill insects and utilize the cadavers as food sources." End Quote.

['An Entomopathogenic Nematode by Any Other Name,' March 2012, Adler R. Dillman, John M. Chaston, Byron J. Adams, Todd A. Ciche, Heidi Goodrich-Blair, S. Patricia Stock, Paul W. Sternberg, PLOS Pathogens, U.S. National Library of Medicine National Institutes of Health]

The relationships between nematodes and bacteria are complex. The immune system of the nematode can distinguish between different types of microbes and must tolerate the mutually beneficial ones while not tolerating pathogenic viruses, bacteria, and fungi.

To paraphrase Murfin, Dillman, Foster, Bulgheresi, Slatko, Sternberg, and Goodrich-Blair in their 2012 NIH article, *Nematode-Bacterium Symbiosis – Cooperation and Conflict Revealed in the Omics Age*:

As for a glimpse into how our selected nematode, C. elegans, protects against pathogenic viruses, C. elegans employs RNA interference mechanisms. In contrast, to protect against pathogenic bacteria, C. elegans employs chains of proteins (i.e., MAPK signaling pathways) to communicate signals from a receptor on the surface of a cell of the pathogen to the DNA in the nucleus of the cell, turning off its ability to reproduce.

The immunological mechanisms of C. elegans controlling pathogenic microbes, such as viruses, bacteria, and fungi, is the ancestral basis of the mammalian immune system that establishes a cooperative balance of organism and bacteria in each organ and body cavity.

['Nematode-Bacterium Symbiosis – Cooperation and Conflict Revealed in the Omics Age,' Aug 2012, Kristen E. Murfin, Adler R. Dillman, Jeremy M. Foster, Silvia Bulgheresi, Barton E. Slatko, Paul W. Sternberg, Heidi Goodrich-Blair, U.S. National Library of Medicine National Institutes of Health]

To paraphrase Holly Evarts and Nandan Nerurkar in their 2019 paper, *How Stem Cells Self-Organize in the Developing Embryo*:

The larvae that hatch from C. elegans eggs lack all microbes, as none of the known species transfer microbes vertically. Luckily, the natural habitats of C. elegans are typically rich in microbes. Notably, the resulting nematode microbiota is a function of the environment and the organism's array of proteins that ultimately repel, disable, attract, and utilize various microbes, without which it could not survive.

As one can begin to see, for any organism to survive, it must remain in partnership with the environment in which it receives the complement of symbiotic microbes (a.k.a. chimera) because those microbes are essential to support the functions of its many tissues and systems, and hence its overall ability to survive.

When it comes to the power of self-organizing systems to cause cells to form tissues and organs, the molecular signals secreted by cells diffuse into neighboring cells that repeat the process to instruct the self-organization of cells into tissues and tissues into organs.

[How Stem Cells Self-Organize in the Developing Embryo, January 16, 2019, Holly Evarts – Director of Strategic Communications and Media Relations, Nandan Nerurkar – Assistant Professor, Biomedical Engineering, Columbia Engineering, Columbia University, New York City, U.S.A.]

THE FORMATION OF THE NEURAL BUNDLE

The fifteenth self-organizing system of the universe, the seventh self-organizing system in the biosphere, was facilitated by the emergence of the nerve cord.

Here, we have the emergence of a new configuration of neurons and the emergence of additional types of neurons and *neuroglia* to form a neural bundle. This new configuration formed the first central processing capability at the head of multicellular organisms.

The symbiotic relationship with bacteria continues to grow and self-organize. Chemical communication mechanisms direct neurons to form a tissue bundle as cells self-organize into new and more advanced tissues and organs supporting over one million species of insects, including our volunteer genus *Apis* (a.k.a. honeybee).

Much research has been conducted on honeybees as these species are essential in the modern multi-billion-dollar agricultural industry.

Regarding self-organizing bacteria, they evolved to collaborate with the insect's immune system to facilitate a more advanced form of coexistence. Honeybee gut microbiota samples collected across different continents are dominated by the same five to nine taxa only present within honeybees.

To quote Zheng, Steele, Leonard, Motta, and Moran in their 2018 NIH article, *Honey bees as models for gut microbiota research*: Quote.

"Once established in the adult gut, the composition of the microbiota changes little, despite seasonal changes and shifts in diet, behavior, and gene expression that occur as workers transition from nurse bees into foragers."

"Pollen is a key component of the bee diet, and the only source of amino acids, fat, vitamins and minerals. Most of these nutrients are absorbed by the host mid-gut, leaving only the compounds that are most difficult to digest, including pollen cell wall components such as cellulose,

hemicellulose, and pectin from pollen cell walls, to be broken down by the microbial community in the hindgut."

"Environmental bacteria are generally unable to colonize the honeybee gut, indicating that gut-associated bacteria have adaptations which enable them to tolerate or evade the host immune system and other stressors within the gut."

"As in the human gut microbiota, most dominant members of the honeybee gut community are found solely in the host gut environment. Gut bacteria in both honeybees and humans are likely to be specifically adapted to these habitats, as they have coevolved with their hosts over millions of years."

"Both bee and primate gut bacteria are primarily transmitted through social interactions. Core taxa of social bees are not found in solitary bees or other related insects such as wasps, nor have they been isolated from other environments." End Quote.

[Honey bees as models for gut microbiota research, Nov 2018, Hao Zheng, Margaret I. Steele, Sean P. Leonard, Erick V. S. Motta, Nancy A. Moran, PMC6478020, U.S. National Library of Medicine National Institutes of Health]

The microbiota of honeybees has self-organized to form a stable symbiotic relationship, participating in the development of the gut, digestion, endocrine signaling, and resistance to pathogens.

To paraphrase A. Desai and T. J. Mitchison in their 1997 NIH article, *Microtubule Polymerization Dynamics*:

Regarding cells that self-organize into tissues and organs, studies of insect embryo development show that physical chemistry at the molecular level of proteins is a significant factor influencing self-organization. The molecular structures of proteins develop via a force that operates at the molecular level, referred to as polymerization.

In cell biology, microtubule polymerization is the molecular mechanism that grows the protein chains of a cell's cytoskeletal microtubules.

One method of polymerization is by a process known as nucleation.

Before the biosphere, nucleation is a molecular force responsible for forming crystals from a solution, liquid, or vapor, such as how ice crystals form from water. Once a crystal forms, it acts as a site for additional crystals to readily form to continue expanding the crystalline structure.

In the biosphere, nucleation is a molecular force often responsible for the growth of cytoskeletal filaments, microtubules, and many protein chains. Many self-organizing forces responsible for forming proteins, cellular structures, tissues, and organs operate at the molecular level following the laws of thermodynamics.

[Microtubule Polymerization Dynamics, 1997, A. Desai, T. J. Mitchison, PMID: 9442869, U.S.A. NIH, National Library of Medicine National Center for Biotechnology Information]

Some insect species demonstrate nucleation of protein molecules to allow unfertilized eggs to develop into adulthood.

To quote Riparbelli, Tagu, Bonhomme, and Callaini in their 2005 book, *Aster self-organization at meiosis: a conserved mechanism in insect parthenogenesis?*: Quote.

"Unfertilized eggs usually lack maternal centrosomes and cannot develop without sperm contribution. However, several insect species lay eggs that develop to adulthood as unfertilized in the absence of a preexisting centrosome."

"We report that the oocyte of the parthenogenetic viviparous pea aphid, Acyrthosiphon pisum, is able to self-organize microtubule-based asters, which in turn interact with the female chromatin to form the first mitotic spindle."

"This mode of reproduction provides a good system to investigate how the oocyte can assemble new centrosomes and how their number can be exactly monitored."

"We propose that the cooperative interaction of motor proteins and randomly nucleated surface microtubules could lead to the formation of aster-like structures in the absence of pre-existing centrosomes." End Quote.

[Aster self-organization at meiosis: a conserved mechanism in insect parthenogenesis? February 2005, Maria Giovanna Riparbelli – (Dept Evolutionary Biology, University of Siena, Siena, Italy), Denis Tagu – (INRA Rennes, UMR INRA/Agrocampus, Le Rheu Cedex, France), Joel Bonhomme – (INRA Rennes, UMR INRA/Agrocampus, Le Rheu Cedex, France, Guilano Callaini – (Dept Evolutionary Biology, University of Siena, Siena, Italy), Science Direct, Elsevier Publishers]

To paraphrase Juliet Eilperin in her 2007 article, *Female Sharks Can Reproduce Alone, Researchers Find*, and Thomas F. Savage, Ph.D. in his 2008 article, *A Guide to the Recognition of Parthenogenesis in Incubated Turkey Eggs*:

The reproduction process from an ovum without fertilization is called parthenogenesis.

Parthenogenesis is not that uncommon. It occurs naturally in lower plants, some invertebrate animal species (including nematodes, some tardigrades, water fleas, scorpions, aphids, some mites, some bees, some Phasmatodea, and parasitic wasps), and a few vertebrates, such as some fish, amphibians, reptiles and on rare occasion some birds if artificially incubated.

[Female Sharks Can Reproduce Alone, Researchers Find, May 23, 2007, Juliet Eilperin, Washington Post, U.S.A.]

[A Guide to the Recognition of Parthenogenesis in Incubated Turkey Eggs, February 11, 2008, Thomas F. Savage, Ph.D. – Professor Dept Animal Sciences, Oregon State University, Corvallis, OR, U.S.A.]

THE FORMATION OF THE PRIMITIVE BRAIN

The sixteenth self-organizing system of the universe, the eighth in the biosphere, further builds upon the neural bundle.

Here, we have the emergence of a new configuration of neurons and *neuroglia* in the form of a primitive brain, which also introduces additional types of neurons and *neuroglia* that form a central processing capability at the head of the organism.

This new configuration forms major functional areas where the neural bundle is more prominent, with polyganglionic neurons divided into tissue groups forming protocerebrum, deutocerebrum, and tritocerebrum.

Equally important, the symbiotic relationship with bacteria continues to evolve and self-organize into new tissues and organs of *Reptilia*. With additional chemical messaging configurations, a combination of advancements results from self-organizing forces that employ trial and error and natural selection.

> *Remember that only a tiny fraction of possible protein configurations exist as many complex permutations did not form or were not successfully deployed and hence did not survive.*

> *Because of this, the self-organizing forces operate within the constraints of the protein chains that have been produced and survived to each point.*

By this time, various organisms have developed relationships with the eleven thousand-plus species of *Reptilia*. It includes relationships with the cells that self-organize into tissues, tissues into organs, and organs into a system of capabilities that support the lives of a diverse community of cells and organisms, including bacteria, fungi, molds, and viruses.

Regarding the prokaryotic members of this relationship, studying bacterial relationships with animals became possible with the development of high-throughput gene sequencing.

High-throughput gene sequencing has provided significant insight into the challenges of protecting endangered species in captivity. Captive populations are more likely to be plagued by unknown diseases, nutritional deficiency, and low reproductive rates mainly due to the differences in the microbial content of their gut, which determines the health status, immunity, and metabolism of their host animal, such as endangered crocodile lizards.

To quote Tang, Liang, Yang, Wang, Chen, Du, Li, and Sun in their 2010 article, *Captivity Influences Gut Microbiota in Crocodile Lizards (Shinisaurus crocodilurus)*: Quote.

"The crocodile lizard (Shinisaurus crocodilurus Ahl, 1930) is a monotypic species in the genus Shinisaurus and monotypic family Shinisauridae, which is the remnant of an ancient lineage from the Pleistocene with around 200 million years of history (Zhao et al., 1999). Because of their narrow distribution, small population, being heavily hunted, and environmental changes, it is listed as a class I protected species in China."

"In recent years, with rapid development of high-throughput sequencing, an increasing number of studies interpreted the health and nutritional utilization of animals by integrating the relationships between bacteria in gastrointestinal tracts and the animals themselves (Mcfall-Ngai et al., 2013)."

"Thus, promoting the conservation of endangered species by studying gut microbiota has been receiving increasing attention and has become a hot topic of conservation biology (e.g., Zhu et al., 2011; Wu et al., 2017)."

"Therefore, in order to explore whether the gut microbiota composition of the crocodile lizard varies along ages and captive environment, it is necessary to analyze its composition of gut microbiota between captive and wild environments, as well as between juveniles and adults."

"Here, fecal samples of crocodile lizards with different ages were collected from captive and wild populations. We aimed to determine variations in gut microbiota of crocodile lizards between wild and captive environments, as well as between juveniles and adults, using 16S ribosomal RNA (rRNA) gene sequencing of gut microbiota. In addition to promoting the conservation of this endangered species, it provides further insight into the ecological and evolutionary relationship between reptiles and their gut microbiota." End Quote.

[Captivity Influences Gut Microbiota in Crocodile Lizards (Shinisaurus crocodilurus), April 2020, Guo-Shuai Tang, Xi-Xi Liang, Meng-Yuan Yang, Ting-Ting Wang, Jin-Ping Chen, Wei-Guo Du, Huan Li, Bao-Jun Sun, Frontiers in Microbiology, Microbial Symbioses, China]

Crocodile lizards (a.k.a. Shinisaurus crocodilurus) grow to a maximum size of sixteen inches and weigh about ten ounces with a diet primarily of worms. In the wild, life expectancy is fifteen or more years, while in captivity, it is closer to ten.

[Chinese Crocodile Lizard, 1996, National Geographic – Animals, Washington, D.C.]

However, as we begin to see, all life depends upon various communities of microbes with vastly different genes than their host animal. This fact helps us realize that all life is a collaboration of systems that operate at many levels, starting with the micro level of the quantum world of quarks and then moving through the many levels up to the macro level of the entire biosphere.

Regarding the cells that self-organize into tissues, tissues into organs, and organs into a system of capabilities, tissues develop and often regenerate when damaged.

To paraphrase the 2018 article in Physics.org News, *Biologists program cells to self-organize into 3D-structures in a first step towards tissues that regrow and self-repair*:

> *Cells must communicate with one another through chemical messengers to develop and regenerate cells of tissues and organs. As a result, intracellular communication provides context to cells that identify the equivalent spatial coordinates of the 'body plan,' such as the head, toe, front, back, left, right, front legs/arms, and rear legs, and the tissue types therein.*
>
> *[Biologists program cells to self-organize into 3D-structures in a first step towards tissues that regrow and self-repair, May 31, 2018, University of California, San Francisco, Physics.org news]*

This communication occurs within components of the same genetic material across the boundary of organisms with vastly different genetic material. As a result, chemical messengering operates simultaneously at multiple system levels across multiple collections of organisms, each with its genetic material.

Consider the difference between self-organizing systems within the biosphere communicating between molecules and with organisms having their distinct genetic code versus the hard determinist's simplistic view that this is the product of billiard balls bouncing off one another on a billiard table.

Self-organizing systems are mindless because there is no agent to design their interactions. It is more like a free economy, not centrally controlled by the government.

A free economy has millions of participants who communicate using various languages, choosing what to produce, consume, or repair. These participants consist of individuals, businesses, governments, and international bodies, many of which operate at different levels with the same overall economic system.

MAMMALIAN, PRIMATE, AND HOMO PHASES OF THE BIOSPHERE

The seventeenth, eighteenth, and nineteenth self-organizing systems of the universe, ninth, tenth, and eleventh in the biosphere continue to build upon the advancements of the primitive brain.

Newer, improved configurations of neurons emerge as brain tissues expand with more types of neurons and *neuroglia* that advance consciousness to new levels.

At the same time, we also have an increase in the sophistication of symbiotic relationships that bacteria have developed in the mammalian class and the *Homo* genus that emerged in the genus *Australopithecus*, which fathered the one extant species of *Homo sapiens* and several extinct species.

Mammals are unique in the animal kingdom for many reasons. Still, perhaps one of the least expected is the extreme degree to which mammalian life depends upon self-organizing symbiotic relationships with bacteria, forming their microbiome.

In studies into *Homo sapiens*, current estimates vary on the ratio of human and non-human cells in the human body. The human body has approximately 100 trillion cells. Estimates vary between 37 trillion and 50 trillion, possessing human DNA, with the remainder possessing the DNA of bacteria, fungi, and molds.

Back in 2012, leading scientific groups had thought the ratio of foreign DNA to be much higher.

To quote the 2012 NIH article, *NIH Human Microbiome Project defines normal bacterial makeup of the body*: Quote.

> *"The human body contains trillions of microorganisms — outnumbering human cells by 10 to 1. Because of their small size, however, microorganisms make up only about 1 to 3 percent of the body's mass (in a 200-pound adult, that's 2 to 6 pounds of bacteria), but play a vital role in human health."*

> *"To define the normal human microbiome, HMP researchers sampled 242 healthy U.S. volunteers (129 male, 113 female), collecting tissues from 15 body sites in men and 18 body sites in women. Researchers collected up to three samples from each volunteer at sites such as the mouth, nose, skin (two behind each ear and each inner elbow), and lower intestine (stool), and three vaginal sites in women; each body site can be inhabited by organisms as different as those in the Amazon Rainforest and the Sahara Desert."*

> *"Historically, doctors studied microorganisms in their patients by isolating pathogens and growing them in culture. This painstaking process typically identifies only a few microbial species, as they are hard to grow in the laboratory. In HMP, researchers purified all human and microbial DNA in each of more than 5,000 samples and analyzed them with DNA sequencing machines. Using computers, researchers sorted through the 3.5 terabases of genome sequence data to identify specific genetic signals found only in bacteria — the variable genes of bacterial ribosomal RNA called 16S rRNA. Bacterial ribosomal RNA helps form*

the cellular structures that manufacture protein and can identify the presence of different microbial species."

"Recently developed genome sequencing methods now provide a powerful lens for looking at the human microbiome," said Eric D. Green, M.D., Ph.D., director of the National Human Genome Research Institute, which managed HMP for NIH. "The astonishing drop in the cost of sequencing DNA has made possible the kind of large survey performed by the Human Microbiome Project."

"HMP researchers also reported that this plethora of microbes contribute more genes responsible for human survival than humans contribute. Where the human genome carries some 22,000 protein-coding genes, researchers estimate that the human microbiome contributes some 8 million unique protein-coding genes or 360 times more bacterial genes than human genes." End Quote.

[NIH Human Microbiome Project defines normal bacterial makeup of the body, June 13, 2012, Contact Raymond MacDougall, U.S. Department of Health and Human Services, NIH, National Institutes of Health, U.S.A.]

However, most scientists agree that foreign DNA is between one-half and two-thirds of the human body. Regardless of the precise ratio, self-organizing systems of bacteria, human tissues, and organs are required to support life in the mammalian class, particularly the *Homo* genus.

To again quote the 2012 NIH article, *NIH Human Microbiome Project defines normal bacterial makeup of the body*: Quote.

"Genes carried by bacteria in the gastro-intestinal tract, for example, allow humans to digest foods and absorb nutrients that otherwise would be unavailable."

"Humans don't have all the enzymes we need to digest our diet," said Lita Proctor, Ph.D., NHGRI's HMP program manager. "Microbes in the gut break down many of the proteins, lipids and carbohydrates in our diet into nutrients that we can then absorb. Moreover, the microbes produce beneficial compounds, like vitamins and anti-inflammatories that our genome cannot produce." End Quote.

[NIH Human Microbiome Project defines normal bacterial makeup of the body, June 13, 2012, Contact Raymond MacDougall, U.S. Department of Health and Human Services, NIH, National Institutes of Health, U.S.A.]

However, the metabolic process of bacteria is essential as opposed to the specific species of bacteria that participate in support of our self-organizing systems. In other words, like in any large organization, the overall function is essential, not the specific participant.

Curtis Huttenhower, Ph.D., of the Harvard School of Public Health and lead co-author of the HMP papers in Nature, writes, "It matters whether the metabolic function is present, not which microbial species provides it."

[NIH Human Microbiome Project defines normal bacterial makeup of the body, June 13, 2012, Contact Raymond MacDougall, U.S. Department of Health and Human Services, NIH, National Institutes of Health, U.S.A.]

Most of us see ourselves only as the part having our human DNA. However, our bodies are a complex community, much like a colony of ants, a flock of birds, or a school of fish, many of which, in our case, belong to different species.

From a distance, a swarm of ants, a flock of birds, or a school of fish may appear as a single visual thing, but when one gets much closer, one realizes that it is a community of many individuals, potentially of many types.

Likewise, we initially view each human or animal as an individual thing. However, nothing could be further from the truth. When one gets closer, one realizes that these are a community of organisms, many belonging to different species. Still, without the human and non-human parts collaborating, the entire community we perceive as an individual organism could neither develop nor survive.

Recall self-organizing systems within the biosphere simultaneously operate at multiple levels. In the case of a human embryo, simple organic molecules stem from self-organizing atoms.

Likewise, complex proteins stem from self-organizing smaller molecules and atoms.

Likewise, cells and their components stem from self-organizing proteins, smaller molecules, and atoms.

Likewise, tissues stem from self-organizing cells, proteins, smaller molecules, and atoms.

Likewise, organs stem from self-organizing tissues, cells, proteins, smaller molecules, atoms, and microbiota.

Eventually, an entire organism emerges from self-organizing organs, microbiota, tissues, cells, proteins, smaller molecules, and atoms.

The formation of yet higher-level self-organizing systems by no means stops with the emergence of *Homo sapiens*.

But let's pause to look at how our scientific methods have instead come to look at the world through the lens of reductionism.

REDUCTIONISM, EMERGENTISM, AND LEVELS OF SYSTEMS

LEVELS OF SYSTEMS

Given the levels of self-organizing systems described thus far, we see how they support higher-level self-organizing systems.

This concept also exists for all things, both natural and artificial.

As an example, an engine has many parts, of which many of those parts have parts. At the same time, an engine is just one part of a Greyhound bus, and a Greyhound bus is just one part of a fleet of Greyhound buses.

Simultaneously, the Greyhound fleet is part of a more extensive ground transportation system. Ground transportation is just one part of an even more extensive transportation system, including marine, air, and space transportation.

In computer science, these levels going up and down are a 'bill-of-materials' structure or systems of systems, where parts have parts, and those parts have parts.

ORIGINS OF REDUCTIONISM

Based on the historical record, reductionist thought can be said to have first emerged in the East around 500 B.C.E. as a prominent theme when the Buddha reduced *consciousness* into its parts.

In the West, reductionist thinking can be seen just a hundred years later, with the Greek philosopher Democritus putting forth the idea that everything in the world is composed of indivisible units called atoms.

However, reductionism and scientific inquiry halted in the West during the Dark Ages, precipitated by the fall of the Western Roman Empire in 476 AD. During this period, the church endeavored to fill the void of influence as the civilizing effects of the Western Roman Empire dissipated.

After a dormancy of over five hundred years, reductionism slowly emerged again in the West as empirical methods returned when Christians regained control of Toledo, Spain, in 1085.

The retaking of Toledo included one of the great Islamic libraries that safeguarded much of the ancient knowledge lost when Rome fell. This one library reintroduced a wealth of previously lost information back into Western civilization, including the works of Aristotle, Plato, Arabic numerals, alchemy, philosophical thought, and logic, much of it contradicting the mystical teachings of the church that had replaced it.

The church's last desire was for its subjects to be encouraged to participate in secular thought and question religious doctrine in any manner that could threaten their coexistence. However, despite the efforts of the church to suppress scientific thought, the rediscovery of ancient knowledge laid the groundwork for empiricism and reductionist thinking to take root once again.

To address this secular challenge to its religious doctrine, the church helped establish a secular institution to create a body of thought to reconcile religious doctrine and secular thought formally like a legal system.

The goal was to develop a compelling explanation for the issues that emerged within various subjects, such as science, philosophy, and cosmology. In the 1090's, this institution became known as Oxford University.

The most significant aspect of this institution was that it represented the first time secular men could learn material that had never been available to men without becoming monks, priests, or clergy members.

After being in existence for about a hundred years, one prominent story was that a town rape precipitated a young woman's death. The suspect was a student at Oxford who had escaped the authorities.

In the wisdom of the authorities, justice came in the form of hanging the suspect's roommates by the neck.

In protest of the student hangings, many professors abandoned the town of Oxford and five years later created a new institution in Cambridge, which we know as Cambridge University.

Unlike its predecessor, which had limited its course offering to science, philosophy, and cosmology, Cambridge offered more diverse subjects, including 'logic and reasoning,' science, mathematics, and philosophy. It unleashed knowledge at a rate never experienced previously and unilaterally propelled the town of Cambridge into becoming a center of commerce, culture, and scientific thought.

During this time, in particular, the open spread of scientific thought generated yet new conflicts with church doctrine. To mediate the growing tension, Thomas Aquinas, an Italian Dominican friar, Catholic priest, and philosopher, proffered that God did not control everything. Instead, he argued that God created the natural laws that governed animal and plant life, laying the groundwork for science.

This explanation and perspective satisfied most church officials until the 1200s and the advent of Roger Bacon.

Roger Bacon was a Franciscan friar, English philosopher, and inventor who studied at Oxford and later became a master at Oxford, lecturing on Aristotle.

A brilliant scientist in his own right, Bacon made significant advances in the empirical methods discovered by the Arab mathematician, astronomer, and physicist Hasan Ibn al-Haytham (a.k.a. Alhazen).

Using empiricism, Roger Bacon performed experiments that disproved predictions rendered by Aristotle, such as Aristotle's assertion that a heavier object falls faster than a lighter object.

His scientific findings and conclusions motivated his enemies, including the church, to successfully petition for his imprisonment. The old establishment, however, was thoroughly unsuccessful at stopping the ensuing wave of scientific progress.

Even though the East had a five-hundred-year head start, the renaissance that blossomed on the heels of the end of the Dark Ages did more to propel science and empirical thinking in the West than had occurred in the East, primarily because our Islamic brothers did not share and spread knowledge in universities and scholars outside the clergy, but instead diligently and competently worked to curate and protect it.

Today, the explosion of knowledge is fueled by the Internet spreading information at rates not previously imagined. A vast amount of public information is now available in seconds, and a significant body of proprietary information is available in minutes with a simple online payment.

However, collecting vast amounts of information and putting it together in a consistent framework that explains how the universe was formed and works is quite a different discipline. From its beginnings, scientific methods made use of reductionistic methods.

But can reductionism resolve every scientific inquiry?

One of many scientific inquiries that reductionism cannot explain is how self-organizing systems operate in the biosphere.

One reason is that self-organizing systems occur in layers dependent upon one another, but all operate according to different rules.

As a result, understanding self-organizing systems is as impervious to reductionism as understanding the global economy is impervious to decomposing a single transaction into its parts. Likewise, a complete understanding of quantum physics does not explain why an apple falls from a tree.

Let's dive in and see what this means.

THE LIMITATIONS OF REDUCTIONISM

Reductionism in the context of science is a methodology that attempts to explain an entire system in terms of its constituent parts.

With the emergence of empirical thinking, reductionism has been the dominant approach employed by Western science.

However, even though we have amassed much knowledge about the fundamentals of chemistry and physics, *reductionism* can neither explain how the biosphere has developed nor what the biosphere will produce next.

One flaw is that reductionism assumes that a 'thing' is only the sum of its parts, and as such, the constituent parts exist independently. Those independent parts interact with one another to operate together. However, in this case, the whole is not a solitary thing in and of itself that operates in the same way, following the same rules.

> *For example, neuroscience looks at the brain and its processes as neurons and the parts that comprise them down to quantum particles.*

> *However, it is incorrect to assume that neurons behave like quantum particles.*

One intellectual trap with this reductionist reasoning is that it naturally brings one back to the hard deterministic view that all things in the universe are the same as billiard balls independently reacting on a gigantic billiard table.

Reductionism conveniently ignores multiple factors. One is that self-organizing systems within the biosphere actively communicate with one another to drive self-organization within each level of abstraction (e.g., tissue, organ, system of organs). In other words, self-organization occurs at different levels, all simultaneously.

> *For example, self-organization occurs at the atomic level, molecular level, cellular level, tissue level, organ level, at the level of a system of organs, and so on, all at the same time.*

More importantly, reductionism ignores that each self-organizing system self-organizes at its level to a completely different set of rules.

It does not mean the end of reductionism is here. However, it does mean that scientific disciplines are undergoing a transformation that considers and includes alternatives, and computer modeling is partially helping to lead the way.

Let's carefully consider the following.

THE EMERGENCE OF EMERGENCE

Emergence is said to occur when a collection of things demonstrates one or more properties that none of the individual parts of the collection demonstrate on their own. Emergence occurs naturally, or an intelligent being can manufacture it.

There are three categories of 'man-made' emergence.

Simple emergence refers to a human-designed system that is simple enough to be entirely predictable. A simple example of emergence that is 'man-made' would be a balloon, basket, ropes, pilot, and a means of heating air to make a hot air balloon that can sail a pilot through the air with the breeze.

Weak emergence refers to a human-designed system that is sufficiently complex that the resulting behavior is not entirely predictable from just knowledge of its components.

Strong emergence refers to a human-designed system that is sufficiently complex that its resulting behavior will be unknown until the final system is simulated or tested in each situation and under the conditions it will encounter.

Natural emergence, such as each layer leading up to and including the emergence of a biosphere, goes beyond 'man-made' emergence.

Full emergence occurs naturally and operates according to its own set of rules independent of the rules that its parts operate by.

> *An example of naturally occurring emergence is a vast cloud of hydrogen and helium of sufficient mass together under the influence of a gravitational force to coalesce over a prolonged period to form a primordial star.*

The tricky part is predicting the product of natural emergence.

However, this does not dissuade scientists from trying. One technique found useful to explore self-organizing systems is computer modeling for its ability to simultaneously represent the interactions at each level of a multi-level organizing system. At the same time, it also attempts to monitor the whole.

THE REDUCTIONISM EMERGENTISM DEBATE

Few people realize that at the time of Darwin, science had not yet understood the reductionist underpinnings of natural selection.

Therefore, Darwin's reasoning in 1859 was not dependent on the laws of physics, chemistry, or genetics. Instead, he relied on logic and reasoning mainly in reaction to what Thomas Malthus had written in 1798 about members of species competing for survival.

As such, the science of how organisms give rise to organisms with heritable variation as genes came along a lot later.

To paraphrase Jou, Haegeman, Ysebaert, and Fiers in their NIH 2006 article, *Nucleotide sequence of the gene coding for the bacteriophage MS2 coat protein*:

> *Gregor Mendel theorized the existence of genes in 1866.*

> *In 1910, Thomas Hunt Morgan showed genes reside on chromosomes.*

> *James Watson and Francis Crick determined DNA structure in 1953, and gene sequencing first emerged in 1972 by Walter Fiers and his team at the University of Ghent, Belgium.*

[Nucleotide sequence of the gene coding for the bacteriophage MS2 coat protein, May 2006, W. Min Jou, G. Haegeman, M. Ysebaert, W. Fiers, Nature, PMID: 4555447, NIH, National Library of Medicine, National Center for Biotechnology Information, U.S.A.]

The point here is that the theory of natural selection did not come into being using reductionism, with an understanding of any lower-level parts. It also was not a product of forecasting emergentism.

Similarly, proteins emerge from the activities of self-organizing forces. These self-organizing forces operate within the envelope of the laws of physics, though the result of self-organizing force is not predictable.

Recall that if the entire mass of the Earth consisted solely of the building blocks of proteins, there would be insufficient molecular mass to manufacture one of every protein possessing just forty-one amino acids.

Hence, only a tiny fraction of possible proteins have been self-organized into existence on this planet.

While the implications of this statement can lead us to a myriad of fascinating topics, we will remain focused on our journey.

As all levels of self-organizing systems must, the formation of proteins operates with support from the lower levels of self-organizing systems that preceded it.

However, the laws governing those self-organizing systems do not themselves determine which specific proteins emerge and the varieties of proteins that will never exist in this biosphere.

Instead, it will be the activity of the chemical messengers communicating at a molecular level that will determine which proteins to manufacture.

Stated in reverse, the underlying laws of chemistry and physics and their underlying laws of quantum mechanics underlie self-organizing systems. However, the determining factor for which proteins to manufacture does not occur at those lower levels, as reductionists and hard determinists would assume.

Instead, those lower self-organizing systems only provided the ecosystem, or the operating system, within which chemical messengers freely communicate.

For the chemical messengers to operate, they needed the lower levels of systems first to emerge, ultimately requiring all the preceding levels to form new proteins. Also, like bacteria, any of the lower levels could have been different technically and still achieve the same result if the lower level provided the same function. Recall it is function and not the specific individual.

The new self-organizing system that emerges on top of those layers operates according to its rules and not the rules of the parts that comprise it.

It is like a program running in the Windows operating system. Windows does not determine what the program will do. But simultaneously, without the Windows operating system, the program could not interact with the laptop's hardware.

Likewise, if the same program were running in a Linux operating system, Linux would not determine what that program would do.

The necessary function that supports the program is an operating system. It doesn't matter which one it is. Once the program exists, it follows its unique set of instructions.

The point is that if the laws of physics were different, self-organizing forces would operate within the envelope of the alternate laws of physics. However, the resulting biosphere would still propel itself forward, developing new levels of self-organizing systems with either the same or different sets of proteins.

The concept is not unlike the idea of a television using vacuum tubes instead of solid-state transistors. Regardless of the alternative, the same programs will be available to the viewer.

In these examples, the underlying systems provide an ecosystem where things may operate. However, the underlying systems do not determine or influence the programs that will or will not exist on top of them.

With this perspective in mind, let's take a moment to understand how levels of self-organizing systems relate to one another and what we can learn from lower and or higher levels.

One scientific debate regarding reductionism versus emergentism began in the 1960s and 70s during the budget allocation process during the Cold War to construct a superconducting super collider (SSC).

The super collider represented the ultimate reductionistic area of research into the smallest components of matter and energy.

The super collider was so expensive, however, that it would leave scarce funding for other scientific initiatives, such as solid-state physics, which, when proposed, placed emphasis on research involving higher levels of complexity in solid-state physics, including lattice structures, energy bands, phonons, and electron-phonon interactions.

During that competition for Cold War funding, those scientists focused on higher levels of complexity realized that reductionism could not render an ability to reveal how higher levels already known at that time worked.

To quote Joseph D. Martin in his 2015 book, *Fundamental Disputations: The Philosophical debates that Governed American Physics, 1939-1993*: Quote.

"The main fallacy of this kind of thinking is that the reductionist hypothesis does not by any means imply a 'constructionist' one: The ability to reduce everything to simple fundamental laws does not imply the ability to start from those laws and reconstruct the universe."

Anderson's emergence-based view of fundamentality granted the concepts and laws of solid-state physics independence by virtue of the fact that they could not realistically be derived from lower-level concepts and laws alone."

"He claimed that the laws of solid-state physics could never practically be extrapolated from quantum mechanics without reference to empirically established, higher-level phenomena; he fought shy of the stronger claim that high-level laws could never in principle be derived from below." End Quote.

[Fundamental Disputations: The Philosophical debates that Governed American Physics, 1939-1993, Nov 1ˢᵗ, 2015, Joseph D. Martin – Lyman Briggs College, Michigan State University, Historical Studies in the Natural Sciences (Volume 45, Issue 5), University of California Press, University of California, CA, USA]

The assertion here is that levels of self-organizing systems that preceded the biosphere neither explain nor predict the behaviors of lower or higher levels of self-organizing systems.

In other words, the only way to understand any self-organizing system is to study the properties and behaviors of that level.

Hence, to understand solid-state physics, one needs to study solid-state physics. Even though the underlying self-organizing systems support the physics of solid-state physics, understanding those underlying levels (e.g., quantum physics) is insufficient to facilitate an understanding of solid-state physics.

Similarly, the self-organizing systems within the biosphere determine which proteins get formed and operate independently in support of the self-organizing systems above and below them.

Although science cannot yet predict what that next higher self-organizing system will be, computer modeling shows that if our laws of physics were different, self-organizing forces would continue to operate within the envelope of the alternate laws of physics.

The lesson learned is that reductionism has its limitations.

As examples:

- If scientists had started with today's knowledge of how pure energy formed the first particles of matter driven by the *particle creation force*, they could neither predict the formation of quarks, electrons, or any of their properties.

- If scientists started from quarks and electrons driven by the *strong nuclear force*, they could neither predict the formation of protons and neutrons nor any of their properties.

- If scientists started from protons, neutrons, and electrons driven by the *strong nuclear force*, they could neither predict nor explain the formation of hydrogen, helium, lithium, beryllium, and boron atoms and their properties.

- If scientists started from clouds of hydrogen and helium, lithium, beryllium, and boron atoms driven by the forces of *gravity* and a *strong nuclear force*, they could neither predict nor explain the formation of photons and the formation of ninety-three heavier atomic elements with weights greater than boron, starting with carbon, silicon, oxygen, and iron, nor any of their properties.

- If scientists started from clouds of the first ninety-eight atomic elements driven by the forces of *gravity* and the *weak nuclear force*, they could neither predict nor explain the formation of ten radioactive elements that came into existence from the process of radioactive decay nor any of their properties.

- If scientists started from the first one-hundred and eight atomic elements driven by the forces of *electromagnetism*, they could neither predict nor explain the formation of molecules and chemical compounds nor any of their properties.

- If scientists started from the initial molecules and chemical compounds driven by the forces of *electromagnetism*, they could neither predict nor explain the formation of the fluidic phase of the biosphere to form amino acids and proteins, nor any of their properties nor could they predict an ability to communicate via chemical messengers.

- If scientists started from the initial amino acids and proteins and their chemical messengers driven by the forces behind the prokaryotic phase of the biosphere, they could neither predict nor explain the formation of the many prokaryotes (a.k.a. bacteria and archaea), nor any of their properties.

- If scientists started from the initial prokaryotes driven by the forces within the biosphere, they could neither predict nor explain the formation of the many eukaryotes nor any of their properties.

Fast forward to Homo sapiens.

- If scientists started with the initial *Homo sapiens* and their many symbiotic relationships with prokaryotes driven by the forces of the biosphere, they could neither predict nor explain the formation of the next level of life that will evolve nor any of its properties.

The question arises: what will be the next thing that self-organizing forces produce?

The observations of self-organizing systems we can make are:

- Each level has its own rules.

- There appears to be a finite number of self-organizing systems outside a biosphere, though more than what we've identified.

- In a biosphere, new self-organizing systems are limitless.

- New self-organizing systems are unique in a biosphere because they result from communication.

- The value of any self-organizing system is solely its reusability by a higher self-organizing system.

As additional evidence that self-organizing systems within the biosphere have independence from their underlying self-organizing systems, let's consider Darwinian preadaptation.

> *Preadaptation in biology is an adaptation that ends up serving a completely different purpose than the purpose for which it originally evolved.*
>
> *An example would be the development of feathers, believed by scientists to have evolved to serve as insulation from cold temperatures but eventually served as a mechanism to support the ability to take flight over short distances and then eventually longer distances in some species.*
>
> *As another example, some organisms have a swim bladder to tune the ratio of air and water in the bladder to control buoyancy, believed to be an adaptation of lungs from lungfish, thereby coopting the lung for a new function.*

As Professor Stuart Kaufmann explains in a 'Closer to Truth' interview, once the swim bladder existed in its new role within the biosphere, it represented an adjacent niche to all living organisms. In this sense, natural selection operated to create a functioning swim bladder in fish, but natural selection did not operate to create an adjacent niche in the animal kingdom. Yet this preadaptation may have significantly changed the direction of evolution within the biosphere.

It means that the biosphere is self-organizing beyond the influence of natural selection. Any self-organizing systems can create future possibilities that cascade into a cycle of radically new directions that lead the biosphere in new directions.

> *[How Complexity and Emergence Create a Cosmos, 2016, Professor Stuart Kauffman, M.D., Biochemistry and Mathematics, University of Vermont, Vermont, USA, interviewer Robert Lawrence Kuhn Ph.D., https://www.closertotruth.com/interviews/49855]*

Professor Kaufmann is on the correct path. The biosphere is self-organizing beyond the influence of natural selection. It is evolving independently at multiple levels, creating future possibilities that cascade into cycles of new possibilities.

As a member of the *Homo sapiens* species, you are just one result of many that have preceded you and just one result of the many that will follow.

The study of self-organizing systems is fascinating.

Within each level of each niche of the biosphere, self-organizing forces are operating with their own set of rules and guiding principles. Analyzing each niche of the biosphere will reveal the guiding principles at work at each level of the self-organizing system.

Within any eukaryotic species, self-organizing systems comprise atoms, molecules, organelles, cells, communities of organisms, tissues, organs, and beings, each with its own rules.

Medical disciplines recognize the need to specialize at various levels of self-organizing systems and are continuing to expand to address ailments at the appropriate level.

To paraphrase Professor Neil D. Theise, M.D., in their 2016 article, *How Complexity and Emergence Create a Cosmos*:

> *To help illustrate this, a physician may interact with the body at each self-organizing level, so if I broke my arm, an orthopedist who puts it in a cast is operating at the macro level of the body.*
>
> *In contrast, if I have an infection and need an antibiotic, the doctor operates at the body's molecular and organism levels.*
>
> *However, if my doctor uses electricity on my broken bone to accelerate healing, that is at the electromechanical or quantum level.*
>
> *[How Complexity and Emergence Create a Cosmos, 2016, Professor Neil D. Theise, M.D., Pathology and Medicine, Gastrointestinal & Hepatobiliary Pathology, Anatomic Pathology, Columbia University College of Physicians & Surgeons, New York Presbyterian Hospital – Columbia Campus, New York City, NY, USA, interviewer Robert Lawrence Kuhn Ph.D., https://www.closertotruth.com/interviews/49855]*

SELF-ORGANIZING DESIGNS

In our discussion of 'design,' we began by exploring the well-understood notion of a designer conceptualizing a thing. Then, we explored the idea of a self-organizing system, which is also a self-designing system by its very nature.

We cede the point that self-designing systems have deterministic and probabilistic aspects, which, at some point, can form the conditions that facilitate the emergence of a biosphere. However, within a biosphere, self-designing systems become less reliant upon their foundational deterministic and probabilistic forces as they initiate various levels of communication to self-direct their new organizations.

While most self-directed designs fail, repeated trial and error attempts occasionally survive in the circumstances they find themselves in.

One theoretical difference between the trial and error that results from a designer conceptualizing a thing versus the trial and error that results from self-designing forces designing a thing is that a conceptual design driven by intelligence, in some cases, can arrive at a working solution more rapidly.

However, the self-designing forces of a biosphere have the advantage of a seemingly infinite capability for many more self-driven design decisions at multiple levels of abstraction, conducted in a massively parallel manner over vast periods.

While simple self-organizing systems formed the initial universe up to the emergence of the biosphere, these forces still form the foundation upon which a biosphere continues to be designed and built.

However, these foundational forces do not influence how levels of the biosphere operate. Even though every self-organizing system in the biosphere depends upon the self-organized systems that preceded it, the biosphere and each self-organizing system that emerges within it operates by its own rules.

Likewise, each level of the biosphere does not influence how each level of the biosphere above it operates, and the patterns of dependency are not that simple. Levels do not stack on top of the other, but rather, a self-organizing system may depend on many other self-organizing systems. It all depends on the capabilities they provide and whether reuse is possible with a sustaining outcome.

Within our biosphere, we find various forms of life consisting of many different self-organizing systems.

Importantly, each of the twenty-four levels of consciousness results from several self-organizing systems that collaborate to create a sustainable outcome

Consciousness could only emerge within the biosphere for three crucial reasons.

First, only the biosphere's self-organizing systems can create the function necessary to support *freedom of attention, will, action*, and other freedoms.

Second, primordial self-organizing systems operate sequentially. For the most part, when one self-organizing system is completed, the next begins. It is only in the biosphere that self-designing systems operate in parallel.

Third, only the self-organizing systems of the biosphere create reusable functions that can operate simultaneously at multiple levels.

In short, a biosphere is necessary to transcend the deterministic forces of the primordial self-organizing forces. That positioned it to create the functions necessary to support the first level of *consciousness* and subsequent levels to build and improve upon.

As we can see more clearly now, the argument that *free will* cannot exist because the universe is purely deterministic fails to recognize that the biosphere transcends the hard determinism of primordial self-organizing systems.

The billiard balls or pachinko machine analogy of consciousness falls apart when the biosphere emerges with proteins communicating via chemical messengers to direct the formation of new proteins, new functions, and, ultimately, new levels of *consciousness*.

The deterministic view of the universe cannot predict the formation of self-organizing systems that preceded the biosphere, and those were the simple ones. In the case of self-organizing systems in the biosphere, it appears more complex and more challenging to predict what will form and how it will behave.

Now that we have equipped ourselves with the basics of self-organizing and self-designing systems let's return to our design discussion.

One of the first issues we may wish to explore is whether a designer can conceptualize a design of something that is, in one or more ways, self-organizing.

As it happens, there are types of software systems that also have aspects of self-organization. The most common of these are operating systems. Computer platforms, both large and small, have operating systems.

The operating system in most home computers is either Windows or Mac OS. The operating system in most smartphones is either Android or iOS. One can find operating systems on other computers, such as Unix, Linux, VMS, or z/OS.

An operating system is a system of programs that support other programs that run on top of the operating system. As such, every program that runs on your home computer sits on top of Windows or Mac OS, and when the program needs something, it asks the operating system for it.

This way, each program does not need to know anything about the hardware environment but instead relies on the fact that the operating system knows everything about the hardware.

In today's modern operating systems, if the operating system is unfamiliar with a particular hardware component, it will look for the software component that is compatible with it so that the operating system can communicate with it.

Another aspect of an operating system that makes it self-organizing is that, unlike most programs, operating systems actively manage the resources on the computing platform, such as the scheduling and sequencing of tasks, management of memory, storage, data movement services, hardware devices, and their interfaces, as well as management of system performance, error handling, and system security.

Additionally, operating systems, including those on your smartphone, will automatically look for updates and patches to fix bugs and to better protect against security threats.

Although operating systems and mini-operating systems have aspects of self-organizing systems, most programs that run on top of an operating system are not self-organizing in any aspect, as they typically ingest data, typically transform the data in some way, and then typically output or store the data somewhere.

In our heads, both the operating system software and the physical hardware demonstrate self-organizing capabilities. In contrast, only a computer's operating system tends to demonstrate self-organizing capabilities, as computer hardware typically does not.

However, this changed with the advent of certain cloud computing services.

There are three categories of cloud computing.

These are Software as a Service (SaaS), Platform as a Service (PaaS), and Infrastructure as a Service (IaaS).

SaaS and PaaS demonstrate a small degree of self-organizing features in that they can add and remove computing resources, such as additional processors, as needed to address their workload. Aside from this, computer hardware currently cannot demonstrate many of the self-organizing capabilities that the physical brain is capable of.

Occasionally, a program will ask the operating system for something it cannot provide. However, the program can do as many things as possible, assuming the availability of resources. Although the operating system might run out of resources, usually, the only limit is one's imagination.

> *For example, while a physical robot's body has limitations due to its physical size and strength in what it can pick up or move, the physical world does not limit the intellectual problems that software can solve.*
>
> *Unlike the physical world, software can render an artificial physical world without physical limits.*

If someone can dream up a software architecture and system design, developing the software needed to achieve it is typically possible.

Hence, we will assume that the foundation of our software architecture must start as a self-organizing software system, like an operating system.

From this as our starting point, let's see if we can imagine a way to support our first level of consciousness while using computer hardware and software.

UNICELLULAR CONSCIOUSNESS REVISITED

UNICELLULAR REQUIREMENTS

With our understanding of self-organizing systems and self-organizing operating systems, we will work towards a conceptual design (i.e., a high-level design) that will meet the requirements of our first level of *consciousness*.

As a caution, this chapter must get into the weeds, but if you are a software developer, you will understand why. However, if you are not, it is sufficiently high-level that anyone can follow along.

Let's review the sensory array of *Paramecium* (i.e., *Paramecium caudatum*).

Paramecium caudatum can sense various environmental substances and their concentrations, indicating physical proximity with its chemical sensors. It includes the presence of microorganisms, such as bacteria, algae, and yeast, and the presence of predators, including amoeba, didinium, the water flea, and other *Paramecia*.

With other sensory nodes, it can detect light and energy, including temperature differentials, brightness levels of light, and electrical current.

Modern mechanical sensors can support the sensory capability of *Paramecium caudatum*, including the detection of the chemical substances and the range of concentrations that *Paramecia* can detect, as well as the levels of light, temperature, and electrical current that *Paramecia* can detect.

These sensors can generate a stream of sensory stimuli that can replicate what a *Paramecium* can sense from various locations about its body that it can transmit to a central collection point.

The ability to reliably determine the source and direction of a stimulus will require our artificial *Paramecium* to be equipped with multiple sensors around its body, as do actual *Paramecia*. Thus, the difference between the strength of stimuli from sensors in one location and another may support an ability to perform various degrees of source triangulation.

Notably, the sensors of our artificial *Paramecium* need not detect the same stimuli to identify the same things in the environment. However, for comparison, it may be more convenient to stay as closely aligned to the capabilities of the actual organism as possible.

UNICELLULAR REQUIREMENTS - FREEDOMS

We may begin by eliminating the freedoms that real *Paramecium* cannot demonstrate. As previously established, *Paramecium* lacks *freedom of mind, emotion, thought,* and *paradigm.*

It leaves us with the ability to support *freedom of attention, will,* and *action,* the three freedoms our framework of *consciousness* supports up to the emergence of neural bundles.

Let's briefly review the forms of freedom present in *Paramecium* and any additional functions we need to support each of them appropriately.

With *freedom of attention,* having the focus one wants, our *Paramecium* demonstrates the focus one wants by choosing which stream of stimuli to focus on and demonstrates that the organism could have chosen otherwise.

As such, the ability to choose which stimuli to focus on will require us to support the capability to detect multiple streams of stimuli and to determine the relative importance of these streams of stimuli.

The relative importance of any given stimuli will need to consider the direction of the source of the stimuli and their relative distance as a function of the strength of the stream of stimuli.

Here, we will incorporate genetically built-in factors that associate a degree of importance and a learning capability to support any learned factors that may have caused some modifications to the degree of importance from the organism's experiences.

Therefore, the ability to store memories and the ability to learn from those memories must also be present to support *freedom of attention* appropriately.

With *freedom of will,* having the volition one wants, real *Paramecia* amply demonstrates this in controlled experiments cited within the section on *Unicellular Consciousness* by freely choosing a direction to move while demonstrating that the organism could have chosen otherwise.

The direction chosen is not random and represents the self-interests of the organism in that it shows a strong correlation between moving toward sources of nutrition and away from predatory organisms.

We also have established that *Paramecia* can learn and modify its behavioral choices as influenced by its learning ability.

Although scientific experiments have not differentiated whether *Paramecia's* ability to learn is explicitly associated with the organism's *freedom of attention* or *will,* we will assume the more demanding requirement that the ability to learn is associated with both freedoms.

As a result, we will include the requirement that the organism's capability to support a degree of importance must apply to the organism's *freedom of attention* distinctly from the organism's *freedom of will*.

The justification for two separate capabilities to support importance is that an organism's *freedom of attention* can have a distinct level of importance from its *freedom of will*.

In other words, the organism will have a distinct ability to manage the importance of having the focus one wants distinct from its ability to manage the importance of having the volition one wants.

It allows separate learning for what to pay attention to versus what the organism wants.

With *freedom of action*, *Paramecia* demonstrates this in the experiments cited within the section on *Unicellular Consciousness* by choosing a direction in which to move and then moving in that direction, such as moving towards sources of nutrition or away from sources of unpleasant stimuli.

Demonstrating *freedom of action* is somewhat different than demonstrating any of the other freedoms in that *freedom of action* is ultimately determined by external factors that might constrain the organism's ability to enact the volitions one wants.

Recall the plant *Mimosa pudica* (a.k.a. the sensitive plant) can enact the volition one wants in having the option to close its leaves. In contrast, *Dionea muscipula* (a.k.a. The Venus flytrap) is not given control over its actions and acts neither with choice nor the ability to choose otherwise.

Similarly, if we apply *Mimosa pudica* with a substance that physically prevents the motion of its leaves upon choosing that volition, it would also lose its *freedom of action* and ability to choose otherwise.

Like our unicellular *Paramecia*, *Mimosa pudica* can enact the volitions one wants in having the ability to move in various directions within a liquid substrate physically and may do so within a range of different velocities.

However, our *Paramecium* cannot enact the volition one wants if it enacts movement in a blocked direction.

That aside, choosing to enact the volition one wants may also be physically possible, though it could encounter an encumbrance presenting unanticipated difficulty.

> *For example, the viscosity of the liquid substrate could be thicker and more challenging to move through.*

> *Such an encumbrance could influence the organism's ability to enact its wants by significantly impeding it while not preventing it entirely.*

Therefore, for completeness purposes, we will still need to incorporate a requirement to support a level of importance associated with enacting the volition one wants while maintaining an ability to have enacted a volition other than the volition chosen.

It will support the ability to enact the volitions one wants while maintaining an ability to determine the relative importance minimally of two or more alternative volitions if the chosen volition to enact meets with an encumbrance.

Our *Paramecium* will also need additional capabilities to support these freedoms.

In addition to the capability to memorize and recall streams of stimuli, our unicellular organism must match up streams of incoming stimuli with stored streams of stimuli to interpret them.

Unlike conventional information systems that ingest structured data records, a stream of stimuli has neither a fixed beginning nor an end.

> *For example, a transactional record of a bank deposit has a fixed set of data points of known data types arranged in a fixed sequence within a record. It may minimally contain the known data points of a Customer Account Number, Transaction Date, and Transaction Amount in that sequence within the data record.*
>
> *A stream of stimuli is like repeatedly having a temperature reading every tenth of a second with no beginning and no end.*

As such, our streams of stimuli consist of an ongoing flow of signal data for each type of sensory organ with no beginning and no end. It always generates a data stream for whatever it detects and only during the detection period.

The environmental stimuli that each sensory organ detects will be specific to the type of stimuli, such as chemicals or forms of energy like light, electric current, or heat.

Additionally, each type of sensory organ must correspond to a set of genetically stored memories of initial patterns that have interpretations of those patterns not yet influenced by learning.

Unlike transactional records that can match exactly, like our bank deposit example with a given Customer Account Number on file at the bank, the patterns stored in memory and the patterns ingested by our sensory organs can never match up perfectly. Instead, the patterns will resemble a memory of a pattern to varying degrees.

Therefore, the requirement will be to perform a 'fuzzy match' or other approximate matching with the identifying features within the streams of stimuli for each type of sensory organ.

For example, the sensory organ may detect a particular combination of chemical molecules that represent a source of nutrition versus the combination of chemical molecules that represent the detection of a predator.

The precise ratio of the combined stimuli may be unique, though its meaning may be apparent.

We can match the prominent features found in the signal data against the genetic memory of the prominent features for what is already known to the organism. If the 'fuzzy match' is sufficiently similar, such that it resembles one pattern more than any other, it should conclude that it matches.

Once a match occurs, the organism must determine whether the matching stream of stimuli represents a pattern of stimuli that is favorable, unfavorable, or indifferent to the organism.

Aside from genetically stored patterns, *Paramecia* has a learning capability that allows it to classify stimuli distinct from prior patterns in some discernable way.

Newly learned patterns can be subtly or substantially distinct from previously stored patterns and may have a different classification (i.e., favorable, unfavorable, or indifferent) than previously known patterns.

Newly learned patterns of stimuli may have a different classification.

Consider if the classifications were always the same for subtly distinct patterns of stimuli, then there may never be a reason to establish distinct items with distinct patterns.

It is difficult to determine whether *Paramecia* experiences stimuli beyond their ability to classify sensory input as favorable, unfavorable, or indifferent. Even though it appears clear that the organism can detect physical proximity from signal strength, it is difficult to determine whether the organism has an experience that varies with proximity instead of simply classifying the stimuli as favorable, unfavorable, or indifferent.

It is what we referred to previously as *Type One Qualia* (Unicellular Qualia), which is supported solely by the cytoskeletal structures within one eukaryotic cell.

We will assume that this form of *qualia* is so primitive that it cannot render anything other than the most fundamental determination of stimuli being favorable, unfavorable, or indifferent, though potentially with simple weights, such as high, medium, and low to reflect the proximity or concentration of the stimuli.

While it is fair to point out that this assumption may be patently incorrect, we will err on being conservative without evidence to support an ability to experience *qualia* beyond this.

We will also assume that the intensity of stimuli will observably affect acceleration and rate of movement.

UNICELLULAR CONSCIOUSNESS CAPABILITIES – CONCEPTUAL DESIGN

The design must support the requirements we've identified. We will address each requirement in a conceptual design that a non-technical expert would comprehend.

One of the advantages of software is that the imagination is its only limitation. It begins with a design concept that can depict a minimum of one method that can support each requirement. Alternative design concepts are almost always possible, but ensuring they accurately support each requirement is critical.

Each design concept can have building blocks that work together.

A logical architecture identifies capabilities independent of specific technological components, such as brands of operating systems, programming languages, or computer hardware. Instead, the physical architecture would identify the implementation specifics most appropriate to work together.

A simple example would be a logical architecture illustrating that data should be transferred from a sensory device to a computer as quickly as possible.

The physical architecture would specify that the computer receiving that data will have a CPU with a complex set of instructions (CISC), a CPU with a reduced instruction set (RISC), a GPU (integrated or discrete), or a combination of many of each with specific memory sizes and processing speeds.

Let's begin by describing a conceptual design for each major component that will comprise our logical architecture, the first step being the *'interpretation of stimuli.'*

The design to interpret stimuli must parse a given stream of stimuli into segments that contain a recognizable feature, which can match up to known features using fuzzy matching. The step following that is to determine whether the segment of stimuli, individually or in a sequence of segments, represents something within the environment that is favorable, unfavorable, or immaterial.

The software functions that recognize the presence of recognizable features can support several related capabilities.

Let's begin with the detection of chemicals.

Chemical detectors must detect the chemicals associated with food, predators, and salt levels on contact. The concentration of detected stimuli must be commensurate with the concentrations *Paramecia* appears to detect.

Various technologies already exist to detect chemicals in liquid and gaseous forms.

To paraphrase Julian W. Gardner and Philip N. Bartlett in their 1994 book, <u>*A Brief History of Electronic Noses*</u>:

> *For example, machine olfaction (a.k.a. electronic nose) devices analyze airborne chemicals as an intelligent chemical array sensor system.*
>
> *Such a device can sense chemicals, including concentrations from various sides of our artificial paramecium, and pass this information along as electronic sensory stimuli.*
>
> *["A brief history of electronic noses," March 1994, Julian W. Gardner – Center for Nanotechnology and Microengineering, Department of Engineering, University of Warwick, UK, Philip N. Bartlett – Department of Chemistry, University of Southampton, UK, Elsevier Publishers,* <u>A brief history of electronic noses - ScienceDirect</u>*]*

As an example of a related capability, one can ignore a sensory node when it is either not detecting anything or is detecting a steady state for a prolonged period.

In contrast, imagine if the signals from every sensory node of your body had your attention. You don't feel every article of clothing or anything touching your body at any moment.

Another is that recognizable features have a data pattern associated with them that may have many valuable attributes. These attributes likely include sequence, frequency, and magnitude of recognizable features. The sequence of recognizable features has potential significance.

Still, the proportions of recognizable features present at any given moment and the sequence of different proportions may be significant.

Therefore, this conceptual design will detect and track these basic statistics by analyzing the sequence, timing, and proportions of recognizable features within both a segment and a sequence of segments.

Various techniques in data processing can support feature recognition.

As discussed in an earlier chapter, two primary methods for pattern recognition involve using either statistical models or neural networks. We will choose neural networks for their speed of recognizing patterns Jand flexibility in learning new patterns and changes in those patterns.

> *An early adopter of neural network technology was American Express for credit card application processing.*

Many neural network algorithms, each with strengths and weaknesses, vary based on the types of data and problem space. At this point, our conceptual design will assume that the exploration to determine the most effective algorithms for the particular use case will occur later.

Each neural network chosen would then be trained for its associated segments of recognizable features, whether they specialize in detecting chemical molecules, concentrations of nutrition, a nearby predator, temperature differentials, brightness levels, or levels of electrical current.

Once we match each segment of stimuli to the appropriate type of known segments, the next step is to determine the pattern as favorable, unfavorable, or indifferent.

Here, we can assume that our *Paramecia* comes genetically equipped with the basic patterns associated with commonly encountered stimuli, such as nutrients and predators.

In separate design steps, we can address the capability of *Paramecia* to learn new patterns of stimuli and to determine how best to categorize them as favorable, unfavorable, or indifferent.

A significant aspect of establishing a recognizable feature from among a stream of sensory stimuli is that it represents the first step toward forming the concept of a symbol.

Recall sensory organs create a stream of stimuli with neither a beginning nor an end. The ability to extract features from the noise of a pattern is an ability to form basic logical operations with established symbols, and learning can potentially support an ability to establish new symbols that are different in some significant way.

Although we have just scratched the surface of *Paramecia's* capabilities, it is already impressive to recognize that within our unicellular *Paramecium*, various cytoskeletal structures residing within a tiny eukaryotic cell already perform these functions.

The following function we will address is memory and learning.

There are many ways to store data in a computer. Selecting the best one depends on whether the data is structured, semi-structured, or unstructured.

> *Structured data has a fixed record layout with set data points, such as an account number, a date, a debit/credit indicator, and an amount.*
>
> *Semi-structured data has a flexible record layout that adds or removes data points. Because of this, semi-structured data also includes the name of the data point and its corresponding value, such as <Account Number> "01002502" and <Transaction Date>" January 15, 2024."*
>
> *Unstructured data is a stream of data, such as a video feed from a camera or an audio feed from a microphone.*

In our use case, the sensory organs produce unstructured data, which we will parse to identify segments of stimuli that we can correlate to a recognizable feature, such as food, when the pattern of stimuli closely resembles that of food being present.

Once the pattern is detected, we can create structured or semi-structured data points to represent the concepts present within the stream of data, such as the sensor's location on the body's surface, the type of food, and its concentration.

In contrast, we may use a different technique called triples to support the memory of recognizable features with their associated meaning. Triples are perhaps one of the most intuitive formats available.

In a sense, each *triple* is an individual piece of knowledge about data that shares the structure of simple spoken language.

Triples belong to a branch of semantics and represent an easy way to understand facts composed of three parts.

Each triple includes a subject, predicate, and object.

A triple's 'subject' and 'object' are always nouns. Rules determine the things permissible to use as a 'subject.' The subject can be as simple as a person or organization or include places or things.

The 'predicate' of a triple is always a trait or aspect of the 'subject' expressed in relationship to the 'object,' which is a verb. Permissible predicates must be consistent, defined, and well-understood.

It represents a collection of use cases closely aligned to intelligence-gathering activities on individuals and organizations. The resulting knowledge management capabilities offer a variety of commercial and government capabilities.

Imagine the possible applications for triples in the intelligence community, such as:

• 'Jim'	'knows'	'Peter'
• 'Peter'	'attends'	'downtown NYC WOW'
• 'Peter'	'owns'	'Firearms Inc.'

[Pragmatic Enterprise Architecture: Strategies to Transform Information Systems in the Era of Big Data, 2014, James V. Luisi – independent scholar and author, Morgan Kaufmann Publishers - Elsevier Inc., MA, U.S.A.]

In our use cases involving our artificial *Paramecium*, the triples could look like the following triples:

• 'Predator'	'harms'	'Paramecia'
• 'Nutrition'	'feeds'	'Paramecia'

However, given our artificial Paramecium and our design needs, our subjects will be a 'recognizable feature' (i.e., 'Predator'), our predicate will be a verb (e.g., 'is'), and our objects will be the genetic or learned assessment, (e.g., 'favorable,' 'unfavorable,' and 'indifferent').

- *'Predator'*   *'is'*   *'unfavorable'*
- *'Nutrition'*   *'is'*   *'favorable'*
- *'Light'*   *'is'*   *'indifferent'*
- *'Electricity'*   *'is'*   *'unfavorable'*

As we can see, there are many ways to represent information. Likewise, a solution architect may choose from many technologies for storing that information when they develop the physical architecture and design.

The understanding here is that the experiences of our artificial *Paramecium* are limited to specific segments of stimuli. It is not likely that we need all experiences from all sensory organs, as we may only need to retain the experiences associated with certain segment types of sensory stimuli.

In storing each segment of stimuli, which we will term 'recognizable feature,' we must also store the genetic or learned assessment (e.g., *'favorable,' 'unfavorable,'* and *'indifferent'*).

We will also need to store an identifier of each sensor and its location on the body for triangulation purposes to facilitate a potentially more useful interpretation. However, storing information is only helpful if there is an ability to retrieve it subsequently.

The role of memory retrieval is to retrieve information from memory immediately when needed.

Several functions require retrieval from memory.

Perhaps the most basic is retrieving recognizable features from memory that have a fuzzy match with new segments of stimuli to look up their assessment (e.g., *'favorable,' 'unfavorable,'* and *'indifferent'*).

Another function of memory is to support learning.

Generally, it is essential to identify recognizable features versus new unknown segments. Unknown segments must still be categorized to determine if they are favorable, unfavorable, or indifferent, depending on the patterns they most closely resemble in general and present circumstances.

This design step provides our artificial *Paramecium* with the ability to retrieve information that resides in memory, whether that information was initially present due to genetic factors or later learned through experience.

Retrieval from memory will occur from inbound stimuli from many sensors simultaneously. The result is a real-time assessment of things within the environment that are 'favorable,' 'unfavorable,' and 'indifferent' in every direction within the range of each type of sensor.

However, we may need more complex types of retrieval involving correlations among related recognizable features to draw even more meaningful conclusions to leverage the results of learning.

The capability to store or memorize information is quite distinct from the capability of learning, as it is possible to store vast amounts of information without learning, though the capability to learn also requires some minimum capacity to memorize information.

Being educated assumes more than memorization and includes establishing a depth and breadth of knowledge, where knowledge is information that forms a familiarity or an awareness within one or more domains.

Yet, the ability to apply knowledge in one's behavior and choices is quite distinct from simply acquiring and reciting it on demand.

For our purposes, the significance of learning is for the organism to benefit from each experience. Hence, we are only concerned with applied knowledge, which involves using knowledge to help *Paramecia* make choices.

As we will see, each function, such as learning, depends on one or more other functions.

> *For example, learning depends on the capability to determine recognizable features from among streams of stimuli.*

> *Without the ability to recognize features among streams of stimuli, the sensory inputs are just noise.*

Once the ability to determine recognizable features is present, the organism can demonstrate learning by showing that it can associate meaning to the recognizable features to use in some way.

> *For example, if the unicellular Amoeba were able to demonstrate that it knows a particular location lacks the presence of nutrients, then it would be demonstrating that it has both memory for previously determining that the location lacked nutrition and an ability to learn from that fact by not returning to the exact location searching for the presence of nutrients.*

> *Scientific experiments have not determined whether the Amoeba lacks the functions to form a memory, learn, or both.*

One of the first differentiators involved in learning is determining which recognizable features are pertinent. Sensory arrays may stream vast amounts of information, but few, if any, may be pertinent. The ability to determine the pertinent features is a core function of *freedom of attention*.

Similarly, when neural networks receive training on learning sets, such as identifying the patterns of data that represent a credit card applicant that is a reasonable credit risk versus those that are not, they 'learn' to identify even the most esoteric parts of the pattern that are pertinent versus extraneous for differentiating between patterns.

To paraphrase Choi, Coyner, Kalpathy-Cramer, Chiang, and Campbell in their 2020 article, *Introduction to Machine Learning, Neural Networks, and Deep Learning*:

We can analyze recognizable features statistically to determine whether a significant correlation exists between excellent or bad credit risks.

There are four learning methods within machine learning, each helpful in solving different types of problems. They are supervised, unsupervised, semi-supervised, and reinforcement learning.

Supervised learning tasks are typically for classifying inputs and for regression, which helps predict numerical data, such as prices and scores.

Unsupervised learning tasks are typically for detecting patterns to categorize individual instances, which is helpful for clustering, association, and anomaly detection.

Semi-supervised learning tasks are essentially a combination of supervised and unsupervised learning, where some data requires too much effort to categorize.

Reinforcement learning tasks involve problems with no correct answer but several, such as moving a gaming character from one location to another where multiple paths are possible.

[Introduction to Machine Learning, Neural Networks, and Deep Learning, February 2020, Rene Y. Choi, Aaron S Coyner, Jayashree Kalpathy-Cramer, Michael F Chiang, J Peter Campbell, Translational Vision Science & Technology (TVST), https://tvst.arvojournals.org/article.aspx?articleid=2762344]

The next factor in learning is associating segments of stimuli with meaning. This may mean forming relationships with other recognizable features and assessing those features (e.g., 'favorable,' 'unfavorable,' and 'indifferent') or determining a new assessment more appropriate to the current circumstances.

Learning may involve forming relationships between new or existing recognizable features, potentially involving some combination across sensor types. Some recognizable features may be reliable predictors of other recognizable features of different sensor types.

The degree of complexity for learning can range significantly. It may involve an exact moment in time or many, involving one or more sequences of events and potentially involving similar highly variable time intervals.

Ultimately, forming a new relationship among segments of stimuli and their sequences may create relationship-based recognizable features that can mean either *'favorable,' 'unfavorable,'* or *'indifferent.'*

As predictive recognizable features and their relationships gain an interpretation, the meaning of these recognizable features will continue to develop, further assisting our artificial *Paramecium* to learn. However, as soon as something has meaning, it also has some level of importance, low or high.

The role of *importance determination* is to determine the relative level of importance of recognizable features within each stage of learning and in support of each type of freedom.

Even at this early stage, *importance determination* is a supporting component for several functions. Hence, the conceptual design of *importance determination* must support an ability to interface with many other components to support their needs.

Once the *interpretation of stimuli* has identified *recognizable features* from the various streams of stimuli, it is the role of *importance determination* to help our artificial *Paramecium* identify the relative importance of the *recognizable features*. The *recognizable features* with greater importance than others are 'pertinent features.'

> *As a starting point, the design of pertinent features (a.k.a. pertinent symbols) can be determined statistically, such as with standard deviations (a.k.a. root mean squares usually represented by the abbreviation "SD" or the symbol "σ" called sigma) of importance that are above the mean level of importance.*

> *Our conceptual design of importance determination can make it reusable to handle the many use cases that need to determine a feature's relative importance or priority, whether recognizable or pertinent.*

Pertinent features may individually represent a particular idea or concept, or a pattern of *pertinent features* may represent an idea or concept. Patterns of *pertinent features* are necessary to support functions such as *freedom of attention, freedom of will, freedom of action*, storing memory, retrieval from memory, and learning in several ways.

> *In this example, let's assume many recognizable features are present within streams of stimuli from various sensory organs from being stored genetically.*

> *Some sensory organs on one side of our artificial Paramecium may recognize pertinent symbols representing food. In contrast, some sensory organs on the same side of our artificial Paramecium may recognize pertinent symbols representing a predator.*

> *While both are pertinent symbols, the relative importance of the predator may depend upon its proximity.*

> *The closer that the predator is, the higher its relative importance. However, in most circumstances, the predator in the same proximity should have a higher relative importance than food.*

The first role of *importance determination* would be to support *freedom of attention* to inform the organism that the recognizable features are more noteworthy than other recognizable features.

At this point, the organism can still choose another recognizable feature to focus on. However, it would only do so because that is what it wants compared to what it might need more urgently.

The process of 'wanting' to pay attention to a recognizable feature stems from a different capability within the organism that also relies upon *importance determination*, which we will discuss in the conceptual design section for *freedom of attention*.

Let's consider a slightly different example involving recognizable features.

In this example, many recognizable features are present within the streams of stimuli from sensory organs that exist via learning.

Like before, some sensory organs on one side of our artificial Paramecium may recognize pertinent features representing food, while others on the same side of our artificial Paramecium may recognize pertinent features representing a predator.

Let's add that there are pertinent features representing the presence of additional Paramecia.

Here, the relative importance of the predator may depend upon the presence of many Paramecia and their ratio.

It is analogous to a State Trooper amidst a large amount of vehicular traffic, all driving above the speed limit. The State Trooper can only capture one driver from among many, making the probability of being stopped by the State Trooper insignificant.

In this situation, if the Paramecium 'wants' food, it may approach the food source with little risk of harm to itself.

The first question, of course, is whether *Paramecia* can learn this. Like many things, the answer is that it depends.

One hypothetical where this may be possible is as follows.

Our individual *Paramecium* is among a sizable cluster of fellow *Paramecia* that initially is void of predator features. After some time, our *Paramecium* detects the pertinent features associated with an individual predator while noticing that most other *Paramecia* are not fleeing.

Let's try another example where importance is associated with other learned concepts.

In this example, concepts may result from something learned when a combination of recognizable features is present, though located in opposite directions.

Different than before, some sensory organs on one side of our artificial Paramecium may contain pertinent features representing food and Paramecia. In contrast, some sensory organs on the opposite side of our artificial Paramecium may contain pertinent symbols representing predators.

The first question in this situation is whether one *Paramecium* can warn others to flee.

Suppose a collection of *Paramecia* can detect that a *Paramecium* is moving at its fastest possible pace in a particular direction. Would this pertinent symbol get processed as something sufficiently urgent to join the fast-moving *Paramecium*?

As one would imagine, the response can and would be different for different individual *Paramecium*, though the ratio of these behaviors may differ among young populations versus experienced *Paramecia*.

Let's say one population of *Paramecia* has previously encountered the pertinent features of a fast-moving *Paramecium*, subsequently to be followed by the pertinent features of a cluster of predators. This population would be in an excellent position to have previously learned to flee with a fast-moving *Paramecium*.

In contrast, another population of *Paramecia* that has not encountered the same learning opportunity would not be in an excellent position to have previously learned to flee.

Controlled experiments with live *Paramecium* would need to be conducted on populations of *Paramecia* to determine whether the response to flee in those circumstances is always genetic or subject to learning.

Once learned, a level of importance would be associated with detecting the appropriate pertinent features that indicate the appropriate circumstances. Separate from the *importance level* of these stimuli, the organism must also determine the relative importance in the context of everything happening at that moment.

Separately, *importance determination* is associated with what the organism wants and considers essential for its self-interests.

We can see that *importance determination* operates at many levels concurrently, even within the cytoskeletal material of a unicellular organism absent neurons.

Hence, the importance of pertinent stimuli, either genetic or learned, can vary. Encountering pertinent stimuli at the moment is much more significant than encountering them in the past.

So, let's explore the conceptual design of *importance determination* using the following thought experiment.

> *We will begin by imagining the image of an old-fashioned mercury thermometer, and we will associate this image with each recognizable feature, whether genetic or learned.*
>
> *As such, an old-fashioned mercury thermometer has a hollow, vertical glass tube containing a bulbous reservoir of mercury at its base. It has evenly spaced horizontal markings extending up its entire length.*

> *Likewise, the column of mercury rises and falls as it expands and contracts in volume with temperature changes.*
>
> *Given that we have created the appropriate mental image, let's refer to the mercury column as representing levels of importance in place of temperature.*
>
> *In this simple model, an increase or decrease in temperature would be analogous to a corresponding increase or decrease in the degree of importance.*

Now that we have our visualization let's look at the requirements of our *importance determination* thermometers.

To begin, let's envision two thermometers supporting *freedom of attention.*

The role of thermometer #1 will be to activate or deactivate *attention* that may have had its level of importance thresholds established either genetically or learned.

> *The top-down threshold lines on this thermometer are a) attention activation, above which attention will activate; b) attention deactivation, below which attention will deactivate.*

The role of thermometer #2 will be the activation of Want of Attention that may have had its level of importance thresholds established either genetically or learned.

> *The threshold lines on this thermometer top-down are similar: a) want of attention activation, above which want of attention will activate; b) want of attention deactivation, below which want of attention will deactivate.*

The idea is that this general design will support the ability to bubble up stimuli from the most rudimentary level through the levels necessary for each level of freedom, including learning and the various other functional capabilities the organism may require to support.

First, *importance determination* supports *freedom of attention* by prioritizing pertinent segments of stimuli (i.e., symbols) from the many *recognizable features.*

The second is to prioritize pertinent features among one another.

The third is to prioritize sequences and combinations of features as they occur. It helps identify potential physical responses in the present.

The fourth is to prioritize sequences and combinations of features from among other recent sequences and combinations of features.

Fifth, its role is to prioritize adding new sequences and combinations of pertinent features in the learned set of knowledge. Therefore, new learning can occur safely after the organism has addressed its immediate survival needs by acting first and reorganizing its knowledge shortly after.

For example, suppose our Paramecium learns that certain light levels foretell an unpleasant electric force. In that case, the pertinent feature associated with that light level will be designated as 'important' in a general sense.

When pertinent feature detection occurs, the learned importance for in-the-moment will rise potentially 'Activating Attention,' 'Activating Will,' and potentially 'Activating Action.'

Likewise, when detection of the pertinent feature ceases, then the level of importance will decrease 'Deactivating Action,' 'Deactivating Will,' and potentially 'Deactivating Attention.

[Sensitive by Nature: Understanding Intelligence and the Mind, 2002, James Luisi, 1ˢᵗ Books Library Publishers]

While the actual algorithms are somewhat more nuanced and complex, at a high level, this accurately depicts the types of issues *importance determination* must address and how.

Thus far, the conceptual design of our artificial *Paramecium* includes:

- Interpretation of stimuli
- Storing memory
- Retrieval from memory
- Learning, and
- Importance determination

Now, we will cover the three forms of freedom that a *Paramecium* possesses. These include *freedom of attention, freedom of will,* and *freedom of action.*

We saw that *importance determination* supports the core function of our *Paramecium's* ability to choose the focus one wants.

Specifically, *importance determination* is responsible for identifying pertinent features from many *recognizable features.* Separately, it then determines the relative importance of pertinent symbols from among other pertinent symbols.

Then, it prioritizes the importance of sequences and combinations of symbols from other sequences and combinations.

However, this sequence of separate *importance determination* instances did not fully address our artificial *Paramecium's* ability to have the focus one wants as a function of what it "wants."

One additional component is a conceptual design for a component to house the "wants" of our artificial *Paramecium.* We will support this with another instance of our *importance determination* component, which tracks the relative importance of what the individual organism "wants" and how much it wants something.

Here, the organism may or may not have a "want" that may be so important that it can, if necessary, override its attention to focus on something other than what the organism will focus on if left to genetic or learned factors.

The 'want' *importance determination* instance is solely responsible for representing the relative importance of the various things the organism wants to focus on.

The second is a conceptual design for a component to determine the organism's " want " degree. However, before we depict the conceptual design for this component, we will need to discuss how any individual organism determines its "wants."

Among somewhat more advanced organisms, emotions influence the "wants" of the individual organism. We can support this using an additional instance of an *'importance determination'* component driven by emotions.

Among even more advanced organisms, reasoning may influence individuals. We can support this with an additional instance of an *'importance determination'* component set by each of the various forms of reasoning.

> *Recall that forms of reasoning include deductive reasoning, inductive reasoning, abductive reasoning, reductive reasoning, hypothetico-deductive reasoning, analogical reasoning, metaphorical reasoning, creative reasoning, holistic reasoning, reductionist reasoning, categorization reasoning, generalized reasoning, and logically fallacious reasoning.*

However, to have any given form of freedom in the sense that we have defined freedom, the organism must have one or more methods for determining what it wants independent of its genetics, learned body of knowledge, emotions, and reasoning.

> *In this manner, Paramecia may "want" to choose freedom due to none of these influences, but instead for no reason except that it "wants" it.*

> *As such, this instance of importance determination must support the ability to choose a want because that want may be so important that it should override all other importance determination instances.*

To better understand this, let's consider the following simple thought experiment.

> *An individual is in a circular room surrounded by identical ten doors that may lead out of the circular room.*

> *The individual gets to choose one door to open and move through.*

> *The individual may choose any door they "want" solely because they want that door.*

It is necessary to have the freedom to override all other influences that may point to a particular choice to support the ability to choose otherwise. The ability to choose based on what one wants provides the freedom to override all other influences.

Luckily, our *importance determination* component records any amount of 'want.'

In our real *Paramecium,* this choice would occur within the cytoskeletal structures of the individual organism. However, our overall conceptual design framework must determine this in our artificial *Paramecium.*

The key word in understanding this form of influence is the word 'want,' as it is a choice bearing no identifiable influence that the individual must choose based solely on what they want.

Therefore, it supports the scenario when the many influences may or may not point to any choices; however, the want decision can potentially override every identifiable influence within the individual, whether genetic, learned, emotional, or based on a form of reasoning.

Interestingly, the event that can prioritize avoiding other forms of *importance determination* is another *importance determination* component. The distinction here is that what one wants can be built up from different experiences, such as the repeated failure of using a genetic, learned, emotional, or reasoned-driven *importance determination* technique, breaking away from the possibility of a never-ending repetition, or just wanting to be different.

Although just wanting to be different is itself a reason, it does not belong to the realm of reasoning, such as deductive reasoning. The want could be to be more random or to explore. While it is true that genetic predispositions may strengthen or weaken one's level of importance to explore, a simple 'want' can override any genetic predisposition.

Even though the factors that can influence behavior for unicellular organisms are relatively limited, this provides a glimpse into how dynamic the *freedom of attention* and the freedom to choose can be as we advance through each level of consciousness.

Like *freedom of attention, importance determination* also supports our *Paramecium's* ability to choose the focus one wants.

Here, *importance determination* is tracking the degree to which the organism wants each volition it is aware of, which is a combination of built-in genetic knowledge and subsequent learning.

Like with *freedom of attention,* the degree of importance for each volition may continually adjust in either direction due to genetic and learned factors and by the stream of recognizable features being focused on in real-time by *freedom of attention,* which ultimately comprises what can motivate the organism.

For example, some potential motivations for a simple organism may be the well-being of oneself, possibly one's offspring, family, or collective, or it could be competing with other Paramecia or other organisms for potentially limited resources.

However, the flow of information between *freedom of attention* and *freedom of will* is not unidirectional. *Freedom of will* is also continually adjusting the importance levels of *freedom of attention* for the recognizable features that *freedom of will* considers more significant or less significant in real-time.

Even in our artificial *Paramecium*, we may begin to recognize the beginnings of a chaos engine.

Chaos theory is a branch of mathematics that describes many systems, such that even when the rules controlling them are fully known, their path and outcome are not predictable.

Unlike hard determinism, which is entirely predictable, like the interaction among billiard balls on a billiard table, chaos theory softens the deterministic characteristics to such an extent that it creates reliably unpredictable behavior and outcomes.

Even when an underlying process can be fully deterministic, the process can be fully chaotic, generating unpredictable results and unique outcomes every time.

> *Perhaps the easiest way to understand the chaos of a fully deterministic process is to consider the design of snowflakes.*
>
> *Every snowflake is a symmetrical design formed by an entirely deterministic process with a unique and symmetrical geometric pattern. Even though the process is deterministic as governed by the laws of physics, not only is there no way to accurately predict the resulting geometry of any given snowflake, but the pattern of every snowflake is unique to every snowflake that formed before it.*

Although the factors that motivate the possible volitions in our artificial *Paramecium* are relatively limited to a comparatively small number of possible outcomes, like *strong emergence*, it is impossible to predict its behavior in advance accurately.

It means that identical artificial *Paramecium* coexisting in the same environment will begin to deviate due to even the tiniest differences in experience.

For example, two identical *Paramecia* can never simultaneously occupy the same position.

> *Consider identical twins interacting with one of their parents who are placing them into their crib. One of those twins will be first, and one will be second, creating a unique experience for each.*

In this way, our artificial organism can still have a fully deterministic set of computerized processes that are sufficiently chaotic that its outcome is uncertain.

Also, like predicting the weather, each successive probability of a projected outcome is less predictable. So, while rainfall projections for today may be relatively accurate, the projections for each additional day into the future will have less accuracy and less certainty.

Also, as with *freedom of attention*, *freedom of will* supports the ability to override genetic and learned influences based on what the individual wants and the degree to which it is wanted.

But what about *freedom of action*?

Like *freedom of will*, *importance determination* supports *Paramecium's* ability to choose to enact the volition one wants, but in a different way.

Freedom of action is primarily a consequence of one's circumstances as to whether an external influence has imposed a constraint restricting the individual from enacting the volition they choose. The role of *importance determination* shifts from influencing the enactment of a volition to how much effort to apply to the enactment of a volition, potentially influencing *freedom of will* to choose a different volition.

Like before, the flow of information between *freedom of action* and *freedom of will* is not unidirectional. *Freedom of action* also continually adjusts the importance of *freedom of will* for volitions that *freedom of will* considers more significant or less significant in real time.

> *An example of this for Paramecia would be to enact a volition to swim in a direction where the viscosity increases, thereby impeding its ability to move. Upon recognizing this, the next choice of the Paramecium is to either increase its effort to move in the impeded direction or to change its volition to choose another direction.*

Ultimately, the choice requires communication with *freedom of will* to determine the steadfastness of maintaining the enactment of the already chosen course or to choose a different volition to enact.

Hence, the conceptual design of *freedom of action* does not allow one to enact the volitions one wants. Instead, it determines whether the organism possesses *freedom of action* and the continued will to enact its volition.

It might cause our artificial *Paramecium* to increase the level of effort it needs to exert to enact its volition or to choose a different volition in which to enact.

At this point, we have established a conceptual framework of how we would design an organism that supports the capabilities of *Unicellular Consciousness* with its appropriate degrees of *freedom of attention, will,* and *action*.

A systems engineering team can develop a logical design from this conceptual design. The logical design will guide the physical design process, directing the engineering team in a physical implementation of our artificially conscious *Paramecium*.

Simultaneously, a test planning team can take the requirements and conceptual design to develop a test plan to determine the success of the design and implementation.

UNICELLULAR CONSCIOUSNESS TESTING

The test planning of requirements and conceptual design can be highly detailed, with positive and negative test outcomes planned.

To spare the reader from excruciating details that will add many pages without advancing the journey, we will provide only a brief glimpse into the test planning of *Unicellular Consciousness* to convey the basic idea of test plans and testing.

Testing is first performed on each function by itself. It is called Unit Testing. Often, this requires the development of a testbed that makes it possible to test each action the function is supposed to perform. Upon passing Unit Testing, the next round of tests requires various functions to be integrated and tested as a larger unit.

Testing complex systems requires a test bed that can support computer modeling of factors, such as *importance determination* settings and the combinations and permutations of external stimuli.

When the various functions represent a complete unit, incremental testing is necessary. It can begin with individual stimuli, such as stimuli denoting the presence of nutrition located in various directions and distances, and then introduce additional stimuli denoting the presence of a predator in various directions and distances.

Again, many of these tests have not yet been scientifically conducted in controlled experiments using real *Paramecia* as a baseline.

When outcomes for our artificial *Paramecium* correlate appropriately to testing individual stimuli on real *Paramecium*, more complex scenarios of simultaneous stimuli should follow. These can start with tests having multiple sources of the same type of stimulus, such as nutrition in one location and another source of nutrition simultaneously in another location, and then proceed to simultaneously introduce different types of stimuli, such as a source of nutrition and the presence of a predator.

During these tests, the level of importance associated with the symbols associated with the various types of stimuli can be varied.

> *For example, an increased level of importance for nutrition can represent greater hunger.*

To test an ability to focus on segments of stimuli other than food or the presence of a predator, one could alter the *level of importance* of another factor within the environment that may have a higher degree of importance factors possibly a frequency of light that is within the detectability range of *Paramecia*.

When individuals participating in the test have identical genetic settings, outcomes may vary solely due to learned responses.

Many test cases are necessary to isolate the effect of various influences.

For example, various tests can adjust internal and external variables to the *Paramecium*.

Some additional internal factors might include things like the *levels of importance* associated with pertinent stimuli; the number, physical positioning, and types of sensory organs; the varying genetic factors, such as the segments of stimuli already known, and the amount of learning (or pre-learning) that has occurred.

Some additional external factors might include the types, number, timing, sequence, intensity, direction, and distance of stimuli.

When we examine the dynamics more closely with a test bed, we should also determine whether Chaos Theory is participating in any of these functions and which ones.

Even though our consciousness is not some weather system, this scientific inquiry is profoundly valuable for advancing our understanding of the various factors that support *consciousness*. Chaos Theory may explain some of the components that support *consciousness*. Therefore, identifying which components are prone to Chaos Theory and which are not may be essential for understanding the mechanisms that support each level of *consciousness*.

To summarize testing, we are designing our artificial *Paramecium* to be as representative of real *Paramecia* as possible. Toward that objective, we also have the advantage of incorporating various traces and audit logs to monitor the activity within every design component. It affords us the luxury to see into the inner workings of each component as they interact with one another.

Given the scientific questions that will arise as we proceed in our journey, we can devise new experiments on *Paramecia* to provide further details into how their freedoms operate.

Additionally, as we continue to add to our knowledge, we can potentially answer questions about the role of Chaos Theory and our overall probabilistic framework.

Luckily, speed and high performance are not factors in these tests, as there is nothing wrong with the various events playing out in a type of slow motion, as we can always address processing efficiencies later.

However, as we gain insight into this level of the biosphere where *consciousness* emerges, we will be better equipped to support our remaining levels of *consciousness*.

SECOND LEVEL REVISITED
(MULTICELLULAR CONSCIOUSNESS)

Recall our two examples of multicellular *consciousness* belonging to the plant kingdom.

The first is the species *Dionea muscipula* within the genus *Dionea*. This plant occurs in a tiny subtropical wetland region along a 700-mile stretch of coast where North and South Carolina meet (a.k.a. The Venus flytrap).

The second species is the *Mimosa pudica* (a.k.a. sensitive plant), native to South and Central America. However, it has become a pantropical (i.e., of the tropical regions of both hemispheres) as a problematic weed.

As we did with our unicellular example, let's begin by identifying the senses that these organisms possess to interact with the environment in which they reside.

The sensory capabilities of *Dionea muscipula* and *Mimosa pudica* both involve tactile receptors. *Dionea muscipula* detects two stimulations of a given trigger hair with a thirty-five-second elapse time as the signal to initiate a response. This two-step trigger helps the plant avoid mistaking a grain of sand or a drop of rain as prey.

In contrast, *Mimosa pudica* detects either touching, jarring, shaking, sudden blowing, or rapidly warming of even a single leaflet as a potential signal to initiate a response to being attacked. However, it learns when the stimulation's characteristics do not result in an attack that uselessly causes *Mimosa pudica* to expend energy.

Although both plants can demonstrate visible motion in reaction to tactile stimuli, we will continue focusing on *Mimosa pudica* as it involves the more advanced organism that demonstrates *freedom of attention, freedom of will,* and *freedom of action.*

MULTICELLULAR REQUIREMENTS

We begin again by putting aside the freedoms that *Mimosa pudica* cannot demonstrate, ceding that *Mimosa pudica* lacks *freedom of mind, emotion, paradigm, and thought.*

Let's begin by highlighting the differences in freedoms concerning multicellular organisms compared to our unicellular organisms.

The first difference we encounter with multicellular organisms is that they have multiple cells forming a community, each with cytoskeletal structures supporting *consciousness.*

Mimosa pudica demonstrates the focus one wants by choosing which stimuli to focus on, such as its ability to ignore certain types of tactile experiences over others, and demonstrates that the organism could have chosen otherwise. However, being multicellular means that not all cells must have the same focus.

Hence, the requirements include an ability to independently determine the relative importance of stimuli within each cell.

It means that one part of the plant may be focused on tactile stimuli, while another may not, as only one part of the plant may be experiencing harmful stimuli, thus allowing it to preserve the energy reserves in that part of the organism.

Regarding *freedom of will*, multicellular organisms can have different volitions among different cells. The relative uniformity of behavior of the leaves seems to indicate that the volitions of cells local to stimuli tend to perceive that stimulus together either as a non-threat or as a threat, causing the leaves to fold, unfold, or not react.

As such, it is essential here that the cells of multicellular organisms do not all have the same volitions at the exact time, as each has the freedom to choose a volition and may not choose the same volition.

Regarding *freedom of action*, a multicellular organism has many cells that may or may not be able to enact the volitions one wants.

One part of this involves the cell type. Many cell types lack the freedom to enact volitions that translate into physical movement.

The other aspect involves whether an external influence inhibits or prevents the ability to enact the volition of cells that can demonstrate physical movement.

The essential factor here is that there are multiple cells, and while some may lack the ability to enact one's volition, other cells may possess *freedom of action*.

Our *Mimosa Pudica* also requires a few additional capabilities to support these freedoms.

Once multiple cells are present, one new issue that arises is communication between them. At this point in the biosphere's evolution, communication mechanisms had already developed much earlier among an assortment of molecules known as chemical messengers.

While all organisms, prokaryotes and eukaryotes, leverage molecular communications, additional forms of communication also developed within multicellular organisms, initially involving adjacent cells and then nearby cells that were not physically adjacent.

Multicellular organisms, such as *Dionea muscipula* (a.k.a. the Venus flytrap) and *Mimosa pudica* (a.k.a. the sensitive plant), employ the release of ions to signal other cells to enact a volition, such as folding their leaves.

The design of *Dionea muscipula*, like most plant life in our biosphere, internally lacks *freedom of action*. However, many cells of *Mimosa pudica* do not share that limitation.

Although it is unclear the extent to which the *Mimosa pudica* cells can act alone versus communicating locally with adjacent or nearby cells, we will assume that *freedom of attention*, *freedom of will*, and *freedom of action* are always determined locally within their cell and that only a collection of cells collaborating can trigger physical motion.

Ion flows cause the physical response to act mechanically via the physical forces of turgidity to support the observed behavior in organisms that share that mechanism, such as *Dionea muscipula* and *Mimosa pudica*.

MULTICELLULAR CONSCIOUSNESS CAPABILITIES – CONCEPTUAL DESIGN

The functional components we designed for *Unicellular Consciousness* are the same here with a few additions, such as intercellular communications involving chemical messengering and waves of ions to alter turgidity in the plant's local area, involving perhaps only a portion of the physical plant.

Also, many capabilities in our example of *Multicellular Consciousness* need to be restricted with limitations placed on *freedom of action*.

> *For example, Mimosa pudica cannot choose to enact a volition involving direction or movement rate. The only possible actions are to fold and unfold.*

Unicellular Consciousness and *Multicellular Consciousness* share many of the same design capabilities, with the addition of intracellular communication via chemical messengering and waves of ions to alter turgidity.

For all practical purposes, they also share the same freedoms, as they pertain to *freedom of attention* and *will*, though a somewhat more restricted *freedom of action*.

As a result, the design steps of these two levels of consciousness are the same mainly because each successive level of consciousness builds upon the capabilities of each earlier level of consciousness.

THIRD LEVEL REVISITED
(NERVE NET CONSCIOUSNESS)

NERVE NET REQUIREMENTS

This level of consciousness marks the emergence of a new type of cell, the neuron. These new cells form strands that act as an expressway to support the high-speed transmission of electrical signals to various locations within the organism.

The flow of information accelerated well beyond the capabilities of prior eukaryotes, making an evolutionary leap over *Multicellular Consciousness* modes of communication.

The species chosen for *Nerve Net Consciousness, Tripedalia cystophora* (i.e., box jellyfish), demonstrates the first sensory organs that are themselves comprised of multicellular structures (e.g., eyes), equipped with specialized parts such as a sophisticated lens, retina, iris, and cornea.

Instead of chemically sensing the direction of food or predators, the box jellyfish can see them visually to rapidly transmit the information along their high-speed network of neurons to other cells within the organism.

Although *Paramecia* can detect light, this is the first time in the evolution of consciousness that an organism evolved the ability to detect objects within its environment visually.

However, we must be careful in that this does not mean that Box Jellyfish can create a visual landscape the way we can. It only means that instead of chemical receptors providing chemical clues as to the direction and distance of an object, such as food or predators, a more efficient means with potentially more significant range and lower latency is available.

As for the breadth of visual detail that Box Jellyfish possess, it is at least sufficient to distinguish prey from its species, its few predators, and the canopy of trees that it uses as a reference for navigation purposes.

Tripedalia cystophora (i.e., box jellyfish) enjoys a higher degree of genetic intelligence to navigate using visual clues and advances its learning capabilities, providing an enhanced ability to capture prey.

The natural habitat of Box Jellyfish is among the roots of mangrove trees, where they eat tiny crustaceans called copepods that tend to collect in the shafts of light that form by the opening of the canopy. If they stray far enough from their habitat, they have difficulty finding food and starve.

As such, scientists have studied various circumstances that test their ability to navigate to stay in their habitat or return to it if they find themselves some distance away but within range of their visual system.

Even though Box Jellyfish have twenty-four eyes of four different types, grouped in six clusters on the four sides of their bell, these eyes form separate visual systems instead of a unified one.

Recall four of the twenty-four eyes of this species are exclusively to peer above the water surface and support navigation to remain within its habitat. Separately, its other eyes support navigation in shallow waters around the various obstacles they encounter using the location of the tree canopy above as a point of reference.

However, some of these eyes support navigation to capture prey. These separate sets of eyes provide segments of stimuli that determine which are pertinent and sufficiently significant to act upon.

Regarding freedom, we will begin by eliminating the freedoms that *Tripedalia cystophora* (i.e., box jellyfish) cannot demonstrate, thereby ceding that *Tripedalia cystophora* lacks *freedom of mind, emotion, paradigm, and thought.*

Tripedalia cystophora demonstrates similar freedoms to previous levels of consciousness to have us conclude that the basic requirements remain the same.

One significant difference pertains to the ability to enact the volitions one wants. The physical mobility of *Tripedalia cystophora* is more significant, with several muscle groups that control its movement in the water and its arms for capturing and ingesting prey.

Again, this involves the available cell types. In our previous organisms, not only did they lack neurons, but they also lacked muscle tissues of any type to affect physical movement.

To support *freedom of attention, will,* and *action, Tripedalia cystophora* also requires a few additional supporting capabilities.

As with our first two levels of consciousness, *Unicellular Consciousness* and *Multicellular Consciousness, Nerve Net Consciousness* can learn and modify its behavior in response to stimuli and does so with an increased set of learning strategies, such as to improve upon its ability to intercept prey.

At its disposal is a more extensive and complex collection of cells requiring a network of neurons to quickly transport signals from sensory organs and muscle tissues.

We should also note that the role of neurons in this early form of consciousness appears mostly limited to supporting high-speed communications from one physical location to another. The cytoskeletal structures of some of those neurons support various calculations and signal-routing decisions, while others are simply acting as links in the relay chain of communication.

NERVE NET CONSCIOUSNESS CAPABILITIES – CONCEPTUAL DESIGN

The essential components developed for *Nerve Net Consciousness* are the same, with a few additions, such as signal routing calculations performed in the cytoskeletal structures of neurons and high-speed intercellular communications involving neurotransmitters that travel through the length of each nerve cell and across the synapse between the axon and dendrite of the next neuron(s).

The conceptual design for signal routing and communications is a simple message broker that can select the appropriate destination and transfer data over a small network.

Another addition will be sensory organs that support visual pattern recognition capabilities for each set of eyes. It represents a modest expansion of neural network capabilities to correctly identify the types of images each set of eyes must detect from various angles and distances.

FOURTH LEVEL REVISITED (NERVE CORD CONSCIOUSNESS)

NERVE CORD REQUIREMENTS

Nerve Cord Consciousness began with the emergence of bilaterians when organisms developed a left and right side that mirror one another that descended from a common marine wormlike ancestor some 600 million years ago.

Today, most animals are bilaterians, sharing the design pattern of a neuronal nerve cord traversing from the organism's front to back, with a hollow gut cavity running in the same direction from mouth to anus.

Perhaps the most significant advancement involving *Nerve Cord Consciousness* is the emergence of the first forms of *neuroglia* (a.k.a. glia, glial cells), which introduced a new dimension to the phenomenon of *consciousness*.

The species chosen for *Nerve Cord Consciousness*, *C. elegans* (i.e., nematode), has significantly advanced sensory capabilities starting at its nose. It supports the detection of light, touch, temperature, osmotic pressure, and tiny amounts of electrical current.

In addition, it chemically detects excitatory neurotransmitters and, even at this primitive stage, demonstrates social behaviors, mating, sleep, motor skills, drug dependence, learning, and memory-supporting behaviors.

Also, as recently as 2021, it has been determined that nematodes can also sense a range of airborne sounds.

To quote Iliff, Wang, Ronan, Hake, Guo, Li, Zhang, Zheng, Liu, Grosh, Duncan, and Xu in their 2021 article published by Elsevier Publishers, *The nematode C. elegans senses airborne sound*: Quote.

> *"Unlike olfaction, taste, touch, vision, and proprioception, which are widespread across animal phyla, hearing is found only in vertebrates and some arthropods. The vast majority of invertebrate species are thus considered insensitive to sound. Here, we challenge this conventional view by showing that the earless nematode C. elegans senses airborne sound at frequencies reaching the kHz range. Sound vibrates C. elegans skin, which acts as a pressure-to-displacement transducer similar to vertebrate eardrum, activates sound-sensitive FLP/PVD neurons attached to the skin, and evokes phonotaxis behavior."* ...

> *"Thus, the ability to sense airborne sound is not restricted to vertebrates and arthropods as previously thought, and might have evolved multiple times independently in the animal kingdom, suggesting convergent evolution. Our studies also demonstrate that animals without ears may not be presumed to be sound insensitive."* End Quote.

> *[The nematode C. elegans senses airborne sound, Aug 2021, Adam J. Iliff, Can Wang, Elizabeth A. Ronan, Alison E. Hake, Yuling Guo, Xia Li, Xinxing Zhang, Maohua Zheng, Jianfeng Liu, Karl Grosh, R. Keith Duncan, X. Z. Shawn Xu, PMID 34555314, PMCID PMC8602785, Elsevier Publishers]*

The phylum *Nematoda* is surprisingly vast, representing millions of species. It amounts to roughly eighty percent of all known animal species, making nematology a distinct discipline within zoology spanning a wide range of marine and land-based habitats.

> *[Caenorhabditis elegans, 2001, J. Hodgkin, Encyclopedia of Genetics]*

The learning capabilities of nerve cord organisms are more advanced, demonstrating highly plastic behavior (a.k.a. quick learning abilities), including associative (i.e., classical conditioning like with Pavlov, operant conditioning based on reward and punishment, non-associative or habituation which is desensitizing with repetition, and sensitization which oddly is sensitizing with repetition.

This more advanced form of learning leverages a broader array of sensory types while using chemical signaling internally within its own body and externally among other individuals.

This significant jump in learning capability may be related to the prospect that the first forms of neuroglia may potentially play an important role in enhancing the ability to learn by enriching the experience associated with each stream of stimuli. Alternatively, my leaning is that it may be the ability of neuroglia to reprogram connections among neurons that significantly enhances learning.

Neurons act in two significant capacities resembling the capabilities of a network server and a network to transport data, even in an organism whose entire body is a millimeter (one-thousandth of a meter) in length and diameter of approximately 50 micrometers (fifty-millionths of a meter), the average diameter of human hair.

While a network transports and delivers data, a network server can rapidly analyze it to determine where and how to route it.

To quote a 2021 Science Daily article, *Scientists map the brain of a nematode worm*: Quote.

> *"Researchers have mapped the physical organization of the brain of a microscopic soil-living nematode worm called Caenorhabditis elegans, creating a new model for the architecture of the animal's brain and how it processes information. The scientists say the worms' brains might have a lot more in common with larger animals than previously thought."*

> *"Created by neuroscientists at the University of Leeds in collaboration with researchers in New York's Albert Einstein College of Medicine, the brain map reveals that different spatial regions support different specialised circuits for routing information in the brain, where information is integrated before being acted upon." End Quote.*

> *[Scientists map the brain of a nematode worm, February 24, 2021, University of Leeds, West Yorkshire, UK, published by Science Daily,* https://www.sciencedaily.com/releases/2021/02/210224143517.htm*, and the scientific journal Nature in the Feb 24, 2021, issue]*

Regarding freedom, we will eliminate the freedoms that *C. elegans* cannot demonstrate, ceding nematodes' lack of *freedom of mind, emotion, paradigm, and thought.*

For the fourth time, this leaves us with the ability to support *freedom of attention, will,* and *action.*

C. elegans demonstrates the focus one wants by choosing which of many types of stimuli and specific stimuli to focus on, including mating signals, while demonstrating that it could have chosen otherwise.

As with the organisms that preceded it evolutionarily, the ability to have the focus one wants necessarily comes with an ability to determine the relative importance of two or more sets of stimuli. In the case of *C. elegans,* the organism must choose from a wider variety of sensory types than organisms that preceded it.

Additionally, introducing *neuroglia* facilitates experiential phenomenon as an additional influence for the first time. It represents a new factor that can influence *importance determination.* It can have a profound effect on the *freedom of attention* to repeat any experience that is deemed pleasurable.

Perhaps this begins to explain why there are so many nematodes.

C. elegans demonstrates having the volition one wants ranging in volitions, such as moving in a direction or mating, while demonstrating that it could have chosen otherwise.

As with our first three levels of consciousness, nerve cord organisms also have abilities to learn, so they may modify their volitions to override genetic influences.

Again, the introduction of *neuroglia* represents a new factor for influencing '*importance determination*,' ultimately impacting the volition one wants, such as for mating.

Regarding *freedom of action*, *C. elegans* demonstrates having the ability to enact the volitions one wants when it is unconstrained to enact its volitions and demonstrates that it can choose otherwise.

Without artificial constraints, *C. elegans* can enact the volitions one wants that its body, musculature, and environment physically permit.

Since *neuroglia* first emerges with this level of consciousness, let's explore the topic of the experiential phenomenon more deeply here as a design requirement.

One of the most debated topics in psychology and artificial intelligence is the subject of *qualia* and identifying what it is. It is mainly because many of us readily conflate our experiential phenomenon (a.k.a. *qualia*) with what we know of as reality.

First, every aspect of *qualia* we experience has nothing to do with reality.

It is a problematic fact for many to comprehend, and even though we've touched upon this topic earlier, let's unpack it to explain this as simply as possible from our experiences and perspectives.

When we position our eyes to look upward into the sky and see the color we know as blue, the color we know as blue is merely a narrow range of the electromagnetic spectrum.

One of the physical characteristics of the electromagnetic spectrum is that it exists all around us. We can measure it in terms of wavelength, usually in units ranging from nanometers to kilometers. The part of the spectrum that is visible to us is pretty tiny, just the wavelengths that are between 380 to 700 nanometers.

Below that range is a vast array of wavelengths we know as gamma rays, x-rays, and ultraviolet light, while above is a narrow band of longer wavelengths that are visible as other colors and a vast array of wavelengths we know as infrared, microwaves, radar, radio, and the broadcast band.

The color we perceive as blue is among the shortest wavelengths we can detect, starting with indigo starting at a wavelength of 380 nanometers and blue having a wavelength of 480 nanometers.

So, when our eyes receive light having a wavelength of 480 nanometers, our *neuroglia* help give us the illusion of blue light. The operative word here is 'illusion.'

When a blue ball is thrown at us and strikes us, we feel it strike us. However, the tactile sensation of it striking us is also an illusion.

Yes, the fact it struck you is indisputable, but the sensation itself is not.

If the ball strikes us with sufficient force, we conclude it hurts. However, that pain is also an illusion.

Yes, the blue ball as an object is real in that it has a size and mass, and the light that reflects off its surface has a wavelength of 480 nanometers, but how we perceive the ball and how it feels when it strikes us is all an illusion.

These illusions are our interpretation of the hormones, chemicals, and signals that *neuroglia* cause within the body.

These illusions are all part of a capability we refer to as imagination. Our glial cells imagine an experience that is supposed to represent the environment and the things that comprise it, at least to the extent our sensory organs can support, which is somewhat limited.

C. elegans, a nematode equipped with a few *neuroglial* cells and a nerve cord, has no neural bundle or brain whatsoever. It represents the first level of consciousness to have experiential phenomena. It is the first to experience *qualia*.

What does that *qualia* feel like?

While we cannot know the answer to this question, since we have *neuroglial* cells that are distant descendants of those of the phylum *Nematoda*, we can speculate that it can be somewhat like the primitive forms of *qualia* we experience.

To support *qualia* and the notion of illusory interpretations of *recognizable features* as being within the range of recognizable streams of stimuli that the sensory organs of the phylum *Nematoda*, we will need to develop one or more foundational components needed to support an imagination.

This primitive form of imagination must create an illusion of sensations that depict a fundamental interpretation of one or more *recognizable features*.

NERVE CORD CONSCIOUSNESS CAPABILITIES – CONCEPTUAL DESIGN

We continue to build upon much of what has preceded.

The incremental design components to address here include the advancements of sensory organs, enhanced learning capabilities, interpretation of stimuli, importance determination, *freedom of attention*, *will*, *action*, and a fundamental imagination to address the illusory capabilities of *neuroglial* cells.

To address the sensory advancements of *C. elegans* (i.e., nematode), we now need to include sensory devices capable of operating within the range and tolerance of *Nematodes* for light, tactile capabilities, temperature, osmotic pressure, tiny amounts of electrical current, and airborne vibrations.

In addition, we need chemical sensors capable of detecting excitatory neurotransmitters to support related behaviors.

To address the improvements in learning capabilities, we must introduce more advanced neural networks and machine learning techniques available in artificial intelligence technologies.

The improvements need to support highly plastic behavior (a.k.a. quick learning abilities), including associative (i.e., classical conditioning like with Pavlov, operant conditioning based on reward and punishment, non-associative or habituation, which is desensitizing with repetition, and sensitization which is sensitizing with repetition.

The incremental conceptual design for interpreting stimuli pertains to the effects of glial cells that help create those illusions.

The illusions created are limited to the interpretations of *recognized features* within *Nematoda*. As we will discuss in the conceptual design of a fundamental imagination, there are different ways that a conceptual design can support these requirements.

The key takeaway from this section is that there will be at least one additional layer of interpretation of *recognized features* that represents the illusory effects that manifest within the imagination.

Regarding *importance determination*, the incremental conceptual design has to do with the effects introduced by *glial* cells creating illusions, as the illusions themselves have an additional influence on the importance of *recognizable features* to repeat the most pleasurable experiences.

These illusions' influence on *importance determination* may stem from *recognizable features* individually or as aggregates. As this represents the most basic form of *neuroglia*, for this level of *consciousness*, we will assume that these early *neuroglial* cells are limited to creating illusory interpretations for individual *recognizable features*.

For example, suppose multiple recognizable features are simultaneously present.

> *In that case, the influence of the illusion itself will be limited to its additional effect upon importance determination based upon the illusory manifestation of the multiple recognizable features individually rather than as a composition that combines them.*

> *In simple terms that we can more easily relate to, it is one thing having an experience viewing different items of food individually, such*

as a freshly baked loaf of bread, versus having an experience also viewing them as a bakery, market, or feast.

The distinction that *qualia* add is that *recognizable features* become an influence based on the pleasantness or unpleasantness of the illusory experience, impacting another conceptual thermometer illustrating importance determination.

As one would expect, this will also influence *freedom of attention*.

Hence, the incremental conceptual design supporting *freedom of attention* includes the '*importance determination*' for the illusory effects of *neuroglial* cells that influence levels of importance for *recognizable features* with degrees of pleasantness or unpleasantness.

Likewise, the incremental conceptual design supporting *freedom of will* includes *importance determination* for the illusory effects of *neuroglial* cells that influence the importance of *recognizable features* for degrees of pleasantness or unpleasantness.

Regarding *freedom of action*, the effects of glial cells should be minimal. The illusory interpretation of stimuli should not influence the ability to enact the volitions one wants, at least not directly.

Additionally, this is the first time *freedom of action* includes the ability of neurons to perform calculations and have neurotransmitter signal routing volitions.

As the number, type, and configuration of neurons increase, this form of *freedom of action* at the cellular level of neurons will influence consciousness more, particularly as the number of *neuroglia* expands around advanced layers of neurons.

NERVE CORD CONCEPTUAL DESIGN – BASIC IMAGINATION

In this framework, the introduction of *qualia* corresponds to the emergence of a primitive imagination.

Even a fundamental imagination plays a significant role in supporting *qualia* and influences many intellectual functions, such as improvements in learning and coordination across sensory organs.

Our conceptual design of imagination is much like a 3-D holographic audiovisual space that adds a tactile dimension, such as wind, moisture, and vibration, much like a virtual reality system, such as Oculus or Quest, with additional environmental factors added, including scent and taste.

The intent is to establish a conceptual design that will readily support an interface to allow humans to experience the imagination corresponding to each level of *consciousness* in the framework.

This way, the data format within the imagination can include the same as modern commercial formats for storing and transmitting data, including audiovisual, temperature, or barometric data. Using these formats makes it relatively seamless for humans to experience the contents of the imagination corresponding to each level of *consciousness* shared by our artificial organisms or beings as we work our way up through each successive level of *consciousness*.

However, to build it properly, we must work through each successive step in the same way that each level of *consciousness* does, from the bottom up. Some call this incremental process: crawl, walk, and run.

Recall our chapter on the ear and hearing and how the inner ear leverages vibrations of distinct frequencies into electrical impulses. These electrical impulses representing different frequencies are then processed through different sets of neurons, as is their sequence and temporal data (a.k.a. timing and duration) and amplitude.

Even though the processing of these stimuli is separate, they are eventually integrated back together again by the imagination as a unified interpretation. As organisms become more advanced, consciousness automatically fills in many missing parts to render a complete interpretation.

Our visual system works in much the same way. Our sensory organs, comprised of rods and cones, only perceive certain features of the actual visual landscape, such as edges, angles, and distinct frequencies of light. The processing of these stimuli is separate and will only be integrated downstream by the imagination as an interpretation.

The conceptual design of the fundamental imagination for *Nematoda* represents the starting point for what eventually becomes a highly advanced imagination that can support the successive levels of *consciousness*.

The ability to render the integrated interpretation in the same format as modern commercial formats for storing and transmitting audiovisual data will allow us to experience how each of our organisms perceives their environment in the areas where the imagination of the organism can overlap with our own.

> *For example, if an organism can perceive vibrations outside our range of hearing, we would need to alter the frequencies to facilitate some degree of perception of those vibrations for ourselves.*

The remaining issue is determining how to design the experiential aspects of the fundamental imagination to mirror that of nematodes. It is one thing for a unified imagination to re-integrate the many stimuli as data, but it is another to determine how nematodes experience that integrated view.

Given the specification details of *C. elegans* sensory organs, it may not be safe to assume that the experience is a severely downgraded version of our own. Still, the issue of supporting experiential phenomenon is yet to come.

To this aim, since all experiential phenomena are an artificial interpretation, we can also imagine that the experiential phenomenon of the phylum *Nematoda* can be an interpretation that we can programmatically render as detailed as we wish.

In other words, we get to choose how much and what types of data we can fill in to compensate for any gaps in the streams of stimuli from each sensory organ. We also get to choose how to interpret the complete integrated rendition of stimuli as an experience.

Remember that there is no physical experience of hotness or coldness, lightness or darkness, quietness or noisiness, or tastiness or tastelessness. Hence, we can create any interpretation of these phenomena we want.

Perhaps for convenience, we can start with the interpretations we are familiar with, namely our own, including the variances resulting from genetic influences.

To summarize the conceptual design of *Nerve Cord Consciousness*, it positioned the biosphere for the emergence of many new animal species equipped with a centralized neural expressway that led to the emergence of neural bundles and the formation of numerous specialized collections of neurons.

Equally important is the emergence of *neuroglia* that collaborated with neurons to create the illusion of experience. It paved the way for streams of stimuli to create a fabricated rendition of the environment.

At some point, an interpretation of a narrow portion of the electromagnetic spectrum became the experience of light, and then, in some species, select frequencies became the experience of color.

Similarly, at some point, an interpretation of kinetic energy became the experience of warmth and cold, while tactile signals became the experience of touch.

Likewise, at some point, an interpretation of chemical signals became the experience of taste and smell. And the interpretation of vibrations became the experience of sounds. Each of these fabricated interpretations is a psychological experience.

These fabricated interpretations are relatively attainable, primarily because they are genuinely fabricated and not actual, and they all live in the imagination.

Many of us have read that creating the sensation of experience is the holy grail of artificial intelligence, and it appears to be beyond our technological grasp. But is it?

Intellectually, we understand that the sensation of experience is an illusion. Yet we are confused by feeling each of these illusions.

Yet, these experiences are far from perfect.

We can see things that are not present in the environment and not see things that are present. We can taste or smell something appealing, yet it can harm us. We can feel cold when physically we are dangerously overheated. We can feel pain when we are unharmed. We can feel emotions that are false interpretations of reality.

But as imperfect as experiences may be, whether pleasant or unpleasant, we hold onto what we know as our experiences as if they were real. However, none of these experiences are there in any sense with the physical universe.

The blue waters and green leaves we experience in our mind's eye are not actual. The secondary emotions we experience when experiencing blue water and green leaves are also unreal. But in the end, we know we experience and feel them; therefore, they must be real.

We can appreciate the various flavors we experience in a small sip of wine. We can appreciate the notes and chords of musical tones. We can appreciate the artistry of a fine painting. And we can appreciate appreciation's effects on our mind and body; most of it is a fabricated illusion.

Why most, not all?

Even though the experiential phenomenon is a fabricated illusion, there are at least two types of aftereffects.

One aftereffect is that one experiential phenomenon often leads to another, creating a chain of fabricated illusions.

Another aftereffect is that one experiential phenomenon, anywhere in the chain, can manifest itself as a physical effect within the body. These physical changes may include a change in heart rate, blood pressure, eye dilation, or involuntary muscle contractions.

The physical effects that occur in response to experiential phenomena represent a physical manifestation that can extend the chain of fabricated illusions and physical effects.

Reproducing a chain reaction of downstream psychological and physical effects is undoubtedly attainable.

In addition, creating the illusion of experience is a requirement that starts with *Type Four Qualia* (a.k.a. *neuroglia qualia*) in *Nematoda*. As a result, let's explore exactly how far we can take this capability that has science so thoroughly baffled.

This illusion of experience has multiple components. To explore this, let's consider the sense of taste in humans and *Nematoda*.

Humans know that our sense of smell influences our sense of taste. Both senses involve chemical sensors with different capabilities for what they can detect.

In ourselves, taste is limited to sweet, salty, sour, bitter, and savory (a.k.a. umami).

The brain structure known as the gustatory cortex supports the sensory organs that detect these chemical structures. The size of the molecules primarily influences the speed with which sensory organs can process chemical structures. The smaller the molecule, the more rapidly it can be detected.

> *In wine tasting, molecule size influences the sequence of flavors, with the flavor of the smallest molecules occurring first and the largest last.*

To paraphrase Kobayashi in the 2006 book published by Elsevier Publishers, *Functional Organization of the Human Gustatory Cortex*:

> *The gustatory cortex comprises the anterior insula and frontal operculum (a.k.a. AI/FO). The neurons in the AI/FO respond to sweetness, saltiness, sourness, and bitterness, including their concentration levels.*

> *[Functional Organization of the Human Gustatory Cortex, 2006, Kobayashi M – Department of Physiology, Osaka City University, Graduate School of Medicine, Osaka, Japan; Journal of Oral Biosciences, Elsevier Publishers, Volume 48, Issue 4]*

Not surprisingly, like our auditory system with neurons dedicated to specific vibration frequencies, sensory neurons are also dedicated to specific taste categories (i.e., sweet, salty, sour, bitter, and umami).

To quote the 2014 NIH article, *Smell Disorders*: Quote.

> *"Each olfactory neuron has one odor receptor. Microscopic molecules released by substances around us—whether it's coffee brewing or pine trees in a forest—stimulate these receptors. Once the neurons detect the molecules, they send messages to your brain, which identifies the smell. There are more smells in the environment than there are receptors, and any given molecule may stimulate a combination of receptors, creating a unique representation in the brain. These representations are registered by the brain as a particular smell." End Quote.*

> *[Smell Disorders, Updated April 2014, NIH Pub. No. 14-3231, NIH National Institute on Deafness and Other Communication Disorders, 31 Center Drive, MSC 2320, Bethesda, MD USA 20892-2320, https://www.nidcd.nih.gov/health/smell-disorders#:~:text=Each%20 olfactory%20neuron%20has%20one,brain%2C%20which%20 identifies%20the%20smell.]*

The science of taste is surprisingly mathematical, with theories that point to the effects of various concentrations of categories of flavor as well as their sequence and timing.

In our framework, neuronal interactions stimulate *neuroglia* not only to render the illusion of an experience of taste but also to create the illusion that the location of that experience is where the sensory organs are in the mouth, as opposed to in the brain's substructures responsible for processing the sensory signals some distance away.

The point here is that everything about *qualia* is an illusion. Yet, even though the experience is an entirely fabricated illusion, the illusion is based on actual chemicals in the environment that come in physical contact with our sensory organs.

Do these chemicals taste the way that they do in reality?

No, of course not.

In physical reality, there is no taste, never mind the taste that certain chemicals evoke within our imaginations or the imaginations of other eukaryotic forms of life.

Returning to our *Nematoda*, recall, *C. elegans* has a total of 302 neurons comprised of a small number of neuron types with four sensory neurons, a small collection of first and second-layer interneurons, a small collection of command neurons, a ventral cord of motor neurons, and the first forms of *neuroglia* (a.k.a. glia, glial cells).

Though the number of possible molecules that nematodes can detect is relatively few, they can detect more than 100 molecular compounds from a variety of chemical classes, including alcohols, ketones, esters, aldehydes, and aromatics, some of which attract while others repel the animal.

> *For example, Nematodes can detect a simple terpene named prenol, which, to a nematode, is an odor that is repulsive because it indicates that the insect encountered is already infected, indicating that no nutrients remain.*
>
> *However, to humans, the odor of prenol is pleasant and used in some perfumes.*

As we can see, the experience of prenol is different for nematodes and humans. Hence, the most crucial aspect of an experience is whether it tends to be pleasant or unpleasant in correlation with whether it is favorable or unfavorable to the organism as an aid to survival.

There are always exceptions where something pleasant is unfavorable to the organism's well-being. However, the general rule holds that most pleasant experiences are favorable, and unpleasant experiences are unfavorable to the organism's well-being.

Can the hardware and software of an artificial organism fabricate an illusion of pleasant and unpleasantness in an artificial organism?

The answer is yes. The combination of hardware and software is the only way to fabricate any illusion, especially on a scale that *neuroglia* supports.

To quote R. Douglas Fields and Beth Stevens-Graham in their 2002 NIH article, *New Insights into Neuron-Glia Communication*: Quote.

"In contrast to the serial flow of information along chains of neurons, glia communicates with other glial cells through intracellular calcium waves and via intercellular diffusion of chemical messengers. By releasing neurotransmitters and other extracellular signaling molecules, glia can affect neuronal excitability and synaptic transmission and perhaps coordinate activity across networks of neurons." End Quote.

[New Insights into Neuron-Glia Communication, Oct 18, 2002, R. Douglas Fields and Beth Stevens-Graham, US National Library of Medicine National Institutes of Health, PMC1226318, https://www. ncbi.nlm.nih.gov/pmc/articles/PMC1226318/]

A GLIMPSE INTO CREATING A PSYCHOLOGICAL STATE IN NERVE CORD CONSCIOUSNESS

Imitating a psychological state within a computer-based organism can leverage many mechanisms that have evolved in the biosphere, such as releasing ions, chemical messengers, neurotransmitters, and extracellular signaling molecules used by *neuroglia*.

Every ion, chemical messenger, neurotransmitter, and extracellular signaling molecule has a chemical formula. Our artificial nematode's *neuroglia* can release digital quantities of the desired combination of chemical formulae into the signal stream for ingestion by other 'automated' *neuroglia* and neurons in the immediate vicinity.

Upon ingesting this electronic stimulus, other cells can use neural network technology to pattern-match the combination of chemical formulae in the quantities received and respond with their streams of stimuli.

In this manner, streams of stimuli generated from our artificial chemicals, in turn, can create their cascade of downstream effects as appropriate, thus causing a relatively endless stream of interactions.

It then serves as a sort of inner voice for the nervous system where certain parts of the nervous system interact with certain other parts in the near-perpetual balance that participates with consciousness.

FIFTH LEVEL REVISITED (NEURAL BUNDLE CONSCIOUSNESS)

NEURAL BUNDLE REQUIREMENTS

We are taking the conceptual design part of our journey to *Neural Bundle Consciousness* to address a requirement that will allow us to introduce an essential reusable function that supports many capabilities among the more advanced forms of consciousness.

The neural bundle of the honeybee is sufficiently advanced to be organized into three regions: a protocerebrum, deutocerebrum, and tritocerebrum. This more advanced insect brain coincides with two significant advancements: active communication among individuals and the emergence of complex social behaviors that are multigenerational.

In the end, this means that the honeybee, particularly the worker honeybee, performs several tasks to support their role. However, they are not born into a set of tasks that they perform during their lifetime. Instead, the set of tasks they perform is age-dependent.

According to the American Bee Journal in their 2015 article, *The Tasks of a Worker Honey Bee*, this phenomenon is known as *temporal polyethism*, where *temporal* refers to time, *poly* refers to many, and *ethism* refers to behaviors.

The set of tasks tends to follow a chronological order, though they can skip tasks. Of particular interest is that they spend a portion of their time looking for things that need doing within the colony.

Inside the hive, a new adult will perform cell cleaning, capping, brood and queen tending, comb building, cleaning, and handling food.

To paraphrase Jaime Ellis in the American Bee Journal in their 2015 article, *The Tasks of a Worker Honey Bee*:

> *The young worker bees polish and clean cells between two and sixteen days of age.*

> *Starting from the rear of the cell and working forward, they remove any cocoons and excreta left by previous cell occupants, repair any damage to the cell walls with a thin layer of wax, and polish the cell walls.*

> *These tasks prepare the cell for its next occupant, which, when seeded with an egg and food, will be capped with a thicker layer of wax to protect the egg as it matures and eventually hatches.*

> *[The Tasks of a Worker Honey Bee, 2015, Jaime Ellis, The American Bee Journal,* https://americanbeejournal.com/the-tasks-of-a-worker-honey-bee/*]*

NEURAL BUNDLE CONSCIOUSNESS CAPABILITIES - CONCEPTUAL DESIGN

While we continue to build upon earlier levels of consciousness, we must introduce a new conceptual design function to support the behaviors of the genus *Apis*.

If we recall the artificial intelligence chapter on generative artificial intelligence, we encountered vectors, vector databases, LLMs (large language models), RAGs, and embeddings.

Embeddings are a way to capture meaning, such as the topology of a graph and the meaning of relationships between nodes (vertexes) on a graph, by encoding information into a graph vector.

Although there are many types of embeddings, at a high level, there are two types: node (vertex) embeddings that transform a node into a distinct vector and graph embeddings that transform an entire graph into a single vector.

The graph may be mathematically simple, like a cartesian plane of two dimensions that is easy to visualize, or it can be complex, consisting of hundreds of dimensions.

Here, we can introduce a new reusable algorithm, stimuli2vec, which will rapidly recognize stimuli segments to help influence a task's importance.

We introduce this vector-based capability here because, unlike previous levels of consciousness, *Neural Bundle Consciousness* must tackle a more comprehensive array of stimuli that generates more highly varied behaviors.

For example, the honeybee represents the first level of consciousness that must support memorizing a flight path and translating that flight path into dance movements.

Other honeybees must memorize the dance movements and translate them into flight instructions.

Here, the algorithm will recognize the dance movements from various angles and relate them to a series of flight instructions.

Whether it is a stream of data representing an image or a sound, the pattern will invariably correlate with vectors already in its database. When those vectors have a meaning associated with them, albeit semantic, then that meaning can raise or lower the importance associated with the following task the honeybee should perform.

FAST FORWARD (HOMO CONSCIOUSNESS AND BEYOND)

HOMO CONSCIOUSNESS REQUIREMENTS

We will fast forward to *Homo Consciousness* to take a glimpse into how we will address software levels of *consciousness*. It is here that we begin to develop software layers that support successively more advanced levels of consciousness.

Whether *Meditative Consciousness, Compartmentalized Consciousness*, or any other software-based level of consciousness, here we encounter a requirement to program ourselves.

In *Meditative* and *Compartmentalized Consciousness,* we must add software to help filter out unwanted thoughts. Also, in *Meditative Consciousness,* we need to add software to support additional aspects of meditation to help manage our focus and volition.

Eventually, we will also need to add software to support the *freedom of emotion, mind, thought,* and *paradigm.* The challenge is how we will create a framework that will facilitate the generation of software that can readily integrate into the *conscious* and *subconscious* levels of the mind.

HOMO CONSCIOUSNESS AND BEYOND – CONCEPTUAL DESIGN

Again, we build upon earlier levels of consciousness. But here, we need some additional things to support our newest conceptual design function to support our artificially conscious creation of programming itself.

First, we need a software architecture that allows adding, modifying, and removing additional programs. At a high level, we can design application program interfaces or APIs. An API is a location in a program where it can call another program to do something customized to meet some additional requirement not previously known.

The somewhat more formal version of this is an API gateway.

An API gateway is software that accepts a request for a function, routes the request to one or more backend services, completes the function, and returns to wherever the request originated. In addition, a gateway may capture statistics, create analytics, and provide security services.

For our purposes, we will need the ability to capture statistics and perform subsequent analysis.

Second, we need the ability to generate and move programs into a backend services library. These are programs that our generative AI will create on demand.

However, in addition to these programs, our generative AI must generate acceptance criteria to help evaluate new backend services. Depending on the score, the generative AI may need to modify or regenerate the backend service.

Third, to support the ability of the generative AI to generate functions and their acceptance criteria, we will need an extensive set of examples that can train our generative AI. A large body of examples serves as the foundation for the AI model to learn from to create new programs and acceptance criteria with the necessary characteristics and level of quality.

Ultimately, generative artificial intelligence is an essential component supporting our notion of a self-organizing system.

This chapter offers a glimpse into the conceptual design of our initial levels of hardware-based *consciousness* and a portion of the more advanced software-based levels.

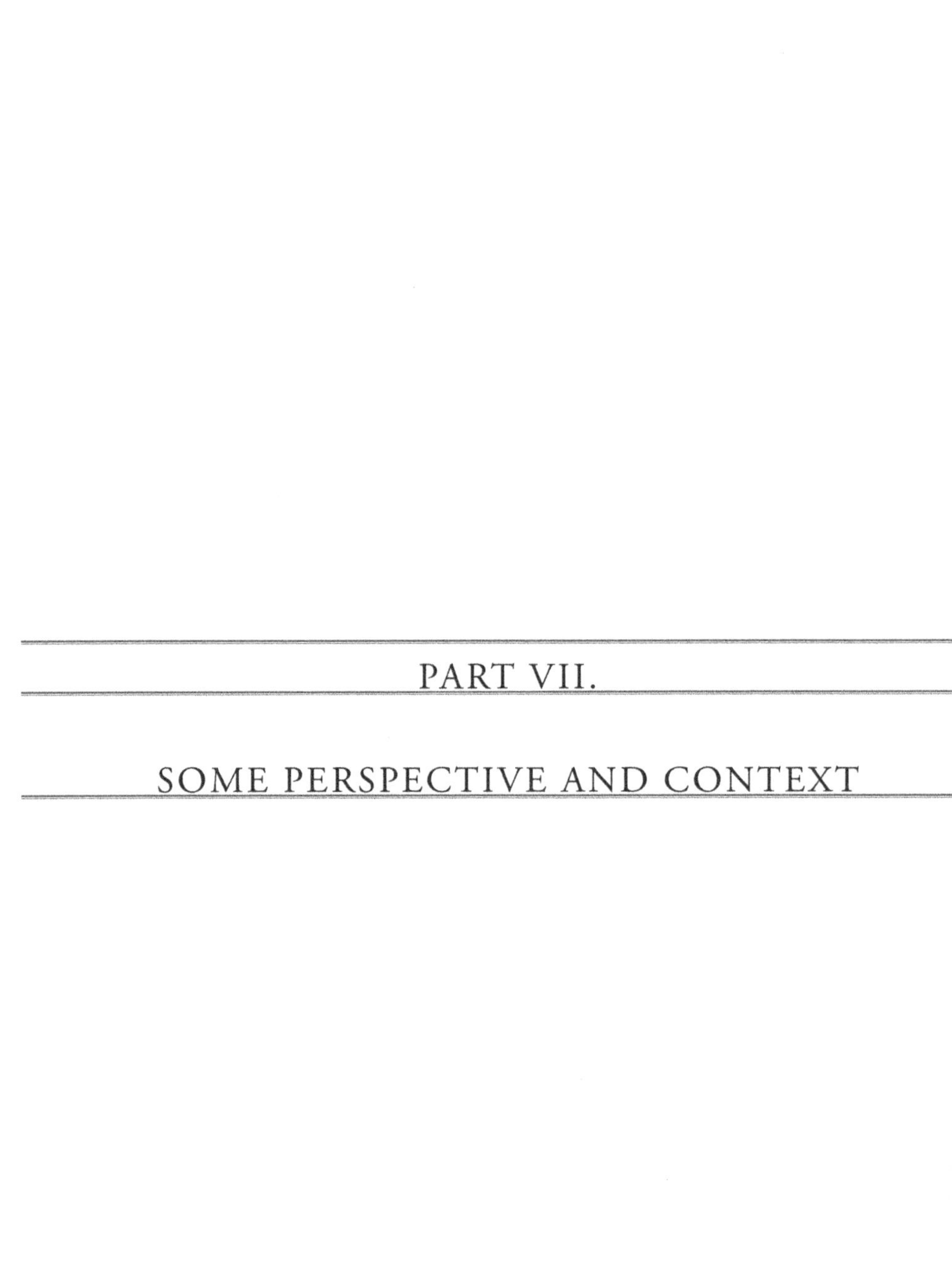

PART VII.

SOME PERSPECTIVE AND CONTEXT

CONSCIOUSNESS IN PERSPECTIVE

Our journey into *consciousness* represents a perspective that differs significantly from the most vocal neuroscientists who serially publish their views on this subject.

My goal is that this journey will help motivate and prepare you to continue the journey in your own way to evaluate and organize your thoughts and ideas on the subject.

Perhaps the most important takeaway is that the reader has a framework of ideas and concepts to start from that may prove helpful in many ways. Some of these ideas we've shared may even be helpful in our day-to-day lives.

Other ideas may allow some to reflect on how they want to proceed with their lives, both in how they interact with others and in their direction, potentially adjusting how they spend their spare time learning, reading, writing, creating, and thinking.

I hope you agree that this journey can also influence one's views regarding oneself, our role in life, our family, our culture, humanity, life on Earth, and the fate that awaits all our descendants.

Let's recap our time together.

In <u>Part One</u>, we began by exploring how ancient people understood consciousness and thought about it from the dawn of written history.

For additional perspective, we saw where life began with prokaryotes.

We climbed the stepping stones from prokaryotes, where *consciousness* originated with eukaryotic life. Our first step into *consciousness* began with single-cell eukaryotes (i.e., *unicellular consciousness*) and the most advanced unicellular organism known to science, *Paramecium caudatum*, which can learn.

Our second stepping stone was *multicellular consciousness, Mimosa pudica* (a.k.a. sensitive plant), with another eukaryote belonging to the plant kingdom also possessing an ability to learn.

The third stepping stone was our exploration of *nerve net consciousness.*

It marked the first appearance of neurons in the phylum *Cnidarian,* focusing on jellyfish, where we chose the most advanced species, *Tripedalia cystophora* (box jellyfish).

The box jellyfish has no fewer than twenty-four eyes of four different types, grouped in six clusters on the four sides of their bell, with each cluster including a pair of eyes already equipped with a sophisticated lens, retina, iris, and cornea.

Our fourth stepping stone, *nerve cord consciousness*, saw the emergence of bilaterians, where a long line of organisms developed a left and right side that mirror one another, stemming from a common marine wormlike ancestor of some 600 million years ago.

Again, we selected the most advanced species, *C. elegans,* within the phylum *Nematoda*, class *Rhabditda*, family *Rhabditdae*, and genus *Caenorhabditis*.

The importance of this stepping stone is that the first forms of *neuroglial* cells emerged with *Nematoda*. With it, the fundamental imagination emerged as *neuroglial* cells paved the way to fabricate an artificial interpretation of the stimuli sent from the organism's sensory nodes.

Our fifth stepping stone, *neural bundle consciousness*, marked a leap in intellectual capabilities with the genus *Apis* (a.k.a. honeybee).

It saw the emergence of communication between individual organisms, including a vocabulary, conceptualization, a sense of time, object use, social behaviors, and the early primitive emotion of becoming agitated.

Equipped with a vast array of sensory types, the genus *Apis* expands upon a fundamental imagination supporting a rich fabrication of reality that includes colors, specifically yellow, blue-green, violet, ultraviolet, and 'bee's purple,' a mixture of yellow and ultraviolet.

Worker bees have a probiscis (i.e., straw-like tongue) equipped with taste buds that distinguish between sweet, sour, bitter, and salt.

Our sixth stepping stone, *primitive brain consciousness*, marks the emergence of the brain. Appearing first in marine invertebrates, the brain's overall structure became fully organized in the vertebrate phylum *Chordata* subphylum *Vertebrata* (e.g., chordates with backbones), numbering about 69,300 species.

Here, we selected the class *Reptilia* equipped with a primitive brain where the term 'brain' is defined as an organ (i.e., a group of tissues adapted to support a functional capability). The first brain began by fusing polyganglionic neurons divided into protocerebrum, deutocerebrum, and tritocerebrum.

In *Reptilia*, we see many early structures of the mammalian brain. Though the mammalian brain did not evolve from *Reptilia*, they share an extinct amniote ancestor (i.e., *synapsids,* a.k.a. *theropsids*) that lent *Reptilia* many of the same brain tissues present in mammals. Likewise, we also see the evolution of more specialized types of *neuroglia*.

The primitive brain supports an initial form of dreaming (i.e., REM sleep) and an active imagination while sleeping. Another advancement is that this stepping stone supports a set of emotions, including sexual attraction, fear, aggressiveness, and social status.

Our seventh stepping stone was *mammalian consciousness*. The first mammals were soft-shell egg-laying organisms that evolved approximately 225 million years ago (mya). Then, at about 160 mya, a marsupial branch emerged, creating placental mammals.

Though the definition of mammals in biology is vertebrates having mammary glands that produce milk in females for feeding their newborns, here we are concerned with the advancement of the brain with a significant increase in neural layering, numbering between fifteen to twenty specialized cortical areas.

The example we chose was the genus *Rattus* for its extreme levels of awareness and curiosity, high levels of object use, significant advancements in memory and learning, the development of a complete dreaming pattern, and the emergence of empathy-driven behavior.

Our eighth stepping stone, *primate consciousness*, marks a leap in communication skills, demonstrating three of the four design components of language. At their peak, primates can achieve a language competency equivalent to that of a three-year-old human child, though with little or no understanding of grammar.

Here, we have chosen the species *Pan troglodytes* (a.k.a. *'common chimpanzee'*) of the genus *Pan*. The genus Pan demonstrates an ability to learn American Sign Language (ASL), and can learn approximately 350 signs of ASL and can unassisted teach a child chimpanzee some signs.

[Teaching Sign Language to Chimpanzees, 1989, R. Allen Gardner, Beatrix T. Gardner, Thomas E. Van Cantfort, State University of New York, State University of New York Press]

[The Study of Signed Languages, 2002, David F. Armstrong, Michael A. Karchmer, John Vickrey Can Cleve, Gallaudet University Press, Washington, D.C.]

[Attitudes to Animals, 1999, Francine L. Dolins, Cambridge University Press, Cambridge, UK]

Likewise, Dr. Francine Patterson of Stanford University taught a female Western lowland gorilla approximately 1,000 Gorilla Sign Language (GSL) signs, similar to American Sign Language (ASL), and understood approximately 2,000 English words.

[Francine Patterson Ph.D. psychology, Stanford University, Stanford, CA]

Pan also demonstrates complex social behaviors, self-recognition, lucid dreaming (i.e., becoming aware of oneself in the dream), and a keen ability to deceive. *Pan* also makes the transition from object use to fabricating tools.

On a physical level, *Primates* continue developing more brain subregions, neuronal layers, neural circuits, neuronal cell types, and *neuroglial* cell types.

Our ninth stepping stone, *Homo consciousness*, marks the most recent step in our journey based solely on advancements in physical hardware with a significant increase in brain mass. The brain of *Homo sapiens* has more neuronal tissue layers, distinct subdivisions with over 200 areas in the neocortex, many more neuronal circuits, higher neuron density, and a significant increase in the types of neuronal cells and *neuroglial* cells.

Among the ten species of the genus *Homo*, only *Homo sapiens* survive though *Homo neanderthalensis* overlapped and interacted with *Homo sapiens*. With *Homo sapiens,* we see the emergence of the learned cultural construct of spoken and, eventually, written language.

Even with all its ambiguities when shared with others, language facilitated an explosion of shared ideas and knowledge. But more importantly, it helped lay the groundwork for programming the brain with layers of software that augmented how we think and understand the world.

Our tenth stepping stone was *meditative consciousness*. Within our journey, this marks the first software-based step into *consciousness*, which pertains to the discipline of programming oneself.

It is a software layer where an individual learns to direct their *freedom of attention, will*, and *action* as an observer to tame their relentless stream of thoughts from the subconscious.

Our eleventh stepping stone, *reason-driven consciousness*, is a learned process that extends the programming of oneself to distill out the emotional effects upon one's thoughts. Reasoning facilitates using any of several disciplines belonging to logical reasoning, including detecting contradictions.

Our twelfth stepping stone, *persona consciousness*, relates to roles. Behavioral roles emerged with neural bundles and expanded with primitive brains to include roles involving one's status within a group. Roles further expanded with the mammalian brain to include new roles for members of herds, packs, prides, and family relationships.

The primate brain saw another expansion of societal roles that exploded with the *Homo* brain as the variety of societal roles skyrocketed. However, this level of software expanded the ability of an individual to create new roles on demand beyond societal roles to meet ad-hoc requirements.

Our thirteenth stepping stone, *compartmentalized consciousness*, emerged as a defense mechanism to control cognitive dissonance involving incompatible systems of thought, such as incompatible beliefs, value systems, emotions, or ideas.

We learned how unconscious compartmentalization permits conflicting thoughts that would otherwise cause cognitive dissonance to co-exist by inhibiting direct or explicit acknowledgment and interaction between the compartmentalized self-states.

In contrast, conscious compartmentalization is an extension of this defense mechanism to either help manage one's focus to enhance productivity on a task or to help manage one's focus to protect information not permitted for sharing outside a given compartment.

Our fourteenth stepping stone was *in-the-moment consciousness*. It can be surprisingly difficult for many who focus incessantly on something that happened in the past or on something in one's imagined future.

A learned skill, *in-the-moment consciousness,* sets one's focus precisely on the present. Upon achieving *in-the-moment consciousness*, interactions with others significantly improve as other individuals sense the rare experience of someone fully and intensely focusing on them without distraction.

Our fifteenth stepping stone marked the first in the sequence of paradigms, starting with *Level Zero* paradigmatic *consciousness*, where individuals become entrapped with zero paradigms representing their self-interest. Once entrapped, individuals require assistance from a third party to re-establish a paradigm that includes one's self-interests.

Our sixteenth stepping stone is the second in the sequence of paradigms, *Level One paradigmatic consciousness*. All humans start constructing their one base paradigm with rules to interpret all sensory stimuli, including which ones to focus on and their relative importance.

Our seventeenth stepping stone, the third in the sequence of paradigms, is *Level Two paradigmatic consciousness*. Attaining *Level Two paradigmatic consciousness* provides an awareness of paradigms starting with one's own and occasionally the paradigm of another.

Here, we began to see the power paradigms can unleash upon oneself and others with the differences between productive, egoistic, problematic, and evil *Level Twos*. Even though we could dedicate an entire book to the behaviors of *Level Two* individuals, we have painted the broad strokes that convey the basics to progress along our journey.

Our eighteenth stepping stone, the fourth in the sequence of paradigms, is *Level Three paradigmatic consciousness*. This level of *consciousness* emerges only when the individual realizes that paradigms can be destroyed and reconstructed. Having experienced the reconstruction process, these individuals soon realize they can construct alternative paradigms on demand.

Soon, the *Level Three* individual learns that multiple paradigms can coexist simultaneously. Upon realizing many interpretations simultaneously, the enlightened *Level Three* will eventually learn to choose the most constructive interpretation.

Our nineteenth stepping stone of consciousness, *Level Four paradigmatic consciousness*, is the fifth and final in the sequence of paradigms.

This level of consciousness is achievable through metta meditation, which is a genuine concern for the well-being of others by tapping into a spiritual realm of consciousness that softens the boundaries of 'Me.'

This level of consciousness belongs to one of the learned levels associated with the mind's software, and sufficiently affects the brain's hardware in ways that neuroscience can physically detect.

> *I practice this level of consciousness regularly regarding individuals I naturally dislike until I no longer dislike them.*

Our twentieth stepping stone is *Buddhist consciousness* (a.k.a. *primordial wakefulness*). Though this level of *consciousness* is achievable by relatively few experts worldwide, it is reportedly the closest we can ever get to experiencing actual reality.

As such an essential step in the journey of *Buddhist consciousness*, it could not be left unmentioned from our consciousness framework.

Our twenty-first stepping stone is *unconscious consciousness*. It is the layer of the mind that is entirely inaccessible to the *conscious* mind and is the only interface in direct contact with physical hardware of the body. It supports the interface with every sensory node and muscle fiber in and about the body.

Only present in organisms possessing a brain, its primary role is to offload work that results from the flood of incoming streams of stimuli that would otherwise overwhelm them and the myriad interactions with the body's muscle fibers.

We designate this as an architectural layer of software for its pre-processing of raw stimuli, message routing, and filtering capabilities.

Our twenty-second stepping stone is *subconscious consciousness*. Another architectural layer, the *subconscious*, performs vast processing supporting many bodily functions below the *conscious* level. Additionally, it pre-processes stimuli and integrates stimuli across sensory organ types.

It performs many roles, such as supporting *compartmentalization*, *personas*, *paradigms*, and their interpretation, without which the *conscious consciousness* level would become overwhelmed.

Our twenty-third stepping stone is *conscious consciousness*. It is the third architectural layer and supports all capabilities an individual is aware of.

The two most prominent capabilities of *conscious consciousness* are one's agency regarding the *conscious* application of freedoms (e.g., *freedom of attention* and *will*) and the imagination.

The illusion facilitated by *neuroglia* centrally manifests itself in the imagination. It expresses the integrated interpretation of stimuli representing one's environment or recalled memories and imagined fantasies.

Our twenty-fourth steppingstone addresses *group consciousness* or group think, was depicted in three different ways by three theories, namely *'r/K Selection Theory'* developed by Robert MacArthur and E.O. Wilson in 1967, *'Affluence Theory'* developed by the British historian Sir John Bagot Glubb, and *'Coddling Theory'* developed by Professor Jonathan Haidt and Greg Lukianoff.

Part One left us with a bright new shiny toolkit, ready to see what we can do.

In <u>Part Two</u>, we set out on the next leg of our journey. Now armed with twenty-four levels of consciousness, we go into how we experience *qualia*.

The body can fabricate an illusion of what our sensory organs perceive as stimuli. But if those sensory organs are defective, we neither get those stimuli nor the illusion they get turned into. Hence, neither a blind nor color-blind individual can ever experience color.

We encountered our first form of *qualia, unicellular qualia*, where eukaryotic cytoskeletal structures fabricate an interpretation of favorable, unfavorable, or indifferent as streams of stimuli enter the cell. We then encountered the second form, *multicellular qualia*, where the experience occurs across adjoining cells.

Next, we engaged a high-speed communications network supported by neurons, which made it possible to share an experience with many non-adjacent cells some distance away, which we termed *neuronal qualia*.

Then, our journey found collections of a new type of cell called *neuroglia* that enriched experience to a whole new level with *neuroglia qualia*. Here, streams of stimuli became fabrications of localized experiences, replacing pleasant, unpleasant, or indifferent with an increased richness of illusion previously unimagined.

The trail then led us to *collective neuroglia neuronal qualia*, where various *neuroglia qualia* are integrated into a broader unified experience as new types of individual *neuroglia* cells physically reach across a greater expanse to other collections of *neuroglia* and neurons to create a unified imagination.

Together, *neuroglia* and neurons increased vastly in the number of cells that could create psychological states and illusions by leveraging many chemical mechanisms available to the body that tied experience to bodily responses, causing yet additional experiences in a chain reaction.

Then, we explored how experiences are fabricated differently among individuals based on their genetics. We saw how the taste sense varies with gene variations and how males and females sense colors differently.

We then looked more deeply into one of the fascinating parts of a cell, the cytoskeletal structure comprised of microtubules, intermediate filaments, and microfilaments, including how cytoskeletal structures use vesicles to transport specialized materials within the cell.

We explored the types of vesicles and the types of materials they transport, such as enzymes, co-factors, peptides, and hormones, and their role in *qualia*.

We then saw how specialized vesicles, called exosomes, travel outside the boundary of cell membranes to many cells and how they chemically communicate with many cells. We saw how they leverage different transport mechanisms, such as the low-speed circulatory system, medium-speed neurons lacking a myelin sheath, and a high-speed communication network supported by neurons equipped with a myelin sheath.

We then crawled into the inner workings of the ear, consisting of an outer ear, middle ear, inner ear, and the three parts of the auditory cortex, namely the primary, secondary, and tertiary auditory cortex.

We concluded this part of our journey by pondering how the characteristics of auditory stimuli, including their frequencies and sequence, can establish meaning.

In <u>Part Three</u>, we continued our journey by further exploring the early linkage and eventual divergence of philosophy and science, noting the decline of philosophy.

We then began to explore the value of philosophy in support of science, starting with some examples of how philosophy can bring perspective, as shown in the interaction of r-individuals and K-individuals as defined by '*r/K Selection Theory.*'

We touched upon the subject of *consciousness* and *free will* and the ability of *free will* to influence our life's path in our choices.

We then challenged the neuroscientist frame of hard determinism, hard indeterminism, soft determinism, and soft indeterminism and explored how quantum computing works.

We followed up by discussing overcoming hardware bias highlighting the learning capabilities of software, such as neural networks. We then equip our *Modern Learning Thermostat* with learning, though it moves it no closer to achieving freedom or consciousness.

Notwithstanding, we provide a spoiler alert that the learning capabilities of software, such as neural networks and machine learning, are essential for supporting *consciousness.*

Our journey then took us through the seven freedoms: *attention, will, action, emotion, mind, thought,* and *paradigm.*

Armed with these definitions, we revisited the twenty-four levels of *consciousness* to determine the emergence point of each freedom. We concluded with the inability of our *Modern Learning Thermostat* to support any form of freedom.

At this point, we questioned whether life can exist without *consciousness.*

We revisited the story of our doctor kneeling beside the unresponsive patient and friend in Part I. Here, the patient is *conscious*, clearly possessing *freedom of attention* and *will*, though lacking *freedom of action*.

We concluded this part of the journey by considering the many types of eukaryotic cells not as fortunate as *Paramecia* that cannot express *freedom of action* to consider their potential for possessing *freedom of attention* and *will*.

In <u>Part Four</u>, we set out anew by defining, exploring, and comparing the concepts of *consciousness, sentience, intelligence, awareness,* and *sapience.*

Here, we established that *sentience* is when the organism possesses *freedom of attention* and *will* to freely choose ideas, opinions, feelings, and tastes. We also noted that *freedom of action* is not required because lacking the ability to enact the volition one wants does not determine whether an organism is *sentient,* as we learned in the previous chapter.

The minimum criterion for *sentience* emerges in *primitive brain consciousness,* where we take a moment to consider the importance of *sentience* in life forms lower and higher than ourselves.

We then consider how perceptions involving *qualia* can be remarkably different when evolving in a different biosphere than our own compared to an extraterrestrial.

Our journey then took us into *intelligence,* which we defined as the ability to acquire and apply knowledge and skills to achieve one's objectives with the proviso that it doesn't undermine the long-term survivability of oneself, one's collective, species, and biosphere.

Here, we learned that *intelligence* could exist with or without *freedom of attention, will, action,* or any ability to choose otherwise.

We learned that the foundation of *intelligence* rests upon *thought,* which is any process that stores, retrieves, or manipulates information in response to stimuli regardless of its source and underlying hardware substrate. Also, the stimuli may originate externally, internally, or both, and the hardware substrate can be biological or non-biological.

It means that when unicellular *Paramecia* detects something within its environment, determines whether it is favorable, unfavorable, or indifferent, and responds to it, at least one rudimentary thought has occurred, such as whether to eat, run, or perhaps to eat and run.

The aspect that makes this a thought, instead of a preprogrammed line of programming, is the concept of understanding.

As such, *Paramecia* understands at a fundamental level that stimuli indicating a predator means its existence is at risk. In this situation, one intelligent response is to flee.

As we progress to higher levels of *consciousness* possessing a physical brain, we see the brain's self-organizing systems delegate its functions to *unconscious, subconscious,* and *conscious* levels.

Next, we defined the *Evolution of Intelligence Argument*, where intelligence could only evolve in the presence of *consciousness* because awareness alone lacks the freedom to grow beyond an initial set of programming, such as the *Modern Learning Thermostat*.

Without the freedom and the ability to choose otherwise, even if equipped with understanding, all *thought* would be limited to ones in which the being could not have thought otherwise. Hence, creative thought could not evolve as all such beings would be limited to non-creative thoughts where they could not think otherwise.

Hence, the *Evolution of Intelligence Argument* means that no matter how aware the *Modern Learning Thermostat* may become, it could never evolve intelligent thought without first being equipped with *consciousness*, which could only be provided by beings already equipped with *consciousness*.

Our journey continued to two thought experiments involving identical intelligent beings equipped with *awareness* but not *consciousness*. Here, we see how difficult it can be to distinguish between an intelligent being equipped with *awareness* versus *consciousness*. However, we also see that an artificially intelligent being can act intelligently equipped only with *awareness*, albeit with 'awareness-related' bug fixes.

Then, a third thought experiment pitted a team of artificially intelligent beings equipped with *awareness* against a team of intelligent humans equipped with *consciousness* in a contest to invent something useful. The humans won the contest, inventing a non-sticky glue, while the artificially intelligent beings and their laboratory were lost in several simultaneous explosions.

As we neared the end of our journey into *intelligence*, we saw how *intelligence* began evolving in partnership with *consciousness* in our first five levels of *consciousness*, beginning with unicellular to neural bundle *consciousness*.

Although distinct concepts, this allowed us to see how the level of *intelligence* invariably increases with a corresponding increase in the levels of *consciousness*.

The next leg of our journey took us to *sapience,* where we learned that to achieve *sapience,* an organism must demonstrate an ability to integrate the *memory of stimuli* and *learning of stimuli* from disparate types of experience and then demonstrate *intelligent* use of those experiences together in some integrated way.

Exploring this, we discussed taking lessons from the history of the Roman Empire and the science of global warming without politics, psychological trickery, or fear-mongering.

We then zeroed in on the frequent use of *common sense* in the definition of *sapience*. Here, we realized how difficult it is to provide concrete examples of *common sense* that do not involve learning. In the end, common sense is simply a vague concept everyone thinks they understand but doesn't.

Finally, we took our knowledge of *sapience* to species other than *Homo sapiens* looking for examples of them demonstrating *sapient* behavior.

To paraphrase Christopher Krupenye in his 2016 article, *Humans aren't special – apes can guess what others are thinking, too*:

> *An example of a sapient skill is to make inferences about what others are thinking, referred to as the 'theory of mind.' Here are closest relatives – chimpanzees, bonobos, gorillas, and orangutans –who have revealed they possess capabilities that rely upon the 'theory of mind.'*
>
> *[Humans aren't special – apes can guess what others are thinking, too, October 6, 2016, Christopher Krupenye – Ph.D. candidate in Evolutionary Anthropology, Duke University]*

Since primates easily qualify as *sapient*, we continued to *Mammalian Consciousness*, where we saw that dolphins demonstrate *sapience* when collaborating to create the illusion of a barrier to capture faster and more agile prey.

Given that mammals easily qualify as *sapiens*, we continued to *Primitive Brain Consciousness*, where we saw *Crocodilians* using knowledge of their prey by balancing sticks on their heads, lying in wait for a bird to claim the stick during nesting season.

As we neared the end of our journey into *sapience*, we explored the *Sapient Paradox*, which asks why it could have taken so long to develop a human culture in the hundred thousand years or more of our existence.

Renfrew's *Sapient Paradox* assumes that *Homo sapiens* were fully developed as the species we are today, just as we were between seventy and a hundred thousand years ago. However, we know this assumption is flawed, as it fails to recognize the software-based levels of *consciousness* that also contributed to our development.

We completed Part Four of our journey into consciousness, sentience, intelligence, awareness, and sapience.

In <u>Part Five</u>, we embarked again on our journey into the landscape of opposing arguments beginning with exploring the concept of a straw man and steel man argument.

Here, we presented the opposing argument that attacks the existence of *freedom of attention*, *will*, and *action*, with five rebuttals.

In the second opposing argument, we proffered that *Dionea muscipula* (a.k.a. The Venus flytrap) and the *Modern Learning Thermostat* cannot express *freedom of action* solely because they physically lack a mechanism to demonstrate it.

Our rebuttal pointed to the fact that many eukaryotic organisms are also unable to express *freedom of action*, but that while there are examples where they can, there are no examples of where neither a *Modern Learning Thermostat* nor any of the millions of other mechanical devices can express *freedom of attention, will,* and *action.*

In the third opposing argument, we cede that a mechanical being that could demonstrate *freedom of attention, will,* and *action* would have achieved *consciousness.*

In the fourth opposing argument, we face the claim that the expression of genetic encoding in behavior and the expression of mechanically programmed behavior are equivalent.

Our rebuttal clarifies that genetic encoding only influences one's behavior, whereas mechanically programmed behaviors are deterministic.

We then ended Part Five of our journey into opposing arguments by highlighting the value they can provide, especially when presented and handled using the framework of a steelman argument.

In <u>Part Six</u>, we continued our journey, blazing a trail into the jungle of *artificial intelligence* and exploring some of its core ideas.

Again, we faced many challenges with how definitions have been crafted without consistency and clarity, citing scantily explained capabilities.

We discussed commercially available speech recognition applications, including Alexa, Siri, and Hey Google. The good news is that these commercial products have great utility for communicating using a spoken language as the user interface instead of a keyboard.

> *Expect this trend to continue with eventually accepting commands by gaining an awareness of physical gestures and adding features such as stereo surround sound and video.*

> *Also, expect additional interfaces, such as the ability of all of these services to place telephone calls and send text messages, as well as engage emergency services providers.*

But as we learned, natural language processing (NLP) has much in common with our *Modern Learning Thermostat.* They both lack *consciousness* and the ability to understand meaning in what their sensors detect or in the actions they perform.

We explored conventional computer technology to provide context for understanding more advanced NLP versions, such as IBM Watson, which can be customized to perform intermediate steps to automate activities requiring multiple steps. Ultimately, it can perform repetitive tasks faster and more consistently at a lower cost with economies of scale.

However, we also saw that IBM Watson could not read legal documents such as contracts, to reliably identify the contract's expiration date, as there are too many ways in which an expiration date can occur in natural language.

Our journey then took us into the world of commercially available robotic consumer products, where we met Roomba from iRobot, the type of computer system known as a *control system*. Here, we saw that the iRobot Roomba, and products like it, have at least one more capability than an amoeba, as it can remember where it has been and not been.

We then delved into the development of robotic products with Honda Corporation's robot named Asimo. Here, a humanoid robot that, although not autonomous, can traverse inclines, declines, and stairs without losing balance.

We also learned that Asimo can recognize moving objects, human postures, gestures, sounds, faces, and much about its surrounding environment, including the direction from which sounds come.

In summarizing artificial intelligence, many involve specialized robot types for commercial and government use. Whether its function is to detect financial fraud, dispose of bombs, or automate multi-step business processes, artificial intelligence represents a wide array of intellectual and physical activities that rely on computers.

At this point in our journey, we began the design process necessary to support *consciousness* by delving into requirements.

We began with *Unicellular Consciousness,* where we analyzed the capabilities of *Paramecia* as a combination of control and information systems. It included the detection of stimuli, memory, pattern recognition, categorization, learning, importance determination, freedom of attention, will, and action, followed by a test plan of these capabilities and then a conceptual design.

The journey led us to the essential concept of self-organizing systems. It began with the first eight primordial self-organizing systems that formed the universe as we know it.

The <u>first</u> was the particle creation force, the first self-organizing system that formed unstructured matter consisting of quarks and bosons and then hadrons and electrons.

It created the conditions for the *strong nuclear force*, the <u>second</u> self-organizing system that formed *semi-structured matter* consisting of protons and neutrons.

The *strong nuclear force* continued by facilitating the <u>third</u> self-organizing system, which consisted of simple *structured matter* in the form of vast clouds, mainly of hydrogen and helium, with relatively trace amounts of lithium, beryllium, and boron, which is everything below the atomic weight of carbon.

The <u>fourth</u> self-organizing system followed 150 to 200 million years later, created by the *gravitational force*, pulling massive clouds of hydrogen and helium together that increased in density eventually to form the first primordial stars.

The <u>fifth</u> self-organizing system then followed billions of years later, driven by a combination of extreme *gravity, heat, nuclear reactions,* and a *strong nuclear force* that formed complex *structured matter* in the form of ninety-three heavier atomic elements with weights greater than boron, such as carbon, silicon, oxygen, and iron.

The <u>sixth</u> self-organizing system was responsible for the formation of heavily structured matter. It was driven by what scientists call the '*weak nuclear force*,' which formed another ten elements considered heavy elements (e.g., Polonium, Plutonium, and Radon), which only came into existence due to the natural process of radioactive decay.

The <u>seventh</u> self-organizing system was responsible for forming molecules driven by *electromagnetism*. The simplest is when two atoms come together to form an ionic or covalent bond held in place by an *electromagnetic* force, such as O_2.

When atoms of different elements come together, the *electromagnetic* force holds the bonds that form molecules called chemical compounds.

The <u>eighth</u> self-organizing system, the reformation of unstructured matter, was driven by extreme *gravity* that forms in black holes. While the underlying driver is still the *gravitational force*, a new process emerges that strips atoms apart into a new unstructured form of super-dense matter that doesn't resemble anything we have encountered and experienced.

Then, our journey led us to an entirely different type of self-organizing system. This self-organizing system emerged specific to planet Earth 3.8 billion years ago, 10 billion years after the prior self-organizing systems formed the universe. It marked the birth of our biosphere.

The <u>ninth</u> self-organizing system, the fluidic phase, formed the first bio-chemicals, marking the first activity within our biosphere producing carbohydrates, lipids, nucleic acids, and amino acids, eventually combining in ways to produce proteins.

It was the first time that self-organizing components communicated with one another through chemical signaling using chemical messengers.

Communication was a significant advancement in self-organizing systems as the complexity of molecular systems is due to the ability of molecules to coordinate with one another to assemble parts that, once assembled, are compatible with one another as building blocks for the emergence of the next self-organizing system.

The second of our biosphere, the <u>tenth</u> self-organizing system, formed the first primitive cells we recognize as the first life forms, prokaryotes.

The only known form of life for the first several million years were two types of prokaryotes, bacteria and archaea, of which the scientific estimates for the number of species range between ten thousand and five hundred thousand.

The <u>eleventh</u> self-organizing system, the third of our biosphere, formed the first advanced living cells we know as eukaryotes, marking the birthplace of *consciousness*.

Scientists estimate that eukaryote species range between seven million and eight million, where the first eukaryote fossil dated 2.1 billion years ago. The first eukaryotes to emerge were yeasts, molds, and fungi, followed later by plant and animal eukaryotic cells.

Our <u>twelfth</u> self-organizing system, the fourth of our biosphere, formed the first multicellular eukaryotes within the plant and animal kingdoms.

The self-organizing forces that propelled the emergence of multicellular organisms were due to the *symbiotic force* and *biological advantage*, where *symbiotic force* involves the emergence of symbiotic relationships among previously independent organisms with distinct genetic material, also known as chimeras.

The <u>thirteenth</u> self-organizing system, fifth with our biosphere, saw the formation of the first neuron network, significantly accelerating communication throughout the multicellular body of animals.

Jellyfish evolved with several types of bacteria between 500 and 700 million years ago, making them one of the oldest multi-organ animals built upon a cooperative system of jellyfish and bacteria.

The <u>fourteenth</u> self-organizing system, sixth within our biosphere, witnessed the emergence of the nerve cord and primitive *neuroglial* cells to support *Type Four Qualia* in bilateral nematodes.

Self-organizing bacteria continue the development of an increasingly complex array of relationships serving as food, pathogens, and mutualists by aiding nematodes in development, defense, reproduction, and nutrient acquisition.

Here, we see how all organisms are an integral part of the biosphere, where our survival depends upon a community of cells of various genetic materials.

The larvae that hatch from *C. elegans* eggs lack all microbes, as none of the known species transfer microbes vertically.

Luckily, the natural habitats of *C. elegans* are typically rich in microbes. Notably, the resulting nematode microbiota is a function of both the environment and the organism's array of proteins that ultimately repel and disable or attract and utilize various microbes, without which it could not survive, thereby firmly linking it to this biosphere.

The <u>fifteenth</u> self-organizing system, seventh within our biosphere, marked the formation of the neural bundle, expanding the role of neurons into bundles to support more advanced calculations of environmental stimuli, further expanding the symbiotic role of microbes and advancing into new levels of consciousness.

The <u>sixteenth</u> self-organizing system, eighth within our biosphere, brought us the primitive brain by further expanding the role of neurons into layers to support yet more advanced calculations of environmental stimuli and more customized microbes to support more 'complex organisms while generating further enhancements into higher levels of consciousness.

The <u>seventeenth</u>, <u>eighteenth</u>, and <u>nineteenth</u> self-organizing systems, ninth, tenth, and eleventh within our biosphere brought us to this point in our journey. Here we found ourselves equipped with deep layers of neuronal tissue and advanced *neuroglial* cells for the physical equipment supporting *Mammalian*, *Primate*, and *Homo Consciousness*.

However, this does not mean that self-organizing systems stop here.

If we have learned anything, the biosphere will continue evolving new and exciting self-organizing systems until it meets its ultimate fate.

We then traveled back in time to 500 B.C.E. to see the emergence of the scientific process of reductionism to recall how the Buddha reduced consciousness into its parts, while a hundred years later, the Greek philosopher Democritus put forth the idea that everything in the world is composed of indivisible units called atoms.

We saw that religious doctrine delayed scientific reductionism for five hundred years. Still, the renaissance that blossomed at the end of the Dark Ages did more to propel science and empirical thinking in the West than had occurred in the East.

We saw that our Islamic brothers did not share and spread knowledge in universities and scholars outside the clergy but diligently and expertly curated and protected it.

At this part of our journey, we learned that scientific reductionism could not explain the formation and operation of self-organizing systems in the biosphere. We saw that self-organizing systems occur in layers dependent upon one another, and all operate according to different rules unpredictably.

We saw that reductionism first ignores that self-organizing systems within the biosphere actively communicate to drive self-organization within each level of abstraction (e.g., tissue, organ, system of organs) and simultaneously at each level.

Second, we saw that it ignores that each level of the self-organizing system self-organizes at its level to a completely different set of rules that, before their emergence, are unpredictable.

However, our journey then took us to the emergence of emergence, which occurs when a collection of things demonstrates one or more properties that none of the individual parts of the collection demonstrate on their own.

We saw that there are forms of artificial and naturally forming emergence, including naturally occurring self-organizing systems.

Thus equipped, we considered the *reductionism-emergence* debate, where we saw that Darwin's theory of natural selection was not reasoned using reductionism and not the result of understanding emergentism.

Instead, Darwin had to draw his conclusions from observations to understand what would eventually become known as genetics and its continuous trial-and-error process.

In other words, the only way to understand any self-organizing system is to study the properties and behaviors of that level, which is what Darwin did.

Hence, understanding the formation of unstructured matter does not help one anticipate the formation of particles and the way they behave, and understanding how particles behave does not help one anticipate the formation of semi-structured matter and the way it behaves, and so on.

The critical concept is that each level of a self-organizing system within a biosphere invokes a non-deterministic form of self-determination that leverages some form of communication among the parts at each level within that biosphere. Also, these parts are reusable functions.

We saw each level's independence by visiting Darwinian preadaptation, where feathers evolved as an advantage to serve as insulation from cold temperatures and then utilized it to take flight.

We also saw where the lungs of a lungfish evolved as an advantage to hold a supply of oxygen and then utilized it to act as a swim bladder to control buoyancy. Again, reusable functions.

Within each level of each niche of the biosphere, self-organizing forces operate with their own set of rules and guiding principles. Only by analyzing each niche of the biosphere can we reveal the guiding principles operating at each level of the self-organizing system.

We summarized system design by exploring the well-understood notion of a designer conceptualizing a thing. Then, we explored the idea of self-organizing systems and the advantage they enjoy employing millions of trial and error exercises conducted in parallel under various conditions, building upon the successful ones.

Hence, the self-designing forces of a biosphere have the advantage of a seemingly infinite capability for many more self-driven design decisions at multiple levels of abstraction, conducted in a massively parallel manner over vast periods.

Equipped with this knowledge, we returned to our path, pondering our ability to design self-organizing systems and then take that to the next level of self-designing systems.

We observed how operating systems organize, deploy, and reclaim computer resources and how an operating system can run various other programs.

Given our knowledge of self-organizing software, we revisited the requirements of *Unicellular Consciousness* and our *Paramecium,* beginning with its senses, *freedom of attention, will, action*, and support capabilities.

It led us to conceptualize a design for supporting interpreting streams of stimuli, storing and retrieving memory, learning, *importance determination, freedom of attention, will,* and *action* before briefly illustrating how to develop a test plan for the first level of consciousness, our artificial *Paramecium.*

We then revisited *Nerve Net Consciousness* to support signal routing and high-speed communication using a simple message broker to select the appropriate destination and transfer data over a small network. To support the advanced visual system, we also needed to add neural network capabilities to correctly identify the types of images each set of eyes could detect from various angles and distances.

Next, we revisited *Nerve Cord Consciousness* to support the emergence of a primitive imagination to fabricate illusions from streams of stimuli involving light, tactile capabilities, temperature, osmotic pressure, tiny amounts of electrical current, and airborne vibrations.

We also had to strengthen the learning capabilities to support associative and non-associative learning.

Then, we revisited *Neural Bundle Consciousness* to introduce semantic search capabilities to support vector-related capabilities to rapidly process streams of stimuli related to honeybees' more advanced communication skills.

Finally, we fast-forwarded to *Homo Consciousness,* where we unleashed the power of generative artificial intelligence to self-organize new software-based functions to support the remaining levels of *consciousness.*

We then concluded Part VI of our journey by conceptualizing a design to support self-organizing and self-programming, including an API gateway, a backend services library, and generative artificial intelligence capabilities generating backend functions and acceptance criteria.

In Part VII, we find ourselves recapping our journey.

Our memories are fresh with the many ideas we've experienced along our journey together. Most of all, we wonder what is next, as this is not the journey's end.

A few of us will not continue the journey, as some lose their way when hard determinists reframe the argument as a mind trap. Another few will go on to their next book to eventually forget much of the experience of this journey though not all of it.

However, some of us will come away retaining a great deal of this journey and will build upon it, incorporating various valuable concepts into our daily lives. Even as the author, this includes me as well.

Having taken this journey with you, like yourself, I am more alert for news and science articles that delve into the nature of *consciousness*. I am more sensitive to the ethical treatment of organisms with levels of *consciousness* capable of being *sentient* and am more alert to levels of *intelligence* that potentially demonstrate *sapience*.

With this journey, I have more interest in the rights of artificially intelligent organisms and ponder the rights of artificial organisms that might possess *consciousness* as opposed to the rudimentary awareness of *Alexa, Hey Google*, or our *Modern Learning Thermostat*.

We also have a heightened awareness of how paradigms affect us and our fellow humans and an appreciation of the differences among productive, egoistic, problematic, and evil *Level Twos* and some sense of the influence they can exert within organizations.

Some of us have a heightened sense of duty to protect *Level Ones* from egoistic, problematic, and evil *Level Two* individuals, and we may desire to share these concepts with our family and close friends.

Also, we are prepared to detect and embrace evolutionary change and the emergence of the next self-organizing system, as it is almost assuredly already in progress.

Perhaps most importantly, we now realize that our biosphere and possibly an incredible number of additional biospheres have worked, are working, and will continue to work in parallel to create and evolve new levels of *consciousness* as we take the first steps in the journey to create artificial *consciousness* and to understand what it means on multiple levels.

EPILOGUE

The realization that biospheres are incubators for increasingly new and more powerful levels of consciousness is fascinating for several reasons. Perhaps foremost is the fact that it is science instead of science fiction.

By now, we realize that our biosphere is not likely to be the first to form and most certainly is not the last to form.

While this perspective upsets the sensibilities of those who are more comfortable assuming we are the apex species of the universe, it does not mean that we are not unique.

Of the parallel efforts of many biospheres, we are likely among the top deciles of biospheres *conscious* of continually emerging levels of *consciousness* and still in the competition among biospheres to evolve ever more advanced levels of *consciousness*.

Some will ask why. What does *consciousness* do? What can *consciousness's* purpose be, and where does that purpose come from?

The answer starts with the basic fact that *consciousness* and its levels have formed to make sense of what our senses can perceive. As individual organisms, we do this to improve our survivability, allowing our continued participation in the evolution of *consciousness*.

However, unlike the competitions of survival we see on television where a sole survivor is the declared winner, the actual competition in which the universe has placed us is different. To win, we need our biosphere to survive.

Hence, our biosphere competes in parallel with other biospheres. Also, to make the competition more interesting, each biosphere has a clock tied to it, as every biosphere initially depends on an energy source like our sun.

Like ourselves, the life of any biosphere in its solar system is ticking down to its eventual destruction.

It raises several questions. It raises a question as to whether our biosphere will extend beyond the energy source of our one star. It also raises the question of how many other biospheres will extend beyond the energy source of their star.

Ultimately, it raises the question of the purpose of these surviving biospheres and their drive to reach newer and newer levels of consciousness.

It raises the question as to whether surviving biospheres could ever link up with one another and collaborate.

However, another possibility exists, one born of science fiction and the future.

It is the notion that we can create artificial *consciousness* and that it can expand beyond the boundaries of our biosphere to explore other biospheres or a place where we can export our biosphere.

But maybe it is bigger than that.

The ultimate question it raises is whether it is all about the universe gaining an understanding of itself.

Perhaps the giant experiment of deploying a massive number of parallel biospheres to attain new levels of *consciousness* represents the only theoretical journey for the universe ever to understand itself, and who can imagine what that level of *consciousness* could even look like?

AUTHOR'S NOTE

I sincerely thank every reader who has shared in this journey. Every moment of your time, attention, and *free will* to intellectually engage these ideas is much appreciated.

I also thank the neuroscientists who had no choice and shared in this journey against their wishes.

In closing, I hope to have many stimulating conversations with as many individuals who wish to share their thoughts on these subjects. A little food, wine, and someone to share ideas with is one of life's greatest pleasures to knowledge-thirsty beings such as ourselves.